THE UNSINKABLE
TITANIC

THE TRIUMPH BEHIND A DISASTER

ALLEN GIBSON

Titanic and *Olympic* were virtually identical. From the outset White Star marketed their brand as a byword for decadence in sea travel. *Olympic* with her Promenade Deck open to the elements was partially enclosed on *Titanic* to afford passengers shelter from sea spray. *Titanic* (right) – pictured with her sister at Harland & Wolff in March 1912 prior to fitting the screens – was built to embody the pinnacle of comfort at sea. (© National Museums Northern Ireland Collection Harland & Wolff, Ulster Folk & Transport Museum)

First published 2012

The History Press
The Mill, Brimscombe Port
Stroud, Gloucestershire, GL5 2QG
www.thehistorypress.co.uk

British Library Cataloguing in Publication Data.
A catalogue record for this book is available from the British Library.

ISBN 978 0 7524 5625 6

Typesetting and origination by The History Press
Printed in Great Britain

CONTENTS

LIST OF TABLES

PREFACE

'In building the *Titanic* it was the hope of my associates and myself that we had built a vessel which could not be destroyed by the perils of the sea or the dangers of navigation.'

Joseph Bruce Ismay, 21 April 1912

The summer of 2003 found me on a train bound for London to attend a *Titanic* artefact exhibition at the Science Museum. Heading there against my better wishes I was doggedly opposed to all the hype surrounding the show. Yet, burning curiosity had me standing in line eagerly awaiting my 11.30a.m. entry to the exhibits. With my White Star Line 'boarding pass' in hand I wandered round the exhibition from one hall to the next, pausing by various meticulous arrangements of familiar items of salvage. Although outwardly aloof, secretly I was entranced by it all. The disaster that I studied so intently had with this visit suddenly transformed my solitary interest into an experience very striking, very real.

I began my research into the *Titanic* disaster in 1987 upon reading Robert Ballard's book chronicling his discovery of the wreck. The encounter awakened a hunger that embarked me on a journey gathering material that before long transformed my bookshelves into a library devoted to *Titanic*. What a world I had discovered. I became a purist, growing firmly withdrawn from the increasing frenzy now usurping her legacy. Yet I found myself drawn to this exhibition, mesmerised by the allure of a ship none of us have seen nor would otherwise know of had she not encountered that infamous iceberg. Meandering around the exhibition, passing displays of silverware here, of playing cards and shoes there, these assortments of everyday once-personal possessions whose survival today owes itself to their presence on that tragic maiden voyage, resonated both awe and sadness for everyone to reflect at the enormity of loss in their time-frozen past. For the first time since my study began, *Titanic* was no longer the intangible monochromatic photograph I knew from my books.

I made a beeline for the exhibition's store. Shelves primed with all manner of glossy merchandising – fridge magnets to reproduction chinaware – I tried desperately to remain detached. I loathed the fickleness of sudden and promiscuous interest in my much-cherished passion; it being the latest merchandising fad, sensationalised to grab attention as if it was some fairground attraction. But for this day I was prepared to risk just that and finally meet face-to-face these treasures that once travelled on history's most fabled voyage. I comprehended then as I glanced at the faces of those about me, wide-eyed and venerating the exhibits as if sacred relics, *Titanic* had always been far more than a mere casualty of overconfidence. The experience found me realising that *Titanic* rests inextricably within our conscience. An existence so familiar that we recognise her silhouette long before discovering its detail. We intimately know of her plight without studying it. We will inherently forever know *Titanic*.

As I depart the exhibition my heart suddenly begins to race. I see a piece of hull visitors are allowed to touch. To the uninitiated, a nondescript shard of scrap, but seconds later I eagerly squeeze my finger through a tiny hole cut into its protective Perspex shroud, stretching to touch it. I am elated. I had made contact with *Titanic* – a lifetime ambition accomplished. With this the exhibition comes to an end. However, there remains one final duty still to perform.

Each boarding pass handed out on entry bore the name of a *Titanic* passenger, and as I make my exit the reason for this becomes suddenly apparent: each visitor would adopt the name of that passenger and as a finale to the exhibition we search the lists of names of those who boarded the ill-fated voyage to discover our individual passenger's fate. I was well aware of the math: the one in three chance of survival. It was sobering facts such as these that were the very reason I became drawn to *Titanic*, astonished how a ship of the twentieth century could brazenly head to sea carrying so few lifeboats, and discovering why its passengers would later willingly cede salvation in them. I yearned to discover how Victorian fastidiousness left this path to disaster so unguarded and if we, with modern hindsight, unjustly attribute her demise to ineptitude from management and navigation.

With a brief look at my boarding pass I peered up at the boards; the 2,000 names printed upon them invoked a poignant display. Eager to discover if mine was a millionaire industrialist or high-society luminary, I scanned the list. Almost believing the name on my card did not exist at all my eyes suddenly arrived at my passenger, a third-class émigré. He had not survived. The game was an effective tool to bring home the reality that had all the people surrounding me travelled on *Titanic*, two thirds of us, including myself, would have perished. With mixed feelings I returned the boarding pass to my pocket and exit the museum, pondering how many others that day would bear the name of my passenger.

Like me, the multitudes converged and marvelled at these artefacts that had been heaved from the resting place of this terrible disaster. Yet this international fascination with *Titanic* will long surpass her physical existence, for these ever-swelling ranks of visitors and those of the generations following them, will all sedulously ensure that the name *Titanic* shall endure in the consciousness of humanity for evermore.

Allen Gibson, 2011

INTRODUCTION

'When anyone asks me how I can best describe my experiences of nearly
40 years at sea, I merely say – uneventful… I have never been in an accident
of any sort worth speaking about. I never saw a wreck and have never been
wrecked, nor have I been in any predicament that threatened to end in disaster
of any sort.'

Captain Edward Smith, *New York Times*, May 1907

If there is ever a vision that depicts the awesome power of nature it is the fury
of the sea churned by tempest and our perennial futility taming it. As humans
we share an instinct that inheritably pulls us seaward. Throughout history the
oceans have conjured the enduring lure of adventure, change and opportunity.
The oceans cover 70 per cent of our globe, and mankind has learned to harness
and traverse them, but to its frustration failed to control them. From hewing out
tree trunks to building floating cities of steel, the cultivation of man is forever
entwined with his tumultuous bond with the sea.

Since the advent of the steam engine, ships have evolved in both scale and
speed, fostering with each an irrepressible desire for builder and nation alike to
impose both technological superiority and political authority. Coupled with mass
migration, sea travel has reshaped our world and one ocean in particular, the
North Atlantic, became the battlefield between the old and new world economies and host to almighty skirmishes between corporations vying for control of
the great 'ocean railway'.

As passenger numbers escalated, shipping companies emerged and multiplied
to meet this demand. Competition intensified. Disaster at sea became increasingly
inevitable. As ocean liners grew, the regulations governing their supply of lifeboats
failed to keep pace and by the twentieth century its outmoded methodology
proved to be to the detriment than the protection of life. Such was the complacency concerning safety.

Against this backdrop two great adversaries became immersed in a battle royale
for their very survival: White Star Line and Cunard. In order to better the other,

Britain's two largest operators produced fleets of floating palaces over the course of half a century; each larger in scale, out-sizing its rival and with ever-faster engines. One such ship was the second of a trio of sisters known as the Olympic Class of liners. She boasted an imposing pedigree. Owned by one of the most influential financiers the world has ever known, she was built by the foremost craftsmen of the age and operated by one of the premier shipping operators on the North Atlantic – the Liverpool-based White Star Line.

Hailed as 'Queen of the Ocean', she was marvelled at as the greatest, most luxurious and safest liner ever to grace the sea. The largest movable structure of her day, she was a seaborne phenomenon, a triumph of engineering and the audacious embodiment of British achievement. However, during her maiden commercial voyage she was embroiled in a tragedy prompted by the very element she was contrived to overcome – nature. It was a tragedy that instead etched her name into the modern psyche as the very synonym of disaster, ill-fortune and catastrophe. The unthinkable had sunk the Edwardian unsinkable.

In just one evening, in April 1912, her name manifested from technological marvel to infamous modern legend. Her loss, the prevalent maritime event of the modern era and one so potent that it bridged society's enormously polarised social structure, spawned the first true global media sensation and was a grisly prelude to the malevolent politic of the new century.

Her wreck laid undiscovered for seventy-three years and to this day remains the most revered treasure on the seabed. She is the most famous ship of all – her silhouette is instantaneously and internationally familiar across all walks of life. Even at the centennial of her demise the scale of her loss prevails as much as ever. She was the icon of the modern age, yet her technological achievements are over-shadowed as the defining monument to misfortune – swathed in an unwarranted tale of calamity, destined to become as timeless as the oceans themselves.

This is the legendary career of a luckless ship that was no failure but the crowning moment of marine transportation. Built to conquer the struggle between nations and corporations alike for power and survival on the North Atlantic, through their conceitedness she became instead its greatest victim.

Casting aside modern preconception and hindsight, and exploring the backdrop to the events and key decisions that were to trigger the most infamous event to take place at sea, we recover the untainted glory of the Royal Mail Steamship *Titanic* and her remarkable footnote in history.

CHAPTER 1

ACCESSION

'All of Europe is crossing the ocean.'

New York diarist, Philip Hone, *c.*1840

RMS *Titanic* was conceived at the close of a period that produced the most crucial development in transportation: the steamship. It is with the growth of this technology that our story begins – a story that witnessed a chain of events that led to the construction of ever larger, faster and increasingly luxurious liners whose vulnerability at sea was not fully appreciated until the occurrence of the sea's most legendary disaster.

Following its conception in the middle of the eighteenth century, the steam engine revolutionised thousands of years of agriculture and industry. On land, steam was rapidly forging a newer, more developed world, and utilising this power at sea would enable ships to power themselves over great journeys, unaided by wind, and change the face of global transportation forever.

That was the dream, though in reality it was quickly realised that to sustain its engines over any lengthy journey a ship would have to accommodate an unfeasibly large supply of coal; such a journey would be an otherwise impossible task should no refuelling points reside along its way. This was until James Watt produced his groundbreaking sensation, the piston engine, in 1765, cutting the fuel consumption of a steam engine by 75 per cent.

The development of the steamship truly began with the first wooden steam powered paddle craft: the 182-ton *Pyroscaphe*, which debuted on the Saône River in France on 15 July 1783. The innovation soon crossed the Channel to Britain where in 1801 the first commercial steamship, *Charlotte Dundas*, was built. Fitted with a 10hp engine it saw life as a tugboat on Scotland's Forth-Clyde Canal.

The first craft to use steam to cross the Atlantic – although predominantly assisted by sail – became the 320-ton 90hp paddler *Savannah*. Departing New York on 24 May 1819, she arrived at Liverpool twenty-seven days later, an epoch followed in 1827 by the 438-ton *Curaçao*, also jointly powered by sail. Setting off from

Rotterdam, Holland, bound for the West Indies, *Curaçao* undertook the first Atlantic crossing of a hybrid powered predominantly by steam. The journey lasted twenty-two days, in contrast to the forty the same trip would have taken by sail.

The next milestone came in 1838 upon the advent of the first transatlantic journeys driven solely and continuously by steam, with two rival shipping companies pitting head-to-head to stake the claim. St George Steam Packet Company's 714-ton *Sirius* departed Cork, Ireland, on 4 April 1838. Travelling at an average of 6.7 knots, her engines paddled the 2,961 nautical miles to New York where she arrived nineteen days later. Meanwhile, from Bristol, England's Isambard Kingdom Brunel on 8 April had dispatched his ship, *Great Western*. Averaging 8.7 knots she reached New York in just fourteen days, as well as making port one day ahead of *Sirius*. The race, turning out to be no mere publicity jaunt, signed off an era that had prevailed for millennia: the age of the sail.

With steam came speed, and with speed came the possibility for more frequent crossings, in particular on the busiest routes: the North Atlantic. During the days of sail most passengers traversing the Atlantic endured forty terribly laggard days at sea, but with steam this same journey was diminished to eighteen. More so, as through *Great Western* Brunel had delivered a ship able to burn fuel economically, and large enough to store a sufficient amount of coal (400 tons) to sustain the entire voyage. The practical long-distance steamship had been born.

By 1852 the advent of high-pressure engines allowed shipbuilders to power even larger craft over greater journeys and at ever-increasing speed. With passengers emigrating westward and additional cargo occupying their vacated accommodation on the return east, transatlantic travel was becoming a highly lucrative enterprise. With 40 per cent of the world's trade passing through its port, Liverpool became the commercial hub of the British Empire, giving rise to numerous shipping lines that emerged to exploit this great new trade, eventually turning Liverpool into Britain's second-largest metropolis. Very soon, one shipping line in particular began striding out ahead of all the others.

Starting life in 1839 as the British & North American Royal Mail Steam Packet Company, Canadian-born Samuel Cunard founded what was to become the most significant shipping line of all time. Samuel's aspirations in shipping began when he took over his father's lumber business in 1814, expanding its operations to include shipping, he established the first timetabled transatlantic services. Travelling from Liverpool to Halifax and onward to Boston, their voyages in 1841 took a mere fourteen days and eight hours to complete. The expansion of his fleet between 1843 and 1845 allowed the inclusion of New York in their schedules from 1847. But, although their ships were fast, standards of accommodation, even in first class, caused considerable disappointment among their passengers: a void in the market had been exposed. With their fleet numbering twenty-eight by 1880, Cunard commanded 15 per cent of the North Atlantic's entire passenger traffic, and in consequence many additional companies formed in the hope of emulating this success.

Yet in the early years of steam it was an American company that would first challenge Cunard's dominance. Edward Knight Collins, who founded the Collins Line in 1845, focussed the design of his fleet on size and luxury as well as speed and consequently won funding from the US government in 1847 to carry their mail. His ship, *Pacific*, snatched the prized Blue Riband in 1851 as the first to cross the Atlantic in less than ten days. Collins would also introduce welcome improvements in passenger accommodation with the first so-called 'floating palace', the hugely expensive *Atlantic*, which, when completed in April 1850, found the bill for her construction amount a bewildering $1.2 million.

Carrying 4,306 passengers across the Atlantic in 1852, the Collins Line outstripped the 2,969 travelling by Cunard, their no-frills counterpart. Collins, however, soon discovered that his ships were burning 40 tons more coal a day than his Cunard rivals, which was particularly unfortunate since his own was turning only half the profit that Cunard was achieving, despite selling far more tickets. Moreover, when Collins lost two of his ships – *Arctic* in 1854 and *Pacific* in 1856 – the US withdrew its $385,000-a-year mail contract. With losses amounting to $1.7 million, high running costs compounded the collapse of the line in 1858. Cunard, however, remained strong, but 1850 saw fresh competition emerge under the leadership of William Inman, although unlike Collins, Inman centred his focus on emigrant transportation. In 1859 Inman had become the first line to add the port of Queenstown, Ireland, as a stop on his schedules to New York in order to cater for the exodus of emigrants fleeing the Great Famine; Cunard followed suit some ten years later. The Inman Line flourished both financially and technologically – their ships attaining the speed record in 1869, 1875, 1889 and 1892 – although economic difficulties forced the company to cede ownership to America, becoming American Line in 1893, which was itself ultimately absorbed into the vast American-owned shipping conglomerate, International Mercantile Marine, in 1902.

Another heavyweight in shipping was Stephen Guion. Establishing his line in 1866, Guion too gained the financial backing of the US government. Basing operations in Liverpool, he harboured an ambition to build liners able to compete for Blue Riband glory, which they won in 1879, 1882 and 1884. However, unlike the Inman Line, Guion put more consideration into the speed of his ships and disastrously less on passenger accommodation. It proved a fatal decision. His ships regularly sailed two thirds below capacity. Falling foul of the maxim – the faster the engine, the higher its coal consumption – spiralling costs steamed the line into bankruptcy in 1892.

Competition on the Atlantic was relentless. To help revive its struggling shipping industry the British government in 1854 awarded Cunard funding to build two fast iron-hulled paddle steamers, *Persia* and *Scotia*, both of which set the speed record in a little over eight days. At this point Cunard began concentrating their focus on operating routes exclusively across the North Atlantic. Abandoning the cumbersome paddlewheel in 1862 in favour of the new innovation, the screw propeller, it was an up-and-coming rival – White Star Line – that in 1872 became the first line to attain the speed record under this new form of propulsion: the 14-knot, 3,868-ton *Adriatic* crossed the Atlantic in a time of seven days and twenty-three hours.

Dedicating the 1890s to modernising their fleet, Cunard's first steel-hulled vessel, the 12,950-ton *Campania*, completed in 1893, set a new Atlantic record of six days and ten hours in 1894, averaging 21.09 knots. In 1905 Cunard became the first line to fit a turbine engine into an ocean-going liner: their 19,524-ton *Carmania*, capable of 20 knots.

It was amid this development that 15 million Europeans had travelled by sea to resettle on the other side of the Atlantic. America's industrial base expanded rapidly, a result of relying heavily on an ever-increasing influx of workers to fill its jobs. A flow of immigration encouraged by a reduction in government red tape prompted unprecedented demands on shipping companies to provide ever larger and faster fleets. Between 1800 and 1900 America's population soared from 5.25 million to 76 million, and from 1900 to 1914 the nation received 1 million people who resettled there each year. Of the total emigrating European population between 1815 and 1930, 20 per cent was British. The Statue of Liberty, brandishing her beacon of light, marketed to the impoverished continent the idyll of hope and escape from the squalor and crowded cities of decaying imperial Europe.

Emigration, however, was not the only driving force behind sea travel. Improving connections found the rich dedicating ever-increasing profligacy and energies on recreation at a time when society's poorest struggled merely to survive. Never before had society become so polarised, and shipping operators competed hard for both spectra of the market. The Edwardian age produced first-class passenger areas on ships themed with rooms reproducing the interiors of the grandest European palaces. Ostentation was the new vogue. To harvest the growing breed of super-rich traveller, shipping operators had their designers build them bigger, better and far more luxurious craft in a race to outdo the creations of their competitors. The newest liners would be brutally opulent in their interiors, yet their outside profiles always maintained graceful elegance and delicate charm. External grandeur masked cramped and spartan accommodation endured by their emigrating third-class companions, cheek by jowl and ensconced well out of sight in the decks below.

One such builder ahead of all others producing luxury and quality for all its would-be elite was Harland & Wolff, the great Belfast shipbuilder who one day would proudly launch White Star's fabled Olympic Class of liners.

The 'Old Firm'

Living his formative years near the shipyards of Scarborough, Edward James Harland developed an early passion for engineering. Beginning his apprenticeship at the age of fifteen in Newcastle at George Stephenson's engineering works, upon its completion in 1851 Edward found employment in Govan, Glasgow, as a draughtsman for a small maritime engine manufacturer, James & George Thompson. In 1854 he then moved to Belfast to manage the yard of Robert Hickson & Co., a shipbuilder on the river Lagan founded the previous year by Mr Robert Hickson. Hickson had been leasing an area of reclaimed land known as Queens Island from the Harbour Commission. However, the company's performance was poor and Harland was hired as general manager to help turn fortunes around. Harland indeed improved business but work at Hickson's remained plagued with setbacks impairing finances, personnel and supplies. All eventually had taken their toll on Hickson, and Harland was offered complete ownership of the yard and its 200-strong workforce. Harland accepted and the deal was finalised on 21 September 1858, with Harland buying the yard outright for £5,000.

Edward had raised the funds from long-term friend and mentor, Gustav Christian Schwabe, a financier from Hamburg who had resettled in Liverpool in 1838. Working during the 1840s as partner of the shipping line John Bibby & Sons (the Bibby Line), Schwabe had known young Harland as a young apprentice. Upon taking over Hickson's the yard became known as Edward James Harland & Co. and soon acquired their first order, a lucrative one at that – three vessels for the Bibby Line: *Venetian* (1,508 tons, launched 30 July 1859), *Sicilian* and *Syrian* (equally 1,492 tons). The size of the contract necessitated the yard to expand and acquire more land, and to give the business a further boost Schwabe injected it with yet more capital. But Harland soon found the yard hard to run on his own, so formed a partnership with his trusted assistant Gustav Wilhelm Wolff – Schwabe's nephew. This was no mere case of nepotism: Wolff had earned Harland's respect securing the yard their building contracts for Bibby.

Born in Hamburg, Germany, in 1834, Wolff had immigrated to Liverpool in 1849 to attend college, after which he undertook an apprenticeship in Manchester at the engineering firm of Joseph Whitworth & Co. Upon completion he remained in the city to work as a draughtsman, but in 1857 he transferred to Hickson's in Belfast, upon Schwabe's request that Harland hire his nephew to head the company's design team. Before long Wolff became Harland's right-hand man, and rising to business partner in 1861: Harland committed £1,916 to the enterprise, Wolff contributed his share of £500. The partnership was formalised on 11 April 1861 and the new business, supporting 2,400 employees, was officially renamed Harland & Wolff on 1 January 1862. By 1864 the yard was outputting 30,000 tons of shipping a year, receiving a further boost in 1867 securing a deal to build several battleships for the Royal Navy following their success producing vessels for the

US government during the Civil War. Harland's meticulous attention to detail – regularly patrolling the yard and appraising his ships for the slightest imperfections – garnered the company an enviable reputation as a centre of excellence.

With significant financial interests in both Harland & Wolff and an up-and-coming shipping operator, White Star Line, during the early half of 1869 Schwabe introduced the two chairmen: Edward Harland and Thomas Ismay, managing director of the Oceanic Steam Navigation Company, parent company of White Star. The meeting was to broker a preferred supplier/customer relationship nurtured and based on a unique and simple understanding. As long as it did not build vessels for a competitor White Star would guarantee Harland & Wolff regular and loyal business. In return Harland & Wolff would build White Star ships of unrivalled quality, at virtually cost price. From this moment on, Harland & Wolff would build every vessel commissioned by White Star Line, not once making an exception. Indeed, so enduring was the alliance to be, from 1869 to 1919, that not a single working day passed without Harland & Wolff constructing a vessel for White Star within their yards. By 1885, Harland & Wolff – outputting in excess of 104,000 tons of shipping a year – was valued at £600,000 and filed for Limited status, offering 600 £1,000 shares.

Edward Harland, a fervent Irish unionist, reaped immense influence in Belfast, allowing him to set deep political roots. Mayor of Belfast during 1885–6, for which he was knighted, he then became member of parliament for the division of North Belfast in 1887, a seat he retained until his death on Christmas Eve, 1895.

To replace Harland, the yard's chief draughtsman, William James Pirrie, joined Gustav Wolff as partner of the business. The Pirrie name was already greatly familiar throughout the town. James' grandfather, William Morrison Pirrie, had from 1820 worked extensively to improve the yard's accessibility and increased the depth of the river Lagan to allow it accommodate larger vessels. In 1852 he was appointed by the Harbour Commission to head the acquisition of land from the Belfast Iron Works Company, which he achieved the following year – the very plot subsequently purchased by Robert Hickson.

Upon William James Pirrie assuming control, he was accorded practical autonomy in running the yard, for Wolff too was devoting his increasing energy to politics. Elected to Parliament in 1892 to represent East Belfast, Wolff would hold the seat unopposed for eighteen years. Mirroring its founders' influence, the yard too grew in stature. By 1900 it had become the largest shipbuilding company in the world, seeing a newly ennobled William James Pirrie succeed Gustav Wolff upon his retirement on 30 June 1906. Owning the yard outright, Lord Pirrie began a series of radical improvements to the business; dividing it into four smaller independent yards – naming them Musgrave, Abercorn, Victoria and Queen's – in a drive to improve overall efficiency. The following year he received their most ambitious and, as it transpired, most infamous project: three new liners for White Star, each of which by far the largest the world had ever seen – the Olympic Class. At that time the relationship between the two companies had never been stronger, and this project would require Harland & Wolff to invest heavily in further alterations to their yard to accommodate White Star's most immense and prestigious new express liners.

Pirrie was well aware that through making these upgrades Harland & Wolff would remain head and shoulders above their contemporaries for years to come. Indeed, since the days of Edward Harland the yard had been regarded as a great innovator of design. They had perfected thinner hulls and straighter bows to glide their ships more efficiently through water. Their ships were strong and durable too, yet the subtle needs of the passenger remained central to their designs. From emancipating the decks of sails, to deflecting sea spray, every consideration was applied to continually improve the passenger experience, down to even the smallest enhancement. In stark contrast to others of the period, the ships of Harland & Wolff were spacious, bright and extremely comfortable.

The team tasked with designing the Olympic Class was headed by Alexander Montgomery Carlisle and Thomas Andrews, with Pirrie himself also paying close attention. The three had progressed quickly through the ranks of Harland & Wolff and were widely considered to be among the best naval architects in the world. On paper, the first of these new ships began to take shape. *Olympic* and *Titanic* were springing to life. Their dimensions and luxury would surpass any other vessel before them, but the means with which to build and launch White Star's new leviathans was an obstacle that the yard had to resolve long before the class's first keel plates could invade the slipways.

None of the yard's existing slipways were large enough to construct one of the new Olympic-Class liners, let alone three – especially as White Star wanted two built in tandem. Therefore preparations began in earnest. Between 1906 and 1908 Pirrie invested £130,000 in transforming slipways 2, 3 and 4 of their facility at Queen's Island, merging them into two to provide a combined working area 840ft long by 270ft wide.

The slips themselves would require colossal frames to be built around them to support a tremendous network of gangways and lifting gear needed to simultaneously frame and plate two of the world's largest hulls. Glasgow-based Sir William Arrol & Co. Ltd – renowned builders of the new Tay (1887) and Forth (1890) rail bridges, as well as London's iconic Tower Bridge (1894) – won the contract to design and install the world's largest double-operating steel gantries to encase these two new slipways. Towering 228ft above the world's longest slips, the skeletal giant required a foundation reinforced with steel piled 40ft deep, topped by a 4½ft bed of concrete to support its 6,000-ton frame. The purpose of the twin gantry was to allow the two slips to operate independently, each having designated cranes, machinery – even workforce. The cost of the gantries would amount to £100,000 and they remained in use until their demolition in 1971, such was their scale and versatility.

With the early designs of *Olympic*, first of the new trio, approved by White Star on 29 July 1908, the 'letter of agreement' for the build followed on the 31st. The collaboration was such that no formal contract for the project existed between the two companies. Construction of the first occupant of the new slipways was soon underway.

Throughout 1909 to 1911 Harland & Wolff had not only to modify their slipways; the Victoria Channel of the river Lagan abutting them was also deepened to provide the 32ft draught required to launch and then float the great 'Olympics' the short distance to the outfitting berth. In order to then install the heavy machinery into the new ships at this berth, in October 1908 Pirrie purchased for £30,000 a floating crane from the Benrather Company of Germany. The crane was the largest of its kind, achieving notoriety for being the first capable of lifting 250 tons. Able to float up and down the full length of the hull at the outfitting wharf meant that only one Benrather would be required for the job. The additions to the yard would not cease there, however.

Their largest dry-dock, the 800ft Alexandra Dock, originally built in 1885, was now far too small to accommodate the Olympic Class. Ever mindful of equipping the yard to handle bigger projects in the future, in 1902 Pirrie petitioned the Belfast Harbour Commission to dig him a new one. With a workforce of 14,000 on his books, Pirrie – the largest employer in all of Ireland – quelled resistance to the plan by threatening to move the yard's entire operations to England should the Commission refuse. Approval was subsequently granted, albeit reluctantly, and work on the new dock began in 1904. By March 1911 the facility was complete, to a cost of £350,000, paid in full by the Harbour Commission, Pirrie naming it the Thompson Graving Dock in a nod to the Commission's chairman, Robert Thompson MP. The new dock was inaugurated quickly on 1 April that year by the largest hull ever afloat – *Olympic*. Measuring 887ft long by 128ft wide the dock housed a flooding volume of 23 million gallons and over time also played host to twins *Titanic* and *Britannic*.

Preparations then focussed on Southampton to improve Harland & Wolff's infrastructure there. The port's Trafalgar dry-dock (originally completed in 1905) was lengthened from 875ft to 912ft. Beginning in the autumn of 1910, work was complete in the spring of 1913 at a cost of £40,000. Becoming only the second such facility in the world large enough to accommodate the 'Olympic' trio, improving the facility in Southampton would allow Harland & Wolff to undertake running repairs to the ships locally rather than returning them to Belfast at the inconvenience of their most cherished and fastidious client, Mr Ismay's White Star Line.

The Ismay Line

Like many shipping operators, White Star was formed during the boom in sea travel. Established in Liverpool in 1845 by business partners Henry Threlfall Wilson and John Pilkington, White Star first concentrated their services between Liverpool and Boston, New York, Charleston and New Orleans. But as Australian gold rush fever took hold in October 1851 their attention was drawn to the more lucrative routes of transporting prospectors outward to Melbourne then returning them to Britain replete with their bounty. Some 41,000 emigrants would make the trip from Liverpool for Australia in 1855, an exodus further bolstered by a similar discovery in New Zealand in 1861. The gold routes became highly competitive and soon enveloped White Star into a fierce price war with the already well-established Black Ball Line. Formed in 1818, Black Ball had become the first operator to offer regular crossings between Liverpool and New York. Although their competition with White Star was unrelenting, the encounter helped propel a battle-hardened White Star into a hugely progressive and innovative line. The staying power of White Star prevailed; Black Ball folded in 1871.

Transferring their ships from sail to steam in 1863, White Star closed two of their routes in 1864 to focus resources on one destination – New York. At that time White Star had only three ships to their flag, but in 1866–7 two of their financiers, from whom they were borrowing to fund construction of a new ship, fell into bankruptcy, leaving White Star half a million pounds in debt to the Royal Bank of Liverpool. The crisis, a significant factor that caused the bank to fold also, forced White Star to sell their fleet as well as its unfinished addition.

The line was saved in 1867 by Thomas Henry Ismay of T.H. Ismay & Co., a shipping line already managing a modest fleet of its own. Coerced in childhood by his father, a shipbroker, Thomas was apprenticed in 1852 at a broker's in Liverpool. In 1864 he was a director of the National Steamship Line, a company established the previous year to operate services between Liverpool and America's south-eastern seaboard, and, with the help of financial heavyweight Gustav Schwabe, benefactor of Harland & Wolff, at the age of thirty purchased the White Star name and goodwill for a token £1,000 on 18 January 1868.

Schwabe convinced Ismay to focus business on the passenger routes to New York that were becoming increasingly in demand, and in 1869 forged the famous meeting between Ismay and his other concern, Edward Harland, knowing that consolidating the resources of the two companies would yield a highly lucrative proposition for all involved. Harland subsequently signed a contract with White Star on 30 July 1869 to build four express liners to operate services between Liverpool and New York.

Following the trend of the time, White Star then began naming their ships to a common theme – opting for the suffix 'ic' – so that the fleet would be easily identifiable as belonging to White Star, as opposed to a rival. Cunard, who had started the practice, were doing likewise, using 'ia' in their names since 1840, while the Inman Line named their fleet after cities, and Guion opted for American states – the concept spawned one of the earliest demonstrations of corporate identity.

To mark the new direction of the business, on 6 September that year Ismay founded a parent company for the line, the Oceanic Steam Navigation Company. On doing so White Star became White Star Line, for which 400 £1,000 shares were allocated for sale, raising the total capital of the firm to £400,000. Purchasing fifty shares for himself, Ismay, the largest holder, was joined by Schwabe and Harland, who took twelve shares each. Ismay also shrewdly appointed Schwabe chairman of Oceanic Steam, in order to ensure the financier's continuing commitment in the success of White Star. The new management would quickly secure the line's niche in the marketplace.

First-class passengers travelling with Cunard, White Star's main rival, felt they were berthed in confoundedly confined spaces that afforded them turgid and tediously slow voyages, a feeling echoed by a disgusted Charles Dickens who in 1842 likened his 'stateroom' on *Britannia* to an 'utterly impracticable, thoroughly hopeless, and profoundly preposterous box'. Seizing the opportunity, Edward Harland convinced Thomas Ismay that White Star must focus on becoming the line recognised for comfort. Ismay consequently permitted Harland to enlarge first-class areas by removing third-class accommodation from the centre of their ships and to transfer these cabins into the bow and the areas around the rudder: thus, steerage class was born.

Alongside Harland & Wolff, White Star played a seminal role in the development of the ocean liner, chalking up a succession of impressive achievements, beginning on 27 August 1870 with the launch of the yard's seventy-third project – the first commission for Ismay's newly created White Star Line – the 3,707-ton, iron-hulled *Oceanic*.

Setting out on her maiden voyage on 2 March 1871, *Oceanic* was squarely aimed at first-class travellers. Costing £120,000, every aspect of her design centred on comfort. Designed by William Pirrie, she was the first to berth saloon-class cabins amidships – away from the interminable vibrations from the engine, which permeated the stern. Also supplying electric light and running water to all first-class cabins, she provided them with larger cabins too, along with improved ventilation, rooftop promenades – even open promenades below the weather deck. Indeed, relinquishing valuable cabin space to a walkway was a huge concession for White Star but the promenades proved hugely popular among her first-class clientele. Having an open area below the top deck vanquished the sense of confinement that passengers habitually experienced aboard other ships, as well as affording unrestricted vistas of the sea, just a few steps from their cabin doors. As the outlook from the Boat Deck was hindered by rigging, crew, lifeboats and their davits (winches) *Oceanic*'s below-deck promenades became an immensely successful, if ingenious, feature, and have been adopted by every passenger liner since. Furthermore, her dining saloon, spanning the full beam of the ship, allowed its windows either side to stream more natural light into the room than was possible on other liners. In addition, its 40ft by 80ft floor space permitted all of her 166 first-class passengers to dine in the same sitting. Gone too were the hard benches lining the saloon's tables; now all passengers in first class had their own cushioned chair.

Measuring 420ft long and 41ft wide, the hull of *Oceanic* also began the 10.2:1 standard, the optimum ratio for minimising water friction – another characteristic still employed by ocean liners today; the hull, thinner than the previous 7:9 and 8:1 standards, measured approximately 10 times as long as its width. Her array of innovations place *Oceanic* as the progenitor of the modern passenger liner.

Ismay's next vessel to cross the Atlantic was the similarly matched sister of *Oceanic*, SS *Atlantic*. Entering service on 8 June 1871, *Atlantic* was wrecked two years later during a storm that forced her upon rocks at Nova Scotia. The sinking claimed 535 lives and became the greatest tragedy at sea until ignominiously surpassed by another White Star liner, *Titanic*.

The disaster did not dent Ismay's desire to give Harland & Wolff carte blanche to create the best ships possible by carefully fusing innovation with tradition. The relationship continued flawlessly and together they forged a reputation for quality that was starting to win over passengers from the popular choice and British staple, the ever-reliable Cunard Line.

Although the rich enjoyed the larger rooms available on board, competition and demand intensified for even larger, faster and more luxurious ships that would meet their ever-growing expectations and the operators' assertions to entice them aboard. The main consideration of the operators was to keep their services competitive with the other major lines, pitting it out in the turf war of transatlantic passenger service. What then followed was a price war, which forced profits lower, while running costs soared ruinously skyward.

To consolidate White Star's revenues, in 1872 Harland & Wolff built the 3,888-ton *Celtic*, their first liner to adopt a near-vertical bow design. Pioneered originally by Brunel's *Great Eastern* fourteen years earlier, the feature boasted dual economical benefits. Firstly, the resulting flatter hull allowed more lower-deck cabins to be sited deep into the bow, but crucially the new shape cut the hull through water with greater efficiency, increasing the ship's speed as well as reducing its consumption of fuel. This too became a standard feature embraced by future generations of liners.

The line achieved recognition in May 1872 with their 3,888-ton *Adriatic*, the first to complete a westbound crossing on the Atlantic within eight days. Because of the pace of their vessels, that October the US Post Office awarded them the contract to carry their mail: White Star injected the proceeds to expand services to South America. The contract boosted confidence, with their ships taking the Blue Riband with their 1,990hp *Baltic* in 1873, the 4,970hp *Britannic* in 1874 and *Germanic* in 1876. With Chairman Thomas Ismay subsequently introduced his two sons, James Hansworth and Joseph Bruce, to the business in 1880, the outfit was universally dubbed 'the Ismay line'.

Harland & Wolff had begun plating ships with steel in 1881. Considerably lighter than iron, albeit weaker, steel paved the way for even faster ships. Yet without any significant orders for a period, in 1885 Harland pressed Ismay to upgrade his fleet and in 1887 was finally commissioned to build White Star's first steel-hulled vessels – incidentally these were also the first craft fitted with twin propellers: the hugely popular 17,500hp twins, *Teutonic* (9,984 tons) and

Majestic (9,965 tons). Upon entering service in 1889 and 1890 respectively, both also achieved the Blue Riband, however these proved to be the final occasions that White Star would actively contend to be the line to own 'the fastest'.

Taking full advantage of the advance in technology since the launch of the now comparatively outdated *Germanic, Majestic* and *Teutonic* were the first liners to feature no sails whatsoever. Opening up the top deck completely for passengers set yet another benchmark in luxury and secured White Star's foothold in the market. The presence of masts diminished to serving a mere decorative function, the two sisters were also among the first liners to introduce second-class fares and be fitted with refrigeration machinery – allowing enough frozen meat to be stored for the entire voyage and negating any future need to carry livestock.

These luxuries saw White Star continue to prosper and by 1891 it become the third-largest passenger carrier to New York. Although vastly overshadowed by the two leading German lines, Norddeutscher Lloyd and HAPAG, White Star was still, crucially, ahead of their British rival, Cunard, which was languishing in fourth place. Ever the visionaries, White Star elevated marine innovation to ever higher plateaus with the launch of their second *Oceanic* amid great fanfare at 11a.m. on 14 January 1899.

The 17,274-ton *Oceanic II* was the first ship to truly personify the concept of a floating hotel. This most significant addition to the White Star stable, at 704ft long, the £750,000 *Oceanic* was also the first craft in forty-one years to surpass the length of Brunel's *Great Eastern*. She was also the first White Star liner to concentrate its design more on passenger comfort than speed. At full power her 28,000hp engines averaged just 19.57 knots, with her voyages taking six days to complete. Marking her owner's tactical retreat from Blue Riband contention she was by no means languid, proving an instant success with the rich, being affectionately lauded as 'the Millionaire's Yacht'. The decision to build a comparatively slow flagship was a risky yet inspired gamble for White Star. No longer interested in producing Blue Riband contenders, they felt her 410 first-class passengers forgave the voyage lasting the extra day, for *Oceanic* was so luxurious and commodious that none aboard her would be in any hurry to disembark.

Apart from the kudos of owning a Blue Riband holder, speed imposed upon the owner a raft of economic burdens in the form of the fuel, space, personnel and machinery needed to achieve it. Ships with fast engines were also prone to increased vibration at high speed, making them noticeably less comfortable for passengers. In 1900 the luxurious 22.5-knot *Deutschland* was striken with it so acutely that she was unflatteringly daubed 'the cocktail shaker'. Requiring less room for machinery, *Oceanic* allowed White Star to fill her space with extra passenger accommodation, maximising profitability. *Oceanic* suffered no vibration, indeed her engines proved extremely reliable, and White Star thereby applied the stratagem to all future express liners.

The popularity of *Oceanic* saw Cunard's finances begin to falter. The market had polarised. Size, reliability and luxury had become the preserves of HAPAG and White Star, whereas Cunard and Norddeutscher Lloyd continued to retail on speed and the no-frills, low cost, emigrant passenger trade. Both camps were praying they had backed the right horse, for there was little rectitude in failure.

Emergence of Morgan

Following Thomas Ismay's death from a heart attack on 23 November 1899, his eldest son, thirty-seven-year-old Joseph Bruce, assumed the chairmanship of White Star. Government contracts transporting British troops and supplies to southern Africa for the Boer War saw the line inadvertently prosper under his leadership. By the time conflict ceased in 1902, White Star's assets amassed a respectable £1 million. Yet still ahead of the game were the German operators, which enjoyed the personal support of their emperor, Kaiser Wilhelm II. His interest in shipping had been further encouraged by a visit to the Royal Naval Review at Spithead on 4 August 1889 when he was shown aboard White Star's armed, albeit barely completed, *Teutonic*. Impressed with her size and speed, the kaiser was particularly enamoured at the ease with which she could be transformed into a fully armed auxiliary cruiser. He was further inspired upon witnessing Sir Charles Parsons appearing, however uninvited, at the Jubilee Review in June 1897 to showcase his invention – the first turbine-driven vessel, the 2,000hp *Turbinia* – where it reached the unprecedented speed of 32.6 knots. The encounters made a profound impression on the kaiser and set in motion a new wave of ships and their counter responses that would eventually culminate in the creation of *Titanic*.

Jealous of Britain's territorial muscle both on land and sea, the kaiser longed for the construction of a new breed of liner fast enough to win the holy grail of trophies – the Atlantic Blue Riband. Although profitable, the existing German fleets were aging and lacked the prestige and speed of their British counterparts. Achieving the speed record would not only draw the international limelight and passenger trade from the traditional holder, Britain, but it would establish Germany as a maritime force and begin the transformation of the predominately landlocked German-speaking nations into a naval superpower.

Decreeing in 1896 that 'Germany's future is on the water', the kaiser petitioned his two largest operators, HAPAG and Norddeutscher Lloyd, to turn this ambition into reality. In 1895 the order had been placed for the first of these liners, doubling as luxury armed cruisers: the 14,349-ton *Kaiser Wilhelm der Grosse*, named in honour of his father 'Wilhelm the Great'. Her launching ceremony, attended by Wilhelm II and 30,000 well wishers, took place in Stettin on 3 May 1897. Able to carry 1,725 passengers and a crew of 480, *der Grosse*, with 28,000hp engines averaging 22.29 knots, wrenched the Blue Riband from Britain on 5 April 1898 by such a margin that the proud maritime nation was stunned. Winning the Blue Riband saw the *der Grosse* become so popular that the 71,118 passengers she carried in 1898 accounted for 24 per cent of the entire movement of passengers in and out of New York that whole year.

The onslaught continued. On her maiden voyage in July 1900, travelling at 22.84 knots, HAPAG's 34,000hp *Deutschland* pushed the speed record even further. These ships exemplified the very best of German engineering and craftsmanship, and Britain's fleets were unable to retaliate. The new German ships boasted the economical advantage too – their leaner hulls and efficient engines consumed much less fuel than their costlier British counterparts and as a result ticket prices were kept mercilessly low. Steady expansion of the German lines also avoided the high costs incurred by their British competitors, squeezed into fewer, more competitive routes on the North Atlantic. Through shoring up their finances on more profitable destinations away from the Atlantic, Norddeutscher Lloyd and HAPAG were able to offer both faster crossings and lower fares. Until the kaiser's interest, however, the two were largely indifferent to building showpiece liners, unlike those regularly produced in Britain. Profit in British shipping was constantly tempered by high running costs, which all too often proved insurmountable for its operators to afford replacements able to compete with the new German 'greyhounds'. Amid intense frustration, there was a slump in passengers using British ships at a time when competition in emigrant transportation was reaching its height.

With reinvigorated pride, Germany began a decade of exercising virtual autonomy over North Atlantic shipping, launching a succession of record-breaking challengers each of which surpassed one another in both size and splendour. Britain's politicians were enraged as they watched their own operators struggling to counter this mêlée. A significant response was sought to rally Britain against a galvanised German mercantile marine and to stem this relentless barrage. The answer arrived in the guise of Clement Griscom, the man who would introduce the formidable J.P. Morgan to shipping and propel White Star into building *Titanic*.

Griscom was a shipping and rail mogul from Philadelphia, who, after procuring the Belgian-based Red Star Line in 1871, founded the International Navigation Company (INC) and through it began building liners under the flag of Red Star to transport large numbers of emigrants westbound, and eastbound to send barrels filled with Standard Oil on the return to Europe. Intense competition on the North Atlantic had embroiled all the major operators in financial chaos; however, backed by the oil barons, Griscom gained advantage by securing a stake in his rivals, Inman Line, buying them outright in 1886. Keen to secure their substantial mail contract he appeased the US government by forming the patriotically named American Line. It worked. They were more than pleased to once more bankroll a home-grown operator for their mail services, their first since the collapse of the Collins Line. Although Griscom's empire consisted of some notable catches he sought to extend its reach further, but doing so would require more concerted support. Hearing that the British Leyland Line was planning to tap into the US cargo market by acquiring the Baltimore-based Atlantic Transport Line, Griscom fielded representatives to lobby the hugely influential financier, John Pierpont Morgan. He had already spoken with Morgan, voicing concerns that the cargo market would be left dominated by Britain should Leyland's deal go through.

Morgan, a prominent banker, had made his fortune funding railroad construction, but he too harboured great personal desire to build an unparalleled transportation network reaching far beyond America to Europe. Rather than start from scratch he set his sights on controlling North Atlantic shipping by acquiring all the major competitors, as well as their infrastructures. His scheme would not only stabilise prices but his incoming ships would also bear passengers and freight directly to his railroads, which now spanned America. For the ships departing the US he intended to use this network of rail and sea to control the export of grain to Europe and onwards to Asia.

Seizing the initiative, Morgan agreed to help Griscom, buying him Atlantic Transport in December 1900. Morgan then offered the Leyland board $3.5 million if they merged with INC. Leyland – who in 1898 harboured ambitions to instead merge with Cunard – declined, but, used to getting his own way, Morgan raised his bid to $11 million, paid not in shares, but cash. Leyland's board relented and the merger marked Morgan's first foray into shipping. The bug had caught him. Morgan began sidelining Griscom, using INC in 1901 to acquire the Dominion Line, Shaw Savill & Albion and a quarter stake in the Holland Amerika Lijn. INC ended the year with a share capital worth $120 million, yet Morgan still needed one of the big names to truly become the force to be reckoned with on the North Atlantic, namely Norddeutscher Lloyd, HAPAG, Cunard or White Star.

Fortunes had turned for Cunard; turnover in 1901 was down by half from the previous year. In 1902 the line, unable to break even, was rapidly losing stock-market value. Urged by unflinching competition from Germany, Cunard discovered themselves entertaining the idea of a buyout with Morgan: an outcome the British government was not prepared to accept.

Since the end of the nineteenth century, Germany's darkening political rhetoric was bringing the inevitability of full-scale European war ever closer. With America officially maintaining a neutral stance on the issue, Britain grew increasingly wary of Morgan, their so-called 'American peril' – the man openly intent on cherry picking Britain's key merchant fleets. The kaiser, conversely, was subsidising Norddeutscher Lloyd for each vessel built with strengthened decks to accommodate heavy guns. Britain, under Prime Minister Arthur Balfour, grew deeply concerned that it too would need to call upon the mercantile marine to carry supplies in the event of war, though many companies were now owned by Morgan, an American. Morgan was used to wielding prodigious influence, frequenting European palaces and political seats at whim. In addition, having originally made his wealth through the steel industry, much of which was needed for British ships, Morgan knew precisely where to apply pressure to leverage his own agenda.

Balfour was perturbed by Morgan's intentions to secure either White Star or Cunard, as his doing so could theoretically deny Britain use of their own merchant fleets in time of war with Germany. Moreover, on 20 February 1902 Morgan had formalised a ten-year alliance with the two main German operators, offering discounted prices to their immigrant passengers using his railroads. Balfour considered Morgan's maritime aspirations to be highly detrimental to Britain's interests.

In Britain legislation forbade shipping lines to receive government assistance for the building of commercial vessels. There was, however, a loophole. Government could indeed fund up to half of the cost of the vessels' construction should these be built to the Royal Navy's specifications and with the proviso that they be requisitioned in time of war. Morgan allowed European politics to play into his hands and began to manipulate Balfour, telling him that he would permit all the shipping operators he acquired to continue trading under their existing names, keep their national identity and man their ships with British crews. Morgan also agreed that should the Admiralty need to commission any of his ships he would allow it at a mere thirty hours' notice. To pacify British anxiety he would emphasise 'International' in the moniker of his shipping trust, in place of 'American'. The plan proved enough to allay fears that Morgan, a man who had openly befriended the kaiser, would no longer deny Britain use of their own fleets at time of war.

Unease over Morgan's influence filtered across both sides of the Atlantic. Although the American government supported Morgan's empire owning swathes of European commerce, quarters there were firmly opposed to the notion of seeing American money financing foreign shipping. Others were also fiercely critical of monopolies. Although antitrust legislation already existed to guard against corporate monopolisation and price fixing no prosecutions would materialise against Morgan's empire, for even its opponents relished the fact that an American enterprise was calling the shots in Europe on Atlantic shipping. The premise that Morgan's company had restored American national pride sufficed to placate his critics at home.

With Morgan courting White Star, Cunard's chairman, Lord Inverclyde, approached Balfour for a loan to build two ships with which to counter their German rivals, warning him that their only alternative was to capitulate to Morgan. In secret Inverclyde had no intention of appeasing the American, indeed he had already rejected an offer from Morgan in April 1902, but Inverclyde knew that Balfour was desperate to keep Cunard out of America's grasp. The gambit worked. On 30 September that year Balfour approved the terms of a £2.6 million loan for Cunard to construct two ultra-modern liners.

The Prime Minister was well aware that should White Star join Morgan, Harland & Wolff would follow suit – perpetually tied up with orders from INC for expanding their fleet. Balfour's loan contained a stipulation that would bind Cunard to build the new ships at two specified British yards, John Brown & Co. of Clydebank and Swan Hunter and Wigham Richardson of Tyneside. In return the government would grant Cunard a low-interest loan at 2.74 per cent, to be paid back over the next twenty years. Armed with the funding they needed, Cunard began work on the two vessels that were to surpass all others in size and speed as well as take on White Star at their own game: luxury.

Operating 213,297 tons of shipping and transporting 29,833 passengers to American ports in 1902 alone, White Star had outsold Cunard by 5,254 tickets that year. They were the most successful British shipping operator as well as the third largest on the North Atlantic. Morgan too had personally favoured White Star, only crossing the Atlantic on their ships since his disappointing experience on Cunard's *Servia* in 1881. As far as he was concerned the British government could have Cunard, and in 1901 he put in the offer to buy White Star. Their board was split, letting months pass by with little indication of a decision. Morgan concerted his efforts. He could not allow this offer – for the only tenable line of note available – to fall through now.

To guarantee the deal's success, Morgan gave Ismay and the White Star board a proposition so enticing that it could only sway their decision in his favour. He would pay its shareholders ten times the value of profit their parent company, Oceanic Steam Navigation, achieved in 1900. In short, considerably more than the company was worth. Denied access to the company's accounts by Ismay, Morgan was unable to discover prior to tabling this offer that 1900 had been an abnormally strong year for White Star. Government contracts for their work in the Boer War had seen profits soar 33 per cent higher than had been achieved over the previous five years. The seventy-five shareholders of Oceanic Steam had purchased 750 shares between them, originally paying £1,000 per share. Morgan was now offering them £13,750 per share at a time profit in shipping was widely falling.

Being the sole builder of White Star's fleet, William Pirrie realised the potential a corporate marriage into Morgan's immense portfolio could produce for Harland & Wolff. Able to build ships 30 per cent more cheaply than its contemporaries in the US, Pirrie knew his yard would become the logical choice for Morgan to populate the fleets of INC. Pirrie also happened to be White Star's second-largest shareholder and exerted pressure on the line's new chairman, Bruce Ismay, to accept the offer. To reject an olive branch of this magnitude would leave both White Star and Harland & Wolff completely without support. But, having just inherited the chairmanship, Ismay was uninterested in selling his father's business. Nor was he in any hurry to turn Morgan down. Withholding White Star's financial records from Morgan, Ismay was in no mind to relinquish ownership of the line and watch it being assimilated into INC. Ismay wanted to retain control, not to cede his father's business to the American on a platter.

Agitated, Morgan slashed the cost of tickets across INC. Abandoned by the government and unable to compete with Cunard's loan windfall or a combatant Morgan, Ismay finally conceded. During a heated meeting in May 1902 three quarters of Oceanic Steam's shareholders voted to accept Morgan's offer of merger.

Morgan was adamant to pacify and immediately prove to the White Star board exactly how central the line was to his plans; so in June 1902 the International Navigation Company was renamed the International Mercantile Marine Company (IMM). Upon doing this, Morgan assumed full control of the organisation, brushing aside the incumbent chairman, sixty-year-old Clement Griscom, reassigning him to a figurehead position as company president. With White Star now under its wing, Morgan's shipping empire and portfolio, encompassing 113 British ships, boasted a formidable working capital amassing £37 million.

Ill at ease with the sale, Bruce Ismay had set the precondition that not only was he to remain as chairman of White Star, but he was also to retain full control of the management of its business. Needing someone to run IMM, Morgan was delighted to accept Ismay's terms. On 1 December that year the sale of Oceanic Steam – parent company of White Star – took place for £10 million ($32 million), 75 per cent of which transferred into IMM shares, the remaining 25 per cent settled in cash among White Star's shareholders. White Star's assets of £750,000 transferred to the International Navigation Company of Liverpool, a subsidiary of IMM set up specifically for the merger, itself worth £25 million, and the new and official owner of the White Star brand.

The merger allowed White Star to undercut Cunard's ticket price for steerage by £1, to an all-time low of £2. During the 1820s the same fare had been £20, falling to just £4 in the 1860s. Prices had become so volatile that a summit between the leading operators was chaired by Bruce Ismay at London's Savoy Hotel from 31 January to 7 February 1908 to address the issue. The outcome resulted in another fierce price war, inflicting even lower profitability on this already battle-weary industry.

White Star immediately became the jewel in the crown of IMM's operations, duly receiving their first instalment, £3 million, on New Year's Eve 1902. White Star quickly diverted the proceeds to commission Harland & Wolff to build them three ships to upgrade their luxury express services. Billed as the 'Big Four', the precursor to the quartet, the 20,904-ton *Celtic* – already in service since July 1901 – was joined in quick succession by three increasingly substantial sisters: *Cedric* (21,035 tons) in 1903; *Baltic* (23,876 tons) in 1904; and *Adriatic* (24,541 tons) in May 1907. As each was launched it surpassed its sister as the largest liner in the world. Managing 16 to 17 knots, they were not only luxurious but also comparably fast, each able to cross the Atlantic in a respectable seven days.

Behind the scenes however, the merger offered a short honeymoon for IMM. Morgan was frustrated by its disorganised management. A price war among IMM's own fleets, as well as paying far more than White Star was worth, had sent finances haemorrhaging from his conglomerate. To add to their woes, 1902 also witnessed a recession throughout the industry, yet White Star's durability shone through, being the sole line within IMM able to return a profit. Despite directly controlling 136 vessels, as well as a further 329 through its alliances with Germany,

IMM's market share still amounted to only 67 per cent of the entire North Atlantic transport. Of that, only 20 per cent was owned by IMM: their German partners commanded the greater 47 per cent share. Morgan even had his bank bridging the shortfalls to keep IMM afloat, but by early 1904 had decided that it was time to retire-off Griscom as president, and he began to seek a replacement, first offering the position to Albert Ballin, current managing director of HAPAG, who had transformed the line into the world's largest. Ballin refused. Morgan's eyes then turned to Ismay, chairman of his new standard bearer. Although he considered Ismay a leader by inheritance only and devoid of entrepreneurial zeal, Morgan appreciated Ismay's natural aptitude for organisation and efficiency, precisely the traits needed to tidy up IMM and get them back on their feet. Bruce Ismay became president of IMM on 21 February 1904, his £20,000 salary soon proving a shrewd investment for Morgan. Ismay stabilised prices throughout IMM and secured Morgan's commitment to continue covering its shortfalls.

To counter both White Star's Big Four and, in particular, the new wave of German liners, on 30 June 1903 Balfour finalised his loan to Cunard. Lord Inverclyde pressed ahead with construction of two new express liners, *Caronia* and *Carmania*, the latter of which was fitted with turbine engines. Cunard were using the sisters – identical in every other aspect – to experiment with the performance of the three Parsons turbines installed in *Carmania* against the conventional quadruple-expansion engines within *Caronia*. Soon after completion, in December 1905, *Carmania* proved her turbines were a considerable advance by markedly outperforming her sister. The experiment paved the way for the next tranche of Inverclyde's riposte, for in May 1904 he had the order placed for two liners that were to comply with the terms set by the Royal Navy's specifications; namely that they exceed 24.5 knots and were thus fast enough to outrun any German craft currently afloat. As first witnessed with *Teutonic*, and now already standard on the new German vessels, Cunard installed specially strengthened decks on their two new express liners to allow each to carry twelve 6in guns and house a magazine for munitions. To resurrect British authority at sea a final condition of the loan required Cunard to make these ships fast enough to recapture the Blue Riband from Germany.

Cunard launched the first of the duo on 7 June 1906: the 31,550-ton *Lusitania* eclipsed the current world's largest liner, White Star's *Adriatic*, by 7,000 tons. Her quadruple turbine engines were able to produce 68,000hp, and in October 1907 they triumphantly propelled *Lusitania* to snatch the Blue Riband in a time of four days, nineteen hours and fifty-two minutes. Averaging a speed of 24 knots she completed the crossing half a day ahead of the incumbent holder, *Kaiser Wilhelm II*. On 20 September that year Cunard then launched her sister, *Mauretania*. At 31,938 tons she was not only larger, but, capable of 26 knots, was even faster.

Mauretania began her maiden voyage from Liverpool on 16 November 1907. During her return from New York, averaging 27.4 knots, she crossed the Atlantic in four days, ten hours and forty-one minutes, setting a record that would remain unbroken for the next twenty-two years. Cunard's latest salvos had brought an abrupt end to a decade of German supremacy, reinvigorating both the line as well as British shipping as a whole. *Lusitania* and *Mauretania* generated in their wake a resurge in patriotic fervour, confidence, and more importantly, ticket sales. British shipping had returned to remarkable form.

Cunard's retaliation proved perfect in its timing. The year 1907 had witnessed 2.5 million passengers cross the Atlantic, out of which 1.2 million had settled in America; on one occasion 11,747 emigrants arrived at New York in a single day. The economy for sea travel was at its zenith. With the Cunard pair making their Big Four suddenly no longer so 'big', a wrong-footed White Star sought an audacious response. This time they would have to strike back harder than ever or risk an irreversible decline into oblivion. It was time for *Titanic* to take centre stage.

CHAPTER 2

INTRODUCING *TITANIC*

'The *Titanic* stood for the "last word" in naval architecture. Not only did she carry to a far greater degree than any other ship the assurance of safety which we have come to associate with more size; not only did she embody every safeguard against accident known to the naval architect … she was built at the foremost shipyard of Great Britain.'

The Scientific American, 27 April 1912

As legend goes, *Titanic* was born on a July evening in 1907 during a dinner party at Downshire House, Lord and Lady Pirrie's mansion on London's fashionable Belgrave Square. Invitations extended solely to Bruce Ismay, chairman of the White Star Line, and his wife, Florence. As the meal came to a conclusion, in typical Edwardian convention, the two wives withdrew from the room to allow their husbands to talk business. Messrs Ismay and Pirrie, operator and builder, immersed themselves in conversation to contrive a plan with which to unseat *Lusitania* and *Mauretania* and with it Cunard's stranglehold on British North Atlantic shipping.

With Cunard raising the standards of luxury at sea higher than ever, Ismay and Pirrie knew that their companies had reached a crossroads; they could either fight back or succumb to mediocrity. There was only one response the two would entertain, and they mused over a long-term desire to build a trio of liners that would surpass the Cunard pair both in scale and luxury. Featuring three funnels and four masts, the new super-ships were to be identical and form the set pieces of White Star's prestigious weekly crossings between Southampton and New York. The new ships would outweigh *Lusitania* and the then-unfinished *Mauretania* by 10,000 tons and out-measure them by 100ft but, more importantly, they would become the most palatial craft ever to strut the ocean.

Launching the most magnificent class of ships ever seen would also allow White Star to replace their aging Big Four express liners and recapture the limelight on shipping's most coveted route. Billed as the Olympic Class of liners they would propel White Star to the pinnacle of luxury travel and underscore Harland &

Wolff's prominence as the greatest shipbuilder of them all. With this new class White Star had played not one ace card but three, hammering down a belligerent statement to their rivals that the stakes in Atlantic transportation had been raised significantly. In addition, each of White Star's 'Olympic' trio would surpass its sibling in size and splendour and widen this margin even further. Their famous counter-attack had begun.

No time was wasted in putting the creation of the Olympic Class into motion. The first would begin its career mid-1911, the second following closely in the early half of 1912, eventually being joined by a third sometime in 1914; together the three would amass a combined tonnage exceeding 140,000. The first two would become Harland & Wolff's fifty-third and fifty-fourth commissions for the White Star Line and, to keep to this schedule, were to be constructed in tandem.

Lord Pirrie would set the general arrangement and dimensions of the ships himself, delegating the more detailed work to his team of naval architects. Preliminary designs increased the number of funnels for each of the 'Olympics' from three to four and reduced their proposed masts to just two, in a bid to instil these leviathans with a more stately and mighty persona.

The names of the first of the class, as chosen by Bruce Ismay, were announced in April 1908. *Olympic* was given to the first ship, with the name for her younger sister confirmed one week later on the 22nd as *Titanic*. Their final blueprints were greeted with approval from White Star's management on 29 July 1908 and two days later signed the agreement to commence construction. Work on *Olympic* began that December and just three months later on *Titanic*, inaugurating a project of unprecedented scale.

Table 1: The Olympic Class of Liners

	Olympic (1911)	*Titanic* (1912)	*Britannic* (1915)
Length (overall)	882ft 6in	882ft 9in	903ft 6in
Beam (extreme)	92ft 6in	92ft 6in	94ft
Load draught	34ft 6in	34ft 6in	34ft 7in
Net Register Tonnage	20,894	21,831	24,592
Gross tonnage	45,324	46,328	48,158
Load displacement (tons)	52,000	52,310	53,820
Bulkheads	15	15	16

Quota of lifeboats (original)	16	20	48
Passenger capacity	2,584	2,603	2,579
Maximum crew capacity	860	944	950
Total engine horsepower	46,000	46,000	50,000
Registry opened	29 May 1911	25 Mar. 1912	8 Dec. 1915
Cancelled	4 Feb. 1939	31 May 1912	18 Dec. 1916

As was the practice with all shipbuilders, Harland & Wolff assigned an identification number to each contract in the chronological order of when the project was commissioned. Bibby Line's *Venetian* of 1859 was Harland & Wolff's first, job number 1, and by the time White Star ordered *Olympic* she had become the yard's 400th, followed immediately by *Titanic* – known throughout Belfast as simply '401'.

Construction on job 401 was begun on 31 March 1909; its steel framing was complete on 6 April 1910 and fully plated by 19 October. With the shell complete the date for the launch of 401 was set for the spring of 1911.

At the firing of a rocket at 12.13p.m. two hydraulic triggers released the empty hull of 401. Sporting her newly incised nameplates, *Titanic* slid stern-first along the Queen's Island slipway, attaining a speed of 12.5 knots. Emblazoned with customary flags spelling out 'SUCCESS' across her bow to wish her luck and prosperity, sixty-two seconds later, at 12.15.02p.m., six anchors eased *Titanic* gently to a halt in the river Lagan. The day of the launch was right on schedule – a gloriously bright Wednesday 31 May 1911. To maximise publicity for the event, after which followed a brief lunch, at 2.30p.m. Harland & Wolff then hosted the rite of signing the now newly completed *Olympic* over to her operator, White Star Line; a moment formally marking the dawn of her commercial service. Two hours later the guests from the launching ceremony departed for Liverpool aboard the proudly finished *Olympic*, closing a day which had seen the wharves of the Belfast yard hold two of the world's largest hulls at the same time, chalking up one of the most significant occasions in the annals of maritime development.

It had taken 23 tons of soap, oil and beef tallow to grease *Titanic* along the 772ft run of slipway number 3. The launch was no mean feat: the 24,600-ton hulls of *Titanic* and *Olympic* were at the time the largest movable man-made structures in existence. And, adhering to company tradition, White Star would resist the fanfare of christening the two ships. Yet the launch of *Titanic* drew vast crowds, vying keenly for a glimpse of the world's largest liner waterborne for the very first time. Across the other side of the wharf, Belfast's Albert Quay was packed with 10,000 onlookers; however, watching from the yard itself was a ticket-only affair. In a specially built stand flanking her vertiginous portside hull sat the VIPs, among them Bruce Ismay, Robert James McMordie (Lord Mayor of Belfast) plus the ship's owner J.P. Morgan himself. Occupying a stand strategically positioned and directly in front of her imposing bow thronged ninety members of the press. Two further stands were similarly filled to capacity.

The launch was a meticulous event, superintended personally by Lord Pirrie. It had proceeded flawlessly, and Belfast was euphoric. The sentiment of occasion was present throughout the town: 'by what it had done in assisting the White Star Line in its great and commendable enterprise, Belfast could lay no small share in the maintenance of the prosperity of the British Empire', proclaimed *The Belfast News Letter* the following morning. With *Olympic* now in commercial service, work completing *Titanic* had still to be done.

Within minutes of making water, *Titanic* was floated to the yard's outfitting bay at the nearby Alexandra Wharf where she would spend the next ten months receiving all her machinery, fixtures and fittings. Work continued apace. Her funnels were added by January 1912, then on 3 February she was towed to the newly completed Thompson Graving Dock – the facility specially constructed to accommodate the Olympic Class – to have her hull painted and propellers fitted.

Building *Titanic* was a huge logistical operation: a total of 4,000 workers were directly involved in her construction between 1909 and 1912, during which time there were eight fatalities. Yet Harland & Wolff would have felt it fortunate to have lost just eight of their men during the course of her construction, for out of experience they anticipated the death of at least one worker for every £100,000 spent on a project. As it cost precisely £1,564,606 to build *Titanic*, Harland & Wolff would have anticipated the loss of at least fifteen men during her construction. One of those deaths was of James Dobbin, a shipwright struck by falling timbers on the morning of her launch. He succumbed in hospital the following day. In addition, of the workforce engaged in piecing *Titanic* together, there would be a further 246 injuries, twenty-eight recorded as serious. As with all shipyards most accidents resulted from falls from staging platforms or by being struck by overhead machinery or falling debris. There were no safety ropes, hard hats or health and safety inspectors; work on *Titanic* was arduous, unrelenting and extremely perilous.

Although the Olympic Class was not intended to attain any speed records, their craftsmanship found *Olympic* and *Titanic* surpassing expectations as the grandest, tallest and largest ships the world had hitherto known: all the accoutrements that White Star sought in order to complete their showdown with Cunard.

Harland & Wolff, indexing the construction of *Titanic* as number 390904, once complete and as with every other British merchant vessel over 15 tons, registered her with the Board of Trade – the body responsible for regulating and licensing merchant shipping. On 25 March 1912, in accordance with merchant shipping law, *Titanic* entered the official register as vessel 131,428, with her port of registry as Liverpool, geographical headquarters of the White Star Line and home to many of the major shipping operators since the early days of steam. The design of *Titanic* conformed to all the requirements of the Merchant Shipping Acts in force at the time, those dated 1894 and 1906.

Painted in the typical scheme applied to most liners of the day, *Titanic's* exterior comprised of four colours. Her keel was protected with red copper oxide anti-fouling paint, the hull's upper portion was black and the decks extending above (the superstructure) contrasted in white, and were separated from the blackened hull by a thin gold band. Her four elliptically streamlined funnels, 24ft long and 19ft at their widest diameter, were painted in the livery of the White Star Line: buff-yellow, topped with a black anti-soot rim at their upper quarter. The funnels, rising 74ft from the Boat Deck and spaced equally apart, reclined regally to an angle of 10 degrees.

Measuring 882ft 9in from stem to stern – the equivalent of 268.8m, or one sixth of a mile – *Titanic* boasted a breadth of 92ft 6in. Towering to a height of 104ft between the keel and the highest deck, the full extent of the ship soared 175ft from the depth of the keel to the tips of the funnels, standing her 30ft taller than London's Nelson's Column. To remain afloat when fully loaded, *Titanic* would require a draught some 34ft 6in. Grossing 46,328 tons (21,831 NRT), her water displacement would amass 52,310 tons, increasing to 60,250 fully laden. In short, *Olympic* and *Titanic* were 31 per cent larger than the next largest vessel afloat, Cunard's *Mauretania*.

The cost to build the Olympic Class was budgeted at £1.5 million apiece. Much of the capital raised from IMM's purchase of 1902 had, however, long since been depleted in producing White Star's Big Four. To finance the construction of the Olympic Class, in 1908 the line mortgaged their existing fleet and also released £1.5 million worth of shares in their parent company, Oceanic Steam Navigation.

Harland & Wolff's own fee for building vessels for White Star was intended to recoup the full cost of its construction plus an additional 4 per cent commission placed on top: the 'cost-plus' arrangement. Since first meeting in 1869 White Star and Harland & Wolff agreed this structure under which the construction of all their ships was to be paid. Namely, although the combined cost for building *Olympic* and *Titanic* was set to £3 million, any additional materials or alterations to their design requiring this price to increase, Harland & Wolff could incorporate such changes without forfeiting their commission. So effective was this arrangement that it continued unchanged until 1927. Such an agreement required a huge element of trust, for it allowed White Star to ensure that Harland & Wolff source only the best materials for their ships, regardless of cost, by removing risk of the builder having to scrimp or reduce quality in order to meet a fixed budget.

Titanic formed half of the initial £3 million investment committed by White Star to build both her and *Olympic*. Valued at £1 million, the hull and machinery of *Titanic* was insured across several institutions – as no single entity would carry the risk alone – namely, Commercial Union Assurance and Atlantic Mutual Insurance of New York, affording *Titanic* one year's cover starting 30 March 1912. The insurance for both *Titanic* and *Olympic* had been underwritten since early 1911 by Lloyd's of London at £1 million apiece, two thirds of their respective costs. Securing the lowest premium available (approximately 3 per cent) White Star would not, out of habit, fully insure their vessels; IMM self-insured the unprotected balance. However, as a precaution White Star would customarily remind each captain in their employ that their livelihood as well as the reputation of the line was at stake should their ship become either damaged or lost. This was considered a sufficient form of insurance in its own right and to ingrain this culture into their captains White Star awarded them a generous annual bonus if the vessels under their command had not come to any harm.

As well as being a publicity draw and cosmetic statement, the bigger the ship meant the more commercial carrying capacity it was able to house and, with that, the greater the income it would generate for its owners. *Titanic* was designed to carry 2,603 passengers accommodated throughout 762 rooms: 905 in first class, 564 in second and 1,134 in third, as well as occupancy for 944 crew: 3,547 in total, the maximum number she was later certified by the Board of Trade to carry. Of the crewmembers that *Titanic* was licensed to accommodate, the full complement she was able to carry comprised of seventy-four sailors, 326 engine room staff, plus 544 others working directly with the passengers. Although able to accommodate more, the optimum number working across these three departments was 887, half of which (494) were engaged in passenger service: cooks, waiters, maids, pursers and stewards. The remainder comprised sixty-six sailors, including officers, and an army of 327 maintaining and supplying the engines and boilers.

Working in teams of fifty-three men per shift, the firemen would fill in excess of 650 tons of coal, usually Welsh (its smokeless properties and intense combustion were considered best for use at sea), into the boilers of *Titanic* each day of her voyage. Her overall capacity for 7,812 tons of coal was distributed among eleven bunkers, providing the fuel to her twenty-nine steel boilers. The boilers in *Titanic* were the cylindrical Scotch marine variety, a type dating from 1870 and preferred for their compactness and ability to retain high pressures. Tested to 430psi but operated at 215psi, of these boilers twenty-four were double-ended, each weighing 91.5 tons and measuring 15ft 9in in diameter and 21ft in length. In addition there were five shorter single-ended boilers, 11ft 9in in length and 57 tons apiece. Each boiler end contained a trio of openings, each leading to a corrugated tubular Morrison furnace 3ft 9in in diameter. One fireman would feed all three, strewing coal onto their suspended grates, which across all 159 furnaces pooled a combustion surface boasting 144,142sq.ft. The heat from each furnace was drawn to the upper portion of the boiler then doubled back into 430 fire-tubes passing through a water reservoir to produce the steam. The cylindrical Scotch arrangement fully immersed the tubes, combustion chambers and furnaces in water, which across all twenty-nine boilers was maintained at a constant 1,309 tons. Extracted through a smoke box at the front of the boiler, the condensate was siphoned away to the engine cylinders.

The boilers themselves were housed in six separate rooms running back-to-back, occupying floor space in the very base of the ship that totalled 320ft in

length. Each room, its own watertight compartment, contained five of these boilers – the forward room contained four – with each compartment designed to
function independently should another become debilitated by emergency.

Smoke and gas extract from the boilers was removed through flues, rising 150ft
before venting through the tops of the funnels at 600°F. The steam itself passed
into two identical sets of four-cylinder, triple-expansion reciprocating engines, a
type manufactured by Harland & Wolff since 1885 and first employed on *Teutonic*
and *Majestic* in 1889.

The engines driving *Titanic* were huge. Standing 30ft high and mounted on beds
63ft long, each set weighed 720 tons and powered groups of pistons driving one of
her two 2ft diameter port and starboard propeller crankshafts. The steam to each
engine was forced firstly into a high-pressure piston cylinder of 54in bore, kept at
215psi. Releasing its condensate through a slide-valve to an intermediate-pressure
cylinder, 84in bore and 78psi, the steam then passed to two 9psi low-pressure cylinders of 97in. These four piston-valves expanding and compressing steam in 75in
strokes powered vast inverted connecting rods to crank one of two 118 ton wing
propeller shafts. Producing a shaft output of 15,000hp, each of the reciprocating
engines was driven at 75rpm for cruising speed and 78rpm for top speed. Affixed
to each wing shaft was a 38-ton, three-blade propeller, its assembled diameter spanning 23ft 6in. Cast of manganese-bronze, the two propellers were bolted to steel
bosses mounted on wings that in turn flanked a smaller four-blade central screw.

The central propeller was driven by the turbine. Powered by exhaust steam supplied by the four low-pressure cylinders, the 420-ton, 50ft-long Parsons turbine
of *Titanic* was also manufactured by Harland & Wolff. The steam to this engine
was blasted through tightly packed rotor blades to spin its 12ft-diameter 130-ton
steel turbine drum. Run at 165–190rpm, the turbine indicated 16,000hp and was
used exclusively to give the ship forward acceleration in open sea. Fastened to its
27in-wide crankshaft and located directly in front of the rudder, the assembled
central propeller spanned 17ft and weighed 22 tons. Between them the three
engines provided *Titanic* with a total horsepower of 46,000, although she was
comfortably able to produce 59,000hp.

The concept of combining two types of engine – mixed propulsion – was still
experimental in 1912. First appearing on conventional ships in 1909, its use was
not commonplace until 1920. *Olympic* was only the second White Star liner driven
by mixed propulsion, as well as having three instead of two propellers – fruits of
the line's successful tests with *Laurentic* in April 1909. The three engines would
give *Titanic* a cruising speed of 21 knots and, with all twenty-nine boilers lit, a
maximum speed of 23.5 knots, weather conditions permitting. Spread across two
dedicated watertight compartments, separated by a bulkhead wall, the twin reciprocating engines shared space located forward of the turbine room, with the two
compartments running a combined length of 123ft and spanning the full beam
of the ship. At their far end, enormous twin condensers, enclosing 25,275sq.ft of

cooling surface each, converted the final remnants of steam extract back to water for filtering and then returned it to the boilers to begin the expansion cycle again.

Steering *Titanic* was a single elliptically shaped rudder weighing 101.25 tons. The mechanism operating it was powered by a twin set of three-crank Brown engines. Pioneered by the Brown Brothers of Edinburgh these had become the standard type used for this purpose since 1867. Manufactured by Harland & Wolff, those on *Titanic* operated as a pair; one driving her rudder, the other its standby should it fail. These inversed standing engines were kept to a pressure of 100psi, each driving a Citroën spur wheel turning the vast central quadrant steering gear fixed to the tiller atop the rudder.

Above decks, the most noticeable feature of *Titanic* was undoubtedly her four funnels. The use of four funnels had been first employed by Norddeutscher Lloyd for *Kaiser Wilhelm der Grosse* – spaced wide apart in pairs to allow for an as large as possible dining saloon below. The first British ship to carry four funnels – although evenly spaced, unlike the 2/2 signature configuration of their German counterparts – was *Lusitania*, starting a trend that was eventually adopted by a total of fourteen liners, the final of which was Cunard's *Aquitania* in 1914. On *Titanic* only the forward three funnels actually emitted steam. The presence of the fourth, a dummy, was mainly for cosmetic effect. Its sole practical purpose was as a vent for the galleys and the turbine room directly below. Going to the expense of installing a seemingly superfluous funnel in an age of hard-fought profits proved one of the most economically astute features possible to be incorporated into a luxury liner's design. To Edwardians, a liner bearing four funnels encapsulated its size and stateliness, projecting confidence and reliability to the beholder by making the ship appear stronger and thereby safer by directly drawing attention to the size of the ship itself.

Another seemingly unnecessary adornment in 1912 were masts – agreeably a less essential attribute in the days post sail. *Titanic*, however, carried two steel masts spaced 600ft apart, their uppermost 15ft sections consisting of teakwood to give her a more delicate, yacht-like semblance. The foremast housed the crow's nest. Sited 50ft above the deck and 95ft above the waterline the nest was accessed internally by an iron ladder. Gradually tapering, the masthead soared 157ft 5in above the deck, overlooking its after companion – the mainmast, 154ft 6in tall – at the rear of the ship. The overall distance between the waterline and the tips of the masts was 205ft, yet they had served little function since 1889 other than supports for wireless antennae and an array of signal pennants; their presence in 1912 was more for decorative effect. Set at a recline equal to one inch for every foot they were tall, the masts on *Titanic* were intended to add a delicate touch of finesse to her record-breaking bulk.

Everything on *Titanic* was oversized, especially the equipment to control her. *Titanic* carried three stockless steel anchors, two weighing 7¾ tons each and suspended 60ft above the keel either side of the bow. Her third lay directly on deck. Weighing 15.8 tons this 17ft-long 10ft-wide anchor was so large that it had to be moved by its own crane; the 2.66in-thick rope used to lower it was calibrated to lift 289 tons and was able to plunge to a depth of 175 fathoms. The central anchor was more intended for stabilising the bow in rough seas and was therefore stored on the deck's centreline to help maintain the ship's buoyancy.

Capstans, in sets of four on the bow and stern, were used to tighten mooring ropes to the dockside. These, supplied by Napier Brothers of Glasgow, which was the very manufacturer that provided the engines for Cunard's first steam-powered ships. Supporting each of the two side anchors was 96 tons of chain fed through hawse pipes in the hull plating. Stretched out the two sets of bower chain could between them reach a depth of 330 fathoms and weighed a total of 96 tons. With each link weighing 175lb they were the largest of their day, and along with the three anchors, were all manufactured in Dudley by Noah Hingley & Sons Ltd.

Because of her considerable length, strength was a key consideration in design-ing *Titanic*. Her hull was divided by two expansion joints penetrating through her upper decks – the superstructure protruding the main hull (Boat Deck to B Deck) – dividing the ship on these decks into thirds. These three uppermost levels, unsupported by the framing employed so liberally throughout the lower hull, were formed of lighter steel to militate undue weight inhibiting the ship's buoyancy. With the upper decks thereby weaker than the area below, which was reinforced with girders encasing her hull, expansion joints allowed this upper portion to flex against the rigours and motions of the sea. Filled with leather, the joints on *Titanic* permitted her superstructure to contort by as much as 2ft.

The hull itself was sheathed by 2,000 steel plates, fastened together by more than 3 million rivets contributing 1,470 tons to the ship's aggregate weight. Each 1in broad rivet was driven either hydraulically or by hand by teams of four men each setting 200 rivets a day. Fixed to the frame in strakes – rows – along her hull, each plate was joggled – overlapped – horizontally over the one below. Held together by rivets in double and triple banks, they fastened the plates to the ship's frame in quadruple rows of rivets around the keel. Joggling in this manner increased the strength of the hull.

The plates themselves were rolled from a mild-steel compound. Each 1in-thick plate measured 30ft in length, was 6ft high and weighed 3 tons apiece. Larger 36ft plates were used amidships, each weighing 4.5 tons. Those cladding B and C decks increased in thickness to 1.5in to provide even greater strength to the hull.

Although Harland & Wolff first experimented with plate welding in 1907, it was not until the Second World War that the practice would universally replace riveting as a method of joining hull plates together. Although welding made it possible to flush plates against one another and give the hull a completely smooth finish, thereby minimising water friction, riveted plates provided one overriding advantage: rigidity, which afforded the hull far greater durability against collision.

The hull of *Titanic* was formed by a network of steel girders. Each frame, 10in thick, rose to form a ribcage from the keelbar – the backbone of the ship – climbed to the extent of C Deck, 66ft at the top of her frame. The frames were spaced 24in apart at the bow, widening to 3ft apart amidships, before closing up again to 27in toward the stern. Each was interlocked by several longitudinal stanchions creating a formation that gave *Titanic* tremendous support: a practice in which Harland & Wolff were well versed: they had been framing White Star's vessels in this fashion since 1881. As a further measure to increase strength, each deck on *Titanic* would rise gradually by 24in toward the bow, run horizontal through their mid-section then camber by 12in again into the stern. This 'sheer' effect had become a standard feature on all liners since Brunel's *Great Eastern*, affording long hulls rigidity and protection against splintering against the force of the heaving sea. To this effect the hulls on the Olympic Class were designed to withstand a maximum strain of 22,400lb per square inch.

For safety *Olympic* and *Titanic* also featured a cellular double keel. Measuring 5ft 3in deep – increasing to 6ft 3in beneath the engine rooms to provide additional support to the power plant above – the double keel ran the full length of the ship. Extending upwards were double-lined sidewalls. Separated by a 10in void, the walls enclosed a secondary protective layer of plating around the hull. Clearing the load-line by 2ft 6in, the walls ran 447ft to encase the exterior flanks to the six boiler and two engine rooms: the hull's most vulnerable area.

The area forming the double-bottomed keel itself was divided by three longitudinal girders. Laying 30ft outward of a 670ft beam along the centreline of the hull was its outboard companions. Each 447ft in length, these ran parallel to the double-hull sidewalls above. The three girders, partitioned by transverse bulkheads, divided the double bottom into forty-four isolated compartments – tanks. Each tank was utilised. The majority stored non-drinkable water, pumped throughout the ship for washing, bathing and supplying the cooling system for the boilers; the latter alone required 105 tons of water per day. These, as well as other tanks, provided *Titanic* with an overall capacity for 5,754 tons of ballast with which to give her stability at sea. Utilising water as ballast enabled crew to drain, fill or redistribute the tanks at any point in the voyage to fine-tune the trim of the ship and accommodate the changeable sailing conditions, as well as to compensate for the quantity of cargo carried on each particular voyage. For further stability two bilges ran 294ft along the hull, each 25in deep working as fins to prevent the hull from rolling with the sea.

Contrary to popular belief, *Titanic* was an incredibly safe ship, benefiting from all the innovations of the day. At the heart of this safety lay fifteen 1in-thick transverse steel bulkhead walls. Dividing the hull into sixteen separate compartments, each wall spanned the full beam of the ship. A safety wall a mere 1in thick may not seem sufficient to keep the rushing torrents of the sea at bay; however, these were the same thickness as the plating forming the hull and, as with the hull, bulkhead walls needed only be strong enough to restrict the inflow of water to an adjoining compartment. To the builders, incorporating more substantial walls was deemed unnecessary for a civilian vessel; those dividing *Titanic* conforming to the requirements of the day – the British Board of Trade's Bulkheads Committee recommendations of June 1891 – with all fifteen bulkheads clearing her water-line. Labelled A to P (no bulkhead I), the leading bulkhead (A), sited in the bow, climbed to C Deck, clearing her waterline by 30ft. Bulkhead B, then those K to P, reached D Deck 20ft above the waterline. As experience had proven in ships more prone to collision at the bow or stern, her seven middle walls – C to J – reached only to E Deck, clearing the waterline by just 11ft.

The bulkheads were spaced at regular intervals, averaging 54–57ft between them and up to 69ft fore and aft the main engine room. Between them they contained a total of thirty-one watertight doorways to afford crew and passengers access between compartments. A switch on the bridge could electronically close the twelve lowest doors after sounding a thirty-second warning bell, the remaining doors needing to be closed manually to seal all sixteen compartments. Pioneered by Norddeutscher Lloyd Line in 1897 the electric doors were designed to close vertically and slowly using their own weight – like a portcullis – so as not to rely on external power sources which might fail during a breach. Geared closing mecha nisms guiding the fall of the doors were further aided by hydraulics to regulate their speed of descent. The doors would even close automatically should a float inside a switch beneath the flooring be triggered by water. Some ships also included a similar device that engaged automatically if the hull developed a tilt. Of those in *Titanic* the mechanism's hydraulics were maintained at a pressure of 800psi to give her 1,600lb doors sufficient force to sever almost anything that was obstructing their fall, guaranteeing closure at all cost: hence the presence of the warning bell. The doors could also close manually without activation from the bridge and were fitted with a spy-hole to allow crewmembers to peer through and assess the extent of flooding in the adjoining compartment. Should they then wish to regain access to that compartment a trigger was fitted next to the door to allow them to be reopened manually. Doing so would activate an alert on the bridge. Furthermore, escape ladders within each of the engine and boiler rooms ensured that no person-nel could be trapped inside a compartment once the doors had shut.

This arrangement of bulkheads intended *Olympic* and *Titanic* to remain afloat with two of the largest compartments or all of the first four compartments com-promised. This was considered a sufficient safeguard against even a worst-case scenario, a statement of fact that would inspire the press to famously proclaim *Titanic* 'unsinkable': a priceless endorsement for White Star's new leviathans.

Relentless competition in North Atlantic passenger routes had seen ticket prices fall to an all-time low by 1900. Prices remained low and by 1912 the cost of a one-way ticket on *Titanic* was competitively broad. Varying wildly between seasons, White Star charged whatever they could get away with and ticket prices for *Titanic* ranged vastly.

The price for first-class passage began at £23 for a single berth in one of her lower-deck staterooms, rising to £870 for one of the four deluxe Parlour suites

– each boasting private drawing and sitting rooms and two extremely plush bedrooms. Aboard *Titanic* the two B-Deck Parlour suites even indulged their occupants with private open-air promenades. At the other end of the scale, a one-way trip with a bed in one of her 350 second-class cabins would cost their occupants around £13, whereas passage bunked in one of the eighty-four shared cabins or single-sex dormitories in third class was £7.

Despite catering for three passenger classes the Olympic Class were primarily designed with their first-class clientele in mind. The first-class apartments on *Titanic* comprised thirty-nine staterooms offering en-suite bathrooms, with the remaining 350 sharing wash facilities. The interiors of her public rooms featured the most palatial furnishings hitherto experienced at sea: their 12½ft-high ceilings were a previously unheard of extravagance. *Titanic* was designed to lavish upon her first-class passengers all the comforts and trappings they would otherwise have enjoyed at home – if not more opulent. Although designed to accommodate the needs of all classes the standards across her three varying passenger areas were considered greatly superior to those found in other liners of the day. Second class on *Titanic* was deemed as fine as first class on most of her contemporaries. Even her third class was less austere than the period's universally frugal accommodation for second class.

Although almost identical in design, the fact that *Titanic* was marginally newer than *Olympic* meant that she enjoyed the incorporation of several key modifications to enhance her potential profitability. Space left as open areas on *Olympic* was ceded on her younger sister to augment capacity in first class. The modifications were concentrated on B Deck, which on *Olympic* housed two 400ft-long, 13ft-wide fully glazed promenades running outboard along the entire length of the deck. Because a full-length promenade still existed on A Deck above, the B Deck walkways on *Titanic* were supplanted by extra staterooms; however remnants of two 50ft sections, one either side of the ship, were kept as private promenades for her two main Parlour suites. Other improvements integrated into *Titanic* included an extra reception room and an additional restaurant, the Café Parisien, which occupied space originally intended for this now omitted portion of B Deck promenade. In addition to the alterations on B Deck, the after extremity of the officers' quarters on the Boat Deck was shortened by 9ft to allow the addition of six staterooms directly abaft; *Olympic* carried no cabins on her Boat Deck until her refit of 1913. Housing a total of twenty-eight more staterooms than her elder sister, the consequence of the alterations was that *Titanic* became 1,004 tons heavier than *Olympic* and thus officially the largest liner in service at the time of her maiden voyage in April 1912.

Stem to Stern

Titanic housed eleven steel decks, each boasting new standards in innovation, luxury and style. From the Boat Deck at the top to the Tank Top at the bottom, here we shall walk through *Titanic* exploring the layout and content of each deck along our way, starting at the bow then working toward the stern.

The Boat Deck measured 500ft in length. Standing 58ft above the waterline, this was the uppermost deck on *Titanic* and served as her main open area and home to the ship's twenty lifeboats – hence its name. Here two sets of wooden lifeboats, grouped into fours, sat along the deck's outboard edge. In addition to these were four collapsible boats, their sides folded down for neat stowage.

Floored in pine, the Boat Deck gave access to the Bridge House. Positioned 197ft aft of the bow and 60ft above the waterline, the bridge afforded its occupants an unrestricted horizon of the path of the ship. Inside were two wheelhouses, the Chart Room and a cabin set aside for the harbour pilot to await his collection and return to shore. Located behind the bridge was the living accommodation for senior crew. Essentially comprising two corridors running either side of the casing for funnel number 1, the captain's suite of rooms occupied the starboard-side corridor, and those for his officers occupied that on the portside. To their rear the corridors were joined by a transverse passage, itself giving access to three rooms forming the Marconi suite. Behind them a partition sealed off the officers' quarters, with the six newly installed first-class staterooms and adjoining corridor leading onto the upper landing of the forward first-class passenger staircase, topped by a beautifully ornate 26ft by 19ft oval glass dome latticed with intricately curved ironwork. Behind the dome, along the starboard promenade outside, lay the 45ft-long gymnasium. Lit by tall arched windows the gymnasium was resplendent with the very latest equipment, including a rowing machine, exercise bikes, weights, even mechanical horses. The use of the facility was available at no extra cost, although only to first-class passengers. Open daily between 10a.m. and 6p.m., its far inboard wall featured a large illuminated map of the world depicting a line plotting the ship's course.

Further aft on deck climbed a freestanding platform housing the ship's main compass. Raised 12ft above the deck to minimise interference from the steel superstructure, it held the compass a total of 78ft above the waterline to reduce similar interference from the sea; the compass plinth itself contained correcting magnets that required regular adjustment throughout the voyage. Surrounding the compass platform spanned an open area of deck allowing first-class passengers to walk – promenade – and relax outside in periods of clement weather.

The after portion of the Boat Deck housed a large skylight straddling a shaft that channelled light and air to the reciprocating engine room deep below. The skylight was in turn followed by the entrance to the after first-class staircase, as well as the uppermost access to a separate enclosed stairwell and elevator shaft for second-class passengers. At sea the differing classes of passenger never shared the same companionways, accommodation, restaurants, amenities or entrances. Passengers in the three classes were kept stringently apart, the rationale for which is explored in chapter thirteen.

The Boat Deck was divided into three promenades, their boundaries dictated by the two expansion joints. The first-class section, extending 200ft, was followed by a 145ft second-class promenade to its rear, the two strategically demarcated by a brief fenced-in engineers' area surrounding the skylight. The officers' promenade toward the bow occupied the remaining area of deck abutting the Bridge House, giving access to the wheelhouse and navigation wings as well as the ship's two 'emergency' lifeboats.

To extend their height the ceilings of the public rooms directly beneath penetrated the flooring of the Boat Deck. Above these, roofs served as raised promenade platforms, for on *Titanic* luxury was king in the normally utilitarian world of life at sea. White Star prided themselves on the scale of their rooms, some boasting 12ft-high ceilings, which were moulded and stuccoed to disguise the metallic consciousness of ship. Indeed 'cabin fever' was not an axiom that Ismay would risk being associated with *Titanic*.

The deck below the Boat Deck was Promenade Deck A. Also measuring 500ft long, it stood 48ft 6in above the waterline. This, a strictly first-class passenger domain, was winged by two 9ft 6in tall sheltered promenades, which ran the full length of the deck – in places they were up to 30ft wide and during the day would be alive with deckchairs. Portions of these promenades were encased by windows known as 'Ismay screens'. Pioneered by Harland & Wolff in 1909, those on *Titanic* were sited along the forward 192ft outboard sections of deck and positioned to shield passengers from the sea spray emitted from the bow. Intended as an improvement to *Olympic*, whose A Deck was completely exposed to afford its occupants unrestricted panoramic views of the sea, the screens were incorporated late in the construction of *Titanic*.

A Deck began with thirty-six first-class staterooms, followed by the forward passenger entrance, from which led a short corridor linking it with the 41sq.ft reading and writing room. The room, Georgian in style, was lined with elegant white panelling. Its brightness was further enhanced by an 18ft bay window near which stood a marble fireplace that formed the focus of the room. At the after end of the corridor sat the 59ft by 63ft lounge. Essentially serving as a room for gaming and relaxation, the lounge featured a bar and library and was lavishly adorned with high moulded ceilings and a central chandelier topping off intricately panelled oaken walls influenced by the style of Louis XV and the Palace of Versailles. Boasting four bay windows and huge inlaid mirrors, an ornate white marble fireplace provided focal point to the room.

Behind, following a connecting corridor and the first-class staircase, was the 65ft by 63ft smoking room – intended for gentlemen only. Likewise Georgian in style, the walls of the smoking room were sumptuously panelled with mahogany, inset with floral patterns of inlaid pearl. The darkness of the wood was offset by a beautiful white moulded ceiling and stained-glass windows. The room also featured the ship's only coal-burning public fireplace (the remaining hearths aboard were electric imitations), which was drawn up the abutting shaft of funnel 4. Above its richly carved 8ft-wide marble surround hung one of a pair of specially commissioned oils by artist Norman Wilkinson. Entitled 'Plymouth Harbour', its companion 'Approach to the New World' took pride of place in the room's twin aboard *Olympic*. Complete with bar, the furniture for the room was specifically chosen to imitate the ambience of a London gentleman's club. A revolving door placed at its after entrance was intended to reduce draft and provided access to the abutting 30ft long by 25ft wide Palm Court Café.

The café was themed to resemble a veranda, the type often seen on the garden terraces of stately homes. Its walls were festooned with trellises interlaced with real ivy, to compliment its wicker furnishings. The casing of a stairwell, dividing the café in two, allowed passengers the choice of dining either in a smoking or non-smoking section. The large bay windows of the café looked upon an open area of deck containing the after mast, surrounding promenade and inhabited by twin cranes for loading cargo into hold number 4.

Much of the interior for first class was designed by Aldam Heaton & Co.; famed for their considerable eye for detail they were the natural choice for White Star, who wanted no component overlooked for *Titanic*. Fitted with oak, all her first-class staterooms were decorated in a vast array of styles catering for all tastes, traditional and modern – from Italian Renaissance, Tudor, Jacobean, William and Mary, Bourbon (Louis' XIV, XV and XVI), Queen Anne, Georgian, Adam, Empire, Regency to contemporary, and both old and 'modern' Dutch – all fabricated to perfection by artisans across Harland & Wolff's vast assortment of workshops. The staterooms themselves ranged from modest to palatial; but, throughout, quality was never to be compromised.

Further down the ship was Bridge Deck B. Running slightly longer to A Deck at 555ft it stood 39ft 6in above the waterline. Of its ninety-nine B staterooms thirty could adjoin to form larger apartments, each offering en-suite bathrooms. The deck also housed the upper first-class passenger entrance foyer, sealed off by two lobbies, each sporting 4ft 6in openings to allow the quayside gangways to penetrate the sides of the ship. The communicating hall contained the forward grand staircase, splendidly lined with bronze candelabra. Behind the hall ran two inboard white-panelled corridors that began immediately with the most exquisite cabins on *Titanic* – Parlour suites B51/5 (styled Renaissance/Adam) and B52/6 (Louis XVI/Empire) – both sporting drawing rooms, moulded ceilings, faux open fireplaces, bathrooms, two bedrooms and 50ft promenades, even separate accommodation for their occupants' private retinue of servants.

Behind the suites ran thirty-four smaller staterooms and the after grand staircase. Bestriding the landing was a bright multi-themed reception area, the newly incorporated anteroom to the 60ft-long à la carte restaurant, run through franchise agreement by London restaurateur Luigi Gatti. After proving so popular on *Olympic*, whose restaurant seated 122, capacity on *Titanic* was increased to 137, and the restaurant was also granted its own reception space. Unlike the ship's main saloon, the restaurant served food on demand between 8a.m. and 11p.m. Complete with adjoining galley, pantries and stores, the restaurant boasted walls panelled with walnut, carved in the style of Louis XVI. Lit by windows along its portside, it was finished with a lavish moulded ceiling and large windows draped with floral silk curtains, which ran parallel along its starboard flank, overlooking the trendy Café Parisien.

The Parisien was decorated to resemble a French pavement bistro. Inaugurated on *Titanic* and adopted on other liners since, the café was furnished with twenty-one tables and sixty-eight wicker chairs and proved a popular haunt among the ship's more youthful first-class patrons. Behind a wall, sealing off the very rear of the deck, was an open second-class promenade which in turn surrounded the principal second-class passenger entrance and smoking room. Even for second class this 32ft by 64ft smoking room was delicately panelled in the style of Louis XVI, furnished with oak chairs and also boasting its own bar.

Fore and aft, at the extremities of *Titanic* resided the Forecastle and Poop decks, both 39ft 6in above the waterline. Pronounced 'fo'c's'le', this short 128ft deck nestled right in the bow of the ship. On *Titanic* it began with a 16ft-tall stem flagpole, followed immediately by the huge central anchor and its accompanying crane, trailed by four capstans and the winching equipment for its two smaller side companions. Behind, and set deep into the deck, towered the forward mast, encasing a narrow internal ladder giving access to the crow's nest. Suspended from the mast itself was a 64ft-long derrick for hoisting cargo. Just ahead of which lay the wave-break and the covered hatchway for hold number 1. The Forecastle became a popular promenade for third-class passengers, who were allowed access during the voyage via portable ladders leading upward from the forward Well Deck.

Conversely, at the very stern of the ship, sat the Poop Deck. Raised level with the Forecastle and overhanging the rudder, it adopted a design harking back to the sail-driven schooners of old. The Poop Deck on *Titanic* held the Docking Bridge, a raised platform protruding beyond the full beam of the ship and permanently manned throughout the voyage by a quartermaster. Its forward section was flanked by two cranes for supplying cargo into hatchway number 6. The Poop Deck itself measured 105ft in length and, like the Forecastle, housed a set of four capstans and winching equipment for securing the stern to the dockside. Both the Forecastle and Poop Deck ran level with B Deck, and once the crew had vacated, third-class passengers were permitted to congregate on these open areas during the voyage itself.

The highest deck to run the full length of *Titanic* was Shelter Deck C – 30ft 6in above the waterline – and thereby deemed the 'main' deck. Its bow contained the windlass engines for the anchors, a carpenter's workshop, separate messes for firemen (boiler stokers) and sailors, as well as the principal galley for the crew. Behind a cordoning wall to its rear and opposite side nestled an exposed open area of deck, the forward Well Deck. Behind the Well Deck stood a further wall and 135 first-class C staterooms, nine containing en-suite bathrooms, which surrounded the two remaining Parlour suites, C55/7 (Regency/Empire) and C62/4 (Louis XIV/Adam) – both as sumptuously decorated as their B-Deck companions, although sans private promenades. Nearby was the landing for the grand staircase, housing the purser's office and enquiry counter: passenger liaison. Along the starboard corridor sat the Marconi saloon for passengers to compose their wireless messages, abutting which a brightly panelled saloon put aside for the maids and valets travelling with their first-class masters. The doctor's surgery and cabin, and barber's shop were located nearby.

Sealed off to the rear was the deck's second-class area, beginning with the second-class library. Carpeted and panelled with sycamore, the library was furnished with mahogany writing tables, bookcases and chairs upholstered with tapestries. Flanked by glass-enclosed promenades, its two outboard passageways – each 84ft in length – were linked forward by a transverse walkway to encircle the main second-class entrance and stairwell. This comparative decadence showcased a fine example of White Star's atypical standards of comfort across the three travelling classes, for it was irregular at the time to see enclosed promenades in second-class areas.

Further rear was the after Well Deck where third-class passengers would board before turning into C Deck, heading beneath the Poop Deck and into the main third-class passenger entrance, comprising a wide central stairwell channelling its inhabitants to their cabins below; two similar, smaller entrances resided either side of the forward Well Deck beneath the Forecastle. Flanking the main third-class staircase, lay two sheltered areas. Divided into equal halves the portside contained the third-class smoking room – stylishly panelled with oak and teak furniture, whereas its starboard companion was more for general use and was therefore lined wall-to-wall with pine benches, interposed at its centre by an upright piano. The two rooms demonstrated unparalleled luxury to anything hitherto experienced in third class. Behind the bulkhead wall, to their rear, sat the winching gear for the capstans, but dominating the stern was the quadrant gear itself, along with tandem steering engines operating the ship's immense rudder.

The two Well Decks were each situated 30ft 6in above the waterline. Their sunken open sides, which gave them their name, allowed unhindered access for cargo when swung aboard from the quayside to be lowered by cranes into the storage holds deep below the hatchways fore and aft. Also serving as the entrances for third-class passengers, to accommodate their gangways the hull plating in the wells folded flush to the deck to allow their 12–14ft-wide gangways to slide aboard from the quayside. Both Well Decks measured 50ft long and 92ft wide and formed open-air portions of Main Deck C.

The forward Well Deck was positioned directly in front of the bridge. Containing cargo hatchways 2 and 3 it was serviced by two onboard cranes for loading the main holds beneath hatch 3. The after Well Deck, residing directly in front the Poop Deck, contained hatches numbered 5 and 6 and featured two motorised cranes for loading twin hatchways number 4.

Titanic carried her own facilities to load cargo. Eight electric Stothert & Pitt cranes were permanently sited on board, six of which were able to lift 2.5 tons through a reaching radius of 29ft and with a lift of 100ft at 40bhp their motors were able to haul a full load at a rate of 160ft a minute. The two remaining cranes, able to heave 1.5 tons at a radius of 21ft, could, with a lift of 80ft at 30bhp, hoist a full load at 200ft per minute. The Well Decks were utilised during the voyage as open promenades for third-class passengers and below them, running 20ft above the waterline, was Saloon Deck D.

In the bow, D Deck began with stores and quarters for 108 stokehold crew, preceding a capacious area beneath the forward Well Deck which served as a recreational room for third-class passengers, and on eastbound crossings doubled as additional cargo space. Behind a dividing wall to the rear lay forty-nine first-class D staterooms, accessed by twin corridors, each leading to a first-class passenger entrance vestibule, port and starboard. An archway to the rear of each vestibule gave access to a communicating ornate, columned and brightly decorated 68ft-long Jacobean reception room, intended to impress first-class passengers at the moment they stepped aboard. Enlarged due to the popularity of its companion on *Olympic*, the room – furnished with Chesterfield settees, an Axminster carpet and a Steinway grand piano – also housed the main landing for the grand staircase, plus three elevator doors tastefully fronted with oaken panels. The principal function for the reception area, however, was to serve as the formal collecting point for the largest room ever seen upon the ocean at that time: the 113ft-long, 92ft-wide dining saloon.

The 115 tables of the saloon provided seating for 554 diners. Its lavish Jacobean décor featured white moulded ceilings arching elegantly downward to white oak walls intermittently penetrated with large intricately patterned stained-glass windows. The room was modern and brightly lit in comparison to the dark Baronial interiors of the Cunarders. Thickly carpeted throughout and furnished with oak tables and chairs, the saloon on *Titanic* was in essence a single room, although to convey a sense of privacy to its diners alcoves skilfully gave the illusion of an occupancy lower than the number of diners actually present. Use of the saloon was optional however; its cost automatically levied on the price of the ticket. Serving breakfast each morning between 8.30 and 10.30a.m., lunch followed from 1 to 2.30p.m. and a seven-course meal served in sittings rounded off the cycle between 6 and 7:30p.m. The marking of the routine was announced throughout first class by a series of gongs and by Mr Fletcher, the ship's resident bugler. Passengers preferring to dine elsewhere for the entire voyage received a reduction of between £3 and £5 on their ticket.

Behind the saloon sat its vast companion pantry. Containing silverware, china-ware and cutlery stores, this was the plating area for the food and preceded the ship's main galley. Housing a 26ft-long by 8ft-wide cooking range, the galley itself also contained nineteen ovens totalling 96ft. Unbeknownst to discerning first-class patrons, food for both first- and second-class saloons was prepared in this one kitchen. Behind the galley was the bakery, scullery, butchery and dedicated pantry for the abutting second-class saloon. To fuel its ovens the galley also contained a storeroom for 51 tons of coal.

The dining saloon for second class directly behind was 71ft long and similarly 92ft wide. Lined with oak panelling, the room was able to seat 394 and featured a piano for ambience. Just as in first class, any passenger not wishing to use the saloon received a cheaper ticket option. This saloon was followed by thirty-nine second-class staterooms and then by eleven third-class cabins at the very stern of the deck. Each second-class cabin on *Titanic* was finished with white enamelled walls, furnished with mahogany and slept between two and four passengers – lavish for the middling class not normally accustomed to such standard comfort in daily life.

Along the starboard side of the deck was the ship's hospital. Primarily intended for third-class passengers, the facility comprised of four wards, each housing three beds, as well as a segregated six-bed unit for infectious illnesses, which was in turn subdivided into two additional wards of three beds each. Air from the room was extracted through funnel 4 to evade its recirculation around the rest of the ship. Access to the hospital was possible solely via a stairway linked directly to the surgery above on C Deck.

Further down was Upper Deck E, which like D Deck ran the entire length of the ship, 11ft above the waterline. Housed within its bow were stores and living quarters for seventy-two trimmers and forty-four sailors, behind which followed nineteen cabins for fifty-six single third-class travelling males. The main scullery followed, as did the office of the master-at-arms – the ship's policeman. The two main corridors on the deck were isolated to avoid first-class passengers berthed on the starboard corridor chancing upon crewmembers quartered along its portside companion. Because of its forty-five first-class E staterooms the starboard corridor was dubbed Park Lane. Being less salubrious than their upper deck companions, some of the staterooms here could double as second-class accommodation when the need arose. A further nineteen permanent second-class cabins, divided off to the rear, housed quarters set aside for the ship's musicians. Parallel along the deck's portside, the opposite corridor was named Scotland Road – recalling the unsavoury dockside area of Liverpool. The epithet was garnered from the corridor's designation as giving access exclusively to the living areas for the carpenter, quartermasters, stewards, barmen, waiters, bakers, cooks and engineers.

To the rear sat the main second-class boarding entrance. Panelled in oak, a stair-case granted access to seven levels: Boat Deck to F Deck. At its landing on E Deck

The sheer scale of the Olympic Class afforded the largest rooms afloat of the day. Unhindered by bulkhead divisions the expanse of the bright and 'peculiarly English' first-class dining saloon showcased unprecedented generosity for space throughout *Olympic* and *Titanic*. (© National Museums Northern Ireland Collection Harland & Wolff, Ulster Folk & Transport Museum)

was the barber's shop for second-class passengers, which also sold souvenirs. Packed behind a bulkhead wall were another fifty-six cabins accommodating 188 third-class passengers in the stern.

Downstairs was Middle Deck F: perched just 2ft 6in above the waterline. At its bow lay the locker for hawser chains (the void of which yawning downward to the Orlop Deck), preceded by supply stores, accommodation for fifty-three stokers, and eighty-one cabins for 356 third-class passengers. Behind a dividing bulkhead to the rear lay a comparative novelty at sea: the swimming pool.

Ever pushing the boundaries of comfort, in 1907 White Star's *Adriatic* became the first liner to showcase a swimming bath. Sited along her starboard side the pool on *Titanic* was 33ft long, 14ft wide and 8ft deep, although only filled to 6ft and only then in open sea. Available exclusively to first-class passengers at a cost of 1s per session, the facility contained thirteen changing cubicles plus two caged shower units. Behind the pool resided the Turkish steam baths – another seaborne introduction from *Adriatic* – again intended solely for first-class passengers, at 4s per session, its suite of rooms offering varying temperatures. Serviced by two male and two female attendants the design of the baths was based on seventeenth-century Arabian décor, with portholes discreetly concealed behind wooden Cairo screens. The rooms, adorned with teak supports and richly coloured floor and wall tiles, had oak-panelled interiors, finished with matching furniture and wall mounted lanterns to exude the ambience of a Middle-Eastern spa. Nearby lay the ship's laundry and main linen stores.

Along the deck's portside were quarters for the thirty-eight stewards catering third class, followed directly behind, and spanning the full beam of the ship, by their place of work: third-class' 102ft long and H-shaped brightly enamelled dining saloon. Bisected into two because of a bulkhead wall, each half of the saloon was sub-sectioned again port and starboard. The four sections catered a total of 473 passengers seated round forty-seven elongated tables. Serving food in three one-hour sittings, each diner was allotted a pre-assigned seat and time. Its adjoining galley was complete with its own butcher and bakery, but sandwiched betwixt them, were the dog kennels: nine dogs were aboard the inauspicious debut of *Titanic*, two of which even survived!

Flanking the casing of the main engine room, the deck also included the living quarters for the chief engineer plus those for his senior staff. Behind followed sixty-four second-class cabins and, after a bulkhead wall, thirty-four cabins for 110 third-class passengers occupied the stern. F Deck was the highest level penetrated by all fifteen bulkheads.

Facing outward from the deck's portside were twenty-one openings (twenty starboard because of the swimming pool), 2ft square and cut into the plating, they sealed off chutes that lent direct access to the ship's immense coalbunkers below. During the coaling process *Titanic* would be pushed ('boomed') 20ft from the dockside edge to enable barges, each loaded with 1,000 tons of coal, to simultaneously replenish the bunkers via these chutes either side of the hull. Large crane-operated buckets would scoop coal from the barges to pour its contents down these openings, which were then re-waterproofed by a hinged plate of hull. This was the cleanest and simplest method to coal *Titanic*, whose bunkers required approximately 6,000 tons to sustain a single crossing. It was also the reason hulls of ships were painted black – to mask the coal smeared along their sides. After coaling all fixtures and fittings throughout the ship had to be polished and cleaned. Coaling remained a filthy and laborious job, and one keenly despised by every member of the crew.

Nestling 5ft 6in below the waterline was Lower Deck G. Broken into two sections due to the casings for the engine and boiler uptakes below, its 190ft forward half housed stores and living accommodation for fifteen leading fire-men and thirty greasers (crewmembers whose sole purpose was to lubricate the engine's moving parts). Behind these resided cabins for 146 single male third-class passengers; portions of this accommodation could be dismantled to allow extra capacity for cargo. Adjacent to a hold assigned solely for first-class baggage stood the Post Office, behind which was the ship's 30ft by 20ft squash court. Ever keen to provide the latest amenities on their fleet, White Star fitted the 16ft-high court (complete with viewing gallery) and swimming pool into the Olympic Class to demonstrate their stability at sea. Users paid 2s per half-hour session, which also included professional tuition.

Into the stern, trailing the impassable boiler casings, the deck's after section continued for a further 210ft. This area housed the cold and dry food stores, engine workshops, oil and supplies stores, after which preceded the lowest accommodation on the ship: berths for seventy-four third-class passengers.

Running 13ft 6in below the waterline, the next deck was the Orlop, containing within its bow the base of the locker for the hawser chain, then stores and cargo hold supplied by hatchway 1. Immediately behind the abutting watertight bulkhead was the main hold. At 46ft long, it housed 1,341 tons of carrying capacity, as well as an area set aside specifically for motorcars, and was serviced by hatchway 2. The sheer scale of *Titanic* afforded her great commercial potential – the combined capacity of her holds amassed 84,000 cubic feet of revenue-generating space. Behind the holds were further stores providing 19,455 cubic feet for first- and second-class luggage, loaded through hatchway 3. Also here was a separate area for 268 tons of mail – during the maiden voyage housing 800 parcels and 3,364 sacks of letters – and a small Specie room for storing valuable items of cargo which was kept locked throughout the voyage.

The boiler and engine room casings bisected the deck from its stern section, resuming again with the main electrical switch panel and chilled stores for keeping wine, champagne, bottled water, fruit, groceries and meat. The 75,000lb of beef carried aboard the maiden voyage was stored in two compartments – one for the westbound crossing, the other for the return east – sealed within 29,557 cubic feet of refrigerated walk-in compartments insulated with granulated cork. The cold areas were followed by normal-temperature stores offering a 15,505 cubic foot space for bulk provisions and accessed via dual hatchways number 4. Behind, a 54ft-long hold for 390 tons of refrigerated cargo accessible by hatch 5 and again followed by a 57ft normal-temperature hold able to accommodate 366 tons of cargo, accessible through hatchway 6. Sited behind, in the very stern, was the after-peak tank, itself capable of containing 115 tons of saltwater ballast.

The Lower Orlop Deck below was a short mezzanine deck located right in the bow, beginning with the forward 190-ton capacity peak ballast tank. As with the main ballast tanks the fore and after peaks could be filled or emptied as necessary to adjust the longitudinal pitch of the ship. A second cargo hold for hatchway 1 occupied the remainder of this short deck.

Residing 29ft 3in below the waterline and continuing unbroken in the very depths of *Titanic*, was the Tank Top, the ship's powerhouse. Containing in its bow a final hold for hatchway 1, the main hold across its three levels accrued capacity for 730 tons of cargo. The hold's lowest level preceded two bunkers able to store an additional 1,092 tons of coal, their contents utilised only once the main supply had run low.

Slicing centrally through the centreline of two compartments ran a tunnel that provided stokers with direct access to the boiler rooms from their living quarters above. Connected by two steep circular stairwells – one used for upward traffic, the other purely for downward – this 'fireman's tunnel' ended at a vestibule protected by two bulkhead doors. The rear door opened to a 54ft-long compartment, forward boiler room number 6, chamber to four double-ended boilers. Adjoining each other and running aft were boiler rooms 5, 4 and 3 – each 57ft long. Room 2, 60ft long, followed next, containing five double-ended boilers. Directly behind room 2 was the final boiler room, number 1, which at 36ft long housed five half-length single-ended boilers. Each boiler room was transversely divided by a bulkhead wall and similarly lined with coalbunkers fore and aft; all six were designed to function independently should one fall out of action due to fire or water breach.

Behind boiler room 1 stood the largest cavity on the ship. Measuring 69ft long by 90ft wide and extending as high as D Deck, was the cavernous main engine room. Along its portside sat two steam-driven carbon dioxide refrigeration engines, built in Dartford by J. & E. Hall Thermotank Ltd, which maintained the refrigerated cargo holds and storerooms above. But standing parallel and dominating the centre of the room towered two enormous reciprocating engines powering the ship's port and starboard wing propellers. These, the largest at sea, also supplied the steam for the turbine engine, occupying the adjacent 54ft-long compartment, driving the central propeller. Flanking the starboard side of the turbine were three evaporator units feeding two distillers, which purified 14,000 gallons of drinking water per day. The electrical plant followed in the compartment behind. At 24ft high and 63ft in length the plant housed four steam-driven dynamos. Running at 325rpm, each dynamo outputted 4,000amps at 100 volts of current to electrify the ship's 10,000 light bulbs and 200 miles of cabling. The dynamos were in turn winged by six storage tanks for 206,800 gallons of purified drinking water; 75 tons were consumed each day of the voyage. The deck ended with three tunnels housing the drive shafts (supported every 15ft) turning the ship's three colossal propellers.

Beneath the 0.56in-thick floor plating of the Tank Top was the 5ft 3in-deep cellular double hull. Divided into forty-four separate watertight compartments (forty-six including the fore and after peak tanks), this honeycomb network of tanks provided rigidity to the keel as well as an inner waterproofed barrier to guard against any breach to the outer plating. These compartments comprised tanks filled with non-drinkable water pumped throughout the ship for bathing and washing; the majority, however, served as storage for ballast. Water had long replaced stone as ballast at sea because it was easier to adjust the buoyancy and distribution of weight to compensate for the amount of cargo and passengers carried during each particular crossing. Even mid-voyage the tanks could redistribute weight to correct the trim of the ship when changing sailing conditions dictated.

Although her rooms were delectable the true centrepiece of *Titanic* was undoubtedly her two grand staircases. One forward and one aft, both were lit by vast glazed domes and chandeliers and provided first-class passengers access to the ship's sublime staterooms and public areas throughout. The staircases were a sight to behold. Their elaborately carved, pale English oak-framed ornate iron balustrades and bronze fittings intricately styled in Louis XIV, glorified the forward (main) staircase, and also sported a clock inset within a richly carved 12ft oak panel depicting the scene 'Honour and Glory Crowning Time' – images of this panel have in more recent years epitomised the unrivalled interiors of *Titanic*. This grandiose stairwell spanned the 60ft shaft linking the Boat Deck to every deck in between, down to E Deck; its handrails were adorned periodically with candelabra and bronze cherubs brandishing flaming torches. The after first-class stairway, shorter and marginally less flamboyant than its forward companion, provided access between decks A to C.

Abutting the forward stairwell at each landing ran three 15cwt Otis elevators; encased by oak panelling and grille gates, they serviced a 37ft shaft between decks A to E. First introduced on ships by HAPAG in 1905, much to the amusement of their passengers, *Titanic* and *Olympic* were the first to offer elevators in second class. Such was their benchmark. The first-class staterooms, restaurants, lounges and saloons aboard *Titanic* were the finest examples afloat, rivalling the standards of the best hotels of London, Paris and New York. None of the décor would have looked out of place in any palace or stately home.

The tableware for first class was provided by Crown Derby, each item bearing the logo of the White Star Line – not *Titanic* by name – to allow its use on any of their fleet. Company ciphers were routinely etched into every piece of cutlery and enamelled into chinaware in a measure to deter theft. The marks, however, often inspired the reverse effect; items bearing such emblems were purloined by passengers seeking keepsakes of the voyage.

Because of her sheer scale and sumptuous interiors the media's interest with *Titanic* began long before she encountered the iceberg. As soon as construction began on *Olympic*, the press homed in on this great class of liners, and on 14 June 1911 a dedicated 'souvenir' edition of *The Shipbuilder* magazine was issued with *Olympic* as its sole feature: since 1906 this had been the bible for every Edwardian shipping enthusiast. The world was eager to explore these new leviathans. Noel Malachard of Pathé news was dispatched as a second-class passenger to document the maiden voyage of *Titanic*, a ship destined to headline newsreels around the globe.

Following afterthought and in response to teething troubles experienced by *Olympic* during her voyages in 1911, *Titanic*, still under construction, afforded White Star ample scope to grant Harland & Wolff free rein to eradicate any short-comings from the design. The adjustments included increased weather protection on her forward promenades and yet more style and luxury. While travelling aboard *Olympic* Bruce Ismay maintained a journal earmarking improvements to be incorporated into *Titanic*. A stickler for detail, aboard *Titanic* he examined the springs in her first-class mattresses and even noted that an extra potato-peeler was sorely needed in her galley. His new ship, *Titanic*, had to personify White Star's exacting standards of perfection.

Between its merger with IMM in 1902 and March 1912, of the 2,179,594 pas-sengers who travelled with White Star just two perished on their vessels. For their volume of crossings this record of safety was exemplary. With *Titanic* White Star's ambition to impart an indelible imprint on Atlantic transportation had borne fruit. With construction complete, *Titanic* underwent swift final preparations for her maiden voyage. But amid the full glare of an attentive world the fate of White Star's greatest creation was instead to take a sudden and irretrievable turn for the worst

CHAPTER 3

OLYMPIC CLASS

'The 31st of May 1911, will remain notable in the annals of shipbuilding
and ship-owning as witnessing the launch of the *Titanic* and the departure
from Belfast of the *Olympic*, two vessels which may truly be said to mark an
intensely interesting epoch in the history of the mercantile marine.'

The Shipbuilder, 1911

In studying the rise and spectacular fall of *Titanic* the student's journey will invariably embark upon a path that will ultimately lead to her sister ships *Olympic* and *Britannic*. The fact that *Titanic* was no one-off, but represented a third of White Star's Olympic Class of liners, may well be news to some. Built explicitly to secure IMM's stranglehold on high-class transatlantic passage the Olympic Class was intended to be the era's most ambitious icons of oceanic transport.

For two of them, history had marked their card: one suffered a famous encounter with an iceberg, while the other was destroyed on a mercy mission during the First World War. Deemed the safest ships of their day, only one from this trio would eventually cross the Atlantic and perform the life of service she was intended to fulfil. The very existence of this class would reassure both a delicate British economy and an equally politically fractious Europe that the evolution of a new and technical age had finally produced the ultimate floating marvels.

Approval was granted for the construction of the Olympic Class in mid-1907, of which the first two were to be built almost simultaneously. The dimensions and plans of the first of the trio were made public on 11 September that year; they would each gross 45,000 tons and measure in excess of 880ft in length, large enough at the very least to be 15,000 tons heavier than any other craft afloat. It would require the best engineers to create them.

The first of these, *Olympic*, would become one of the very few express liners on the Atlantic to return a profit during the Great Depression, even with newer craft snapping closely at her heels a quarter of a century later. She would be the sole survivor of the Olympic Class and an enduring success. One of the

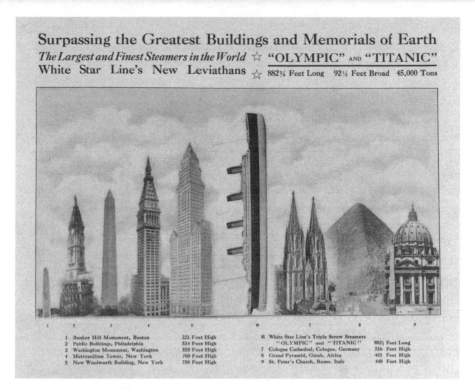

Surpassing the Greatest Buildings and Memorials of Earth

The Largest and Finest Steamers in the World ☆ **"OLYMPIC"** AND **"TITANIC"**

White Star Line's New Leviathans ☆ 882½ Feet Long   92½ Feet Broad   45,000 Tons

1 Bunker Hill Monument, Boston	221 Feet High	6 White Star Line's Triple Screw Steamers	
2 Public Buildings, Philadelphia	534 Feet High	"OLYMPIC" and "TITANIC"	882½ Feet Long
3 Washington Monument, Washington	555 Feet High	7 Cologne Cathedral, Cologne, Germany	516 Feet High
4 Metropolitan Tower, New York	700 Feet High	8 Grand Pyramid, Gizeh, Africa	451 Feet High
5 New Woolworth Building, New York	750 Feet High	9 St. Peter's Church, Rome, Italy	448 Feet High

To highlight the gargantuan scale of their Olympic Class, White Star compared their lengths to the heights of famous landmarks. Towering 792ft skyward, New York's Woolworth building, under construction at the time, was the tallest structure of the day, illustrated here in promotional material dwarfed by *Olympic*. (Mary Evans Picture Library)

most economical vessels of her day, when launched, *Olympic* heralded a class of liners offering White Star the panache, luxury and the viability to propel the line through ensuing economic turmoil and onwards to a new plain of transportation – she epitomised a truly 'Olympic' class.

Olympic: Lady Luck

When White Star commissioned Harland & Wolff in the 1890s to design a pair of liners with the explicit remit to surpass all others in both size and grandeur, the first was to be called *Oceanic* and the second was to be known as *Olympic*. Construction on *Oceanic* began in January 1897, yet by the time of her completion in September 1899 only she had come to fruition. The ailing health of Thomas Ismay and his death that November found the line shelving plans for the ship named *Olympic*. But the name would resurface again in 1907 during the fabled meeting between Bruce Ismay and William Pirrie, while musing over the building of a new class of liners labelled the Olympic Class. Finally able to use the moniker he had put aside almost a decade before, the name of this great class and its first addition was to be 'Olympic', an announcement that was proudly confirmed on 16 April 1908.

Construction on *Olympic* – Harland & Wolff's 400th commission – began on 16 December 1908. Project 400 progressed smoothly. The keel was finished the following February, framing was complete by 20 November and she was fully plated by early April 1910. On the slipway – being the first of the class to be constructed – her immense 26,400-ton hull was painted light grey to give the illusion of appearing even more imposing: having done likewise with *Oceanic* in 1899. The premise was to allow the cameras of the newspapermen to be present at her forthcoming launch ceremony to record every nuance of the world's newest and largest hull.

The Earl of Aberdeen (Lord Lieutenant of Ireland) and his wife the countess headed a VIP guest list that included the Lord Mayor of Belfast (Robert McMordie) and chairmen Pirrie and Ismay, to witness the launch of *Olympic* on 20 October 1910. Joined by 100 members of the press, at 11a.m. the assembled crowd applauded the great hull of *Olympic* as it slid down the yard's specially modified 772ft run of slipway number 2. Reaching a momentum of 12.5 knots, 160 tons of drag chain eased *Olympic* to a steady halt in the river Lagan. As with the launch of *Titanic* a year later, the process had taken just sixty-two seconds, with events typifying Harland & Wolff's boundless endeavour for precision and perfection. Indeed, the remaining stages of her build proceeded just as smoothly.

Shortly after launch the hull of *Olympic* was towed to the yard's outfitting quay where to receive the installation of machinery. On 1 April 1911 she was moved, this time to the newly finished and specially built Thompson Graving Dock to complete final fitting out and have her hull blackened and propellers added.

Among 220 separate accidents during her construction, fourteen were recorded as serious; the project claimed the lives of nine workers. Such incidents were inevitable at shipyards given the volumes of men and machinery moving and working at heights, without safety ropes, and racing to meet both cost and deadline. For such occurrences Harland & Wolff purchased two automobiles especially to ferry the injured to the local city hospital.

Olympic was of monumental scale. None before had come close to her magnitude. When launched her empty 24,600-ton hull required a draught of 18ft, but with engines, boilers and all fixtures added, her draught almost doubled. With outfitting complete, on 25 May 1911 she was registered with the Board of Trade as vessel 131346.

Her trials for seaworthiness followed promptly, requiring two days – 29 and 30 May – with a crew of 250. Reaching a top speed of 21¾ knots, to the delight of all, she passed every test. With paperwork complete, *Olympic* was proudly handed over to her owners at 2.30p.m., the very day the hull of *Titanic* was launched – 31 May 1911; the two events choreographed to maximise publicity on the new class. Fresh from the launch of *Titanic*, Ismay, Pirrie and owner Morgan boarded

Olympic on which they departed Belfast at 4.30p.m. Her port of call was a short 135-mile journey to Liverpool, where, to showcase the ship at her home city for a day, White Star admitted a fee-paying public to explore the newest, largest, most decadent liner the world had hitherto set eyes upon. At 882ft 6in in length, and grossing 45,324 tons (20,847 NRT), *Olympic* overshadowed *Lusitania* as the largest vessel afloat, by a bewildering 14,174 tons.

The designed occupancy for *Olympic* boasted room for 1,054 passengers in first class, 510 in second and another 1,020 in third, as well as accommodation for a crew of 860. Departing Liverpool at 11.15p.m. on 1 June, she arrived in Southampton at 3a.m. on the 3rd to undergo final preparations for commercial service. White Star had *Teutonic* reassigned to their Canadian routes to allow *Olympic* to slot in alongside *Oceanic* and *Majestic* to form their premier trio until *Titanic* and eventually *Britannic* could join her in 1912 and 1914 respectively.

On 14 June 1911 *Olympic* cast off from Southampton at exactly 12.45p.m. to begin her maiden voyage, under the steady hand of White Star's venerable Captain Edward J. Smith. Joining Smith was a senior crew comprising Chief Officer Joseph Evans, First Officer William Murdoch, Second Officer Robert Hume, Third Officer Henry Cater, Fourth Officer David Alexander and Fifth Officer Alphonse Tulloch, and Harold Holehouse serving as the junior sixth officer, 1,313 passengers in their charge. After calling at Cherbourg and Queenstown *Olympic* arrived at New York on 21 June, completing the crossing in a respectable five days, sixteen hours and forty-two minutes, averaging a speed of 21.17 knots. Aboard was a delighted Ismay, who telegraphed back to Pirrie: '*Olympic* is a marvel ... unbounded satisfaction'. Her time was far short of that set by the incumbent Blue Riband holder, *Mauretania*, which had set the current speed record four years previously at four days, ten hours and fifty-one minutes. But that had not mattered. *Olympic* was never intended to attempt the record. Her bulk was utilised to lavish spacious interiors for passenger comfort, not to house machinery for ravenous engines.

Yet, much to the disappointment of White Star, the coronation of King George V on 22 June saw the maiden voyage virtually outshone during the blisteringly hot summer of 1911. The occasion for her younger sister would attract greater media interest on her maiden voyage the following year, long after the euphoria of the coronation had passed. But from the outset *Olympic* looked to have the makings of a highly eventful career.

On 20 September 1911, on her fifth outward voyage, she collided with navy cruiser HMS *Hawke* in a narrow stretch of water between the British mainland and the Isle of Wight, badly damaging her hull. *Olympic* limped to Belfast at a sedate 10 knots and underwent repairs that were to cost White Star £250,000 to complete. The incident postponed work on *Titanic* by six weeks while Harland & Wolff diverted manpower to perform the emergency repairs. For such occasions *Olympic* was insured for £1 million, however in this instance the White Star liner was seen to be at fault for the collision and an insurance payout was denied.

Nevertheless, *Olympic* resumed service on 29 November that year. The incident was not altogether a complete public relations disaster for White Star. Rather than making her seem lumbering and oversized, the collision was viewed as proof of the durability and safety of their Olympic-Class fleet.

Fortunately for *Olympic* only minor incidents would befall the remainder of her lengthy, albeit still highly eventful, career. Engulfed by a wave on 14 January 1912 which damaged her Forecastle, only weeks later – on 24 February – she ran over an uncharted object in the Grand Banks, losing a blade from her starboard propeller and forcing a second return to Belfast for repairs that once again delayed construction on *Titanic*.

When transferred to *Titanic* to captain her maiden voyage Edward Smith's berth on *Olympic* was filled by Herbert James Haddock. Before assuming the command on 3 April 1912 Haddock had served as captain of *Oceanic* since 1907. Having also been appointed commander of *Titanic* on 27 March for her sea trials, on 1 April he was suddenly replaced by old hand Edward Smith.

At 3p.m on Saturday 13 April, with her new commander, *Olympic* departed New York for Southampton, commencing a voyage which 750 miles later received the distress signal from her newly completed sister. *Olympic*, 512 miles away, unable and out of range to assist detoured for fourteen hours in a desperate attempt to reach the stricken *Titanic*. *Olympic* eventually resumed her voyage to Southampton following a decision by Bruce Ismay not to further distress survivors from *Titanic* by having them see her almost identical twin.

Olympic arrived in Southampton at 2a.m. on the 21st, the crew extremely anxious over their ship's safety. Controversy sparked the morning of her next scheduled departure to New York, 24 April, as 284 stokers deserted amid protests over her supply of lifeboats: twenty-four extra Berthon collapsible boats had been hastily installed as a temporary measure to redress her now evident dearth of lifeboat capacity. While the extra lifeboats had earlier received approval from both the Board of Trade and the British Seafarers Union, who represented the stokers, the crew remained unsettled. Heated exchanges ensued, reaching their crescendo at Spithead where the commotion left Captain Haddock having to stop her engines and issue a call for the police. After thirty-six hours of deadlock the voyage was cancelled. *Olympic* would not sail again until her next scheduled departure, 15 May. The public too echoed the apprehension of travelling aboard *Olympic*: departing for New York for the first time since her aborted crossing she carried just 432 passengers – barely 18 per cent of her licensed occupancy.

White Star recalled *Olympic* on 9 October to extricate the faults in her safety so sensationally debunked with the loss of *Titanic*, and to restore the public's confidence in their flagship. The upgrades included a virtual rebuild of her interior to improve its watertight integrity; most notably extending her inner hull layer to provide greater encasement to the engine and boiler spaces above her waterline. Harland & Wolff also raised her bulkheads to Shelter Deck C (five even reaching B Deck) and installed an additional bulkhead within her electricity plant. These modifications, amounting to £156,000, enabled her to remain afloat with six watertight compartments breached as opposed to the original design of four. More crucially, her original lifeboat capacity of sixteen was augmented by fifty-two boats: enough to accommodate 3,510 people, more than the maximum number of passengers she was able to carry. Due to the surge in demand for lifeboats in the wake of the disaster, an ensuing shortage of supply had *Olympic* returning to service bearing just sixteen of the thirty-six additional wooden boats: the remaining sixteen comprised of two types of collapsible boats, tiding over her capacity until the missing permanent ones could be completed.

Not all modifications were to improve safety. The extent of the rebuild also gave White Star the unprecedented opportunity to remodel much of her accommodation. This included the expansion of her à la carte restaurant and the addition of a completely dedicated reception room. In response to its successful airing on *Titanic* a Café Parisien was added, rectifying also the array of teething issues exposed during her first two years of service. Once complete all the amendments raised her overall tonnage to 46,359 (NRT 22,320) although reduced passenger capacity to 735 in first class, 675 in second and 1,030 in third. During this time White Star maintained their Southampton/New York schedule with *Adriatic*, *Majestic* and *Oceanic*, though with work on *Olympic* complete on 22 March 1913 she rejoined service on 2 April as arguably the safest vessel afloat of the day. However, barely a year later normality ceased. Europe was enveloped by war.

As war escalated White Star returned *Olympic* from New York on 21 October 1914 to store her in the safe port of Belfast to evade German U-boats. During her voyage home she deviated from course on 27 October to rescue all the survivors from the third largest dreadnought of the Royal Navy, HMS *Audacious* – fatally crippled after striking a mine. *Olympic* arrived at the distress position and initiated a dramatic rescue of its 600 crew, arriving in Belfast on 3 November amid a blaze of glory.

Acclaimed for his involvement in the rescue, her master, Captain Haddock, was reassigned to war duties. On 1 September 1915 *Olympic* too joined the war effort, commissioned by the Admiralty from White Star at a rate of 10s per gross ton per month: £3,000 a month in total. First she was taken to Liverpool to undergo conversion into an auxiliary transport, work which was underway on 11 September. On 24 September His Majesty's Transport *Olympic*, T2810, returned to service fully equipped to carry 6,000 troops. Under her new captain, Bertram Fox Hayes, she began transporting troops to and from the campaigns against the Turks at the Gallipoli peninsula in the Mediterranean.

From March 1916 HMT *Olympic* brought Canadian troops over to Europe and in December the following year transported some of the first Americans to fight the war. She was also painted in a 'dazzle' scheme, a system of black, white, blue, yellow and grey intersecting geometric lines adopted by the British Admiralty in

1917 to impede U-boat rangefinders plotting the course of ships painted in this fashion; its creation was credited to artist Norman Wilkinson but its effectiveness remained unproven. Her relatively sprightly engines did, however, prove a great success, evading encounters with four U-boats. She even found fame as the only merchant vessel during the First World War to ram and sink an enemy submarine – U-103, near the Scilly Isles on 12 May 1918 – after which all the crew of *Olympic* shared a handsome £1,000 reward. During her war service *Olympic* covered a total of 184,000 miles, once carrying 6,148 troops in a single voyage.

After the armistice she returned to White Star who sent her onward to Harland & Wolff to have her engines upgraded from steam to oil. The work, commencing 16 August 1919, included her conversion back to a luxury passenger liner. Her lifeboat configuration, newly reduced to fifty boats, provided seating for 3,428 occupants. All in all the $2.5 million refit increased her tonnage to 46,439 and by 25 June 1920 *Olympic* was back in commercial service. On 22 March 1924, however, she was involved in an incident in New York Harbour. Causing $150,000 of damage she had reversed into a tourist vessel carrying 275 passengers, Furness Bermuda Line's *Fort St George*.

Olympic, being now in her sixteenth year, during February 1927 underwent a mandatory inspection into her structural integrity which discovered tanks in her double hull starting to suffer the effects of corrosion. *Olympic* was subsequently placed on the Board of Trade's register for ships closely monitored for structural decay.

Changing trends of sea travel also saw her passenger capacity reduced from 2,435, to 2,055 (675 first, 561 second and 819 third class) in February 1928 during her third major refit. Following yet another refit in 1933 accommodation was lowered further again, and significantly so – offering room for just 1,447 passengers in total; 618 first, 447 second and 382 third class. Within months of this fourth refit she struck and sank the Nantucket Lightship, the 630-ton *117*, built in 1930. *Olympic* smashed into *117* on 15 May 1934 while negotiating a fogbank off Cape Cod, killing eight of the lightship's eleven crewmembers. Inflicting damage amounting to $70,000, the incident occurred at a critical moment in White Star's history. Rising debts had recently forced the line to merge with Cunard and the collision with the lightship did not bode well with the new management. Growing ever unwilling to fund a fifth refit to keep *Olympic* in service, her twenty-year-old running mate *Majestic (II)*, herself fast approaching the end of serviceable life, was sold off as scrap on 15 May 1936. With construction of Cunard-White Star's *Queen Mary* now well underway the management reviewed the viability of the career-worn *Olympic*. Unconvinced that she would pass the next Board of Trade appraisal for seaworthiness the line announced on 25 January 1935 that maintaining *Olympic* was no longer economical and she would be withdrawn from service.

Her final roundtrip to New York began on 27 March 1935. Upon return to Southampton on 12 April she was retired: former captains expressing admiration in her reliability which had dutifully provided twenty-four years of steadfast

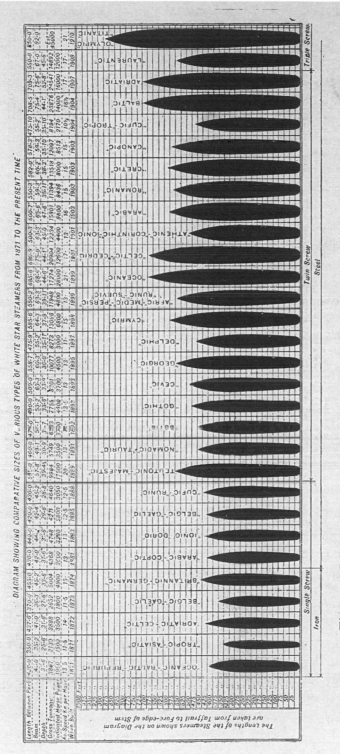

Fig. 2. – Diagram showing Development in Size of White Star Liners.

The epoch of *Olympic* and *Titanic* illustrated in the summer 1911 edition of the periodical *The Shipbuilder*, highlighting the trend in the development of the ocean liner with this diagram of key vessels from the White Star fleet. (SSPL (Getty Images)) service. Moored out of the way at Southampton's Western Docks, unable to attract a buyer, *Olympic* was sold for scrap on 10 October for £97,500 to Sir John Jarvis, MP and owner of Metal Industries Ltd. To reinvigorate employment in the area, the deprived port of Jarrow was selected as the site to dismantle her hull. *Olympic* was transferred the next day to Thomas Ward's scrapyard for demolition, which began on 6 November; the following day a series of auctions started selling 4,456 items salvaged from her interiors.

Her empty hull was towed to Inverkeithing, Scotland, on 19 September 1937 to begin the final stages of demolition, which at the time was the largest hull ever seen at a breakers yard. One month later, Joseph Bruce Ismay, the man who had named her, was himself dead. The era of the Olympic Class had passed over to history. *Olympic's* steel was remoulded and recycled during the Second World War but her sumptuous dining interiors found new lease of life adorning the White Swan Hotel in Alnwick, Northumberland, where they can be admired to this day.

Throughout her illustrious career, *Olympic* had travelled a total of 1.5 million miles and was considered one of the most economically efficient liners of her era. Her almost 260 roundtrips to New York earned the broad affection of the shipping industry, who bestowed on her the soubriquet 'Old Reliable' in honour of a career which boasted a glittering clientele, including Charlie Chaplin and Edward, Prince of Wales.

As the first of the class *Olympic* was the most favoured by White Star and Harland & Wolff, considering her their true flagship of the line. *Olympic* was the realisation of an epoch for White Star who privately revered her over either *Titanic* or *Britannic*, despite the younger sisters surpassing her in grandeur and size. Her long and untiring service befitted her place in history as one of the truly successful merchant ships ever to grace the oceans.

Britannic: White Star/Red Cross

With insufficient funds in 1907 for Harland & Wolff to build all three 'Olympics' at once, RMS *Britannic* was always intended to be the belated addition to White Star's new class. Until her completion White Star planned to leave *Oceanic* working alongside *Olympic* and *Titanic*, temporarily completing their requisite trio until *Britannic* entered service in the autumn of 1914. Delaying the final addition to the class afforded White Star a window with which to assess the running performance of *Olympic* and *Titanic* and evolve and improve the designs for its climax. After all, the Olympic Class was intended to remain operational for a quarter of a century.

The green light to produce the final Olympic-Class liner was given on 20 June 1911. With her designs receiving the stamp of approval on 17 October, Harland & Wolff cleared Queen's Island slipway number 2 on 23 November to begin construction on *Britannic* on the 30th – right on schedule. Her bold and patriotic moniker, however, was not the original preference of White Star. Early promotional material for the final ship of the class planned, like her middle sister, to shout out its bearer's gargantuan proportions. Be it from indecision or heightening suspense through intriguing red herrings it was common for operators to change the names of ships during the course of construction. White Star had first mooted *Gigantic* as a potential in 1892 during preliminary designs for a 700-footer scheduled to enter service in March 1894. Although the ship never materialised the project eventually evolved into *Oceanic* when finally launched in 1899. But the name *Gigantic* would resurface again for the decidedly more voluminous Olympic Class a decade later.

The catastrophe of *Titanic* – another ship evidently named to advertise its size – found White Star hastily withdrawing notions to name the third ship of the class *Gigantic*: plans they hotly refuted, although plenty of traces argue the contrary. The 25 November 1911 edition of the *New York Times* had let the cat out of the bag, publishing the name of the last of White Star's Olympians as being *Gigantic*. The *Liverpool Journal of Commerce* on, of all days, 15 April 1912, likewise affirmed this ship to be named Gigantic. White Star was clearly undecided on the moniker of their new liner, but the loss of *Titanic* provided them with the catalyst to decide which name to plump for.

White Star realised *Olympic* and *Titanic* were not going to be the largest ships afloat for long. To upgrade *Lusitania* and *Mauretania* to operate as a trio and be up to par with the competition – the Olympic Class – early 1911 saw Cunard commence construction on their 909ft *Aquitania*. Work on White Star's now slightly eclipsed 900ft *Britannic*/*Gigantic* followed that November, yet in Germany HAPAG too was preparing to launch their 900ft *Imperator*. To White Star their final Olympic liner had to now outshine its rivals, and naming it *Gigantic* would certainly placate the Edwardian desire to emphasise size.

Sadly for *Gigantic*, her more famous sister, the largest ship afloat at the time, was suddenly lost to an iceberg, leaving the industry, particularly White Star, under intense and highly critical scrutiny. On 30 May 1912, to remove any insensitive reference to *Titanic* – likewise named to vaunt her gargantuan hulk – White Star confirmed that the final ship of the Olympic Class would instead be named *Britannic*. Rumours that plans to call her *Gigantic* ever existed were quickly quelled, fuelling speculation that attracts plenty of debate even today. Yet *Britannic* was no new inspiration either. Amid the hope of reliving the success of a predecessor it was widely common for shipping lines to recycle the names of favoured bygone stars of their fleet. White Star had already launched a 5,004-ton passenger liner named *Britannic* in 1874; Blue Riband holder in 1876, she was subsequently decommissioned in 1903. A third *Britannic* followed in 1930, the 26,943-ton liner becoming the line's first motorised vessel. The occurrence was common: White Star also reprised the names *Adriatic, Arabic, Baltic, Celtic, Doric, Majestic, Oceanic, Republic* and *Runic*. However, their second *Britannic* became Harland & Wolff's

433rd commission and final addition to the Olympic Class, built upon the same slipway formally occupied by *Olympic*.

White Star's timescale intended to see *Britannic* completed by September of 1914, although disaster deferred this until November 1915 in order to apply emergency enhancements to *Olympic* following the loss of their sister. When the *Titanic* disaster occurred, work on *Britannic* had progressed for only four and a half months and was consequently still very much in the early stages of development, construction reaching only as far as her lowest deck, Tank Top. To rebuild confidence in their vessels Harland & Wolff used the opportunity to apply extensive modifications to *Britannic*, more so than they were able to implement during their similar recall of *Olympic*.

At the base of *Britannic* the double keel beneath her already finished Tank Top remained at 5ft 3in deep, but above, her inner sidewalls were widened and raised a further 4ft higher than originally planned. In order to maintain buoyancy, widening the sidewalls of *Britannic* required Harland & Wolff to also broaden her hull. Her bulkheads were also strengthened. An additional wall to divide the room containing her electricity generators was fitted, increasing her number of watertight compartments to sixteen. In addition five bulkhead walls now rose as high as B Deck, 40ft clear of the waterline and 75ft above the keelbar.

Increasing the heights of the bulkheads on *Britannic* was a huge compromise for White Star. It became the first instance in which they permitted the walls to slice through their spaciously sacrosanct areas of first class. These adjustments would allow her now to remain afloat with any six compartments flooded, as opposed to the maximum of four on *Titanic*. As a further precaution extra rows of rivets were applied amidships, endowing *Britannic* with a hull of unprecedented strength. The most visible improvement, however, was the inclusion of eight enormous sets of lifeboat davits.

Intended as very noticeable additions, to thereby restore public confidence in White Star's safety record, each davit was now large enough to house six boats. Perched high upon gantries, these davits would hold among them forty-eight wooden boats; forty-six at 34ft long, with two others as emergency boats 26ft long. To free as much deck for passengers as possible and to better store this vast supply of boats required them to be banked in triples in huge extended latticed davits. The davits were extremely dexterous. Tall enough to reach farther outward and lower boats by avoiding contact with the hull – even if the ship had developed a severe list – the davit's girder arms were able to incline across the entire width of the deck and hook up a boat on the opposite side and hoist it back over. Crucially, to avoid a repeat of the evacuation of *Titanic*, the new davits were strong enough to load passengers into the lifeboats from the deck itself, negating the prior need to swing boats over the side rails and precariously jump passengers into them from the edge of the ship itself.

A further improvement in light of the disaster saw a voice pipe fitted between the wireless room and the bridge of *Britannic* to expedite the communication of ice warnings which had been so sorely ignored on *Titanic*. But not all enhancements focussed on safety. *Britannic* boasted new luxuries for first-class passengers too: a children's nursery and ladies' hairdressers to name but a few. Her second-class passengers would also see an amenity previously unheard of in this class, their very own gymnasium.

The 24,800-ton hull of *Britannic* was launched at 11.15a.m. on 26 February 1914. Reaching a speed of 9.5 knots she was waterborne and brought gently to a halt eighty-one seconds later. The launch was supervised by Lord Pirrie and Harold Sanderson – new chairman of the White Star Line; her hull was painted and her propellers were fitted in the Thompson Graving Dock that September.

The designed capacity for *Britannic* stood at 790 in first class, 836 in second, 953 in steerage and a crew of 950. Grossing 48,158 tons (24,592 NRT) and measuring 903ft in length she remains today the largest four-funnelled liner ever built; the fashion reverted to the three functional funnels soon afterwards. With her forward sections of Promenade Deck enclosed with glass screens, *Britannic's* appearance was more akin to *Titanic* than *Olympic*.

Her reciprocating engines each weighed 990 tons and were capable of indicating 16,000hp. Furthermore, her modified 490-ton turbine could generate 18,000hp. The three engines markedly outperformed those of her surviving sister, *Olympic*, despite all ships of the class sporting the same number of furnaces: 159.

Construction on *Britannic* was initially slow as IMM had accumulated a debt of £585,000 with Harland & Wolff, leaving White Star to announce on 2 July 1914 that she would instead begin commercial service the following spring. However, the onset of the First World War that August found the British government ordering all merchant contracts in its shipyards to be abandoned to clear the way for military projects. *Britannic* sat mothballed at Harland & Wolff's wharves at Belfast for the next fifteen months, safely beyond reach of the Kaiserliche Marine.

Spiralling casualties from British forces sustaining heavy losses combating the Turks at Salonika and Gallipoli on the Dardanelle Peninsula forced the British high command to begin the evacuation from the region on 18 December 1915. Requiring vessels to return the wounded home, the Admiralty ordered that work resume on *Britannic* to bring her to serviceable condition. The work began on 13 November 1915 and, as requested, immediately upon completion, 11 December, Harland & Wolff cordially ceded her to hospital duty.

Registered as vessel 137490 on 8 December, the same day of her sea trials, *Britannic* steamed under escort from Belfast to Liverpool on the 12th to undergo a ten-day and £90,000 conversion into a fully equipped 3,309-bed Red Cross floating hospital. Able to accommodate 4,473 patients, medical staff and crew, and conforming to the terms of the 10th Hague Peace Convention (dated 18 October 1907), *Britannic* officially became His Majesty's Hospital Ship (HMHS) G618 on 6 December 1915. Her supply of lifeboats, increased to fifty-eight, rounded off the cost of conversion, which left her final bill of construction tallying £2 million.

To denote immunity under the Geneva Convention *Britannic* was painted in the colours of the Red Cross: a white hull encircled with a green band and three giant red crosses on each side. To indicate this immunity, as she was not in the commercial service of a British company she was topped off with buff-coloured funnels: unlike those of other nations, British hospital ships did not display white funnels. Also fitted to her hull were rows of green and red lights to identify her as a Red Cross ship at night. One of sixty-four hospital ships in service, the Admiralty would compensate White Star £24,000 per month for her use. Under the command of White Star's Charles Bartlett her maiden voyage began on 23 December 1915, taking her from Liverpool to the safe port of Mudros, Greece, to collect the wounded from the failed campaigns of the Dardanelles. Joining White Star in 1894 as fourth officer upon gaining his Masters Certificate in 1893, Bartlett had risen to captain in 1903. Finding favour at the line, in January 1912 he was appointed its senior marine superintendent for Belfast. With Edward Smith's pending retirement, following a successful maiden voyage of *Titanic*, it was highly likely for Bartlett to have assumed stewardship of her regular crossings. Instead, with the outbreak of the First World War, as member of the Royal Navy Reserve (for which in 1907 he was awarded its decoration, the RD), Bartlett was called upon to command various patrols in the North Sea, a service that earned him recognition in the form of the Companion to the Order of Bath in 1916. However, on 14 December 1915 he transferred to the command of the newly completed *Britannic*.

The maiden roundtrip of HMHS *Britannic* ended in Southampton on 9 January, returning home some 3,300 wounded soldiers. Her second mission – this time to Naples, Italy – began on 20 January. Upon her return work resumed to complete her rushed conversion into a hospital ship; commencing 9 February. She rejoined service for the Red Cross on 20 March that year, collecting troops from Naples and Augusta, arriving safely back in Southampton on 4 April.

With the Allied evacuation of Gallipoli complete *Britannic* was discharged from the Red Cross on 21 May to undergo fitting out in Belfast on 6 June for entry into Atlantic auxiliary service, where she would join four other troop transports, *Mauretania*, *Aquitania*, *Olympic* and the 32,234-ton *Statendam* of the Holland-Amerika Lijn. But an ensuing resurge in casualties following a second British-led offensive against the Turks at Salonika instead found *Britannic* returned to the Red Cross on 28 August 1916. Her sixth voyage, beginning 2.23p.m. on Sunday 12 November, had her departing once more from Southampton, bound for Mudros and Naples. She was not to return to British shores again.

Being an outward voyage no patients were carried, yet on board were 673 crewmembers and a medical staff of 392. After a brief refuelling stop at Naples, *Britannic* departed on 17 November for the final leg of her mission to Mudros.

To keep her course so that she would pass through the Kea Channel, her route was to skirt the Greek island of Makronisos. Travelling at 20 knots, at 8.12a.m. on Tuesday 21 November, she struck a mine on her starboard bow on the wall separating cargo holds 2 and 3; its explosion breaching all leading five watertight compartments.

The damage disabled the bulkhead door connecting boiler rooms 5 and 6, allowing water to fill all six forward compartments; the maximum flooding with which she was designed to remain afloat. *Britannic* then heeled violently starboard, listing so severely that water cascaded through the portholes left open on E and F decks. At 8.35a.m. Bartlett gave the order to abandon her, restarting the engines in a desperate attempt to save *Britannic* by beaching her upon an island nearby. At 8.45a.m. her bow slipped under, heaving her propellers through the water's surface to rotate menacingly in mid-air. Just minutes later, *Britannic* slipped from sight.

Her flotilla of lifeboats was discovered at 10a.m. and survivors were rescued by Royal Navy destroyers HMS *Scourge* and HMS *Foxhound* and the cruiser HMS *Heroic*; respectively rescuing 339, 193 and 494 from the thirty-five boats deployed from *Britannic*. All survivors were transported to the port of Piraeus before ultimately arriving back in Southampton on 4 December. The incident, however, left twenty-one crewmembers and nine medical staff dead, mostly from the two lifeboats drawn into the blades of *Britannic's* airborne and rotating propellers. A further forty-five were wounded.

Britannic had been lost due to a key watertight door that had not closed because of a malfunction caused by the explosion. Protocol required that all bulkhead doors remain sealed when in hostile territory, but *Britannic's* had been open since 8a.m. to allow stokers to change shift. Also, some portholes nearest the waterline had been opened by orderlies to air the wards in the final preparations to receive patients. Opening them was prohibited in war zones as each 18in porthole could admit 3¼ tons of water per minute.

Controversially speculation arose at the time that *Britannic* had been carrying munitions. Being a Red Cross ship, transporting arms contravened her immunity under the Geneva Convention. Suspicion piqued when the British Admiralty surreptitiously altered the co-ordinates of her wreck by 6.75 miles to allegedly prevent discovery of this dubious hoard. It was also counter-posed that a torpedo, not a mine, had struck the fatal blow – another blatant violation of the Convention – although a chain-fixed mine anchored to the seabed remains the likely cause of her loss.

The mine theory was substantiated by the log of Kapitanleutnant Gustav Siess, commander of the mine-laying U-73 between October 1915 and April 1917. Entering service on 16 June 1915, the 58.8m-long submarine displaced 832 tons when submerged. Capable of laying thirty-two mines per mission, Siess recorded planting twelve in the very area that *Britannic* foundered.

The damage inflicted upon *Britannic* however had been exacerbated by the coal-dust within her bunkers igniting from the initial explosion. This was the official explanation anyway. More recent examinations of the wreck to determine the cause of the sinking and to find evidence of her alleged cargo of munitions have all proven inconclusive. Aboard HMS *Duncan* on 23 November 1916 Rear Admiral Arthur Hayes-Sadler chaired the day-long investigation into her loss, his two-page report attributing the sinking to the mine. The report had been prepared for the Admiralty by the commander-in-chief of the Eastern Mediterranean Fleet, Vice Admiral Sir Cecil Feinnes Thursby, filing it in turn with the Board of Trade amid claims of conspiracy. After the war, in 1921, the Reparations Committee awarded White Star the brand new 56,551-ton German liner *Bismarck* as a formal replacement for *Britannic*. Anglicising its name to *Majestic*, White Star put her into service in 1922, partnering *Olympic*.

Through the use of SONAR, the wreck of *Britannic* was eventually discovered from the vessel *Calypso* on 3 December 1975 by famed explorer Jacques Cousteau. Unable to actually visit the wreck himself until September the following year, Cousteau found *Britannic* lying at a depth of 395ft in the Kea Channel of the Aegean Sea, 4 miles from the Greek port of Saint Nikolo. Save for the hole punched by the explosion, her hull remains intact. Other than an additional 60ft rent caused by the bow striking the seabed, *Britannic* is in otherwise remarkable condition, resting at an 85-degree list on her starboard side. To this day she holds the dubious distinction as being the largest complete civilian wreck on the seabed. In 1995 Dr Robert Ballard, discoverer of the wreck of *Titanic*, put plans in motion to designate the resting place of *Britannic* as the world's first underwater museum. It remains his intention to this day.

Lost to the fog of war, *Britannic* sadly had never shone like her sisters. Not once would she carry a fee-paying passenger or sail the Atlantic. She was not even handed to the control of White Star Line. Yet during her brief career she returned more than 15,000 wounded soldiers safely to Britain over her five missions of mercy to the Mediterranean.

Had White Star's Olympians survived they would no doubt have become the predominant force in transatlantic shipping and would have remained so for as long as a quarter of a century. Had they done so, history may have seen White Star's name still emblazoned upon the Atlantic liners today. Ultimately, having lost two thirds of one of the greatest class of liners hitherto conceived, the most ambitious feats of Edwardian engineering, White Star was never able to compete toe to toe Cunard again. History would instead consign them as the failed operator of the doomed *Titanic*, unacknowledged and unsung for the wonderful legacy their great Olympic trio lent the pantheon of maritime development.

Heavy Lies the Crown

The days that followed the *Titanic* disaster heralded the onset of a long and irreversible decline for the White Star Line. The Olympic Class would be their last liners produced prior to the First World War, during which Cunard would remain the sole operator sponsored by the British government to maintain a timetabled service on the Atlantic. But after the war Cunard too faced financial ruin, reeling from the torpedoing of their *Lusitania* in 1915; one of twenty-two vessels lost by the line during the conflict. White Star had suffered greatly too: ten of their ships had been destroyed, most notably *Britannic*. But they were not alone. With 2,749 vessels lost the fallout of war had left the British mercantile marine at the brink of devastation. With *Titanic* and *Britannic* gone, and demand for emigration diminishing, White Star found itself in a new fight for survival, this time a fight they would be unable to win.

To restock the void left by the 12.5 million tons of sunken Allied and neutral merchant shipping, the peace terms of the Treaty of Versailles ordered the surrender of the largest surviving German liners to Allied governments, selling them onward to their operators. These reparations were not billed as spoils of war, but were intended to disable German merchant shipping and stunt the growth of their economy by giving the Allied economies the impetus to recover first. However, despite best efforts, shipping was inadvertently pulled into the economic turmoil of the war's aftermath.

Being one of Morgan's businesses, expectations of IMM's performance were extremely high, if not disproportionately, yet IMM failed to be the tiger that Morgan aspired for it to become. Within just eleven years IMM had witnessed a succession of four company presidents, none able to deliver the revenues the company was anticipated to attain. IMM, in truth, averaged a $2.5 million annual loss, proving after all to be little more than an elaborate vanity project.

Swamped by overwhelming competition on the Atlantic, IMM's overheads spiralled and only the stubbornness of Morgan had kept the entity afloat, topping up its shortfalls from his bank. But with the death of their paymaster in 1913 the handouts ceased. Over-invested, IMM promptly fell into receivership. Coupled with dwindling demand for emigration and the increasingly turbulent economic climate, White Star reduced its departures to New York and Boston to just sixty-six a year; almost halving the 108 timetabled in 1913. Finally, on 17 June 1926 a beleaguered IMM decided to sell its foreign concerns – White Star Line in particular. On 1 January 1927 White Star was sold to the Royal Mail group for £7,907,661, a £2 million loss on IMM's original outlay in 1902.

Lord Kylsant – chairman of the Royal Mail Line and now the new head of White Star – had, coincidentally, also been appointed chair of Harland & Wolff in 1924 following the sudden death of Lord Pirrie. Harold Sanderson, who had served as Bruce Ismay's lieutenant since 1899 and as company chairman since 1913, remained as deputy of the new White Star Line, which on 10 January 1927 filed for Limited status. However, in 1929 the Great Depression followed, biting Kylsant's empire – bloated with over 2 million tons of shipping – particularly hard, and once again shipyard order books fell empty. Kylsant's vast shipping empire was perilously over-resourced to weather the tempest.

To make matters worse, White Star, whose balance sheets of 1930 posted a deficit of £1.25 million, was for a second time in its history overlooked by the

British Treasury, which was again preparing to offer Cunard a loan, this time to fund construction of their Queen class and pull this much-stalled project out of hiatus. Speculation about the arrangement saw White Star increasing efforts in a last-ditch bid to meet the regal splendour of the newly emerging vanguard of 1,000ft liners planned by Cunard and heralded by French Line's almost completed *Normandie*. White Star had plans in motion in 1926 to design a £3.5 million liner to rival the grandeur of these new giants. Construction on hull number 844, *Oceanic III*, finally began on 28 June 1928, however the 1,010ft liner, which was to gross 52,000 tons, proved little more than a pipe dream. Work progressed slowly and the project was aborted the following year. Saddled with debt, White Star was instead forced to sell much of their existing fleet to P&O, and in 1933 while Cunard negotiated with the government for their second loan stimulus, the effects of the Depression had taken their toll. White Star capitulated.

In one final roll of the dice to save the two lines, the chancellor of the exchequer, Neville Chamberlain, agreed to write off White Star's debt of £11 million as well as give Cunard the funding sought to complete *Queen Mary*, whose construction had ground to a halt since 1931, and another, *Queen Elizabeth*. The condition he set was that the two lines must merge. The frailty of the two companies expelled all other options, and Cunard and White Star could do nothing but accept. Formalising the government's terms on 30 December 1933 the merger itself took place on 28 March 1934.

This newly wedded fleet comprised fifteen ships from Cunard and ten from White Star, with Cunard the majority partner, owning 62 per cent of the company's assets. On 17 May the line was renamed Cunard-White Star Ltd and, as promised, Sir Percy Elly Bates, its new chairman, duly received the £9.5 million loan from the Treasury. It was almost too late. White Star's parent company, Oceanic Steam Navigation, declared bankruptcy on 31 August 1939. Forever scarred as the operators of the hapless *Titanic*, Oceanic Steam had finally succumbed to the global economic chaos. With debts amounting to £22 million, their former owner, Royal Mail Line, similarly fell by the wayside in 1936. IMM, renamed United States Lines in 1937, lingered, but folded nonetheless in 1986.

With only nine ships in the whole Cunard-White Star fleet a revived Cunard finally bought out its smaller partner on 16 March 1945, symbolically dropping the White Star motif from the company stationery. Becoming solely Cunard Steam-Ship Company, by 1947 it had absorbed White Star's shares and remaining assets, ultimately phasing out their share of operations in 1949.

A century of precocious existence since its debut in 1845, White Star had succumbed as yet another marred casualty in the changing face of sea travel. In the wake of their remarkable contribution and achievements to merchant shipping, the line was unable to disentangle itself from the tainted association with its greatest accomplishment, their ever indomitable Olympic Class of liners.

CHAPTER 4

LAST MAN STANDING

'Captain Smith having done all that man could for the safety of passengers and
crew remained at his post on the sinking ship until the end. His last message to
his crew was, Be British.'
Memorial inscription to Captain Smith, unveiled 13 April 1913

In addition to the 5,000 workforce directly engaged in the creation of *Titanic*
there was a crew of almost 900 to operate her. *Titanic* was a floating city, a serving luxurious, self-contained bastion of safety to her temporary and transient
populace. Much is known of *Titanic*, but what of the people who brought her to
life: the designers, owners and crewmembers to whose care this symbol of British
fortitude was entrusted.

Titanic was the brainchild of Joseph Bruce Ismay. Born in Crosby, Merseyside,
in 1862, the eldest son of White Star's founder Thomas Henry Ismay, Harrow-
educated Bruce joined his father's company, Ismay, Imrie & Co. (the ship
broking arm of White Star) as an apprentice on 13 September 1880. Dispatched
in May 1887 to serve as White Star's agent in New York, Bruce returned to
Britain, albeit reluctantly, upon his father's insistence in September 1890, so
that he could become partner in the business; the position was formalised on
1 January 1891. A director also of the London Midland & Scottish Railway
he held five additional positions of varying influence elsewhere, but upon the
death of his father on 23 November 1899, as heir to the Ismay legacy, Bruce
duly assumed the chairmanship of the White Star Line. Intent on perpetuating
his father's legacy in North Atlantic passenger shipping, falling profits in this
increasingly competitive industry found Bruce in 1902 selling the parent company of White Star – Oceanic Steam Navigation Company, and with it their
entire operations – to the American shipping conglomerate, IMM. Successfully
negotiating to remain head of White Star, in February 1904 Morgan obliged
him with the presidency of IMM, with Bruce striving to ensure his father's line
remained core to its American owner's interests.

Indeed, Ismay proved a gifted organiser. White Star prospered under him as a result. But the comparative ease of the line's success during his tenure cultivated within Ismay an arrogance in decision making: he ardently believed his personal judgment was beyond reproach. Yet the bonds his father had forged with Harland & Wolff continued White Star's prominence as the most successful British operator at the turn of the twentieth century. An extremely spirited Cunard, however, prompted Bruce, together with Harland & Wolff's Lord Pirrie, in 1907 to begin the creation of a class of ships to counter Cunard's newly upgraded prestige trio servicing New York: the Olympic Class of liners. Although the first of the trio, *Olympic*, enjoyed tremendous acclaim, Bruce's voyage and ensuing survival on her doomed sister, *Titanic*, was widely admonished as an inexcusable act of cowardice and one viewed with utmost disdain throughout the international media. By the time he arrived in New York aboard the rescue ship *Carpathia*, the injury to Bruce's reputation, which was already in tatters, compelled him six days after the disaster to declare in a statement that not 'for one moment' would he have 'thought of getting into the [life]boat if there had been any women there to go in it'.

His plea fell on deaf ears. Despite wanting to remain on IMM's board of directors, Bruce's continued employment was viewed a liability, its management insisting that he take early retirement. Ismay relinquished the presidency of IMM on 2 January 1913, leaving on 30 June 1913 after his notice period – his deputy, Harold Sanderson, succeeded him both as head of White Star and IMM. The line's ensuing vilification in the press also found IMM denying Ismay the post previously promised him as managing director of White Star. On the notion that he of all had survived the disaster, the stigma of *Titanic* would haunt the Ismay name for the remainder of his days. This staunch condemnation would lead to his younger brother's racehorse, Craganour – the 6-4 favourite – being disqualified following a stewards' enquiry upon winning the coveted Epsom Derby – literally by a nose – in 1913 (the very race in which Suffragette Emily Davison perished from wounds after jumping in front of the King's horse, Anmer). The decision was given on the tenuous pretext that Charles Bower Ismay's horse had failed to maintain a straight line. One of the stewards, however, was the Earl of Rosebery (Prime Minister, 1894–5), an ardent detractor of Bruce Ismay in the aftermath of *Titanic*.

Branded 'J. Brute Ismay', his survival from *Titanic* left Bruce harangued and in disrepute until his death. The roots of the smears that condemned him had stemmed from his time as White Star's agent in New York, when he fell foul of the press there upon locking horns with media mogul William Randolph Hearst. Hearst pounced on the disaster to destroy Ismay's character, admonishing him as a self-preservationist, coward and a 'Brute'.

Upon eventually leaving IMM's board, as well as personally donating £20,000 to the families of the surviving and lost crew of *Titanic*, Ismay continued fulfilling directorships for other organisations: one of which processed many of the insurance claims concerning the disaster, the Liverpool & London Steamship Protection &

Indemnity Association, a company founded by his father in 1881. Bruce retired in 1934, dividing his time between London and his secluded retreat in Costello, County Galway. He died aged seventy-four at his Mayfair home on 17 October 1937, three days after suffering a stroke; he was interred at Putney Vale Cemetery on the 21st.

The success of White Star owed much to its almost brotherly alliance with Belfast's inimitable employer, Harland & Wolff, whose yards were run by the redoubtable figure of the Northern Irish establishment, The Rt Hon. Lord William James Pirrie. Born in Quebec, Canada, in 1847, Pirrie's career at Harland & Wolff began in 1862 as a premium apprentice. By 1869 he had risen to the position of chief designer and then became partner in the company in 1874. Following the death of Sir Edward Harland in 1895 Pirrie was appointed managing director. His position as the largest employer in Ireland endowed Pirrie with considerable political influence, consequently securing his selection as lord mayor of Belfast for 1896–7, during which he became a privy councillor, and in 1898 was the first ever recipient to be anointed Freeman of the City of Belfast. But fundamentally Pirrie also held a directorship with Oceanic Steam Navigation and in 1904 joined Bruce Ismay on the board of IMM. Pirrie was a leading and influential voice to the young and inexperienced chairman, Bruce. Inextricably intertwining Harland & Wolff with White Star he cajoled Ismay to sell White Star to IMM in 1902 for fear of harming his yard's interests.

Upon Gustav Wolff's retirement in June 1906 Pirrie assumed the sole chairmanship of Harland & Wolff – and was also invested with a baronetcy on 17 July that year – he garnered commitment for the yard to construct all future ships for IMM; and, intent on retaining its status as 'the best', Pirrie began modernising and expanding its facilities. His work and services as lord lieutenant of Ireland saw him knighted with the Order of St Patrick (KP) in 1909. But at the yard Pirrie proved an autocratic leader. Exerting strict control he kept the design and construction of *Titanic* under his direct supervision, setting her dimensions and general arrangements personally. Yet Pirrie would be too ill to sail on her maiden voyage, sending his deputy, Thomas Andrews, in his place and later donating £2,100 to the Belfast Titanic Relief Fund in the aftermath of the disaster.

With his reputation intact following the disaster, in 1918 Pirrie became comptroller-general of Merchant Shipping, an appointment that saw him ultimately raised to viscount on 9 July 1921, but succumbed to pneumonia on 6 June 1924 during a business tour of South America. The much lauded director of thirty-nine companies left in death personal debts accumulating £1 million. His body was returned to Britain aboard his beloved *Olympic*.

Pirrie's right-hand man and principal designer of *Titanic* was Alexander Montgomery Carlisle, Harland & Wolff's chief naval architect until 1910. Born in 1854, at sixteen he too joined the yard in 1870 as a premium apprentice, and shared family ties with the yard's eventual owner: his sister Margaret married William Pirrie on 17 April 1879. By 1890 Alexander had been made the firm's general manager, and subsequently chairman of managing directors on 7 March 1907. He was also its chief designer, responsible during his tenure for many notable creations, namely *Teutonic, Oceanic II* and *Olympic*. Although Lord Pirrie had drafted the conceptual plans for *Olympic* and *Titanic* himself, Carlisle would devise their finer details and working arrangements, also overseeing the preliminary designs of *Titanic* until his retirement in 1910. An avid Irish Unionist, Carlisle was resoundingly defeated at a parliamentary election in 1906 standing as an independent candidate for the constituency of West Belfast, yet joined his brother-in-law as privy councillor the following year.

Carlisle retired from Harland & Wolff on 30 June 1910 while work on *Olympic* was nearing completion. A fervent exponent of marine safety, he afterward attained a directorship at Welin Davit & Engineering Co. Ltd – the very company tasked to manufacture the lifeboat winches for *Titanic* – and was also co-opted to the government's Advisory Committee on Life-Saving Appliances in 1911. During construction of *Olympic* he twice petitioned White Star to furnish the then unfinished *Titanic* with a greater allocation of lifeboats. Appeals were dismissed by a pious Bruce Ismay as disproportionately cautious. However, in May 1911 Carlisle's advisory committee would controversially draft recommendations that if applied would unwittingly reduce the legal lifeboat capacity for the Olympic Class; a missive that would taunt him in the maelstrom following the disaster. Aged seventy-one, he died in London in 1926.

Carlisle's replacement in the Harland & Wolff design team was Pirrie's cerebral protégé, Thomas Andrews Jr. Second only to Pirrie at the time of the disaster, Andrews became chief designer of the Olympic Class upon Carlisle's retirement. Born in 1873 in Comber, a small town nestling in the outskirts of southern Belfast, Andrews had graduated from college in 1889 to join Harland & Wolff as a 'premium' apprentice (whereby a one-off fee is paid by the family, guaranteeing employment), which he completed in 1894. With his warm and unassuming demeanour, he became highly popular among his peers, as well as the labourers of the yard. He too shared family ties with Lord Pirrie: his mother Eliza Morrison Pirrie was William Pirrie's sister. Andrews' career soared. Joining the yard's design department in 1892 and becoming its manager in 1905, his outstanding proficiency gained him the reputation of master shipbuilder, ultimately earning him the position of managing director of Harland & Wolff in 1907.

Married in 1908, upon Carlisle's retirement in 1910 Andrews assumed the supervision of the design and construction of *Olympic* and *Titanic*. While travelling aboard the maiden voyage of *Titanic* he remained often in his cabin continually drafting improvements to her already palatial interiors; noting intentions to shorten her reading and writing rooms to yield yet further space for additional revenue-generating staterooms.

After the iceberg struck, Andrews refused escape, remaining behind to assist women and children to the safety of her all-too-few lifeboats. Shortly after 2a.m.

on 15 April, he withdrew to the first-class smoking room where he was last seen, appearing to survivors as dejected and broken. Andrews, whose body was never recovered, was succeeded as chief designer at the yard by his deputy, Edward Wilding, who in 1914 also rose to managing director – holding the post until his own resignation in 1924.

In order to compete on equal terms with Cunard and their unrelenting German rivals it became ever clearer to Ismay that if his father's line was to survive it would be unable to do so alone. Ismay sold White Star in 1902 to the financial colossus John Pierpont Morgan. A kingmaker of formidable reputation, J.P. Morgan was born in Connecticut in 1837. Qualified as an accountant in 1857, he rose to eminence upon founding the Fidelity Trust Company of Philadelphia in 1873 to finance the completion of the Northern Pacific railroads: later owning 5,000 miles of track across America. In 1891 he also helped form General Electric. Known for avarice he was first introduced to shipping in 1899 shortly after which he forcibly assumed ownership of the well-established International Navigation Company (INC) – holding company of the Red Star, Inman and American lines. Morgan's immense influence found him befriending the monarchs and political leaders of Europe, affording him unrivalled power. Keen also to dominate the railroad industry he diversified into steel production and in 1901 created United States Steel, the first commercial American entity valued in excess of $1 billion.

To fortify his reach into shipping, in 1901 he used INC to acquire the Dominion, Atlantic Transport and Leyland lines, culminating in 1902 with the purchase of White Star Line – their largest single acquisition. Upon securing White Star he renamed INC the International Mercantile Marine Company (IMM). Morgan then formed a subsidiary within IMM named the International Navigation Company of Liverpool; the element of his empire holding all but six of White Star's newly acquired shares. Morgan also appointed Bruce Ismay president of IMM in 1904, tasking him to produce 'the finest vessels afloat'. Since the purchase, however, Morgan's relationship with Ismay became decidedly strained. As the actual owner of *Titanic*, Morgan was guest of honour at her launch on 31 May 1911, although he cancelled his reservation on the maiden voyage due to a bout of illness, from which he was convalescing at the luxurious French spa at Aix-les-Bains when he heard of her loss. His health never recovered. Following an acute nervous breakdown during a Nile cruise in February 1913 Morgan expired in Rome on 31 March. However, his company, J.P. Morgan & Co., which he founded in 1895, thrived, becoming the largest investment house in the world and twice instrumental in reviving the American economy after the First World War and during the Great Depression. To many, Morgan was widely perceived as the country's unofficial central banker – his name still holds pre-eminence on both sides of the Atlantic today.

Upon its sale to IMM White Star was split into two administrative regions: one based in Liverpool, and the other in New York, with Ismay overseeing both. The man responsible for managing White Star's British apparatus was Harold Arthur Sanderson. As general manager of the line, Sanderson was also Ismay's trusted aide since joining its earlier incarnation, Ismay, Imrie & Co., in 1895. Sanderson, born in 1859 to nautical heritage, was appointed partner in the firm in 1899 – also holding a directorship with Oceanic Steam Navigation. When Oceanic Steam was purchased by IMM in 1902 Sanderson, Bruce Ismay and Lord Pirrie remained as board members of White Star; Sanderson that year was reciprocally appointed vice-president and head of the British wing of IMM. With Ismay's acrimonious departure from both IMM and White Star in 1913 Sanderson assumed the presidency of IMM as well as the chair of White Star. Other than Ismay he was the longest-serving member of White Star's senior management, but within months of attaining the role IMM's board also ousted him as their president. Although allowed to retain the chairmanship of White Star Line, in 1927 a beleaguered IMM sold White Star to the Royal Mail Line, reappointing Sanderson as deputy chairman. An honorary captain in the RNR, he died in 1932.

The head of White Star's American interests and a key figure in the co-ordination of the company's media relations post-*Titanic* disaster was Philip Albright Small Franklin. Born in Baltimore to a wealthy family in 1871, he was introduced into shipping aged eighteen upon taking employment as an office junior at Atlantic Transport. Rapidly promoted and relocated to New York, upon Morgan's takeover in 1902 the banker subsequently appointed Franklin vice-president of IMM and head of its entire American operations. Franklin received the first telegrams reporting the sinking directly from Bruce Ismay from aboard *Carpathia*: the only ship to recover any survivors. Heading White Star's responses to the media in the immediate aftermath of the disaster he fielded their deputation at the ensuing US Senate investigation. Prior to receiving confirmation of the sinking, Franklin had issued statements bullishly exalting *Titanic* as unsinkable. Even during the inquiry he persisted: 'There was nothing further from the minds of everybody than that an accident of this kind could take place … that the ship could go down'.

Franklin became president of Atlantic Transport in 1912, as well as of IMM itself following Sanderson's dismissal in the latter half of 1913. However, by this juncture IMM's finances were in a tailspin, Franklin eventually declared the company insolvent in April 1915, and was consequently appointed its official receiver. He did, however, keep the business afloat and was mainly assisted by contracts and commitments for the First World War, though by the late 1920s the company's faltering performance forced him to dispose of IMM's non-American assets, namely White Star. Appointed in 1918 to head the Shipping Control Committee of the US Shipping Board, Franklin was lauded for his work improving efficiency at American and French ports during the war and was awarded both the DSM and the Legion of Honour that year. He died in August 1939.

In addition to White Star's management their new flagship required a crew handpicked for their experience to oversee the inaugural voyage of *Titanic* to

New York. This principal crew were chosen due to their working knowledge of large ships. After all, the majority posted to *Titanic* had previously served on her identical twin, *Olympic*.

Of this crew the captain and chief engineer were the sole members deemed to be on duty at all times during the voyage. White Star particularly expected their captains to remain present on the bridge during times of inclement weather or when within 60 miles of landfall. To support the captain's potential twenty-four-hour duty, the chief officer, down to and including the second officer, held certificates affording them the authority to command the ship as senior watch officer. These three officers – working in rotations of four-hour shifts, permitting each commander an eight-hour respite – were required to hold the Board of Trade's Extra Master's Certificate (EMC), a standard of competency compulsory since 1850 that qualified the holder to command British ocean-going vessels after passing a written and oral examination. The remaining officers, third to sixth, had only to attain the entry qualification for a deck officer, the Ordinary Master's Certificate (OMC). These more junior officers each undertook a four-hour watch on the bridge, also in strict rotation, permitting each four-hour rest cycles throughout the voyage.

Quartermasters would work in pairs on the bridge, again in four-hour turns – one manning the helm for two hours, the other acting as standby, swapping every two hours. The same pair of quartermasters served the same four-hour duty, alternating between helmsman and relief. Lookouts also worked in pairs, jointly covering a pattern of two hours on duty followed by a four-hour rest. To maintain the twenty-four-hour cycle *Titanic* had six lookouts, working in three pairs.

It was considered by many of the crew that being selected by White Star for a posting on *Titanic* – the flower of their fleet – was a career-enhancing honour. For her maiden voyage they would be headed by the line's prized veteran and stalwart, sixty-two-year-old Commodore Edward John Smith. Known more endearingly among his regular passengers as 'EJ', Smith was born at Hanley, Staffordshire, in 1850. His career at sea began as an apprentice in 1869 at the age of thirteen, and after achieving his Master's Certificate in 1875 he joined White Star in 1880 as fourth officer on their 3,888-ton *Celtic*. Achieving his first, albeit brief, command, *Republic (I)* in 1887, and receiving his Extra Master's Certificate (number 14102), the following year, Smith was awarded his first full-time captaincy, the 3,707-ton *Baltic (I)*. Throughout his service with White Star Smith would command a total of seventeen vessels, accidentally grounding three.

Beneath his dogmatic exterior, Smith cut a figure of a much cherished and good-natured captain and one who keenly demonstrated the trait inherent amongst all his professional contemporaries – showmanship. Serving as an honorary commander for the Royal Navy Reserve during the Boer War, he later received the officer's decoration (RD) in recognition for his long and dedicated service. Smith was further honoured in 1904, with White Star making him commodore of their fleet, a position that saw him awarded command of their then flagship, the 23,876-ton *Baltic (II)*. Following his posting from the 725ft *Adriatic* in May 1911 he duly received the captaincy of the 880ft *Olympic*. By 1912 he enjoyed celebrity status. Drawing a £1,250 annual salary, Smith was the most highly remunerated seafarer of the era, for he was widely regarded as the most proficient commander on the North Atlantic. After forty dutiful years of service, thirty-two of which were with White Star, in March 1912 the line granted him stewardship of the maiden voyage of his 17th command – *Titanic*. Such an illustrious occasion for his final roundtrip would demonstrate the extent of the company's benevolence toward Smith, who afterwards was due to retire from the career that he himself had earlier described as 'uneventful'. But for him, retirement was not to be. Smith did not survive the *Titanic* disaster and is recalled by history as perhaps one of – if not the – most ill-fated captains of all time. A stickler for tradition and the rules of the sea, Smith dutifully went down with his ship. His questionable navigational judgment that evening, however, finds his name well remembered but recalled mockingly in cultural lore.

Following a lengthy campaign, a statue in memory of his honour was unveiled by his daughter on 29 July 1916 in the town of Lichfield, Staffordshire – 40 miles from his hometown. Debate still rages to this day how and where he died on *Titanic*, and especially if his last words were the rallying call to his crew to 'Be British'; Nevertheless Smith's image at the time came to epitomise British fortitude.

Second in command was Henry Tingle Wilde RNR, the thirty-eight-year-old chief officer of *Titanic*, a position responsible for the safekeeping of the ship's logbook. Born in 1872 in Liverpool, Wilde, who joined White Star in 1905, gained his EMC and climbed the ranks swiftly, following a rapid succession of postings, also serving in the Royal Navy Reserve as lieutenant. Little is known of his life prior to his posting on *Titanic* – although he was widowed on Christmas Eve 1910 – Wilde had garnered Smith's respect while chief officer of *Olympic*, where they served together between 9 August 1911 and 30 March 1912. Although not originally chosen to serve on *Titanic*, one day prior to her maiden voyage Wilde was transferred to the crew at the personal request of Smith. It was a temporary, albeit prestigious, sideways shuffle from *Olympic*, but in secret it was one for which Wilde was not particularly thankful. In correspondence written before leaving Queenstown on *Titanic* he prophetically confessed to his sister his 'queer feeling' about the voyage. During the sinking he supervised the readying and lowering of the lifeboats and distributed handguns among senior officers with which to maintain order on the deck. He died on *Titanic* shortly after ushering passengers on the portside of the deck over to starboard in order to counterbalance the ship's list to port.

The next in Smith's chain of command was William McMaster Murdoch, the thirty-nine-year-old first officer on *Titanic*. Born in Dumfries in 1873 he completed his apprenticeship in 1892, attaining both his OMC and EMC in 1896 prior to joining White Star in 1900. He too served as a Royal Navy reservist, and in 1903 his derring-do, when he snatched the wheel of the *Arabic* himself, saved the ship from collision with another vessel. Posted as first officer of *Olympic*, White Star transferred him to *Titanic* to serve as chief officer, his seventh placement with the line; a promotion, however, short lived. Captain Smith replaced him with Henry Wilde at the last minute, temporarily demoting Murdoch to first officer for the maiden voyage. Murdoch would, however, achieve notoriety for being in command of the bridge at the moment *Titanic* struck the iceberg; his earlier luck aboard *Arabic* clearly deserted him. He assembled the passengers on the Boat Deck to have them board the lifeboats, and was subsequently placed in charge of lowering those along its starboard side. But he too died on *Titanic*, leaving much conjecture about his fate, be it from drowning, or shooting himself upon becoming so racked with guilt for failing to avert the collision (the latter more Hollywood sensationalism than truth).

Next in command was Charles Herbert Lightoller, Smith's thirty-eight-year-old second officer and designated supervisor of the lookouts. Born in Chorley, Lancashire, in 1874, he was apprenticed to the sea in 1888. Shipwrecked in the Indian Ocean on a small uninhabited island for eight days in 1889, he signed with White Star in January 1900 as fourth officer. Attaining his EMC in 1902, a decade later Lightoller transferred sideways from *Oceanic* to serve as first officer on *Titanic*. But he too was temporarily demoted to make way for Wilde's impromptu appointment as chief officer.

After the collision, Lightoller was placed in charge of lowering the portside lifeboats. Famously obeying his captain's order 'women and children first' to the letter, even to the point of allowing seats to remain unfilled when neither women nor children were available to occupy them, he allowed just one male passenger into the boats he supervised that entire evening.

Wilde had ordered Lightoller to leave the ship in collapsible lifeboat D, but the second officer characteristically declined. Actually going down with *Titanic*, Lightoller swam to an upturned collapsible, lifeboat B, and took command of both it and the thirty occupants standing upon its capsized hull until they were later rescued by his colleague Harold Lowe. As the most senior officer to survive *Titanic* Lightoller endured the wrath of the inquisitor's probing, fending some 1,500 questions at the ensuing London inquiry. Once the furore had ebbed he was again reassigned to *Oceanic*. Serving in the Royal Navy during the First World War he was promoted captain in 1915, and twice decorated. In peacetime, however, captaincy of a civilian vessel would continually elude him, and he rose only to chief officer of *Celtic*. Disillusioned, he resigned from White Star in the 1920s, subsequently opening a London guesthouse, then later a chicken farm. Publishing his memoirs *Titanic and Other Ships* in 1935, in 1940 he sailed *Sundowner* – his self-designed 58ft yacht – to Dunkirk and rescued 131 British soldiers. He died on 8 December 1952.

Herbert John Pitman was the third officer of *Titanic*. Born in Sutton Mantis, Somerset, in 1877, he joined the sea in 1895, and subsequently White Star in 1906,

immediately upon attaining his OMC. The only deck officer on *Titanic* not a
member of the Royal Navy Reserve, he served previously aboard *Oceanic* as fourth
officer before transferring to *Titanic* aged thirty-four. During the sinking he helped
lower her starboard lifeboats and was placed in charge of boat number 5 by First
Officer Murdoch. Worried about overcrowding, the occupants of his boat refused to
allow Pitman to return to the wreck site to rescue further survivors. After the disaster
he briefly returned to *Oceanic* as third officer although soon afterwards left the deck
officers' department due to failing eyesight, and transferred to the pursers section of
Olympic. He retired from the sea thirty-five years later and was awarded the MBE in
1946 in recognition of a long and loyal career. He died on 7 December 1961.

Joseph Grove Boxhall, aged twenty-eight, was the fourth officer and principal
navigator of *Titanic*. Born in Hull in 1884, he joined the sea in 1899. Gaining his
EMC in 1907 he joined White Star that November. Prior to receiving his posting on *Titanic* he served aboard *Oceanic* and *Arabic*. A highly competent navigator,
Boxhall was Captain Smith's preference to chart the daily position of *Titanic* and
earned notoriety for plotting her infamous CQD wireless distress position. He
was also first to inspect *Titanic* after the impact with the iceberg, albeit failing
to find any damage. Later that evening Boxhall requested use of rockets that he
and Quartermaster George Rowe then launched to summon help. The captain
then ordered him command of lifeboat 2 from which he continued firing flares
to beckon rescue ships, subsequently seen by *Carpathia*. Following the disaster he
joined the Royal Navy before returning to White Star in 1919 where he remained
until 1940. Rising to chief officer of Cunard-White Star's 13,912-ton *Ausonia*, in
retirement he became technical adviser to the movie *A Night to Remember* (1958).
He died on 25 April 1967.

Aged twenty-eight, the fifth officer of *Titanic* was Harold Godfrey Lowe. Born
in 1882 in Conwy, North Wales, he proved an extremely gifted boatsman. Having
joined the sea in 1898 he gained his OMC just prior to joining White Star in 1911
as third officer of the *Belgic*. The maiden voyage of *Titanic* happened also to be
his first Atlantic crossing. Following the collision he was placed second-in-charge
of lowering her starboard boats; assisted by Sixth Officer Moody, who, to ensure
order was maintained in the lifeboats, decided that an officer should accompany
them – Sixth Officer Moody offering him the seat. Lowe took command of boat
14 which became the only lifeboat to return and search for anyone still alive in the
water – it found only four, one of whom soon died. Later tying his lifeboat with
boats 4, 10, 12 and the collapsible boat D he formed the flotilla that rescued Charles
Lightoller. During the ensuing Senatorial inquiry, its investigators famously point-
edly enquired what an iceberg was made of, to which Boxhall replied flippantly:
'Ice, I suppose, sir!' He later became third officer of the 11,948-ton *Medic*, servicing
White Star's Australian routes. After transferring to the Royal Navy Reserve as a
commander during the First World War he left both White Star and the sea, later
serving as a councillor in North Wales. He died on 12 May 1944.

The junior officer of the crew was twenty-four-year-old James Pell (Paul) Moody, the sixth officer. Born in Scarborough in 1887 he joined the sea aged fourteen, and then White Star Line in 1911, occupying the same position aboard *Oceanic* prior to his posting to *Titanic* as her apprentice officer. On the night of the sinking he answered the lookout's telephoned alert, warning 'Iceberg, right ahead', and recorded the time of the collision for the log. Afterwards he circulated boat assignments to the crew and helped supervise the loading of the portside boats. Moody relinquished his seat to his senior, Harold Lowe, and was last seen attempting to loose a collapsible boat stowed awkwardly upon the roof of the Bridge House.

The chief engineer on *Titanic* was fifty-one-year-old veteran, Joseph Bell. Born in 1861 at Maryport, Cumberland, Bell had joined the sea in 1883 and subsequently White Star in 1885. Promoted to chief engineer at the age of thirty, he served on *Olympic* prior to his posting to *Titanic*, which began even while she was undergoing construction. On 10 April 1912 Bell was controversially pressed by Bruce Ismay to run her engines at full speed on the 16th, spawning speculation of the chairman's reckless intention to race *Titanic* through ice fields to reach New York ahead of schedule. During the sinking, to aid evacuation, Bell remained alongside his team of thirty-four engineers to maintain electricity to the ship's water pumps and lighting systems. Relieving his men of their duty at 2a.m., all declined and remained at their posts to the bitter end. Bell consequently perished with his entire engineering staff; a monument dedicated to the team was unveiled in Southampton on 22 April 1914 in front of a crowd 100,000 strong.

Other notable crew aboard *Titanic* were her two wireless operators. The senior operator, twenty-five-year-old John 'Jack' George Phillips, was born in Godalming, Surrey, in 1887. Phillips joined the Post Office as a telegraph operator in 1902 and had gone to the Marconi Company in 1906 to attend a six-month course that August at its training facility in Liverpool. Upon its completion he served aboard *Teutonic*, *Lusitania* and *Mauretania*, after which between 1908 and 1911 he was based at Marconi's Clifden land station on Ireland's west coast. Returning to the sea to serve on *Adriatic* and then *Oceanic* he was posted to *Titanic* along with his assistant, Harold Sidney Bride, twenty-two. Soon after *Titanic* struck the iceberg Captain Smith had Phillips transmit their distress position and he is ignominiously remembered for dispatching the world's first mid-ocean use of SOS. Phillips remained at his wireless until the moment *Titanic* sank. Jumping overboard, even managing to reach the upturned collapsible boat B, he succumbed to hypothermia prior to rescue.

Quartermaster Robert Hichens, aged thirty at the time of the disaster, found unsuspected fame as the man at the helm of *Titanic* at the moment of the collision. Born in 1882 in Whitby, his posting to *Titanic* marked his first crossing of the Atlantic. Executing Murdoch's infamous order 'Hard-a-starboard', he afterwards escaped *Titanic* when given command of boat 6 by Second Officer Lightoller.

Hichens was asked 492 questions at the ensuing British investigation, after which he parted company with White Star and allegedly accepted the position of harbourmaster at Cape Town to evade the media's glare. Following a stint in the Royal Navy he rejoined the merchant service in 1919 as a third officer. Setting up his own business in 1930 its sudden failure due to the Great Depression spiralled Hichens into financial hardship. Taking a variety of other jobs, he turned to alcohol and died at sea on 23 September 1940.

A far worse affiliation in history lay not for the man at the wheel of *Titanic* but for the individual specifically entrusted to warn for icebergs. Frederick Fleet earned distinction as the twenty-four-year-old lookout who first spotted what has since became the most studied iceberg in history. Born in Liverpool in 1887, Fleet joined the sea in 1903 and became lookout on *Oceanic* in 1908. Serving there until his redeployment to *Titanic*, he was the first to sight the iceberg 500 yards ahead and alert the bridge. Following that, his fate and that of all aboard rested in the hands of the gods. Fleet helped load lifeboat number 6 and was subsequently asked to crew it by Charles Lightoller. After the disaster he served aboard *Olympic* until August 1912 when he left White Star to improve his career prospects by joining the Union Castle Line, remaining there until 1936. He then worked as a labourer for Harland & Wolff, but fell victim to depression. Beset with financial difficulties, the death of his wife became the catalyst that ultimately induced him to take his own life just days later. His body was discovered on 10 January 1965.

Surprisingly, the most revered member of the crew was neither a deck officer, doctor, engineer nor sailor, but the ship's thirty-three-year-old bandmaster Wallace Henry Hartley. Born in Colne, Lancashire, in 1878, his father, Albion Hartley – insurance broker and amateur violinist – uprooted the family to Yorkshire during the 1890s. In childhood Wallace became a chorister for the Bethel Independent Methodist Chapel in Colne, but upon completing his education found employment as a clerk at Drewsbury's Union Bank before embarking upon a career as a professional musician with the Carl Rosa Opera Company. Subsequently contracted as a band member for Cunard aboard *Lusitania* and *Mauretania*, in 1912 he accepted a promotion as bandmaster for White Star's new luxury liner, heading the eight-piece orchestra for *Titanic*. Split into two ensembles they performed nightly until 11p.m. in her two reception rooms during her ill-fated voyage. At 12.15a.m. following the collision Captain Smith had them play in the first-class lounge to relax passengers while crew readied lifeboats for deployment. Later moving out to the Boat Deck adjacent to the entrance of the forward grand staircase, they famously carried on performing until the angle of the deck made it impossible to continue. At that point, realising that all chances of survival had elapsed the group purportedly packed their instruments away and calmly departed the Boat Deck. All of them died.

Hartley's body was recovered on 30 April and, amid great publicity, figureheaded the stoicism and self-sacrifice that embodied the disaster. Receiving a state-funded funeral in his hometown, the hearse's procession into his former Bethel Chapel on 18 May 1912 was witnessed by 40,000 people.

In death the crew of *Titanic* transcended heroic status, altruistically accepting their finality while upholding the virtues of Britain: decorum and tradition. Britannia was proud, but she proved far less forgiving to the management of White Star, in particular its chairman Bruce Ismay and his apparent refusal to furnish *Titanic* with additional lifeboats amid dubious concerns that doing so impinged on her external aesthetics.

Titanic was owned and operated by these people, ordinary folk, who in tragedy achieved timeless notoriety due to an iceberg forming ominously upon Greenland's Jakobshavn ice shelf. An iceberg that happened to break free of its glacier two years prior to the maiden voyage and drift indiscriminately into the path of the unsuspecting, over-confident, man-made ocean titan.

The crew of *Titanic* had differed during her sea trials: a complement of forty-one sailors (deck crew), the senior being Captain Smith, Chief Officer Murdoch, First Officer Lightoller, Second Officer Blair and officers Pitman, Lowe, Boxhall and Moody, plus a crew of seventy-eight manning the engine and boiler rooms. This was the proposed constitution of senior crew White Star intended to assign to the maiden voyage but was suddenly and unexpectedly altered a day prior to her departure, 9 April, at the behest of Captain Smith himself.

Wanting to pool extra handling experience for this high-profile trip, Smith petitioned his head office to transfer Henry Wilde, his former chief officer on *Olympic*, to occupy the same rank for the first outward and return voyage of *Titanic*. The move required the original second officer, 'Davy' Blair, to leave the roster and allow Murdoch and Lightoller to step down a rank to free the berth for Wilde. In his memoirs in 1935 Lightoller admitted the decision 'threw both Murdoch and me out of our stride', in having to learn new duties. But the reshuffle was intended to last just the roundtrip to Southampton, after which Wilde was to begin his new posting as captain of *Cymric*. At that time *Cymric* was herself laid up in Southampton due to the resulting shortage of fuel following the recently concluded national coal strike, consequently leaving Wilde available for this crossing. By calling on his experience as chief officer of *Olympic*, Smith seized the opportunity to temporarily return Wilde to his team for *Titanic*.

The profile of the maiden voyage necessitated more than ever the captain's need to have full confidence in his crew's proficiency. Out of White Star's original selection for the crossing Chief Officer Murdoch and Chief Engineer Bell were the sole members of Smith's senior crew that had served aboard a ship of a similar size to *Titanic* – *Olympic*. There, Smith, Bell, Wilde and Murdoch served together. Bringing aboard Wilde, his former chief officer, to the roster for the maiden voyage of *Titanic* redressed, in Smith's view, the shortfall in handling experience of this 45,000-ton liner. For this was far more than a familiarisation voyage. Smith – who appreciated that any commander was only as good as the officers supporting him

– sought for his final roundtrip absolute reassurance in his senior crew. Indeed, the sole officer known to Smith prior to taking charge of *Olympic* was Charles Lightoller – first officer during Smith's command of *Majestic* in 1903–4.

Although, at the time, thirty-seven-year-old David Blair, the original choice for second officer of *Titanic*, was saddened by Smith's decision to supplant him, remarking: 'This is a marvellous ship and I feel very disappointed I am not to make the first voyage'. It was, as events transpired, a blessing in disguise. Impossibly unbeknownst to Blair, Smith's decision inadvertently spared his life – albeit causing his ungracious denial and brush with infamy. Blair had made White Star's original shortlist due to his service on *Teutonic* and *Oceanic*. Smith's decision, by no means harbouring any personal agenda against Blair's ability, was founded on the captain's familiarity with the other officers. After all, one senior watch officer was needed to make way for Wilde. Other than Murdoch and Lightoller, Smith had not previously served with Blair or any junior officer in White Star's original shortlist for *Titanic*.

White Star intended to reinstate Blair as second officer upon the return to Southampton, this eventuality of course was scuppered by events. Blair instead returned to *Oceanic* as her navigating officer. Commissioned to war service as an armed auxiliary cruiser on 8 August 1914, strong currents ran HMS *Oceanic* aground at Foula Island on Shetland's western isles on 8 September; on her bridge were Blair and Commander Charles H. Lightoller. Battering waves destroyed the stranded *Oceanic* two weeks later. The ensuing courts-martial ruled Blair solely negligent for the loss of the much-cherished liner, but unlike his surviving colleagues from *Titanic* Blair would still later attain the rank of captain of a civilian vessel during his career.

Be it fortitude, instinct or just plain resignation to the inevitable, with *Titanic* Edwardians discovered that ordinary people too could exhibit heroism. And history loves its heroes, especially those of ordinary stock whose dying actions embody our greatest values. Edwardian Britain despised weaklings, for its might was founded on a culture of courage and vitality, and notwithstanding the misjudgments individuals made in life, if they died with aplomb all could be absolved in death:

> 'High up on the bridge, at his post to the last, is the liner's captain. Waves sweep him off his feet, but he rises. And when the *Titanic* sinks beneath the waste of waters Captain Smith dies like a simple hero, as a British sea captain should.'
>
> *The Daily Sketch*, 20 April 1912

CHAPTER 5

LEAP OF FAITH

'The *Titanic* is now about complete and will I think do the "old firm" credit
tomorrow when we sail.'

Thomas Andrews, 9 April 1912

To ensure that every vessel was up to standard, both in terms of mechanics and
safety, each registered ocean-going craft was and still is required to undergo a
performance test, or sea trial. *Lusitania* underwent hers off Skelmorlie on 27 July
1907. She did not impress. Severe vibration within the stern had her owners
returning the liner to John Brown's Clydebank shipyard for an extensive overhaul to strengthen her frame; delaying her maiden voyage by a month. Shipping
owners paid meticulous attention to the testing of their latest vessels and viewed
their trials as far more than mere formality.

In Britain each trial took place under the scrutiny of the Board of Trade in
order to satisfy their assessment of the vessel's safety features, operation and handling capabilities before being allowed to begin commercial service. Those for
Titanic were due to commence at 10a.m. on 1 April 1912, though high winds
postponed proceedings until 6a.m. on the 2nd. Surveying her performance was
Francis Carruthers of the Board of Trade, the senior inspector for Belfast.

Along with Captain Smith and a skeleton crew of 120, *Titanic* was towed from
her wharf at Harland & Wolff to a point 6 miles into the wide, 15-mile stretch
of open water at the mouth of the river Lagan, known as Belfast Lough. Steam
valves opened to feed her engines for the very first time, and here the testing of
Titanic officially got underway.

Averaging 18 knots, the session began with a test on her steering responses. Her
turning circle was measured next – 3,850ft. Although her helm response timing was
not tested it was found that while travelling at 20.5 knots *Titanic* required 850 yards
– approximately half a mile – to perform an emergency stop, which took three
minutes to complete. By 2p.m. the trials had taken *Titanic* 40 miles into the Irish Sea
where further running tests would then be conducted, as well as one on her lifeboat

davits. The trials concluded with a test on her anchors and, after covering approximately 120 miles, by 7p.m. the checklist was complete – all to the satisfaction of the Board's standards. Also aboard observing proceedings were Thomas Andrews and Harold Sanderson, who, upon completion of the sea trials, marked the final rite of the builder by signing over the ship to its owner and operator, White Star Line.

For the era, sea trials for ocean liners commonly ranged between one day and one month. Those for *Titanic* were largely based on the successful two-day testing that had already been carried out on *Olympic* at the end of May 1911. Since they were by and large identical ships, the Board of Trade saw no reason to require more than a single day of testing for *Titanic* unless anything fundamental had been exposed during the trials that initial day. Assumptions such as these exposed the deep-rooted complacency that enveloped the shipping community.

The *Titanic* disaster proved the trials conducted on the Olympic Class – which were 31 per cent larger than any other afloat – a woeful indictment of shipping's laissez-faire attitude to safety in 1912. As well as assessing how the liners performed, how they were actually handled by the crew was overlooked, despite being crucial information for craft edging the boundaries of innovation for builder, operator and regulator alike. Mollified by their ship's safety features, the crew and examiners of *Titanic* remained perilously oblivious that within a fortnight such wherewithal on the manoeuvrability and response timings of this very ship would be so instrumental to saving it.

Officially seaworthy, *Titanic* departed Belfast at 8p.m. that evening. Bearing a light crew of 280 she raced to Southampton to catch the midnight high water. Captain Smith used the 570-mile trip to continue acquainting himself with the handling of *Titanic*; a journey which pushed her to 23.25 knots – the highest speed she would attain in her tragically shortened career. Moments after midnight on the morning of 4 April *Titanic* arrived safely at berth 44 inside the purpose-built White Star Dock. Moments prior to docking, tugboats had spun *Titanic* to point her bow downstream and facing the river Test. Turning her under the cover of darkness to avoid performing the manoeuvre under the glare of the hundreds of well wishers anticipated to witness her departure on the 10th, White Star were not leaving anything to chance. Her arrival marked the line's newest addition to their fleet. *Titanic*, their thirteenth vessel engaged on the Atlantic run at the time, was now ready to commence active service.

Unlike Cunard, White Star preferred Southampton over the more traditional choice, Liverpool, as their main European port. Using Southampton as their hub since June 1907 it afforded three key advantages over other British ports: its deeper harbour allowed for larger vessels; the flow of water around the Isle of Wight granted two high tides a day; and, nestling a mere 78 miles from London, Southampton enjoyed a geographical advantage over its northern rival. With France also featuring as a stopover on American express voyages, departures from Southampton abbreviated cross-Channel journeys too.

At Southampton White Star had even excavated its very own dock, and running parallel along its berth 44 towered two boarding gantries, purpose-built for the Olympic Class. Connected to a 700ft-long single-storey passenger terminal, its two gantry towers, 40ft high and 20ft wide, supported retractable gangways unable to rise or fall to meet with any other door, for they had been designed specifically to align with the entry vestibules of the Olympic Class.

On 18 September 1911 White Star had the original date for the maiden voyage of *Titanic* confirmed as Wednesday 20 March 1912. However, within two days of the announcement *Olympic* collided with a Royal Navy cruiser a stone's throw from Southampton. The damage was serious. On 11 October White Star postponed the date for the maiden voyage of *Titanic* by three weeks to the slot of her next scheduled Southampton departure – Wednesday 10 April – allowing Harland & Wolff to delay work completing *Titanic* and carry out emergency repairs to *Olympic*.

With *Titanic* arriving at Southampton on 4 April preparations for her maiden voyage began in earnest with all manner of provisions trailing their way aboard White Star's new ship magnificent.

Observing convention, the 5th – a public holiday – saw *Titanic* 'dressed' with flags to mark Good Friday. On Saturday 6 April cranes loaded her with 11,524 items of cargo, a job traditionally supervised by the second officer. Amassing 559 tons, her cargo was valued collectively at around £84,000. Ranging from golf balls to some of the earliest Renault production motorcars, and even carrying the only copy in existence of director Max Reinhardt's *The Miracle*, his silent movie set in medieval Europe. The most valuable item stowed aboard, however, was the Persian tome *Rubáiyát of Omar Khayyám*. Bejewelled with 1,500 gemstones, the poetry book had been purchased in London for £405 from an auction at Sotheby's by Gabriel Wells, a rare books trader in New York, and was carefully packaged on *Titanic* for shipping to its new home.

Non-permanent crewmembers were signed on the 6th, as was the loading of 4,427 tons of coal from the barges of R&J.H. Rea – a company supplying Southampton's ships with coal since 1893 – their crews requiring fifteen hours to coal *Titanic* alone. This coal was added to the remaining 1,880-ton supply *Titanic* carried from Belfast, for in this particular April, coal was extremely scarce.

Industrial action plagued British politics of 1912. Walking out over pay and working conditions on 22 February 1912 British coalminers' dispute came to an end on 6 April upon a settlement brokered by the government, which promised minimum wages of 5s a week. With the strike resolved the resulting shortage of coal left many ships displaced and dormant, jamming Southampton's quaysides, while they waited for fresh supplies to filter through. To ensure no similar delay to this voyage the coal loaded aboard *Titanic* at Southampton had been gleaned from the bunkers of five incapacitated IMM liners: *Philadelphia*, *St. Louis* and *New York*, as well as White Star's *Oceanic* and *Majestic*. Even at New York *Olympic* had filled her second-class public areas with sacks of coal to return supplies for her sister. *Titanic* would sail at all costs, and was duly supplied with 5,892 tons of coal – just enough to sustain her outward crossing. This provision also included a 10 per cent reserve for emergencies: bad weather, changes in course or unforeseen events requiring extra consumption of fuel. Burning 415 tons of coal while docked at Southampton to maintain her generators during pre-departure preparations, her limited supply would require the speed during the maiden voyage to be restricted to between 20 and 22 knots.

The day of departure drew nearer; 7 April was Easter Sunday, a day of rest for dockside workers and crew. Food for the voyage was taken aboard on the 8th – the day on which Thomas Andrews conducted his own inspection of the ship. The senior crew arrived on Tuesday 9 April, beginning their watch cycle as if out at sea; the officers observing a four hours on, eight hours off rotation. Finally, sailing day arrived: Wednesday 10 April, a day greeted by a fine, bright morning that brought the temperature in Southampton to a cool but pleasant 51°F.

The timetable for White Star's express services scheduled a departure from Southampton every Wednesday, docking in New York the following Wednesday after calling at Cherbourg and Queenstown. This timetable required the ship to remain in New York for a four-day turnaround and commence the return leg that Saturday, arriving back in Southampton six days later. The cycle would be repeated following another four-day turnaround at Southampton, during which a total of three weeks would have elapsed. To guarantee these weekly departures White Star fielded a trio of ships running in relay to maintain this cycle: *Titanic* would Southampton for New York every third week. For instance, in April 1912 *Olympic* had left Southampton on Wednesday the 3rd, with *Titanic* following on Wednesday the 10th. *Oceanic* would trail likewise on Wednesday the 17th. For the return leg *Titanic* was scheduled to leave New York at noon on Saturday the 20th and again on every third Saturday, followed in turn by *Oceanic* then *Olympic*. Cunard operated their trio from Liverpool: *Lusitania*, *Mauretania* and *Campania* departing for New York at 1p.m. each Wednesday.

Due to the increasing frequency of timetabled crossings, sea travel in the Edwardian era had become popular with high-society and business leaders. Thereby, at the turn of the twentieth century, the wealthy were devoting ever more of their energies to travelling, and maiden voyages of high-profile liners became the social equivalents of the big budget movie premieres and grand casino opening nights today. Millionaires were the celebrity of 1912, and thirty from society's uppermost echelons booked themselves staterooms aboard the maiden voyage of *Titanic*. Maiden voyages had become a typical magnet for wealthy Americans, more partial to the glamour of the occasion than their habitually less impervious British cousins who tended to travel with trusty Cunard. White Star, on the contrary, championed the vogue and became the line of choice for Americans. With its glitz, the maiden voyage of *Titanic* proved equally popular and, typically with honeymooners too: twenty such couples chose the crossing to celebrate their marriage, though only two would survive the disaster. Each of *Titanic's* passengers was thrilled to be among the very first ticketed for *Titanic*, the new 'wonder ship' of the era. The malevolent economic and political feeling of the age, however, would give the arrival of *Olympic* and *Titanic* unique significance.

A jubilant media hailed the Olympic Class as proclamation of Britain's rightful return to the forefront of Atlantic shipping, this the palpable exorcism to a decade of German supremacy. Indeed the publicity surrounding *Titanic* attracted a particularly dazzling ensemble of luminaries aboard her much anticipated maiden crossing. The most noteworthy to step aboard was Lt-Col John Jacob Astor IV, the forty-eight-year-old landowner of more than 700 Manhattan properties. Possessing a personal fortune worth $100 million, Astor had arrived in Europe aboard *Olympic* that January and was ticketed for the return voyage on *Titanic* in one of her four ultra-luxurious Parlour suites – C62/4. 'JJ' was returning home amid some controversy after honeymooning in Egypt with his five-months-pregnant wife, Madeleine – just eighteen years old. The Astors were joined in first class by Benjamin Guggenheim, the renowned forty-six-year-old industrial magnate and art collector, also worth $100 million. Booked for cabin B84, he was returning to New York after holidaying in Paris.

Occupying the remaining C-Deck Parlour suite, C55/7, and paying £221 for the privilege, was Isidor Straus, the sixty-seven-year-old owner of Macy's department store in New York since 1888 – whose own personal wealth amassed $50 million. He was heading home with his wife, Ida, following a visit to their ancestral home in Germany. Other notable passengers aboard included fifty-year-old banker and tramway builder George Dunton Widener, worth $30 million, who was returning to New York along with his family in staterooms C80/82. John Borland Thayer, vice-president of the Pennsylvania Railroad Company, was making the journey with his family, berthed in cabins C68/70. Charles Melville Hays, aged fifty-five, president of the Grand Trunk Pacific Railroad, was booked into B69 as a personal guest of Bruce Ismay. Washington Augustus Roebling, thirty-one-year-old heir to the steel cable-making empire, paid £50 for cabin A24. Also with them were Major Archibald Willingham Butt (cabin B38; chief military aide to President Taft), William Thomas Stead (C87; distinguished British journalist), Henry Birkhardt Harris (C83; Broadway theatre producer), Francis Davis Millet (E38; artist and renowned travel writer), and Jacques Heath Futrelle (C121; crime fiction author). Yet irrespective of individual wealth all would perish with *Titanic*.

The illustrious list continued. Notable persons to survive the disaster included Colonel Archibald Gracie IV (C51; military historian), Dorothy Gibson (E22; actress who later starred in the first movie depiction of the disaster), and Karl Behr (C148; professional lawn tennis player). The maiden voyage also attracted the obligatory gaggle of socialites; heading the list was Charlotte Cardeza, paying £512 for the best rooms on the ship – Promenade Parlour suite B51/5. Fashion designer Lady Lucile

Wallace Duff Gordon was travelling with husband Sir Cosmo and occupied cabin A20, and Margaret Tobin 'The Unsinkable Molly' Brown and the Countess of Rothes travelled in cabins B2 and C37. Major Arthur Peuchen of the Queen's Own Rifles, marshalling officer for the coronation of King George V the previous year, booked in C104. Finally, Bruce Ismay, president of IMM and White Star Line took the promenade Parlour suite originally reserved for J.P. Morgan – B52/6 – rounding off a passenger list that was potentially one of the most impressive of the era. New and old money blissfully intermingled aboard maritime's social highlight of the year. Conspicuously absent, however, was the owner of *Titanic* himself, J.P. Morgan. He, along with fifty-four others booked for the voyage, decided not to travel, cancelling their places at the last minute against a myriad of reasons encompassing illness, unforeseen commitments to even just forebodings about sailing on *Titanic* in general.

At the quayside on the morning of departure *Titanic* was inspected by Captain Maurice Clarke on behalf of the Board of Trade. After his assessment and brief supervision of a lifeboat drill he duly issued her certification under the requirements of Section 272 of the Merchant Shipping Act, clearing *Titanic* fit and fully equipped as an immigration vessel for one year. Captain Benjamin Steele, White Star's marine superintendent since 1909, likewise inspecting the ship, received Captain Smith's written report verifying the readiness of the new liner 'loaded and ready for the sea'. *Titanic*, shipshape and fully provisioned, was now all set for her grand departure.

At noon and to schedule, her two giant sets of whistles broadcast the cast-off of *Titanic* from berth 44 of Southampton's newly built White Star Dock, the very spot *Olympic* vacated on 3 April. Aboard *Titanic* were 1,814 passengers and crew, comprising 193 in first class, 234 in second class, 495 in third class and, according to the muster list, 892 crew. *Titanic* was setting sail one third below capacity due to many would-be passengers being disenchanted with travelling in light of the coalminers' dispute; its knock-on effects causing still the cancellation of many voyages. Nevertheless, the tickets sold for *Titanic* were above the seasonal average for a westbound voyage in April.

Turning out of White Star Dock, partly under her own steam and aided by six tugs, *Titanic* headed gingerly down Southampton's river Test. As she moved along the dockside the deepwater channel, narrowed by its precarious sandbanks, found her huge water displacement surging under the passenger liner *New York*, tethered to a nearby berth to await fresh supplies of coal. Her mooring ropes snapped as *Titanic* passed, swinging the loose stern of *New York* toward *Titanic*. The two narrowly averted collision due to the quick thinking of the six tugboat commanders, but the incident delayed departure by one hour while *Titanic* was kept at a standstill to wait until *New York* had been secured once more to the quayside. At 1p.m. *Titanic* resumed her 77-mile voyage to Cherbourg, France.

A port frequented by White Star since 1907, the harbour at Cherbourg was itself too small to accommodate the behemoth that was *Titanic*. White Star had

Harland & Wolff build two tenders solely for conveying passengers to *Olympic* and *Titanic* anchored offshore in deeper water: *Nomadic* (1,273 tons, launched on 25 April 1911) and *Traffic* (675 tons, launched two days later). After collecting 274 passengers *Titanic* turned westward for her second port of call – Queenstown – an ancient harbour nestling at Ireland's southernmost tip.

Originally known as Cobh (meaning 'cove'), the port was renamed Queenstown in 1849 following a visit by Queen Victoria (its name reverted on independence in 1921). White Star had been frequenting the port as a regular stopover on their North Atlantic express services since 1871. But, like Cherbourg, Queenstown Harbour was also unable to accommodate *Olympic* and *Titanic*, having them drop anchor 2 miles offshore to await tenders *America* and *Ireland*, which ferried passengers to and from the ships via a landing stage.

At this moment White Star's future had never looked brighter. *Olympic* was already proving a great commercial success, and now *Titanic*, her new and improved sister, was joining her in service amid a blaze of acclaim. With *Britannic*, their third and even larger running mate, already under construction, White Star had successfully countered Cunard's *Lusitania–Mauretania* partnership. The maiden voyage of *Titanic* had begun and was proceeding delightfully smoothly:

Wednesday 10 April (Sailing Day)

5.18a.m. Sunrise at Southampton.

6.30a.m. Thomas Andrews along with eight representatives from Harland & Wolff board *Titanic*.

7.30a.m. Captain Smith receives pre-sailing report from senior crew. The 'boat train' bearing many second- and third-class passengers departs London's Waterloo station.

8.00a.m. Crew mustered; twenty-two fail to report for duty (inebriated in quayside bars, making the most of alcohol since crew were forbidden to indulge at sea) – substitutes signed in their place. Blue Ensign raised on the stern's 24ft tall flagpole, acknowledging Smith's affiliation with the Royal Navy Reserve.

9.00a.m. Brief drill takes place with two lifeboats.

9.30a.m. Boat train arrives at Southampton: 234 second-class and 495 third-class passengers start boarding *Titanic*.

11.15a.m. Harbour Pilot George Bowyer reports to the bridge.

11.30a.m. 193 first-class passengers begin to make their way aboard.

12.00p.m. *Titanic* casts off: six stokers miss departure. Near-miss with the liner *New York*, which breaks her mooring ropes as *Titanic* passes, delaying departure.

1.00p.m. *New York* restored to the quayside, *Titanic* resumes voyage to Cherbourg carrying a recorded 922 passengers, 892 crew and 1,758 sacks of mail.

6.35p.m.   Arrives at Cherbourg – averaging 16.25 knots in the 89 miles since leaving Southampton. 274 passengers board via White Star's two new tenders; of those, 142 first-class passengers and thirty second-class are ferried out by *Nomadic*, 102 steerage passengers and 1,412 sacks of mail arrive via *Traffic*. Fifteen first-class and nine second-class cross-Channel passengers disembark.

8.10p.m.   *Titanic*, cleared by French immigration, departs for Ireland. Captain Smith conducts manoeuvres to test the handling of the new ship throughout this 315-mile journey between Cherbourg and Queenstown, for which she travels at 20.5 knots.

Thursday 11 April

11.30a.m.   Rides anchor at Roche's Point, Cork Bay, 2 miles offshore from Queenstown Harbour. Seven first-class passengers disembark and are ferried to the pier-head at Scott's Quay, named in memory of local shipping agent, James Scott & Co. Hidden under mail sacks, Fireman John Coffey deserts ship. Tender *America* brings 120 new passengers to the ship, predominately impoverished migrants: 113 third-class plus seven second-class. 194 sacks of mail are loaded. Local immigration officer, Edward Sharpe, records 2,208 passengers aboard *Titanic:* the complement comprises 324 in first class, 284 in second class, and 709 in third class plus a crew numbering 891. He signs her certificate of clearance approving *Titanic* 'seaworthy, in safe trim, and in all respects fit for her intended voyage and that the steerage passengers and crew are in a fit state to proceed'.

1.30p.m.   The Star-Spangled Banner is hoisted on the forward mast to denote the nationality of her final destination, New York. *Titanic* departs Queenstown for her maiden transatlantic crossing with an estimated 2,228 people aboard (excluding the absconder) plus 3,364 sacks of mail and approximately 800 parcels. RMS *Titanic* heads to open sea. She will not reach landfall again.

Friday 12 April

12.00p.m.   Negotiating blustery weather, *Titanic* averages 20.98 knots on her first full day. Engines run at 70rpm, she covers 484 nautical miles. Weather: brightening, becoming calm and sunny. (*Olympic* had accrued 428 miles during her first full day of her maiden voyage.)

Saturday 13 April

12.00p.m.   Engines increase to 72rpm; 519 miles covered averaging 20.91 knots, also in fine weather (*Olympic* achieved 534 miles on the second day of her maiden voyage), a faster run planned for the following day.

Sunday 14 April

12.00p.m. Officers gather with sextants on the bridge to calculate their daily mileage. *Titanic* had covered 546 miles since the previous midday reading – averaging 22.06 knots with engines turning at 75rpm. (*Olympic* had travelled 542 miles on her third day.) Weather: although remaining pleasant is starting to cool.

5.20p.m. *Titanic* reaches the 'Corner', the point the westbound shipping lane marks a crucial change in course.

11.40p.m. A further 258 miles west of her noon calculation, *Titanic* travels at 22.25 knots – engines still at 75rpm. She strikes an iceberg 1,080 miles east of New York on a calm, clear and moonless night. An evening on which Captain Smith had earlier remarked it was the only occasion during his twenty-six years as captain had he seen the Atlantic so peaceful.

Had *Titanic* crossed the Atlantic, she was due to dock at pier 59, opposite West 18th Street at New York's plush Chelsea pier complex in the early hours of Wednesday 17 April. Here she was to remain for refuelling and provisioning before departing for Southampton on the 20th. Sadly for *Titanic* only her lifeboats would eventually arrive at this pier.

The waterfront adjacent to Chelsea was chosen for redevelopment in 1880 to bring luxury liners northward and thus closer to the wealthier suburbs of Manhattan; it would be of greater convenience for their first-class passengers, landing them closer to their Park Avenue mansions or onward rail connections via Grand Central Station. The complex itself served only as a terminus for first- and second-class passengers as those in third disembarked by tender at Ellis Island for quarantine, screening and processing.

Chelsea had also been earmarked as the new main embarkation terminal to ease congestion of shipping traditionally concentrated around the Battery at the tip of Lower Manhattan. With an eye firmly to the future, planners considered the Hudson River wide enough at Chelsea to accommodate lengthened piers, avoiding these dangerously protruding into the western shipping lanes. The major work to develop the complex began in 1902 with the design of the piers concentrated on accommodating the larger liners of the day – particularly *Lusitania* and *Mauretania*, which at the time Cunard had just been granted assistance from the British government to construct.

To emphasise the move of luxury berths to Chelsea, famed architects Warren & Wetmore designed immense grandiose pink granite façades to span the concourse fronting the entire complex of the nine new pierheads; *Lusitania* was their first occupant upon docking at Cunard's newly finished but shed-less pier 54 on 13 September 1907. Construction costs amounting to $15 million when finally complete in 1910, the complex marked its official opening by the arrival of *Oceanic* severing a ribbon strewn across pier 61 on 21 February.

Each shipping line using the facility was designated its own pier, each housing a cavernous two-storey passenger transit depot. Cunard received piers 54 and 56, and French Line had pier 57. IMM owned numbers 58 to 62 which they in turn allotted to the lines of their combine: Atlantic Transport Line pier 58; White Star 59 and 60; Red Star 61; and American Line 62.

The riverbed beneath White Star's piers was deepened specially to accommodate the draught of the Olympic Class. The piers themselves were also temporarily extended by 90ft as a result of Bruce Ismay's meeting with the New York Harbour Board in June 1907. The extensions were to afford his new ships greater protection, their sterns otherwise jutting obtrusively into the busy Hudson River. The modifications to White Star's piers were completed in 1910 well in time for the maiden voyage of *Olympic* the following year: their *Celtic* damaged this new extension on 4 June 1911.

In its heyday Chelsea was the main embarkation point for the cabin classes at New York City, but with the advent of the airliner in the 1960s the area fell out of use and was subsequently abandoned to neglect. Luxury liners visiting New York today use a larger complex further to the north but vestiges of the Chelsea piers survive to this day – most notably the iron edifice of pier 54, the location where survivors from *Titanic* disembarked from their saviour, Cunard's *Carpathia*, on 18 April 1912. As for White Star, these now silent remnants embody the ruination of the line, for *Titanic*, the pride of their fleet, was never to reach New York. Her destiny lay elsewhere.

CHAPTER 6

MAKING WAVES

'I do not think that the wireless waves I have discovered will have any
practical application.'
Heinrich Rudolf Hertz (physicist), 1857–94

Ever since the birth of man, once a craft had departed shore and headed into open
sea it did so in absolute solitude. That craft would have no ability to summon
help should it run into trouble and throughout its long journeys would travel
at the mercy of nature. Its distress would pass unobserved and, barring a miracle,
everyone aboard would be lost, with no one even learning of the craft's fate until
its scheduled arrival in port fell overdue. All who found a seat in its tiny lifeboats
would succumb either to starvation or exposure to the elements unless they were
lucky enough to be stumbled upon in time by a passing ship.

This scenario remained the reality until Guglielmo Marconi's invention of
the wireless in 1895, patenting it 1896. Although electric telegraphy had been in
existence since 1837 and the telephone since 1877, Marconi's device offered one
insurmountable advantage. His system required no wires to link two communicating units together, creating a long-distance method to finally enable ships to
communicate with each other far out at sea.

The first wireless sets were installed on ships in 1897. So impressed with the
equipment, in 1898 Marconi's home nation, Italy, became the first to equip its
naval fleet with the wireless. Merchant shipping followed suit in 1900, *Kaiser
Wilhelm der Grosse* being the first commercial recipient. Demand for the equipment grew, requiring Marconi to establish a manufacturing facility to ramp up
production, and under the name Marconi International Marine Communication
Co. Ltd began licensing the apparatus to private shipping operators.

To showcase its range, on 12 December 1901 from Poldu, Cornwall, Marconi
made the first ever transatlantic transmission: it was received in Newfoundland,
2,100 miles away. Unlike radio telegraphy it did not transmit voice over the airwaves, instead, signals were tapped out by a sprung brass key forming electronic

pulses – Morse code. On 7 January 1904 Marconi announced the creation of a distress call specifically for ships at sea: CQD (-·-· --·- -··). Formalised on 1 February 1904 'CQ' was Marconi short-form for 'seek you', calling 'all stations' to stand by and pay attention for an important inbound message. The 'D' signified distress. Marconi abbreviated common words to allow whole sentences to be transmitted quickly rather than requiring the radio operator to spell out each letter verbatim.

CQD, however – also transcribed as Come Quickly Distress/Danger – found its combination of letters proving too complicated for novices to discern easily as an emergency signal. The Berlin International Convention on Wireless Telegraphy thereby approved its replacement in April 1906 with a signal simplified for decoding and transmission: SOS (··· --- ···), Save Our Souls being its most popular variation. The change was confirmed on 3 November that year and was officially effective from 1 July 1908.

Indeed, it was not long after its invention that the wireless was first employed to summon help out at sea, when the freighter *R.F. Matthews* struck the East Goodwin Lightship 10 miles from shore in the English Channel on a foggy evening of 28 April 1899. The lightship was badly damaged and transmitted a call for help that was received by the South Foreland Lighthouse at Dover, which subsequently dispatched the Ramsgate lifeboat to rescue the lightship's crew. This was the first instance in which wireless had been used to save lives at sea, yet it was not until 1909 that a ship mid-ocean would use the distress call: White Star Line's *Republic*.

In the early hours of 23 January 1909, *Republic*, bound for Genoa, Italy, with 822 passengers and crew, traversing the Nantucket fogbank, was struck by the Italian liner, *Florida* – westbound and laden with 824 occupants. With far too few lifeboats between them the fate of the 1,600 lives aboard the two ships lay at the mercy of Marconi's radio. Jack Binns, the twenty-six-year-old wireless attendant aboard *Republic* hammered out CQD, sending the message along with the call sign identifying the originator as *Republic* – MKC: the very designation subsequently reassigned to *Olympic* in 1911. Binns' CQD was received at 6.40a.m. by the Siasconset wireless station, Nantucket, call sign MSC. The message was then relayed, to which three ships responded.

Apart from the three passengers on *Republic* and three crewmembers on *Florida* killed instantly from the initial collision, the remaining 1,650 survivors from the two vessels were transferred to White Star's *Baltic*, the first respondent to arrive at the scene. Radio had saved the day. And it would not be too long before a distress call at sea was heard again – in fact as early as 10 June that same year, with the sinking of Cunard's 10,606-ton *Slavonia*, mortally wounded after striking rocks 2 miles off Flores Island at the Azores. Two German ships answered the calls and rushed to her aid. All lives were saved.

The incidents underscored the importance of radio aiding vessels in distress. Seeing the wireless as the most significant innovation in maritime safety, military and commercial operators worldwide soon utilised it, and it was increasingly considered a necessity at sea. Sir Edward Sassoon MP tabled a Bill in the House of Commons on 13 July 1910 calling for its compulsory installation on all ocean-going vessels carrying more than fifty passengers. The Bill was rejected amid fears that its cost implications would impose on an already burdened shipping industry. Therefore, by April 1912, of the 20,000 vessels registered in Britain just 410 carried a wireless. It would not be until the aftermath of the *Titanic* disaster that vessels would be legally obliged to carry the equipment and that it be manned at all times.

However, since cost was no concern for White Star's Olympic Class, these were fitted with the most powerful sets of their day. Produced in Chelmsford, Essex, they offered a guaranteed range of 250 miles but in practice averaged 400 miles. During the sea trials of *Titanic* on 3 April 1912 her wireless was also tested, at one point her operators raising contact with Port Said in Egypt, 3,000 miles away.

The call letters assigned to the Olympic Class became MGY for *Titanic*, MKC for *Olympic* and, eventually, MUW for *Britannic* – the prefix letter 'M' the identifier for a Marconi wireless station. Located at the rear of the officers' quarters on her Boat Deck, the radio system aboard *Titanic* comprised of a three-tuner, magnetic reception detector powered by a 5kW generator supplied by the ship's electrical plant. The set on *Titanic* also featuring a 60Hz tone discharger to boost her signal above weaker transmissions was an attribute its slightly older companion aboard *Olympic* did not offer, making the equipment on *Titanic* the most cutting edge and powerful carried at sea at the time of her maiden voyage.

Far above her deck spanned four antennae of silicon-bronze wire. Spaced between 6ft and 8ft apart they stretched 600ft between the ship's two masts, suspending them 205ft above sea level. The masts themselves were designed to this height to afford the aerials a clearance of 30ft above the tips of the funnels to keep interference from all metallic objects to a minimum, thus augmenting the range of their reception.

Adjoining the wireless 'shack' on *Titanic* was a soundproofed silent room housing the rotary spark: a dynamo developed by Marconi in 1908 that created the transmission range of the set. This allowed the operators next door to receive messages from other stations without the distraction of noise from the motor driving the dynamo. Having no printout facility to receive transmissions the room was kept silenced to allow the headphone-wearing operator to manually decode and transcribe each inbound signal as they came in.

Two additional receivers were ensconced between the double hull walls of the Olympic Class to detect signals transmitted by any of Trinity House's 120 submersed navigational bells warning the presence of fog. These in turn were linked to a device in the Chart Room and could receive these signals up to 15 miles away. The Olympic Class benefited from all the modern apparatus of their day.

In lieu of any legal requirement to man wirelesses twenty-four hours a day, most shipping companies employed just one operator per set, but *Olympic* and

Titanic were the exception, each boasting two operators – both employed by Marconi Company Ltd. Guglielmo believed the status of the Olympic Class liners warranted their sets to be manned round-the-clock, and doing so would require two operators. He also wanted *Titanic* to be his marine standard-bearer, and to underline her importance Marconi booked staterooms for himself and his family aboard the maiden voyage. Luckily for the Marconis, Guglielmo cancelled the reservation, opting instead to travel to America on Cunard's *Lusitania* as business commitments necessitated an earlier crossing.

Having already served six years at Marconi, Jack Phillips, able to transmit a rate of thirty-nine words per minute, was appointed senior operator on *Titanic*. His assistant, Second Wireless Operator Harold Bride, had joined Marconi in July 1911 – by the maiden voyage he was able to muster twenty-six words per minute. Both had attended a six-week training course at Marconi's college in Liverpool – in 1906 and 1911 respectively – both attaining full graduation standard. The operators received two monthly wages, one from White Star and the other from Marconi. Working in six-hour shifts, Phillips would man the set between 8p.m. and 2a.m., then from 2a.m. to 8a.m Bride took over. Between 8a.m. and 8p.m. they would take turns on the set, resting in a shared adjoining cabin as and when they could.

Bride and Phillips were responsible for sending and receiving messages – 'Marconigrams' – from *Titanic* via mainland stations or other ships as necessary, relaying them onward to their ultimate destinations. Relaying messages in such a fashion allowed news to travel at great speed. The method had already proven its worth in July 1910 when, travelling from Antwerp to Quebec aboard *Montrose*, Dr Crippen, the infamous London murderer, was recognised by the crew. His whereabouts were relayed back to London at such velocity that Scotland Yard dispatched an inspector to catch the faster *Laurentic*, which managed to overtake the *Montrose* and allow the inspector to apprehend Crippen before the doctor even set foot on Canadian soil.

By 1912 wireless was still very much a novelty among passengers and its presence aboard was, after all, more to serve a commercial purpose than as a navigational tool. Since departing Southampton Bride and Phillips had keyed over 250 rather mundane – sometimes desultory – private messages ranging from hotel reservations to telegram permutations of postcards, or passing snippets of ship-to-ship gossip for the onboard newspaper, *Atlantic Daily Bulletin*. For this service first-class passengers on *Titanic* were charged a rate of 12s 6d for the first ten words of each message, plus 9d for each additional word thereafter. Passengers would compose their messages at a kiosk located along the starboard corridor of C Deck, which the clerk would then affix to a carrier and rocket up to the Boat Deck wireless room through a pneumatic tube: the operator returned the empty carrier down a second tube.

Other than using the sets for private messages, wireless operators were in constant contact with other vessels, exchanging greetings between captains as well as information on sailing conditions and in particular advising the whereabouts of ice, either reported or encountered by themselves or by other ships. To differentiate navigational messages from ordinary traffic the prefix 'MSG' was added: priority mail for the airwaves. This was the serious face of the business and the reason shipping operators installed the sets on their vessels in the first place. Yet tying up operators with navigational messages often infringed the time sending those from fee-paying passengers. Therefore, in the contract between Marconi and White Star, signed 9 April 1909, White Star contributed a portion of the operator's wages to reimburse the use of the equipment for navigational purposes, thus ensuring that these messages were always accorded priority.

Marking the height of winter in the North Atlantic, April witnessed many navigational messages pertaining to sightings of ice. Those received by the operators on *Titanic* for the 13th and 14th are detailed here, along with the originator's call sign:

French Line *La Touraine* (MLT): 12 April, 7.10p.m.
> Captain Caussin: 'Crossed thick ice field 44°58'N, 50°40'W … another ice field and two icebergs 45°20'N, 50°09'W.'
> First Ice warning received by operators, they pass it to the bridge who records on the chart the position of ice reported.

Wireless on Titanic *down due to circuit failure between 11p.m. 12 April and 5a.m. on the 13th.*

Furness Withy Line *Rappahannock*: 13 April, 10.30p.m.
> Captain (Albert) Smith: Passing close by and thus signals message by Morse Lamp: 'Have just passed through heavy field ice and several icebergs.'
> Officers on the bridge of *Titanic* respond also by Morse Lamp, 'Thank you. Good night', but take no further action.

Cunard Line *Caronia* (MRA): 14 April, 9a.m.
> Captain Barr: 'Westbound steamers report bergs growlers and field ice in 42°N from 49° to 51°W April 12.'
> Wireless operators present this message directly to Captain Smith: the position of ice reported is then marked on the chart.

Dutch Line *Noordam* (MHA): 14 April, 11.40a.m. (via *Caronia*)
> Captain Krol: 'Much ice reported in 42°24' to 42°45'N and 49°50' to 50°20'W.'
> Message ignored by Phillips and Bride.

White Star Line *Baltic* (MBC): 14 April, 1.42p.m.
> Captain Ranson: 'Greek steamer *Athenai* [MTI] reports passing icebergs and large quantity of field ice today in 41°51'N, 49°52'W.'

Message handed to the captain by operators but goes uncharted by the bridge. Smith later gives the message to Mr Ismay which he later retrieves and deposits in the Chart Room at 7.15p.m. – remaining uncharted.

HAPAG *Amerika* (DDR): 14 April, 1.45p.m.
  Captain Knuth:'… passed two large icebergs in 41°27'N, 50°8'W …'
  Message ignored by operators. Addressed to the US Hydrographic Office in Washington, *Titanic* forwards to Cape Race but not until 7.30p.m. later that day.

Leyland Line *Californian* (MWL): 14 April, 7.30p.m. Intercepted by *Titanic*, operators oblige and forward the message to Leyland Line *Antillian* (MJL).
  Captain Lord:'… 42°3'N, 49°9'W three large bergs five miles to southward of us.'
  Antillian acknowledges. Both transmissions overheard by *Titanic* and Harold Bride posts them to the bridge, although uncharted by officers.

Atlantic Transport Line *Mesaba* (MMV): 14 April, 9.40p.m.
  Captain Clark:'In 42° to 41°25'N, 49° to 50°30'W saw much heavy pack ice and great number large icebergs also field ice.'
  Message overlooked by operators.

Leyland Line *Californian* (MWL): 14 April, 10.55p.m.
  'We are stopped and surrounded by ice.'
  Message interrupted and subsequently ignored by Jack Phillips as it blocked his outgoing passenger transmissions.

Although the Marconi set was the new wonder of the era, the protocol of what to do with its messages highlighted a fundamental flaw in navigation. Due to the workload of the operator, messages as crucial as ice warnings often received less attention during busy periods. Moreover, because of the technology's infancy, the messages posted to the bridge tended to be ignored by officers too. Of all the ice warnings received by *Titanic*, Fourth Officer Boxhall, her navigational officer who always marked the ship's chart, recalled at the inquiry investigating her loss only charting the position of ice reported by *La Touraine*. Had he marked the locations of ice contained in all warnings received in the twenty-four hours preceding the collision, the chart would have shown *Titanic* following a path leading directly toward the centre of an ice barrier 78 miles wide.

The whereabouts of ice reported by *Caronia* became the only warning received on the day of the disaster that was actually marked on the ship's chart. What happened to the rest of the messages formed a catalogue of errors.

Inexplicably, Captain Smith merely pocketed the warning received from *Baltic*. Instead of charting its ice report he presented the message to Bruce Ismay, where it then remained in his pocket for five and a half hours, until Smith retrieved and returned it to the bridge, where it lingered uncharted. The two other messages passed to the officers on the bridge – those from *Californian* and *Rappahannock* – likewise remained uncharted.

Due to the pressure to clear their rising backlog of transcripts from fee-paying passengers, four remaining messages containing ice warnings received on the day that *Titanic* struck the iceberg, sat in a tray, overlooked by the wireless operators. Since they were primarily employed by Marconi, not White Star, Phillips and Bride shared no formal ties with the crew at all. They were, however, obliged to acknowledge that they had to report messages regarding navigation immediately and directly to the captain. But, famously, on the day of collision, only one of the eight warnings received was ever charted. The two ensuing investigations of 1912 learned to their disbelief the dearth in formal guidelines prescribing the handling and prioritisation of navigational warnings and the communication of them between the bridge and Marconi operators. It became a crucial contributory factor to the loss of *Titanic*, and as a consequence both hearings demanded the practice to be tightened.

Twenty minutes after striking the iceberg (midnight) Captain Smith ordered the wireless operators to stop sending private messages from the passengers and 'send the call for assistance'. When Phillips asked the captain which he should transmit, CQD or SOS, Smith replied simply, 'the regular international call for help. Just that.' The reason for the question was that despite SOS having existed since 1906 and formally so from 1908, Marconi operators still harboured preference for CQD. Mr Marconi himself had developed CQD as the call to summon help, and as SOS had stemmed from Germany – which at the time was growing politically and widely unpopular throughout Britain – Marconi's operators were merely exercising loyalty to both country and company. Thus, the first distress calls sent from *Titanic* became CQD rather than SOS.

The distress call was received first by French Line's *La Provence* at 12.15a.m., hearing the ominous plea: 'CQD require assistance position 41.46N 50.24W, struck iceberg'. Other vessels in the busy lanes straddling the same area of the North Atlantic begin likewise to receive and respond to the calls, listed below in the order they acknowledged receipt, along with the station's call sign (their time of acknowledgement to the CQD is shown in brackets): French Line's *La Provence* (MLP), Canadian Pacific Line's *Mount Temple* (MQL) and Cape Race (MCE) all responded at 12.15a.m. followed by HAPAG's *Ypiranga* (DYA; 12.18a.m.), Rotterdamsche Lloyd Line's *Birma* (SBA; 12.20a.m.), Cunard Line's *Carpathia* (MPA; 12.25a.m.), then Norddeutscher Lloyd Line's *Frankfurt* (DFT) and Cunard Line's *Caronia* (MRA) both 12.30a.m.; next to respond was Norddeutscher Lloyd Line's *Prinz Friedrich Wilhelm* (DFK; 12.36a.m.), White Star Line's *Baltic* (MBC; 12.53a.m.) via *Caronia* (MRA), then White Star's *Olympic* (MKC) and *Celtic* (MLC) and HAPAG's *Cincinnati* (DDC) all at 1a.m., and finally Leyland Line's

Asian (MKL) and Allan Line's *Virginian* (MGN) at 1.02a.m. Responding to help their stranded colleagues, radio waves spiralled into confusion.

Table 2: Vessels nearest Titanic, *14 April, 11.40p.m.*

Vessel	Operating company	Call sign	Miles from CQD
Californian	Leyland	MWL	10–19
Mount Temple	Canadian Pacific	MLQ	49
Carpathia	Cunard	MPA	58
Parisian	Allan	MZN	60
Birma	Rotterdamsche Lloyd	SBA	70
Prinz Friedrich Wilhelm	Norddeutscher Lloyd	DFK	120
Frankfurt	Norddeutscher Lloyd	DFT	150
Virginian	Allan	MGN	170
Mesaba	Atlantic Transport	MMU	200
Baltic	White Star	MBC	243
Olympic	White Star	MKC	512

It has often been incorrectly recorded that *Titanic* was the first ship ever to send SOS as a distress call. Historically, *Slavonia* grounding at the Azores in 1909 saw its first transmission; however *Titanic* did indeed issue the first use of SOS mid-ocean. Yet transmitting SOS instead of CQD on *Titanic* happened only as result of a light-hearted exchange between her two operators. Opting originally for CQD Harold Bride later jested to Phillips to instead 'Send SOS, it's the new call'; cheerily adding, 'it may be your last chance to send it'. Captain Smith was present in the wireless room at that moment, the three laughed, injecting into the situation a slice of graveyard humour.

So, at 12.45a.m., Phillips hammered out: 'CQD CQD SOS SOS CQD SOS. Come at once. We have struck a berg. CQD position 41°46'N, 50°14'W CQD SOS', closing the message as with every other, suffixing their call sign MGY. Perversely this particular message was first received by their colleagues aboard their sister ship *Olympic*, 512 miles away eastbound and heading to Southampton.

Bride and Phillips continued transmitting the distress calls until 2.17a.m., two minutes before *Titanic* disappeared beneath the sea. The position of distress they had been transmitting had been calculated by the ship's navigator, Joseph Boxhall, moments after the collision, determining their location through the imperfect science of 'dead reckoning'. After looking at the last recorded position of *Titanic* on the chart – being the location ascertained through the stellar observations taken at 7.30p.m. that evening – Boxhall then took into account their course (S86°W), speed (22.25 knots) and the mileage accumulated on the Patent Log since it had last been reset (noon: 258 miles). Without using a sextant to fix their position, Boxhall was able only to determine a rough position, which he handed to Captain Smith. Smith in turn forwarded this to the wireless operators to transmit with the distress calls: 41°46'N, 50°14'W. Initially, however, the operators had sent the position as 41°46'N, 50°24'W but the mistake was rectified to 50°14'W by 12.25a.m. As there were no ships in their immediate proximity the error proved not to be life threatening. But by no means had Boxhall's calculation marked the precise location of *Titanic*, the true position was more likely to have been 41°47'N, 49°55'W. The inaccuracy was probably due to not accounting for the southerly drift of the Atlantic known as the Labrador Current, or misjudging the time *Titanic* changed course at the 'Corner'; but, as the term 'dead reckoning' implies, position is attained by pure estimation. Its inexactness was proven in 1985 upon the discovery of the wreck, 13.5 miles from Boxhall's CQD position: a competent achievement nonetheless given the circumstances under which it was arrived.

At 2.17a.m. *Olympic* made the last direct communication with *Titanic, Virginian* afterwards receiving the final signals – hearing just two 'v's, caused by an operator on *Titanic* adjusting the spark on his set. It was exactly this moment that the power on *Titanic* had been severed, for at 2.18a.m. she had sunk.

The to-and-fro of messages that evening generated plenty of confusion. During the sinking operators aboard *Olympic* were unable to decipher the resulting cacophony of transmissions. Out of puzzlement they asked *Titanic* 'Are you steering southerly to meet us?' The volume of wireless traffic they had to contend with exerted unrelenting pressure on Bride and Phillips. Refusing to leave his post Jack Phillips jumped ship only once the water lapped at his feet. Though able to swim to a lifeboat (collapsible B) he succumbed to exposure before daybreak. Harold Bride boarded the same collapsible and survived – albeit sustaining severely frostbitten ankles. While aboard the rescue ship *Carpathia* Bride continued transmitting messages from the survivors in order to give his colleague, the sole Marconi operator of *Carpathia*, much needed respite.

Following the mêlée of the disaster and its ensuing investigations Bride resigned from Marconi, but returned to the sea in 1913 working for P&O aboard *Medina*. After serving in the First World War as an operator for the Royal Navy he uprooted to Glasgow in 1922. Finding employment as a salesman, in later life he grew reclusive to evade the attention of the press, still inquisitive about the *Titanic* disaster. He died in April 1956.

However, the speed of communication had proven its mettle. The first report of the sinking to reach the mainland was received by David Sarnoff, the twenty-one-year-old radio operator at the wireless station that Marconi set up on the top floor of Wanamaker's department store on New York's Broadway, assigning it the call letters MHI. Sarnoff had been listening to the set that evening and happened to receive a signal from *Olympic* at 11.10p.m. New York time (1.50a.m., 15 April on *Titanic*), bearing news that *Titanic* was sinking and appealing to other ships for assistance. Hearing this, Sarnoff telephoned the *New York Times*, which became the first newspaper to report the disaster; the wireless station at Cape Race confirmed the disaster to the Associated Press at 12.40a.m.

Rust had barely been given a chance to speckle *Titanic* by the next time wireless summoned aid to a stricken liner, called to the loss of the *Volturno*, a British-owned, 3,502-ton emigrant carrier, operated by the Uranium Steamship Company since 1910. *Volturno* had departed Rotterdam on 2 October 1913, bound for New York with twenty-two first-class passengers, 539 eastern European migrants and a crew numbering ninety-six. During a storm on the 9th her cargo caught light and consequently exploded. From position 49°12'N, 34°51'W her SOS was sent and was received by eleven ships. Cunard's *Carmania*, detouring some 200 miles, was the first to arrive at the scene, six hours after receiving the signal. In total 523 lives were saved by the responding ships, including two that had warned *Titanic* of ice the previous year: *La Touraine* and *Rappahannock*. Owing to the wake of the *Titanic* disaster the media widely reported the *Volturno* incident, underpinning with it Marconi's sensational contribution to maritime safety. *The Independent* hailed the sentiment of the occasion: 'The rescue of five hundred of the passengers of the *Volturno* is the most impressive demonstration of the value of the wireless telegraph that has yet been made'.

The role Marconi's wireless had played in instigating the rescue of survivors from *Titanic* substantially elevated its commercial and public recognition. The company's share value rocketed spectacularly: their price of £2 8s 9d on August 1911 soared to £9 in the days following the much-publicised demise of their set's standard-bearer. The disasters helped ensure the future of wireless radio. The oceans had indeed become safer, and journalists throughout the globe too had discovered a new medium: long-distance, real-time reporting. As the first headlines of the disaster rolled off presses on both sides of the Atlantic within an unprecedented matter of hours, a new age of communication had truly begun.

CHAPTER 7

PARADISE LOST

'When the dear ones, the dependant ones, had been sent to safety in the lifeboats and had drifted away into the dark night, these true men, calm and courageous, stood alone upon the deck of the doomed ship and went down to death and to glory.'

William Randolph Hearst, 19 April 1912

Being a lookout or crewmember on the bridge of *Titanic* the moment she veered into the iceberg is no claim to fame that most would recount to their grand-children with utmost pride. Fate and circumstance singled out an unfortunate band of people destined to be consigned to history as those who lost the world's most famous and 'safest' ship, and all amid a decidedly avoidable collision. In what began as a routine voyage the events on the bridge of *Titanic* on the evening of Sunday 14 April transpired into the most iconic incident ever to unfold on the North Atlantic Ocean.

Every evening aboard *Titanic* 10p.m. marked a change in roster that began a fresh watch for both the officers on the bridge and the lookouts in the crow's nest. Indeed, today it is hard to imagine that ships of the twentieth century relied upon men aloft masts scanning the horizon for danger. But in 1912 lookouts were still among the key members of the crew. The nest for *Titanic* was located 50ft up her forward mast, standing 70ft forward of the bridge and 95ft above sea level. Accessed by a ladder encased inside the tubular steel mast, the lookout entered through a tiny door into the nest itself. Housing a warning bell and a brass handset affording a direct telephone link to the bridge, the nest on *Titanic* provided enough room for two lookouts; one responsible for the ship's portside horizon, the other for starboard.

With this change of watch lookouts Archie Jewell and George Symons were replaced by Frederick Fleet (port lookout) and Reginald Lee (starboard). An hour previously Jewell and Symons had received a message from Second Officer Lightoller alerting them to look specifically for ice, a warning that Symons

relayed to Fleet at the 10p.m. changeover. Fleet and Lee's watch was scheduled
to last until midnight, by which time *Titanic* was anticipated to be amongst ice.
The evening was extremely cold: the sky clear and moonless, the sea perfectly
calm – hallmarks of a particularly cold winter. The glistening sea and briny headwind kept passengers stubbornly indoors enjoying the warmth of their cabins on
this particularly frigid evening. As *Titanic* ploughed onward at 22.25 knots (about
25mph) – her full speed – lookouts Fleet and Lee during the first hour of their
watch began to notice the horizon ahead of them transform into a haze: ice.

Ice drifting in the North Atlantic as far as south as experienced in 1912 was,
even for winter, somewhat atypical. *Titanic* had been following a more southerly
route intended to avoid it, however the sea temperature around her was 31°F
(0.6°C) – perfectly adapted for allowing icebergs to venture further south in the
abnormally cooled Labrador Current. These were exceptional conditions.

Minutes later this haze manifested into what Fleet later described a large 'black
mass' – an iceberg – one 50–60ft high according to accounts, emerging out of the
dark and into the path of *Titanic*, just 500 yards ahead.

Fleet was first to see the iceberg. His reactions as a seasoned lookout consuming him immediately, he sounded the nest's bell with three hard strikes:
the signal warning that something lay directly ahead. The time was 11.39p.m.
Controversially, in 1964 Fleet admitted first seeing the iceberg 10 miles ahead on
the horizon in front of *Titanic* at 11.15p.m., attempting unsuccessfully for twenty-
five minutes to contact the bridge to inform them of what he had seen. However,
according to testimony he gave under oath in 1912, by 11.30p.m. Fleet and Lee,
unequipped with binoculars, found the horizon ahead of them forming into a
haze – choosing not to report the anomaly to the bridge.

Almost immediately upon striking the bell, Fleet contacted the bridge using
the nest's telephone. 'Is someone there?' he pleaded anxiously.

Answering the call, Sixth Officer Moody responded calmly, 'Yes, what do
you see?'

'Iceberg, right ahead,' followed Fleet's taut reply.

'Thank you,' replied Moody, remounting the handset.

Fleet, rooted to the spot and still clutching the telephone, willed *Titanic* to turn
away from the iceberg looming ever larger upon their bow. And so the world's most
contentious iceberg glides into history. The crew had good reason to be alarmed.

Commonly the mass of an iceberg plunges over 1,600ft deep beneath the
waterline. Protruding just one-eighth above the surface it marks a vast indestructible ice-shelf sliding a matter of inches beneath the waterline. As silently as they
move, icebergs travel too slow to ripple the water's surface, making them frustrat-
ingly difficult to sight in adequate time, especially on a moonless evening – as
was 14 April. The iceberg that struck *Titanic* was particularly hard to spot, having
capsized sometime earlier, revealing only a darker face warmed by water, which
dulled the reflective glare of its ice.

Five members of the crew were present on the bridge at the moment of colli-sion. First Officer William Murdoch (commanding) was assisted by officers Joseph Boxhall and James Moody. Quartermaster George Rowe stood on the Poop Deck in solitary vigil on the Docking Bridge. Manning the helm in the wheelhouse was Quartermaster Robert Hichens, accompanied by Alfred Olliver as relief quarter-master. But at the time the iceberg slid into view three of the watch crew were absent from the wheelhouse. Olliver was out on deck, returning to the bridge after checking the compass on its raised plinth in the centre of the Boat Deck. Just completing writing up his earlier position readings, Boxhall too was about to re-enter the wheelhouse from the Chart Room immediately behind it. Finally, Murdoch, watch commander, stood outside on the starboard navigation wing.

Titanic had three helms, two on the bridge, one of which, inside the enclosed warmer inner wheelhouse, was known as the Captain's Bridge; occupied when in open sea the Captain's Bridge afforded increased protection against the unfor-giving elements of the Atlantic. The third helm stood on the Docking Bridge, a raised platform surmounting the Poop Deck on the stern. Both the outer wheel-house (also referred to as the Navigating Bridge) and the Docking Bridge were used predominantly when guiding the ship into port, the inner wheelhouse thus presided over by Moody and Hichens at the moment of Fleet's sighting.

Upon receiving Fleet's alert Sixth Officer Moody yelled to his watch com-mander by the starboard navigation wing outside, 'Iceberg, right ahead!'

Racing back, Murdoch ordered Hichens to spin the wheel 'Hard-a-starboard!', a command that actually turned the ship to port since the order harked to the age of the tall ships steered by tillers. Tillers turn the ship in the opposite direction to which it is set: positioned starboard would turn the ship to port. Modern and larger vessels used a wheel to steer, as did *Titanic*, turning the ship in the same direction in which it was swung. Confusingly, however, 'tiller' commands remained in frequent use until 1928.

Hichens responded by spinning the wheel, from 289 degrees to 40 – swinging the bow 22.5 degrees to port – confirming as he does so, 'The helm is hard over, sir'. At the same time as giving his now notorious order, Murdoch prised the engine telegraph lever to 'full speed astern', jerking the main engines into full speed reverse, an action known as a 'crash stop'. Turning the engines suddenly into reverse from 21 knots ahead risked them serious damage, particularly unworn engines such as those on *Titanic*. Ordering a 'crash stop' was therefore considered a last resort and thereby performed only in emergencies. Consequently, any engineer below deck seeing the telegraph lurch from 'full speed ahead' to 'full speed astern' with no warning when in open sea intuitively reacted to its instruction instantaneously.

Weighing over 100 tons, the rudder itself required a separate engine to steer *Titanic*. As a failsafe *Titanic* carried two such engines, sited directly above the rudder 600ft abaft the helm on the bridge. Because Hichens had spun the wheel at such velocity, the resulting delay with the command registering upon the steering engine was several chillingly long seconds. The two lookouts braced themselves as the bow began its slow swing to port away from the iceberg drawing ever closer along their starboard hull.

Murdoch then ordered the helm to 'hard-to-port' (a sharp turn to starboard), doing so to attempt to pirouette the stern away from the iceberg; a practice known as 'porting-round'. Coupled with the ship's momentum, reversing the engines, the effect of which would slowly be starting to engage, helped Murdoch do this – although he performed this second manoeuvre too soon. *Titanic* instead pivoted her stern toward the approaching iceberg, with it striking the starboard bow well below her waterline.

Tests on *Olympic* conducted on 6 May during the official British investigation exploring the cause of the disaster attempted to replicate this manoeuvre over the same distance and speed. With her engines run likewise at 75rpm and with the same twenty-four of her twenty-nine boilers fired, it was apparent that between the initial sighting, manoeuvre and impact, the 45,000-ton *Titanic* had just thirty-seven seconds to dodge the approaching iceberg if it were approximately 500 yards directly ahead.

Upon collision small amounts of ice dislodged from the berg, tumbling and skidding into the forward Well Deck as it rasped along the hull passing by. Murdoch then ordered Moody to close the bulkhead's twelve electronically operated watertight doors. Moody did this. Flicking the activation switches on the panel one by one (others required to be closed manually), Murdoch then had Quartermaster Olliver mark the time of collision, Moody noting it in the log: 11.40p.m.

Finally, Murdoch returned to the starboard navigation wing, just in time to see the iceberg diminish from view virtually unscathed. At this moment Captain Smith entered the bridge from his cabin, taking over command from Murdoch upon doing so.

'What have we struck?' he anxiously enquired.

'An iceberg, sir. I hard-a-starboard and reversed the engines, and I was going to hard-a-port round it, but she was too close. I could not do any more.' explained Murdoch.

'Close the watertight doors,' requested Smith.

'The doors are already closed, sir,' confirmed Murdoch.

Smith then enquired if Murdoch had triggered the warning bell for the bulkhead doors. Murdoch already had. The automatic doors had closed fully within thirty seconds following their activation from the bridge by Sixth Officer Moody.

In the moments that followed, *Titanic*, still in motion, eased slowly forward at a much reduced 14 knots. A few minutes later the captain set the telegraph to 'ALL STOP', shutting down her engines. Unbeknownst to him, water was already filling five forward compartments – boiler room 6 was already awash in 8ft of seawater, the forward motion incurring *Titanic* a 5 degree list to starboard. Damage was fatal. Indeed, it has since been claimed Murdoch's actions inadvertently doomed

Titanic – squandering valuable seconds by slowing her from 22.25 knots to just 14 by reversing the engines. Time, it has been argued, that would have been better spent taking advantage of her momentum at full speed, allowing her to turn far more quickly, potentially even avoiding the iceberg. His decision to turn to port, however intentional, did take advantage of the ship's propulsion system. Her clockwise rotating starboard and central screws and anti-clockwise portside, gave *Titanic* a quicker natural turn to port. Moreover, *Titanic* boasted a steel bow strengthened to support the chain housings for her anchors. Coupled with a 190-ton rudder mounting in her stern and the density of framing in these areas *Titanic* was incredibly resilient at the extremities. However, when attempting to avoid the berg, Murdoch exposed the less protected part of her hull – the side – precisely the area glanced by the iceberg.

With engines at a standstill Smith then had Fourth Officer Boxhall go below to assess the damage; on his return he reported finding none, not noticing at that time that the forward boiler room was already awash with floodwater. Unsatisfied with his first, rather cursory inspection, the captain sent Boxhall back, this time to find the carpenter, John Hutchinson, and 'get him to sound the ship'. Soon afterwards Boxhall encountered Hutchinson, who starkly informed him that 'the ship is making water'.

At 11.51p.m. Smith then surprisingly set the telegraph lever 'half speed ahead', limping *Titanic* onward again at 8 knots. At 12.09a.m. *Titanic*, engines bereft of pressure, ground to a halt. Smith then gave the order to 'Shut all dampers', sealing off the airflow to the boilers and closing them down. *Titanic* was motionless, fatally injured and at the mercy of a perilously cold, dark and foreboding mid-Atlantic Ocean.

Embarking on his second assessment, Boxhall explored much further, meeting postal clerk Jago Smith along the way and informing him that the mail room on G Deck was flooded. Instructing the clerk to relay the news to the captain, Boxhall returned to the bridge fifteen minutes later to confirm the damage found. Resigned to the fact that his ship could not be saved, Smith contemplated the situation in silence.

It was at this point that Chief Officer Henry Wilde arrived on the bridge, before departing immediately to inspect the condition of the forepeak tank in the bow. Upon arriving at the peak an engineer already there informed him that air was escaping from it. The tank had been breached. Wilde returned to report this discovery to Smith.

It was bleakly fortuitous for the captain that the designer of the ship, Thomas Andrews, was himself aboard for the voyage. At midnight, Smith and Andrews descended to inspect the damage for themselves. Upon their review Andrews surmised that the damage to the hull extended across the first four to five bulkhead compartments. Returning upstairs, the two examined the blueprints that Andrews had been carrying in his cabin, A36. There they realised the damage had indeed compromised the first five watertight compartments, with flooding already filling the sixth – boiler room 5. Andrews had designed

Titanic to survive with a maximum of four breached. He informed Smith that *Titanic* might last just one hour. The news resonating in his mind, Smith, ashen-faced, ordered the lifeboats to be uncovered and prepared for lowering. The time was 12.05a.m. Andrews and Smith, only too aware of the sobering math suddenly impressed upon them: the ship's supply of twenty lifeboats among them provided enough seats for just half the people on board, and many only on the proviso that the remaining bulkheads held long for the boats available to be filled.

Boxhall left to alert Second Officer Lightoller, who was still in his bunk, albeit restively. Although Lightoller had known the ship had suffered a collision, he reasoned that he should remain in his cabin so his fellow officers would know exactly where to find him if needed. With water now lapping at F Deck, 2ft 6in above the ship's intended waterline, time was running out.

Within thirty minutes of the collision, 16,000 cubic feet of water had surged into *Titanic*, 25,000 tons within the first hour. Capable of collectively discharging up to 1,500 tons of water per hour, her pumps were overwhelmed. As water mounted within each compartment, bulkhead walls began to collapse one-by-one, allowing water into each adjoining section one at a time. The ship was lost. Smith was left with just one course of action to take: evacuate.

Timeline to Disaster

Here we shall explore the full chain of events in *Titanic*'s final hours, starting with the morning on the day of the collision. All times indicated relate to those displayed on the clocks she carried. Continually adjusted according to the line of longitude reached, *Titanic* carried forty-eight clocks, adjusted each midnight by two master Magneta regulators hung on the Chart Room wall. This adjustment, known as Apparent Ship Time, was to gain approximately forty-five minutes a day on westbound crossings.

The day unfolded.

Sunday 14 April

9.00a.m.   Iceberg warning received from *Caronia*. *Titanic* reaches 43°35'N, 43°50'W; ice reported in this message lies 300 miles to their south-west.

10.00a.m.   Captain Smith officiates the daily briefing with senior crew. Afterwards, in accordance with White Star's regulations, Smith begins his daily inspection of the ship; First Officer Murdoch takes command of the watch.

10.30a.m.   With his inspection complete, Smith conducts a forty-five-minute Church of England Divine Service in the first-class dining saloon (*Titanic* carried no chapel).

11.40a.m.   Iceberg warning received from *Noordam*.

12.00p.m.   Routine testing of communication system linking the engine room with the bridge takes place. Captain and officers gather to calculate daily position: using sextants they confirm 546 miles have been covered over the previous twenty-four hours. Fourth Officer Boxhall and Sixth Officer Moody replace Third Officer Pitman and Fifth Officer Lowe as forenoon watch ends.

12.45p.m.   Smith hands the message from *Caronia* to Second Officer Lightoller.

1.42p.m.   Iceberg warning received from *Baltic* indicating ice 250 miles ahead. The captain presents this message to Bruce Ismay. *Titanic* at 42°35'N, 45°50'W, travelling at 22.25 knots.

1.45p.m.   Iceberg warning received from HAPAG's *Amerika*.

2.00p.m.   Chief Officer Wilde begins command of the watch.

4.00p.m.   Officers Pitman and Lowe replace Boxhall and Moody for the watch – First Dogwatch.

5.20p.m.   Heading S62°W, *Titanic* reaches the 'Corner' (42°N, 47°W), the point at which westbound ships alter bearing. Smith instead maintains *Titanic*'s current south-westerly course for thirty minutes more.

5.40p.m.   Air temperature measured at 43°F (6°C).

5.50p.m.   *Titanic* 'rounds the Corner'; changing heading to S86°W 10 miles further south of the official point. Sea and air temperatures begin to drop noticeably.

6.00p.m.   Second Dogwatch begins, Second Officer Lightoller assuming command from Wilde. Lookouts Alfred Evans and George Hogg begin their stint in the crow's nest.

6.42p.m.   Twilight begins.

7.00p.m.   Lightoller withdraws for dinner, temporarily relieving command to First Officer Murdoch.

7.10p.m.   Captain Smith also leaves the bridge to attend a dinner in his honour hosted by George Widener in B Deck's plush à la carte restaurant.

7.15p.m.   Forecastle cargo hatch ordered closed by Murdoch to prevent light emitting from it obscuring the view from the crow's nest. Captain Smith retrieves the message containing the ice warning from *Baltic* which he had earlier given Mr Ismay.

7.25p.m.   Second Officer Lightoller resumes command of the watch.

7.30p.m.   Iceberg warning intercepted from *Californian* to *Antillian*: ice field 50 miles ahead. Lightoller takes stellar reading to plot current position of *Titanic*.

7.35p.m.   Air temperature measured at 39°F (4°C).

7.40p.m.   Twilight ends.

8.00p.m.   Night watch begins: Fourth Officer Boxhall and Sixth Officer Moody replacing officers Pitman and Lowe. Archie Jewell and

George Symons take over the crow's nest shift from Evans and Hogg. Quartermaster Alfred Olliver mans helm, Robert Hichens on hand as standby.

8.40p.m.   Freshwater supply checked by the carpenter, John Maxwell, amid concern that it may have begun to freeze in the rapidly falling temperature.

8.55p.m.   Captain Smith excuses himself from Widener's table and returns to visit Lightoller on the bridge. They note the coldness of the air and the expectant difficulties of sighting ice.

9.00p.m.   Air temperature measured at 33°F (0.5°C). Smith charts the earlier position reading taken by Lightoller.

9.20p.m.   *Titanic* passes the 49th Latitude. Smith retires for the night. Concerned over the likelihood of encountering ice he instructs Lightoller to wake him 'If it becomes at all doubtful'.

9.30p.m.   Lightoller has Sixth Officer Moody telephone the crow's nest to alert them for ice. Concern continues over freshwater supply, which is now beginning to freeze.

9.40p.m.   Ice warning received form *Mesaba*. Pieced together all warnings received depict an ice field 78 miles long and lying directly in their path. Wireless Operator Harold Bride goes to bed, leaving colleague, Jack Phillips, to man the set alone.

9.45p.m.   Lightoller advises new watch commander, First Officer Murdoch, to stay alert for icebergs.

10.00p.m.   Frederick Fleet and Reginald Lee take over from Jewell and Symons in the crow's nest, passing on Lightoller's earlier caution. Murdoch begins his command of the bridge, allowing Lightoller to start his routine inspection of the ship. Air temperature continues to fall; reaching 32°F, freezing point. Quartermaster Hichens takes over the wheel from Alfred Olliver who becomes relief helmsman. Iceberg less than 40 miles ahead.

10.30p.m.   Sea temperature measured at 31°F. *Titanic* is within 30 miles of fatal iceberg.

10.55p.m.   Second iceberg warning received from *Californian*. *Titanic* maintains speed at 22.25 knots, travelling 700 yards per minute in perfectly calm weather on a star encrusted moonless evening. Iceberg 20 miles ahead of *Titanic*.

11.25p.m.   Air temperature measured at 28°F. Iceberg 6 miles away.

11.33p.m.   Lookouts notice a 'dark mass' appearing in the path of the ship and report it to bridge: Captain Smith is not alerted. The iceberg is less than 3 miles ahead.

11.39p.m.   Lookout Frederick Fleet sights an iceberg directly in their path, 500 yards (quarter of a mile) ahead. He telephones the bridge. Murdoch begins evasive action, 'Hard–a–Starboard'.

11.40p.m. Thirty-seven seconds after the sighting *Titanic* strikes the iceberg along her starboard bow; there is damage 20ft below her waterline and all six forward compartments are breached.

11.45p.m. Smith instructs Boxhall to inspect the ship; he finds no damage.

11.50p.m. The waterline has risen by 14ft. First five compartments are completely flooded. *Titanic* sustains a 5 degree list to starboard.

11.51p.m. Smith orders engines 'slow ahead'.

Monday 15 April

12a.m. Keel 24ft below natural waterline, 7,450 tons of water within hull. Boxhall again descends to search for damage, this time finding the mail room flooded. Accompanied by Captain Smith, Thomas Andrews assesses the damage: Andrews surmises that *Titanic* would last just one hour. Cargo holds 1, 2 and 3 are flooded. The contents of the ship's safes are emptied by the pursers, and the items are returned to passengers.

12.05a.m. Keel 32ft below natural waterline. Smith orders lifeboats uncovered and passengers marshalled to the Boat Deck.

12.09a.m. Engines stopped and boilers shut down. *Titanic* is at standstill.

12.10a.m. Last private wireless messages sent. CQD position calculated. Distress location and message ordered by the captain.

12.15a.m. First CQD transmitted: position mistakenly given as 41°46N, 50°24W. The band starts playing on the Boat Deck to calm passenger nerves. Lifeboats are prepared for lowering.

12.17a.m. Surrounding ships begin responding to distress calls.

12.20a.m. Keel 48ft below natural waterline; 16,000 cubic feet of water is now inside *Titanic*.

12.25a.m. Order given to begin loading lifeboats. Passengers assembled. Water pumps started in boiler rooms. Correct CQD position transmitted; 41°46N, 50°14W.

12.30a.m. Lifeboat 4 is lowered to load people through promenade windows on A Deck but glass screens bar access. Passengers wait as Lightoller sends a crewmember to search for the spanner to unfasten the screens.

12.40a.m. Over 25,000 tons of water within hull.

12.45a.m. First lifeboat, boat 7, lowered; few people are willing to get into it, and thirty-eight seats remain empty. Boxhall launches his first distress rocket. *Titanic*'s first use of SOS signal in place of CQD. Bulkhead wall between boiler rooms 5 and 6 fails against the hydrostatic pressure.

12.50a.m. Transmission sent, imploring 'require immediate assistance'.

12.55a.m. Bruce Ismay orders boat 5 lowered but is rebuked by Fifth Officer Lowe for interfering. Third Officer Pitman leaves in this boat, twenty-four of its seats remaining empty. Revolvers distributed among officers to maintain order with passengers. Boat 6 is lowered with just twenty-eight occupants.

1.00a.m.   Boat 3 is lowered with fifty passengers, although fifteen seats remain empty.

1.10a.m.   Radio contact is established with *Olympic*: 'We are in collision with berg. Sinking, head down. Come as soon as possible… Get your boats ready.' With few passengers willing to enter the lifeboats, boat 1 is lowered with just twelve people, seven of which are crew. Boat 8 is also lowered; twenty-six seats are empty.

1.15a.m.   *Titanic* lists to port: water laps at the bow's 18in gold name lettering; the deck angle is more acute. Third-class men granted access to Boat Deck.

1.20a.m.   Lifeboats 9 and 10 are lowered almost fully occupied. Due to the ship's list, passengers have to jump a 1½ yard void to board portside boat number 10. Last distress rocket fired.

1.25a.m.   *Olympic* replies to CQD message, perplexed, 'Are you steering southerly to meet us?' Boat 11 is the first that is lowered over capacity; occupants have great difficulty unhooking it from the falls upon reaching water. Boat 12 is also lowered; twenty-three seats empty.

1.30a.m.   Panic grows for the lifeboats as only half remain. Chief Purser McElroy fires his revolver to stave off a rush for collapsible boat A which crew attempt to slide down to the Boat Deck. Fifth Officer Lowe fires his to evade a similar clamour for boat 14, itself already full, in which he leaves the ship.

1.35a.m.   Wireless transmission sent: 'Engine room getting flooded'. Lifeboat 13 lowered, also full; because the sea is so calm, its releasing mechanism fails to unhook the boat from its falls and is nearly crushed by boat 15, also fully laden, being lowered from above. Crew hear the cries from boat 13 and halt the winch motors just in time for its occupants to cut the boat free. Boat 16 is similarly lowered over capacity.

1.40a.m.   Forward Well Deck awash with water. Passengers start congregating towards the stern. Ship lists 6 degrees to port. Order given by Chief Officer Wilde to straighten the deck by transferring passengers to the starboard side, and 2 degrees are gained in doing so. Murdoch fires his revolver to ward off a group of men attempting to board collapsible boat C, already full, in which Bruce Ismay leaves *Titanic*.

1.45a.m.   Last legible wireless transmission sent: 'Engine room full up to boilers'. Fourth Officer Boxhall leaves in boat 2, fourteen of its seats remaining empty.

1.50a.m.   Water begins to spill through Forecastle railings.

1.55a.m.   Lifeboat 4 is finally launched, twenty-five seats under capacity after trying to load passengers through the windows of the enclosed section of Promenade Deck. Hampered by glass screens, they could not be opened until the eventual arrival of the unlocking spanner.

2.00a.m.   Waterline 10ft from Promenade Deck. Since the collision 39,000 tons of water had spilled into the hull. Desperation intensifies. Crew form circle round last available lifeboat, collapsible D. Lightoller discharges revolver to stop the crowd clambering for it.

2.05a.m.   Last lifeboat lowered from *Titanic*, boat D, leaving with all seats filled. Lightoller fires his revolver skyward to deter people from jumping into it from the decks above.

2.10a.m.   Forecastle submerged. Captain Smith relieves the wireless operators of their duty although both choose to continue. Crew try to prepare canvas boats A and B that have become entangled in their fixings up on the roof of the officers' quarters. When freed both are damaged when dropped to the deck down improvised slides.

2.15a.m.   Bridge dips underwater, generating a wave that engulfs the whole length of the deck, washing many people overboard and also boats A and B.

2.17a.m.   Last wireless transmission sent. Band ceases playing. Captain Smith releases the crew: 'It's every man for himself'. Funnel 1 collapses, smothering the Boat Deck with soot. Along with thirty others, Lightoller pulls himself aboard the upturned hull of boat B. Twenty-three swim and board the upright but severely damaged boat A; ten succumbing to hypothermia prior to rescue.

2.18a.m.   Deck angle reaches 45 degrees. Electricity fails. Huge roar erupts as the hull breaks in two. Bow section starts its descent to the seabed.

2.20a.m.   Afloat still, the stern's rudder rises 250ft clear of the water. The entire stern section then lurches upright, holding an angle of 80 degrees for thirty seconds. Stern pivots then also slowly recedes below the surface leaving behind very little suction when sliding under. *Titanic* is gone. The scene that follows is reportedly one of brief silence, yielding suddenly to the cries of 1,500 people freezing to their deaths in the icy sea. Only boats 4 and 14 return to look for survivors; they recover only four.

Of the 2,228 passengers and crew *Titanic* carried, just 705 survived what became the greatest disaster ever experienced at sea. With the majority of the iceberg extending beneath the water's surface the collision had mortally wounded *Titanic*. Its extent was estimated by Thomas Andrews in the moments following impact and corroborated later at the British inquiry by both Edward Wilding (Harland & Wolff's chief naval architect since 1904) and Leonard Peskett (co-designer of *Lusitania*). All three agree the area breached by ice totalled a mere 12sq.ft of hull spanned over a length of 249ft, averaging but 2cm wide.

The iceberg had pierced the hull above her protective double sidewalls at a point 15ft above her keel. Although neither a gash nor a rent, the damage comprised six 'slits' formed by rivet seams bursting against the pressure of the berg buckling plating inward. Only in contact with *Titanic* for around ten seconds, the iceberg imparted damage of sufficient severity to allow water to pour through these slits at a rate of 7 tons per second. Sustaining damage that extended from the fore-peak tank and all the way to abaft boiler room 5 was beyond the limit of the four compartments with which her designers had equipped *Titanic* to remain afloat. Indeed, the fracture compromised the first six compartments.

Witnesses described the impact as akin to a large object 'rolling over a thousand marbles', their accounts collectively suggesting the actual collision as not an almighty crash but a far gentler buffeting. 'Vibration', 'quiver' and 'rumbling' were all words used by survivors to describe the collision, indeed it was one so delicate that few on board even noticed. Some passengers even attributed the shuddering to a loosening propeller blade – an occurrence by no means unheard of even in 1912: *Olympic* had lost a blade on 24 February by striking floating wreckage.

The majority aboard *Titanic* who felt the vibration from the berg's impact simply ignored it, ruling it out as a trivial, underwhelming affair, one posing greater potential for inconvenience than threat. Unknown to them, their observations were actually describing the type of impact felt when a ship ran aground.

It is unlikely that the holes as described by Wilding were sufficient to sink *Titanic*; the fatal injury was more likely inflicted beneath her hull as it grounded across a submerged precipice of iceberg. This observation is given further credence by the stokers in the boiler rooms reporting water secreting through the floor plating in addition to the torrent entering through the starboard hull itself. With both layers of her double hull compromised, this damage was terminal.

Had Murdoch not attempted to 'port-round' the iceberg, it is argued that the damage would have instead extended far beyond the actual extent of 249ft. Indeed, his porting-round is why survivors found the collision a gentler affair rather than the Armageddon one would expect of a ship displacing 55,000 tons striking a 300,000-ton iceberg. With his manoeuvre still taking hold even at this stage, Murdoch's actions in pulling *Titanic*'s stern away from the path of the iceberg as it bumped into her bow minimised the ship's contact with the iceberg.

Titanic took two hours and forty minutes to sink: almost two hours longer than Thomas Andrews envisioned when assessing the damage with the captain soon after the collision. But once *Titanic* dipped beneath the surface it would have taken just seven minutes for her to reach the seabed 2 miles below. *Titanic*, the Jerusalem of meticulous innovation and homage to unbound perfection, had reached her final resting place amid an abrupt and mangled world of chaos.

With the stern rising high of the surface, lifeboats pulled rapidly away amid their crews' fear of them being dragged into a vortex along with her. Despite what the lifeboats' occupants thought may happen, *Titanic* imparted no vacuum as she made an almost serene exit from view. In every aspect of her existence *Titanic* had defied convention, but from their tiny lifeboats her survivors sat in wonder as they watched the final moments of the unsinkable ship, numb in disbelief at the event they had just witnessed.

Devil-May-Care

The incessant throb of engines gently permeating throughout the cabins on a steamship habitually reassured its passengers of a confident and steady crossing. Only a change to their rhythmic drone or pause in their sound would raise alarm that something was amiss. A restrained angst would follow as quizzical rumours emanated through corridors, companionways and public rooms. Such was the extent of concern with which passengers greeted *Titanic* and her collision with the iceberg. Despite it, most would choose to remain inside their cabins or warm lounges than venture outside and satisfy curiosity. After all, they believed, what could possibly go wrong?

As crew readied the lifeboats they attempted in vain to muster passengers, widely oblivious as to why their ship had pulled suddenly to a standstill in the middle of the Atlantic Ocean, onto the Boat Deck. In his book recounting the disaster, passenger Lawrence Beesley described a convivial scene exuding no sense of impending tragedy at all: 'no one ran a step or seemed alarmed ... nothing was broken or out of place, no sound of alarm, no panic, no movement of anyone except at a walking pace'.

Incredulous passengers clustered and watched as crewmembers unsheathed and prepared the lifeboats. Initially jovial, the realisation of the predicament soon unfurled to all on board: 'the work on the lifeboats and the separation of men and women impressed on us slowly the presence of imminent danger,' Beesley continued; 'it made no difference in the attitude of the crowd, [passengers loitered] quiet and waiting in patience for some opportunity of safety to present itself.'

The iceberg had struck on a very cold evening, close to midnight. Many passengers were already in bed or close to being so: the last public areas closed at 11.30p.m. Too few cared to venture outside as, frankly, no one aboard realised the extent of the damage, dismissing the affair as nothing to rattle *Titanic*. The calm sea, the stable ship and no visible evidence of breakage propagated an illusion of unnecessary alarm. Yet unknown to them, within the first ten minutes of collision the lowest deck in the bow lay awash in 14ft of water.

Describing the laxity of the crew that followed the impact, one survivor would recall: 'The result was complacency, an almost arrogant casualness.' The crew too, along with the ship's builder, exuded unfaltering confidence in *Titanic* – an opinion echoed conjointly by the media as the world's first truly 'unsinkable' ship. Passengers candidly believed the infallibility *Titanic* commanded upon her environment. Safety was, after all, the reason many had specifically booked *Titanic* in the first place. Greeting the collision with little or any deference at all saw most of the first life-boats leaving the ship not even half filled. Even the occupants in these early boats left slightly affronted having climbed into them.

Most did not wish to set foot into the lifeboats, believing that they would only need to return to *Titanic* once the all-clear was given. The mood was unhurried – if anything, inconvenienced. The band played. Lifejackets were donned. The moment briefly transcended into an inconsequential distraction from the routine and monotony of sea travel.

The air temperature on 14 April had reached freezing point at around midnight, leaving many passengers preferring to remain in the warmth and protection that their large and 'safe' luxury liner afforded them. Taunts were exchanged about needing boarding passes to be allowed back on board once the 'all clear' had been given. The passengers genuinely expected the voyage to resume.

Passengers generally felt safer amid the confines and comfort their large, indulgent and technically superior liner offered them; rather there than sitting exposed in a 30ft lifeboat, bobbing aimlessly upon the North Atlantic on a winter's evening. Those already in the lifeboats were told by crew to remain close to *Titanic* in order to easily return aboard. While the first lifeboats were lowered, passengers remained so blasé that crew could not even find enough at hand to cajole into them – let alone fill all of their seats. Often, crew in the first lifeboats that were lowered occupied places intended for passengers since so few were willing to take their seat in one.

It may seem chevalier, but those aboard all appreciated that *Titanic* carried the most powerful wireless of the day, able to summon assistance should her extensive bulkheads be overcome. They were all aware of the figures: the sixteen compart-ments of which *Titanic* could keep afloat even with four breached. Passengers were certainly not placing their wellbeing on twenty miniscule boats.

On paper *Titanic* was unquestionably a very safe ship, if not the safest of her day. Indeed, other than *Olympic*, no other at that time could have survived the damage that *Titanic* sustained from the iceberg. There was no precedent. No other ship equipped with a wireless had experienced a head-on collision with an iceberg, and sunk. Tragically, it was not until around 1.30a.m. that the seriousness of the situation was finally accepted among passengers; once the waterline had crept slowly, palpably and mercilessly higher. Only then did passengers make a greater effort to attain a seat in her rapidly dwindling supply of lifeboats.

The ship's in-house band moved out onto the Boat Deck to perform lively tunes to pacify the anxiety of passengers waiting patiently for a seat in a boat. As the deck's angle increased, crowds began to linger toward the Poop Deck at the stern. Once the last boats had been lowered this was the only sanctuary remaining for the 1,500 people stranded aboard: awaiting divine intervention, miraculous salvation, or a temporary haven where they could delay their inevitable finality for just a few moments more.

At 2.17a.m., on telling the crew that it was now 'every man for himself', Captain Smith purportedly returned to the bridge to await the end. The time had come. At this moment the eighty-four-strong engine room staff fought deep in the belly of the ship to maintain its dazzling electric light display. A truly commendable act, for none of them survived; at 2.18a.m. the mighty *Titanic* succumbed to the sea.

There is little secret that the roots behind the reticence to abandon *Titanic* stemmed from an insurmountable confidence in her watertight compartments. Yet her occupants little appreciated that the fate of all was to rest on one bulkhead in particular, the very wall whose durability had been slowly eroded since sailing day: wall 'E'.

Reports of a fire inside a coalbunker aboard *Titanic* surfaced early during her voyage, breaking out in starboard coal store 'Y' – a bunker aft of boiler room 6 amid a bank of others that lined bulkhead wall 'E'. Here the fire had reportedly been ablaze since departure day, 10 April, if even since 1 April during preparations for her sea trials the following day. Indeed at Southampton twelve extra firemen were transferred from *Oceanic* specifically to restrain this fire, working in pairs over four-hour shifts.

Fire was naturally a constant and omnipresent threat aboard steamships, particularly those with poor coal storage. *Titanic* was no exception. Bunkers were located as close as possible to her 159 furnaces, which between them consumed an average of 650 tons of coal each day of the voyage. And, like all steamships – elemental as they are – coal had to be barrowed as quickly as possible from bunker to boiler. With combustible ingots stored in such close proximity to the furnaces, sparks leaping in the hot air from any unguarded grate could easily ignite the pieces of coal strewn nearby. The consequences of such an occurrence are easy to imagine, for between 1900 and 1919 almost as many ships were lost to fire than through collision.

The main bunkers on *Titanic* provided her with a combined capacity of 6,611 tons of fuel. As well as those in the boiler rooms, *Titanic* housed two additional bunkers in her bow. Sited longitudinally, these extra bunkers provided between them a surplus capacity of 1,201 tons, their contents set aside for emergencies. 'Emergencies' being if the ship was forced to re-route to a different port or the sea had become too rough, *Titanic* would expend more fuel breaking the resistance of tempestuous waves. Both eventualities ran her the risk of running low or out of fuel, but should the need arise these emergency bunkers could also double as additional cargo space, allowing her owners the flexibility to truly maximise her commercial carrying capacity.

All main coalbunkers – labelled A–Z – were banked transversely along the bulkhead walls, dividing her boiler rooms into six separate watertight compartments. The benefit of this transverse arrangement allowed colliers to replenish the same bunker through chutes on either side of the ship, speeding up the coaling process.

With each bank capable of storing 30ft of coal, it was the work of the trimmers (four per boiler room) to keep the bunkers 'trim' – obliterating and dispersing their contents to ensure free and easy spillage for barrowing off to the stokers. To avoid shifting and depleting stocks from unbalancing the ship, trimmers would also ensure the movement of coal within the bunkers remained evenly distributed throughout the voyage. It was not a popular job.

To power a ship the size of *Titanic* each furnace would be filled with 4in of evenly laid coal, which would be allowed to burn for seven minutes, then the embers left behind would be raked out and the grills cleared ('sliced') with a giant 40lb poker for re-stoking. The residual waste removed from the ashpit below (about 100 tons daily) was continuously disposed into the sea through a series of ejectors. Laced with methane from the burning coal, the air temperature inside the boiler rooms was a constantly searing 120°F and was a brutal environment for its occupants, shovelling endlessly through gruelling four-hour shifts. Coupled with the high combustibility of the best Welsh coal, any spark or gas emanating from the boilers found the supply stored in bunkers close by precariously effortless to ignite.

Too large to simply douse with sand, extinguishing the fire that had been smouldering in bunker 'Y' required the removal and jettisoning of the affected coal. This would have been in large quantity, and since coal was already a scarcity following the recently concluded miners' strike, doing so made this a costly measure. This fire, however, was expending less coal than would be jettisoned and was thereby allowed to continue burning, under close supervision.

Allowing coal to remain burning inside a bunker was indeed a tremendous risk. At this early stage of the voyage the affected bunker would still have housed more than 400 tons of fresh coal – a fire taking hold would most certainly cost the ship. Why then had Captain Smith continued the voyage with a fire he knew could jeopardise this high-profile crossing? He believed the fire had been brought under control as early as the crossing to Cherbourg – the afternoon of the first day of sailing, 10 April. Indeed, both Bruce Ismay and the captain were aware of its existence, raising a difference of opinion between the two over how it should be dealt with since it unquestionably threatened the performance and wellbeing of the new liner. Should they remove it and reduce speed to preserve the untainted supply – already scarce by way of national shortage – or should they increase speed and arrive in New York ahead of schedule but expend more fuel in the process? There was no silver bullet to this common problem but this was not the first occasion on which Smith had faced the predicament. Two previous commands had caught alight also. On 7 August 1901 a linen store on *Majestic* had ignited during her approach to New York Harbour, as had a cargo hold on *Baltic* on 3 November 1906. Both fires were extinguished without serious damage. By the time of *Titanic* Smith was only too aware of the spectre aboard ships laden with coal, yet he also appreciated that the voyage was safe to continue as long as any unwelcome fire was kept under strict control.

Smith's chief engineer, Joseph Bell, had indeed reported to the captain that the fire had been fully extinguished by 1p.m., Saturday 13 April, and eyewitness evidence supports this. But less apparent damage had already been sustained. Prolonged exposure to the fire against the adjoining bulkhead wall had left its steel embrittled and weakened. Leading Fireman Charles Hendrickson noted that the bulkhead had buckled from the sustained heat. Recalling the matter at the ensuing inquest Hendrickson described the fire's effect on the wall: 'it was dented ... warped'.

Although the bulkheads on *Titanic* were stronger than required to withstand and contain large volumes of water, their single-inch thickness still left them susceptible to buckling. The fire, incontrovertibly, weakened the adjacent bulkhead, incapacitating its watertight integrity and rendering the wall virtually useless as the iceberg pieced its adjoining compartments. Why this fire was particularly significant to *Titanic*, however, is that it occurred in the bunker adjacent to the wall dividing boiler rooms 5 and 6 – bulkhead E.

The damage the iceberg imparted as it breached the hull brought the heated steel of wall E into immediate contact with torrents of ice-cold water. The bulkhead, already expanded and thinned by the fire, contracted at such a rate that it literally exploded. Indeed 116 of the 328 bodies later recovered from the wreck site yielded injuries sustained from an explosion, instead of death by drowning or hypothermia as one might expect.

It began a series of explosions, as other bulkheads overwhelmed by the weight of water spectacularly followed suit. At the two official inquiries any survivors recounted the crescendo of explosions as a chain of bulkheads collapsed.

Crewmembers:
 Third Officer Pitman: 'I heard four reports [of explosions].'
 Fifth Officer Lowe: 'I heard explosions ... about four.'
 Quartermaster Olliver: 'I heard several little explosions.'
 Lookout Jewell: 'heard some explosions ... two or three.'
 Able Seaman Scarrott: 'Then followed four explosions.'

Passengers:
 Henry Stengel: 'four sharp explosions.'
 Mrs J. White: 'four distinct explosions.'
 Catherine Crosby: 'repeated explosions.'

For *Titanic* the weakened bulkhead was all that shielded her forward-most compartment, unaffected by the iceberg's damage. Designed to remain afloat with her forward four adjoining compartments flooded, the iceberg had ruptured her leading five. The failure of bulkhead E gave water access to the all-important sixth consecutive compartment. Furthermore, ten minutes after their collision Captain Smith continued *Titanic* onwards for a further twenty minutes. Unknown to him, doing so exerted considerable pressure on this already weakened bulkhead. The failure of this crucial wall and its contribution to the demise of the ship proved a cruel twist of fortune: the very bulkhead Smith would rely upon to save his ship was rendered ineffective by the fire he believed no longer posed a problem.

After the disaster an internationally attended conference was held in 1914 to re-evaluate safety at sea. Named SOLAS, it demanded the stress-testing and fire-proofing of bulkheads to be mandatory and their regulatory criteria to be more stringent. But what of Smith's motivation for continuing the voyage of a high-profile liner threatened by fire in one of its freshly stocked bunkers? One would hope it to be impossible that a captain boasting forty-three years of service, and who also risked forfeiting a substantial £1,000 annual bonus if any vessel under his command came to any harm, would knowingly endanger a ship in his change. Would Smith have left landfall or sail with course and speed unaltered had he honestly considered the fire to pose sufficient danger? Doing so would have reaped untold damage to his company's £1.5 million ship. A captain of Smith's stature, or Ismay the company director, amid the full glare of the press, perhaps would have aborted the voyage and attempted the crossing another day. Instead they pressed on, gambling their ship and the lives aboard it for the sake of pride.

Notwithstanding fire, the greatest failure in the disaster was the evacuation of *Titanic* itself. The crew's breakdown in their chain of command led to spur-of-the-moment decisions dictating ultimately how many lives would be saved and, indeed, lost. Smith's stewardship that evening proved negligible and when filling lifeboats his officers believed their supply to be unable to cope with a full complement of occupants and thought that they could potentially disintegrate before reaching water.

Across the industry, lifeboats built prior to the disaster were not renowned for their quality. As a result many crews exercised unwarranted caution when filling lifeboats during evacuations: on *Titanic* famously sending them away below capacity amid an unsubstantiated fear that they could not sustain the weight of a full load. Here the crew had failed to be informed of a test conducted in Belfast by Harland & Wolff on these very boats on 25 March 1912. Supervised by Francis Carruthers, the Board of Trade's chief surveyor for Belfast, the test on *Titanic* comprised swinging all sixteen wooden boats out, lowering them, then winching them back into position in the davits. Lowered with weights equal to sixty-five people (5½–5¾ tons) the test simulated the burden endured by the lifeboat if filled to capacity in its davit. The 'falls' themselves – made from Manila rope, a natural fibre favoured for its strength and durability against saltwater – were likewise calibrated and could withstand a strain equal to 60 tons. Shared among the sixteen sets of davits on *Titanic*, four electric motorised winches were able to safely lower and raise a full boatload of occupants at a rate of 100ft per minute. Harold Sanderson, White Star's general manager, confirmed that during this particular test in Belfast her boats were deployed safely in nineteen attempts out of twenty.

Again in Belfast, on 9 May 1911, a similar test was performed on one of the boats on *Olympic*, which was successfully lowered and raised six times while bearing weights equal to sixty-five people. Yet no officer on *Titanic* was made aware of either test, rendering the process of testing the apparatus woefully redundant for the actual evacuation, and their subsequent concern needless. As a result both the British official investigation into the disaster and the ensuing SOLAS convention of 1914 demanded that the maximum load calibrated for each lifeboat be clearly marked on its bow.

Titanic was fitted with sixteen wooden lifeboats, eight placed on either side of the top deck, all numbered for identification. Boats with even numbers were sited along the portside, those with odd numbers along the starboard. Stowed on the Boat Deck 60½ft above the waterline, they were divided into two sets of eight, fore and aft. The first set of boats flanked the officers' quarters and the first-class section of the deck. Interposed by a 190ft gap, the second set followed within the second-class promenade section toward the rear. Being nearest the bridge those numbered 1 and 2 acted as 'emergency' boats and, being smaller than the remaining wooden ones, were permanently swung out in readiness for speedy deployment. In addition to the main boats were four 'collapsible' additions, lettered A to D. A and B sat either side of funnel 1 on the roof of the officers' quarters, with the remaining pair, C and D, stowed directly upon deck adjacent to the davits bearing emergency boats 1 and 2.

The boats and distress rockets installed on *Titanic* received the Board of Trade's stamp of approval from Carruthers on 3 April 1912. Each lifeboat was further examined by Fourth Officer Boxhall to satisfy curiosity that all were adequately equipped. They were. The fourteen wooden boats were each supplied with sails, oars and a removable mast and rudder. In addition, inside small onboard lockers, was a supply of preserved biscuits and a compass.

Despite this preparation only one lifeboat drill would be held on *Titanic* during her tragically shortened commercial service. Under the instruction of Captain Maurice Clarke of the Board of Trade this drill was jointly observed by White Star's marine superintendent, Benjamin Steele, at her Southampton berth at 9a.m. on 10 April, two and a half hours prior to the noon cast-off for her maiden voyage.

Prior to the disaster the actual extent of lifeboat drills varied freely between captains: Edward Smith routinely conducted his with two boats on the morning of each departure. Alternating between different pairs each time, on this occasion he chose boats 11 and 15 for the sailing-day drill. Fifth Officer Lowe and Sixth Officer Moody each commanded a boat along with eight handpicked crew-members in each. Loaded and lowered the boats were rowed around for twenty minutes then raised back into position. At 9.30a.m. Captain Clarke, satisfied with the demonstration, approved *Titanic* fit for sailing.

A further safety test, this time during the voyage, focussed on *Titanic's* bulkhead doors. Overseen by Thomas Andrews and First Officer Murdoch, it took place on the second day – 11 April – but, famously, no lifeboat drill was conducted during the maiden voyage itself. Perversely, Captain Smith cancelled the full-scale one scheduled for the morning of 14 April. Although there was no actual legal requirement to conduct such drills with passengers, White Star, however, always requested that one be performed on all of their vessels each Sunday. However on this particular Sunday (14 April) Smith felt conditions too blustery to attempt the drill safely and cancelled it. Later that evening, with lifeboats lowered and over 400 seats remaining empty, the evacuation of *Titanic* transpired as a disastrously imperfect demonstration of the abandonment of a vessel, with Britain's supposedly best crew. With no predetermined plan for the crew to adhere to, the actual evacuation was primarily superintended by two officers, First Officer Murdoch and Second Officer Lightoller, delegated on the spot as marshals by the captain.

The evacuation and the supply of lifeboats became the disaster within itself, and in its wake admonishment turned to the body responsible for maintaining and imposing the standard of safety at sea: the British Board of Trade. Questions needed to be answered. Widespread complacency was found skulking at the very heart of government. Whisperings turned into demands, in desperation to learn how so many people were left to die on *Titanic*. Why, pleaded retrospect, had *Titanic* not carried enough boats?

CHAPTER 8

SAFETY IN NUMBERS

'Unsinkable – indestructible, she carried as few boats as would satisfy the laws.'
Futility: The Wreck of the Titan, 1898

Nothing could better highlight the pomposity of man than picturing their mere mortality when attempting to tame nature – particularly when casting a less than cautious eye to their own safety. Throughout the industrial heartlands of Victorian and Edwardian Britain, safety was considered more obtrusiveness than necessity. It was an age of workhouses, child labour and lookouts perched in crow's nests. Yet the Victorians were also masters of engineering and mechanisation, going to great efforts to modernise and mechanistically advance every aspect of life, be it architecture or zoology. Likewise the application of safety at sea joined the obsession with complexity and methodology – choosing to calculate the supply of lifeboats carried by the ships' cubic capacity than by the actual number of passengers potentially requiring one of these seats.

Since the 1850s the number of lifeboats carried at sea had been determined by providing a prescribed minimum cubic carrying capacity – volume – among the supply of boats aboard each ship. All measurements for sea transportation was (and still is) calculated by volume – empty space – rather by actual weight. The overall tonnage of 46,328 bears no relation to the weight of *Titanic* herself but translates to the number of cubic tons of space her structure enclosed. The principle was thereby to determine the total (gross) volume of commercial and non-commercial capacity available in any given vessel. Lifeboats to this effect were likewise measured in this fashion, although in smaller units of square feet instead of tons.

Titanic entered service bearing a total of twenty lifeboats comprised of three varieties, categorised by the Merchant Shipping Act according to their build. Of this allocation fourteen were classed as Section A. Measuring 30ft in length by 9ft 1in wide, their hulls were moulded to a depth of 4ft. Formed from elm and oak, this particular supply was designed by Harland & Wolff's chief draughtsman, Roderick Chisholm, and constructed in the yard's own boat shop. Built in full accordance with existing regulations they each contained a copper-lined air chamber for buoyancy, and for stability they were based on a clinker design harking back to the double-bowed whalers of old. Indeed, the quality of Harland & Wolff's lifeboats was reputed to be among the best, if not the best, of the era.

The cubic capacity of lifeboats was derived using what was called Stirling's Formula. Named after its creator, the esteemed eighteenth-century mathematician, James Stirling, the formula multiplied the length of the lifeboat by its breadth and depth by 0.6. Applied to the hulls of the fourteen wooden boats of *Titanic* it afforded each a volume of 655.2 cubic feet, enough space for sixty-five occupants.

In addition to the Section A boats there were two cutters, classified as Section D. Slightly smaller to the main set and without buoyancy chambers, these were likewise constructed of wood. One, 25ft 2in long, 7ft 2in wide and 3ft deep, the other all but identical, was 1in narrower; their respective capacities 326.6 and 322.1 cubic feet. The cutters were intentionally smaller, thus lighter than the remaining wooden boats so to be faster in water and aid their hasty deployment during an emergency. For this purpose the cutters flanked the bridge port and starboard and were kept swung in the outboard lowering position at all times in readiness in the event of someone falling overboard. Despite this difference in dimension the two cutters were able to accommodate forty occupants each. Positioned and ready for use, the sixteen wooden boats on *Titanic* were permanently stowed in a dedicated set of lowering winches (davits); eight were placed either side of the Boat Deck.

The third type of lifeboat aboard *Titanic* were the 'collapsibles'. Patented in 1900 by Valdemar Engelhardt, founder of the Copenhagen-based Engelhardt Collapsible Life Boat Company, the first prototype was completed in 1901. Following interest from several governments, full-scale production moved to Germany shortly afterwards but by 1912 their use commercially was still relatively new. Consisting of a wooden frame and hull not dissimilar to a regular lifeboat, their sides, however, were canvas, allowing the boat to telescope down for easy stowage on the deck; those for *Titanic* were manufactured in Glasgow by McAlister & Son. Classed as Section E, these were the only boats on *Titanic* not afforded their own set of davits, for in the eyes of the law collapsible boats were construed as life-rafts, not life-boats. Each collapsible measured 27ft 5in long by 8ft wide and 3ft deep, and with Stirling's Formula applied each provided capacity of 376.6 cubic feet: enough room for forty-seven people.

Also installed around *Titanic* were forty-eight lifebuoys and a supply of 3,560 cork lifejackets. The regulations required that *Titanic* carry at least sixteen lifebuoys and provide as many lifejackets for as many people as she was licensed to carry: 3,547. Controversially, however, the maxim 'provide for all' did not apply to the provision of lifeboats.

Table 3: Combined lifeboat provision and cubic capacities for Titanic

Type	Quantity of boats	Seating capacity	Cubic capacity (ft)
Wooden (A)	14	910	9,172.8
Emergency (D)	2	80	648.7
Collapsible (E)	4	188	1,506.4
Total	20	1,178	11,327.9

The most widely known fact concerning the *Titanic* disaster is her alarmingly short supply of lifeboats, such that it turned a mid-ocean incident into an unequalled catastrophe. It is as equally recognised that *Titanic* carried too few boats to save even half of the passengers aboard her maiden voyage despite the fact that the crossing was not even booked to two thirds of her capacity. Today, and probably because of *Titanic*, we think it inconceivable for any passenger liner to lawfully head to sea without enough boats to accommodate everybody on board. However, the attitude a century ago was entirely different.

It may appear surprising, but for half a century before disaster consumed *Titanic*, not a single incident on the Atlantic resulted in heavy loss of life: 1854–1904. Indeed, of the total crossings on the Atlantic by British-registered ships between 1892 and 1901 just 183 lives were recorded as lost at sea. It was an improving statistic also witnessed over the following decade, which saw the loss of fifty-seven lives on those same routes. Moreover, by 1904 the carrying of wirelesses had become commonplace – albeit not compulsory. Its use lurched to the fore in 1909 during the sinking of White Star's *Republic*, an incident that had seen all but a handful of her occupants saved because other ships were able to answer her distress calls and rush to her aid. Her wireless radio and bulkhead structure had proven their mettle, becoming a media sensation, hailing its success as the 'shipwreck of the future'. It was a model rescue.

High running costs at the turn of the twentieth century found shipping operators increasing their carrying capacities for cargo and passenger accommodation as efficiency measures to maximise their fleets' profitability. In this endeavour to boost revenue, ships grew larger, and amid the age of Victorian diligence, this progress was mirrored by their builders continually raising the standard of safety integrated into ever more voluminous, Herculean craft. As a result, watertight subdivision became progressively more sophisticated, so much so that with each passing year sea travel was consistently becoming a markedly less perilous affair.

Yet in the intervening years spanning 1876–85 an incredible 25,528 lives would be lost at sea. To stem this unacceptable toll a Royal Commission was established in 1886 to report on the causes of 'Loss of Life at Sea'. Reviewing existing legislation that in Britain required every passenger liner grossing 1,500 tons 'and upwards' to carry only seven lifeboats, regardless of the number of persons carried, the Commission was startled to learn that Section 27 of the Passengers Act of 1855 had become perilously outdated with reference to modern shipping.

On 26 March 1886, against the backdrop of the Royal Commission, the Board of Trade established its own panel comprising of its three senior officials for Glasgow, Liverpool and Hull tasked with reviewing the current state of lifeboat provision. The following year a Parliamentary Select Committee was also established, chaired by Admiral-turned-politician Lord Charles Beresford, for the sole purpose of evaluating the Dickensian laws governing the quantity of life-saving equipment carried by British ocean-going passenger vessels.

Presented on 28 October 1886, the resulting survey of the Board's internal review itself acknowledged the woeful state of existing legislation: 'the time has passed when boat scales should be regulated solely by tonnage' and stated that at sea a sufficient supply of lifeboats must provide for 'all on board' – though it warned of the great costs to the shipping operators to facilitate the improvements needed. Beresford's report followed on 29 July 1887, and brought to light the Board's alarming survey revealing that the majority of existing craft were unable to accommodate enough lifeboats for everybody on board nor did they provide enough crew to man the boats available, let alone to launch them safely in bad weather. Starkly warning that 'fresh legislation is essential', Beresford branded existing laws 'totally inadequate' and 'obsolete'. His findings called for the Board to establish a separate committee to formulate a series of provisos that ensured that ships of all varieties carried as many boats and rafts as possible and provide enough life-saving devices for everybody on board. Beresford's recommendations formed part of the Merchant Shipping (Life-Saving Appliances) Act which came into law in 1888.

As required under the new Act, the then president of the Board of Trade, Sir Michael Hicks-Beach, formed a committee that November to establish the regulations – Rules – with which to govern life-saving appliances. Its membership comprised fifteen professionals nominated by various maritime bodies, such as the Chamber of Shipping and the ship-owner's institutions of Glasgow and Liverpool, as well as various naval architects, insurers, societies and seafaring unions. By June 1889 the Committee on Life-Saving Appliances had drafted its Rules, the Board enacting them into law on 31 March the following year.

The Rules set a formula to determine the minimum number of lifeboats that ships were to carry. They had, however, based their calculation not on the number of people the ship was able to carry but on the gross tonnage of the ship itself. The rationale of basing the calculation this way was because the Board of Trade classed passenger ships into different categories, ranging from those bearing emigrants to international destinations, to craft engaged as small coastal pleasure cruisers. For that reason the Board was looking for the committee to form separate requirements for each category of vessel. Should the committee base the Rules on passenger capacity doing so would then demand them to specify separate requirements for every type of ship on the Board's extensive list. The committee instead preferred the Rules to be as rudimentary as possible; determining the quantity of lifeboats on the size of the ship itself. Homogenising the Board's categorisation evaded a need to create individual Rules and distinctions between each kind of vessel and for the nature of service in which it was engaged. The committee also believed that basing the calculation on size would automatically reflect the number of lives potentially aboard any particular voyage since larger craft invariably accommodated more occupants than smaller craft.

Covering matters stipulating the lifeboat's quality of build and the formula to measure its cubic capacity, the committee's Rules also contained a table determining the minimum quantity of boats to be carried by ships within prescribed increments of tonnage. It became the first major revision to a smaller scale first seen in the Act of 1855. To cater for the increasing sizes of modern liners the extent of the new range ended at ships grossing 9,000 tons. Any vessel nearing the top or exceeding this range had now to carry at least fourteen boats, each stowed permanently under their own set of davits. That ship must then ensure the total cubic volume of these lifeboats provided a minimum combined capacity equal to or exceeding 5,250 cubic feet. Thinking more to the present than of the sizes that ships were likely to gross in the future, the limit in the table harboured a disturbing flaw in the Rules: a ship grossing, say, 13,000 tons, would be legally obliged to furnish the same capacity of lifeboats as a ship of only 9,000 tons.

Since 1889, the chairman of the committee formulating these Rules happened also to be the owner of White Star Line, Thomas Henry Ismay. Thomas shared the industry consensus that ships were many years from grossing much beyond 10,000 tons. They were soon proved wrong, when in 1893 Cunard launched *Lucania* as the world's largest ship. Boasting 12,952 tons, *Lucania* was approved by the Board of Trade to carry a total of 1,857 people. The committee was recalled to revise their regulations, although submitted a solitary amendment: raising the scale from '9,000 tons and upwards' to '10,000 tons and upwards'. Ships exceeding this new ceiling were now obliged to carry at least sixteen lifeboats and among them provide capacity totalling a minimum of 5,500 cubic feet.

There was at the time the general belief that during emergencies sixteen boats were all a ship could deploy safely and within adequate time. The revision was deemed appropriate for *Lucania* and the Rules remained famously unchanged until the loss of *Titanic* eighteen years later.

The committee presented their modified regulations to the Board of Trade on 9 March 1894, including this new cap for lifeboat capacities. The amendments came into effect on 1 June under Section 427 of the new Merchant Shipping Act; adherence to them by all British-registered vessels was therefore required by law. Receipt of Royal Assent came on 25 August 1894, the Act itself had come to fruition to allow the Board to amalgamate and simplify the panoply of some twenty-seven existing codifications governing merchant shipping into one all-encompassing Act. One of those superseded was the original requirements and Rules on lifeboat provision set previously by the Merchant Shipping (Life-Saving Appliances) Act of 1888.

Therein lay the problem: measuring lifeboat capacity by volume rather than by the actual number of occupants the ship itself was potentially able to accommodate. As well as not raising the minimum tonnage capacity to pre-empt any inevitable increase in size of future craft, the edict was proved particularly precarious by the arrival of *Titanic*. *Titanic* shattered the 10,000-ton cap of the 1894 Act by 36,328 tons. Yet still the law obliged her designers to provide the base minimum of only 5,500 cubic feet throughout her sixteen lifeboats; exactly the volume a ship 36,328 tons smaller was similarly required to carry.

The sixteen wooden boats *Titanic* was obliged to carry gave her a combined lifeboat capacity of 9,821.5 cubic feet; exceeding the mandatory requirement by 4,321.5 cubic feet. Still the Act would remain unaltered – *Lucania* proving no anomaly when she was first to smash the revised 10,000-ton limit. Hot on her heels came her sister, the 12,950-ton *Campania*; White Star following suit in 1901 with the first of their Big Four liners, although across the wider industry the tonnage of British ships had increased marginally, leaving the Board seeing no urgency to extend the cap since to them the problem was not endemic. By 1904 White Star had launched their Big Four, each clearing 20,000 tons; Cunard famously replied in 1907 with their *Mauretania* and *Lusitania*, both topping 30,000 tons. Still regulations remained unaltered.

The reason for the Board's impermeable resistance to increase the scale was rooted in a series of recent dynamics. Universally defined shipping lanes had been in use on the North Atlantic since 1899. By 1904 wireless radio was commonplace on larger passenger liners (Cunard fitting their first set in 1901 – the recipient being *Lucania*, 15 June). More importantly, bulkhead design in general was seeing boundless improvement. Sea travel was becoming safer. However the fact remained that the world's largest passenger steamers were still legally being supplied with lifeboats offering capacities well below the number of persons – lives – they routinely carried aboard. The rate at which the tonnage of ships had grown in the new century attested, if anything, to the inadequacy of the regulatory system in keeping step with this advanced and rapidly evolving method of transportation. Had the regulatory system ground itself to obsolescence?

The Board of Trade was far from oblivious to the fact that their regulations were behind the times. They were instead relying on the series of Rules from Section 427 of the 1894 Act that detailed the individual lifeboat requirements each class of ship was to carry: the very Rules that had remained largely unaltered since 1890, receiving only cursory revision in 1894. The classes ranged from large 'emigrant carrying' vessels, down to tiny barges used on inlets and river ways – the 'home trade'. *Titanic* fell into the highest category: emigrant class 1. Any vessel of this category not providing enough lifeboats to accommodate its entire certified capacity of passengers and crew would see Rule D of Section 427 spring into play.

Titanic was licensed by the Board to carry 2,603 passengers, as well as a maximum crew of 944: 3,547 in total. Clearly, with sixteen lifeboats she would not provide sufficient capacity for everyone on board. Thus with Rule D *Titanic* would be required to carry in addition to her lifeboats enough rafts and floatation devices to provide for three quarters of the Act's compulsory 5,500 cubic minimum capacity for boats. Thereby in addition to the cap, Rule D would require *Titanic* to supply a further 4,125 cubic feet of lifeboat/raft accommodation to raise her new legal minimum capacity to 9,625 cubic feet: enough space for 962 people. However, this too would represent just 27 per cent of the maximum occupancy that *Titanic* was intended to carry and was licensed by the Board of Trade to carry on any given voyage.

The calculation used in the Act was based on the assumption the average person (above the age of twelve, or two children: 'statute adult') would each occupy space in a lifeboat equal to 10 cubic feet. For example, dividing the increased cubic capacity of 9,625 by 10 produces 962, once rounded down. The seating capacity of each of the fourteen boats of Section A was therefore calculated by dividing 655.2 cubic feet by 10 (65.52), which, once rounded down, determined its seating capacity as adequate for sixty-five persons. The figure rounded down to ensure each statute adult occupied a seat of equal size in the lifeboat.

The Act also contained a set of General Rules that applied across all classes of British vessels. Of these, Rule 12 contained the exemption that should an emigrant-carrying vessel – *Titanic* – be deemed by the Board to contain less than satisfactory watertight subdivision (that in moderate weather was unable to remain afloat with any two of its compartments flooded), Rule D would apply as normal to augment its life-raft capacity. Should the Board, however, consider the compartments of sufficient quality, deeming it a safer ship, Rule 12 would reward the shipping operator by halving the number of additional rafts required under Rule D. As the sixteen compartments on *Titanic* were considered more than satisfactory, White Star was only obliged to install just half the 4,125 cubic feet – 2,062.5 cubic feet – of Rule D's additional capacity in reward under her qualification for Rule 12: if applying this rule to *Titanic* it legally required her to carry an aggregate lifeboat/raft capacity totalling 7,562.5 cubic feet instead of the Act's original base requirement of 5,500.

Under the rule for statute adult this revised capacity of 7,562.5 cubic feet would provide *Titanic* with seating for 756 people – 21 per cent of her potential travelling occupancy. If filled to her licensed capacity *Titanic* could still head lawfully to sea with 2,791 of her passengers and crew with neither a seat in a lifeboat nor access to a life-raft. Even so, her actual supply of boats exceeded the combined requirements of Rules D and 12 by 3,765.4 cubic feet: still providing at full capacity a seat in one of her lifeboats/rafts for just 33 per cent of occupants aboard.

As it transpired, because *Titanic* was furnished with a supply of boats amassing a capacity of 11,327.9 cubic feet, as well as boasting sixteen watertight compartments, she not only doubled the legal base minimum but exceeded the extended provisions of Rule D by 15 per cent. To this effect, when considering the matter for *Titanic*, the Board felt her sufficiently undeserving to warrant application of either Rule D or 12 since she had already more than satisfactorily fulfilled its criteria. *Titanic* was thus obliged to carry only the minimum capacity set by the Act – 5,500 cubic feet of lifeboat space – enough room for 550 people, 15 per cent of the total occupants she was designed and licensed to accommodate.

Rule 12 was included in the Act to induce shipping operators to build their ships to be more invulnerable. The Board between 1890 and 1912 only applied the Rule on sixty-nine occasions, and as an outcome of the investigation into the loss of *Titanic* this seldom employed but controversial proviso was repealed. Lord Mersey, chairman of that investigation felt it naive for a government body to reward shipping operators by reducing the number of lifeboats as a method of coaxing them to improve safety on their liners. Mersey instead insisted upon simple logic: even if a ship was considered suitably protected by watertight compartments, installing them still did not eliminate its possibility of sinking and thereby requiring its original quota of lifeboats.

The under-regulation of lifeboats was not only a British issue. In America the legal minimum for vessels grossing 10,000 tons stood at 11,520 cubic feet. For Germany it was 13,343 cubic feet, and France 9,625 cubic feet. All major nations, in fact the majority of others as well, based their calculation for lifeboat supply on cubic capacity than by the people their ships were actually licensed to carry. Since craft of all nationalities had also to comply with the laws of the nations they were visiting, regulations governing shipping were largely standardised. For instance, following American law to the letter would require *Titanic* to supply 2,142 seats in her lifeboats, still, however, leaving 1,405 (40 per cent) of her designed passenger occupancy without guarantee of a seat. In Britain, Section 4 of the Merchant Shipping Act of 1906 granted the Board the authority to impose their Rules for life-saving appliances to all foreign craft visiting British ports. This, mutually agreed with America in 1905, was in 1907 widened to include Belgium, France, Holland, Germany, Denmark, Japan and Norway. The problem was global. But in the aftermath of *Titanic* the British regulatory system found itself under intense scrutiny, with other nations bracing themselves for similar outcries at home. The law had to be changed.

The extent of the death toll resulting from the loss of *Titanic* posed serious ramifications for the Board of Trade. First and foremost they were the body responsible for the administration of the Merchant Shipping Acts in force at the time of the disaster, which since their most recent revision in 1906 had not kept up with modern development. Furthermore, the Board had to convince Mersey's court that their inspectors had not neglected their duties through inadequate supervision and subsequent approval of the blueprints of *Titanic* and *Olympic*. Known to them as early as 1907 the Board left their regulations unaltered when *Titanic*, the largest ship ever afloat, departed Britain's busiest port on 10 April 1912 bearing a deficient supply of lifeboats. Luckily for the Board Mersey did not find them culpable, ordering them only to append their regulations to require lifeboat accommodations allowing for the maximum occupancy of people carried on any given vessel. Restraining his criticism, Mersey had been appeased that by the time of the disaster the Board had already instigated measures to update the regulations of 1894 but had not happened to implement them in time to benefit *Titanic*. To the relief of the British establishment, Mersey's verdict was enough to keep the groundswell for compensatory claims at bay.

A Matter of Record

For many years prior to the loss of *Titanic* it was widely considered that far too few lifeboats were carried at sea and that it was a case of when, rather than if, disaster would strike. Journalist William Thomas Stead, who in a wicked twist of fate lost his life on *Titanic*, forewarned in the 22 March edition of the *Pall Mall Gazette* in 1886 that a great loss of life 'will take place if the liners are sent to the sea short of boats'. His earlier short story 'From the Old World to the New', published in the Christmas of 1892, depicted the disaster of a fictional transatlantic-bound ship stricken by an iceberg – its survivors rescued by White Star's *Majestic*.

In May 1898, Morgan Robertson's book *Futility* was published, its ship, named *Titan*, all but accurately prophesised the *Titanic* disaster. Followed in 1911 by *The White Ghost*, penned by Mayn Clew Garnett, both narrated tales of hundreds of lives drowned because of a shortage of lifeboats following the collision of a large Atlantic liner. The prospect of disaster was becoming far more than fictional fare, and many commentators began lobbying operators to equip ships with enough boats to provision for all lives on board. The shipping operators themselves however appeared less concerned. Blinkered by a complacency in which consequences garnered no priority, the industry continued plying traditionally outmoded ideologies to build ever-modern and larger craft, clouded by a precipitating arrogance which was to reach its dramatic culmination in 1912.

Titanic boasted 'everything for enjoying life, but not much for saving it', exclaimed *The Detroit News* in the wake of the tragedy, echoing the media's astonishment with shipping's lassitude toward the number of lifeboats carried by their steamers. Yet until the loss of *Titanic* shipping companies considered lifeboats highly unsuitable to saving life in the middle of a potentially volatile North Atlantic Ocean. They shared a belief that lifeboats should only be employed to ferry passengers to and from a rescue ship, shunning the need to install dozens of superfluous boats to provide a separate seat for each person aboard. Both the shipping industry and the Board of Trade preferred to instead expel the anticipation of disaster through corrective engineering, and more modern alternatives: increasing the ship's floatability through improved compartmentalisation, thereby no longer having to rely on lifeboats in the first place. To them, legislating for more boats was no remedy for poor subdivision. The ship itself would become the lifeboat.

The capacity of the sixteen wooden boats installed on *Titanic* totalled 9,821.5 cubic feet, comfortably exceeding the Board's base requirement by 44 per cent. Although bettering a legal standard was a positive initiation by the operator, that act is belittled when the original standard was itself deficient. The fourteen Section A boats on *Titanic* afforded enough space for 910 occupants. Even with her two emergency cutters (categorised Section D and the maximum number of this type permissible), providing an additional eighty seats between them the total of number of places among all sixteen boats stood at just 990. Less than 1,000 spaces for a ship officially certified to carry passengers three-and-a-half times that number. Of her allocation 72 per cent (2,557) of the passengers and crew able to board *Titanic* would have done so with no guarantee of a place in one of these boats.

The four additional Engelhardt collapsible boats for *Titanic* (Section E) each offered capacity of 376.6 cubic feet. The computation used in the Act of 1894 for boats of Section D and E reduced the cubic capacity for statute adult for these from 10 to 8. Divided by eight the capacity of each collapsible provided room for forty-seven occupants: 188 across the four boats. Although boats of Section E did not qualify towards the ship's legal obligation, the additional Engelhardts raised the aggregate capacity for *Titanic* to 11,327.9 cubic feet, generously double the legal base minimum. Their installation increased the lifeboat occupancy of *Titanic* by 16 per cent, raising the maximum possible accommodation in her lifeboats to 1,178; however this still left 2,369 passengers and crew without guarantee of a seat among her now twenty available boats.

Fortuitously, the coalminers' strike at the outset of 1912 left ticket sales sluggish. The resultant strikebound journeys, cancelled at short notice, discouraged many would-be travellers from planning voyages. As it transpired, only 2,228 passengers and crew boarded *Titanic* for her ill-fated maiden voyage – 37 per cent below her potential maximum occupancy. Nonetheless, total lifeboat capacity still found 47 per cent of the persons aboard this voyage with no access to a seat in her boats. The four Engelhardts proved in the event to be little more than a woefully inadequate gesture from White Star as *Titanic* would require as many as sixty-three boats to provide enough seats for all if she had carried a full passenger complement.

Between October 1909 and January 1910 during the construction of *Olympic* and *Titanic*, disparity of opinion had grown between the chairman of White Star Line – Bruce Ismay – and the then general manager of Harland & Wolff – Alexander Carlisle – over the issue of the lifeboat capacity intended for them. During this time Carlisle, as principal designer of *Olympic* and *Titanic*, was responsible for contriving the ships' working arrangements. Believing, like many others, the regulations of 1894 to be dangerously antiquated, Carlisle began openly articulating concern: 'As ships grew bigger, I was always in favour of increasing lifeboat accommodation'.

When details were made public for the allocation intended for *Olympic*, she was due to be installed with just fourteen wooden boats and two emergency cutters. Providing an overall capacity of 9,752 cubic feet between them these sixteen boats afforded *Olympic* enough seats for only 990 of the 3,444 people she was licensed to carry. When entering service in September 1907 Cunard had likewise let their 31,550-ton *Lusitania* marginally surpass her legal minimum quota for lifeboats. The sixteen aboard *Lusitania* each provided an average capacity of 611.25 cubic feet (9,780 cubic feet in total) – enough seats for just 978 (32 per cent) of the 3,025 people she was licensed to carry. The year 1910 then saw the launch of *Olympic*, a 45,000-ton vessel. *Olympic* and *Lusitania* afforded enough lifeboats for only a third of the passengers and crew that each were able to accommodate. The figures laid bare an alarming math and sparked a wave of calls demanding the industry consider a dangerously overdue review into the quantities of lifeboats routinely carried by their fleets.

Concern about the allocation of lifeboats intended for the then unfinished *Olympic* would prompt questions in the House of Commons. During November 1910 Horatio Bottomley MP lodged his misgivings to the Board of Trade over the fourteen boats planned for *Olympic*. The answer received from the minister attempted to allay his fears by confirming White Star's consignment for *Olympic* was already 'in excess of the requirements of the Statutory Rules'. Dissatisfied, Bottomley presented a supplementary question in February 1911 appealing that *Olympic* and *Titanic* had thereby proven the regulations of 1894 to be gravely out-dated for modern express liners. The Board duly responded, promising that internal reviews on the tonnage cap were already receiving their 'serious attention', and passed the matter to the Merchant Shipping Advisory Committee for investigation.

The Merchant Shipping Advisory Committee was the consultative body of the Board of Trade. First appointed in 1907 it assumed the responsibility of review-ing the Rules pertaining to life-saving appliances that had barely evolved since their inception twenty years previously. The committee's membership comprised largely of shipping operators, but for examining matters concerning safety it appointed a specialist sub-panel, the Committee on Life-Saving Appliances. The group met on 19 and 26 May 1911 specifically to conduct a review to upwardly amend the tonnage cap for lifeboat capacities carried by the larger liners. In answer to Bottomley's appeal their findings were presented to the Board of Trade on 4 July that year.

Alexander Carlisle had specifically designed the Boat Decks of *Olympic* and *Titanic* to each accommodate forty-eight lifeboats, shared among their requisite set of sixteen davits. Also asking Axel Welin, owner of the Swedish firm Welin Davit & Engineering Co. Ltd, to design him a winch able to handle this number of boats, these new davits could store four each and thereby enable *Titanic* safely to stow as many as sixty-four boats: three on deck, with a fourth suspended over the side of the hull. In October 1909 Carlisle mooted these plans to his client – Bruce Ismay – to demonstrate that the Boat Decks could easily accommodate forty-eight lifeboats within sixteen sets of davits housing three boats each.

Carlisle preferred the davits to store just three boats apiece rather than the four they were able to accommodate. It allowed *Olympic* and *Titanic* to pre-empt any likely revisions to the Board's regulations and increase capacity to sixty-four boats without involving any rearrangement to their existing layout or equipment on the Boat Deck. Unconvinced, Ismay rejected the proposal on the grounds that current regulations required the new liners to carry just sixteen lifeboats each. Any plan suggesting to install as many as forty-eight or even sixty-four boats on the new Olympic Class would be a number far too profuse for the chairman to even remotely entertain.

Their respective drawings approved, the agreement to proceed with construction of *Olympic* and *Titanic* finalised between White Star and Harland & Wolff on 31 July 1908 placed all matters pertaining to safety appliances at the prerogative of the builder. Any subsequent change such as installing additional lifeboats to the sixteen contractually agreed was consequently outside this agreement. Any additions or alterations to the project beyond the scope of the original contract would therefore require the express approval of the client, cynical White Star Line. During his two meetings with Ismay, Carlisle had shown the drawings of the proposed lifeboat arrangements but failed to verbally validate his view. His senior, Lord Pirrie, also present, had led the presentation, with Carlisle reduced to silent bystander. On lifeboat supply Ismay was resolute.

Comfort was the mainstay of White Star's stratagem. Ismay firmly believed that cluttering the sun decks of the 'Olympics' with as many as sixty-four boats – four times the number they were legally obliged to carry – severely undermined any aspiration to offer more space than their competitors. White Star was, after all, the first shipping operator to free their decks of masts and rigging and to open the sides of their ships in a highly successful bid to offer passengers unobstructed vistas of the ocean. To Ismay, Carlisle's notion was a reversal of the company's past innovation and he was in no mind to allow dozens of superfluous lifeboats to ingloriously invade an otherwise clutter-free Boat Deck, unless he was obliged by law to do so.

The chairman insisted the North Atlantic was no place for forty-eight tiny lifeboats to be left sailing exposed to the elements for prolonged periods of time. He shared the industry standpoint that lifeboats were only necessary to ferry passengers between the damaged ship and its rescuer. Carrying more boats, the industry reasoned, was pointless. Furthermore, the boats built for *Olympic* and *Titanic* each weighed 1½ tons, and siting large numbers of them high on the top deck risked compromising the ship's buoyancy. Installing all sixty-four would require additional ballast to raise the waterline a quarter of an inch to compensate for this

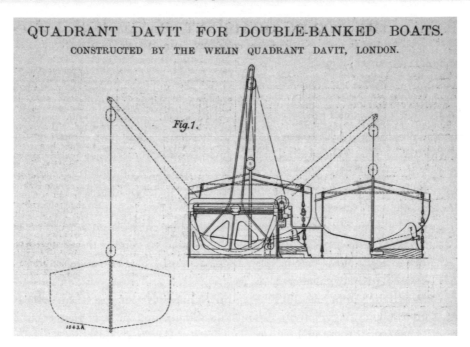

QUADRANT DAVIT FOR DOUBLE-BANKED BOATS.
CONSTRUCTED BY THE WELIN QUADRANT DAVIT, LONDON.

Sixteen sets of Welin's double-acting quadrant davits were installed on *Titanic*, each able to accommodate three lifeboats. The arm's opposable action angled the davit both inboard and out to easily hook adjacent boats to its falls, illustrated here in the 1910 periodical, *Engineering*. (The National Archives, Kew (ZEPR 50/90))

increase in weight to the upper decks. Allowing just for that would not only sacrifice valuable commercial carrying capacity but expend additional fuel to drive this now unavoidably heavier ship through water. Ismay's underlining reason to reject Carlisle's additional boats, however, was neither inspired by economics nor hydrodynamics, but by ascetics.

Adverse to the banks of lifeboats brutalising the veneer of his dapper new liners Ismay felt an increase in their lifeboats would also subversively trigger a sense of vulnerability in the new class, singling them out as less safe to the point of arousing suspicion that the additional boats compensated for hidden flaws in the design.

Carlisle redrafted his plans to have the sixteen sets of davits store just two boats each, reducing the total aboard to thirty-two, even commissioning the Welin Davit Company to produce a mechanism able to deploy them. On 9 March 1910 Welin confirmed that the double-acting quadrant davits ordered by Carlisle for the Olympic Class were indeed able to store thirty-two boats, two per set: one stowed directly beneath the davit's arms, the other inboard lying parallel on deck. The opposable 'double-action' of the davit permitted its arms to extend over the side of the ship as well as inboard to connect and hoist the second lifeboat stowed adjacent on the deck and swing that to the newly vacated lowering position.

Hoping to reach a compromise by reducing the proposed lifeboats to thirty-two he presented the revised drawings to Ismay in January 1910. These too were swiftly rejected.

It is possible that Ismay was considering the implications of these extra lifeboats from a legal standpoint. Laying additional boats on the deck parallel to a set of davits already occupied by another nested within, ran the risk of the inboard set being completely disregarded by the Act of 1894. Of the minimum sixteen sets of davits the Act required that the class of which *Titanic* was categorised – Division A, Class 1 – 'shall carry boats placed under davits', and qualified further in the General Rules that 'boats placed under davits are to be attached to the davit tackles and kept ready for service'. This condition was widely interpreted throughout the industry to infer that none of the unattached adjacently placed inboard boats counted towards the ship's legal capacity. Not wishing to confuse the issue Ismay remained steadfast to the original plan, keeping just the sixteen wooden lifeboats nested within their own dedicated davits.

Carlisle retired from Harland & Wolff on 30 June 1910 leaving no one else at the yard willing to champion his cause. White Star finalised the deck plans regarding the configuration of lifeboats for *Titanic* on 5 May 1911. Carlisle's specially commissioned davits, able to store three boats each – which, due to their arms' reversible action intended to nestle each bank 'under davits' – were ultimately installed on *Titanic*, but instead of housing sixty-four, forty-eight or thirty-two, just sixteen boats were subsequently provided: one per davit. Indeed, during her evacuation, crew found it difficult to operate this new design of davit since only a few had been inducted to its use.

Prior to the disaster the Board of Trade initiated a rethink of the regulations regarding lifeboat capacities but its implementation was stalled until after the sinking. The sixteen rigid boats and their four canvas additions were installed on *Titanic* in January 1912: twenty-eight fewer than their davits were able to accommodate. Even in retirement Carlisle remained committed to advocating safety at sea. His views found him co-opted onto the Board's seven-member Committee on Life-Saving Appliances, and he attended its final two sessions in May 1911 to redraft the controversial tonnage scale of the 1894 Act. On 4 July 1911, twenty days after the maiden voyage of *Olympic*, the committee issued its findings suggesting the upper limit for the total lifeboat capacity of ships grossing more than 10,000 tons be increased to accommodate the tonnage of ships upwards of 45,000 tons. They went on to request that all vessels over 45,000 tons provide a minimum lifeboat capacity of 8,300 cubic feet, distributed among sixteen lifeboats permanently nested in their own set of davits.

Perversely, as a member of that committee, had its proposals been enacted Carlisle's permutation of the regulation would have required *Titanic* to carry enough seats in her lifeboats for only 830 people, actually reducing by 132 the 962 seats she was already obliged to carry. A fact Carlisle would magnanimously recant at the ensuing inquiry: 'I was very soft the day I signed that'.

Had the Board chosen to apply Rule D to *Titanic*, under Carlisle's recommendations she would be required to carry an additional 75 per cent to her capacity of 8,300, namely 6,225 cubic feet – an accumulative capacity of 14,525 cubic feet. But of course Rule D would never have applied to *Titanic* as she already more than satisfied its benchmark for subdivision. As history would demonstrate, events superseded the reviews and Carlisle's version of the Rules was never incorporated into law. Even as late as March 1912 recommendations catering for ships exceeding 50,000 tons oscillated among Board of Trade officials.

The amended Rules would have certainly increased the maximum 5,500 cubic feet of lifeboats a ship the size of *Titanic* would be required to install, but the Board's reviews still fell short of providing an adequate solution to the shortfalls routinely carried. As pointed out at the British inquiry into the disaster, William Archer – the Board's principal surveyor, tasked to review these regulations – acknowledged that a ship the size of *Titanic* would require a capacity of 24,937 cubic feet: twenty-four boats totalling 14,250 cubic feet as well as the extra 10,687 cubic feet implemented through Rule D. Only then would the lifeboats provide enough seats for the 2,201 people aboard her maiden voyage, notwithstanding the maximum number *Titanic* was licensed to carry. Unaware at the time of the loss of *Titanic*, on 16 April 1912 the Board of Trade approved the subcommittee's proposal to increase the threshold in their Rules. However, disaster pulled these plans to a halt.

Once news of the sinking reached London, Sydney Buxton, cabinet minister for the Board of Trade, swiftly declared: 'There will not be a moment's delay in preparing and issuing revised regulations with regard to the number of boats'. On 4 September 1912, in the aftermath of the disaster and its ensuing inquest, the Board issued a new set of Rules. Effective from 1 January 1913, this final iteration set a simple requirement that first and foremost required all emigrant-carrying vessels launched after that date to provide enough lifeboat seats for every passenger and crewmember on board. No longer employing cubic capacity to determine the provision of lifeboats, the new Rules instead obliged ships of equal size to *Titanic* to carry a minimum of twenty-four sets of davits and a boat ready for lowering within each set.

The pains to align the capacities of lifeboats with the numbers of people travelling at any given moment at sea offers fascinating insight into the Edwardian mindset: considering safety more nuisance than life-saving necessity. That external appearance leveraged precedence over a ship's safety apparatus. Demoted to mere clutter, lifeboats were installed not so they may be relied upon to save lives, but because the operating companies were obliged to supply them. To the operator safety was neither a right nor a guarantee, if excessive lifeboats drew attention to their craft's vulnerability and demeaned the owner's claim to its resilience. Imagine an airline today routinely distributing parachutes prior to takeoff – it would hardly inspire confidence among passengers. The rationale behind why *Titanic* carried so few lifeboats may in hindsight seem nonsensical, but when examined alongside the facts of the day, her quota may not appear so impenetrably indefensible. Yet staggeringly the maritime industry twice witnessed startling precursors to the *Titanic* disaster during key incidents in 1904 and 1909 from which it seemingly turned a blind eye.

Norge was a 3,318-ton liner owned from 1898 by the Scandinavian America Line. Operated out of Denmark, she transported emigrants to New York from a variety of Scandinavian ports. Built in 1881, *Norge* was designed to carry fifty passengers in first class, 150 in second and 900 in third, including a crew numbering sixty-eight. Subsequent concerns over her safety found her total licensed occupancy decreased to 800.

Since 13 February 1903 Danish law had required all vessels grossing more than 2,400 tons to provide a total lifeboat capacity of between 2,000 and 2,500 cubic feet. *Norge* supplied 2,538 cubic feet from her eight 22ft-long lifeboats, which in total housed enough seats for 251 of the 800 people she was licensed to carry. Like *Titanic*, despite this shortfall, *Norge* still exceeded legal requirements for lifeboat capacity.

Norge departed Copenhagen with 727 passengers and a full complement of crew (sixty-eight) on 22 June 1904. During the voyage she ventured off course and on the 28th struck a submerged reef amid a dense fogbank at Rockall, 400 miles off the western shore of the Scottish mainland. Promptly beginning to sink at the bow, just 161 of the 795 people aboard survived. The incident became the then greatest loss at sea and was a grisly prelude to the *Titanic* disaster eight years later. But during these eight succeeding years a lucky reduction in the number of deaths at sea laid the foundations of a complacency that was to engulf the entire shipping community.

Before the demise of *Titanic*, White Star listed safety as their highest concern. They were proud of the features incorporated into *Titanic*. 'These steamers were considered tremendous lifeboats in themselves,' remarked a stupefied Philip Franklin – Ismay's lieutenant in New York – when speaking of the Olympic Class at the Senate inquiry investigating the disaster. White Star's earlier confidence in denying Carlisle his proposal to increase the number of lifeboats intended for the 'Olympics' had stemmed from the successful abandonment in 1909 of another liner in their fleet: *Republic*. Following her collision with *Florida* the bulkheads on *Republic* held long enough for her crew not only to launch every lifeboat she carried but to transfer safely all but three of her occupants to one of the many ships responding to help.

Republic was among the very first vessels to use wireless radio to summon help; thus facilitating a highly successful rescue. *Norge* carried no wireless. As a result no one on the mainland would learn of her loss until six days after her collision at Rockall. Her six bulkheads, keeping her afloat for just minutes, provided too little delay for crew to free one of her eight lifeboats and, due to the rapidity of sinking, few of her remaining lifeboats could be launched either. Urged by the success of the evacuation and rescue from *Republic*, neither the Board of Trade nor leading shipping operators found the need to extend the regulations of 1894 governing lifeboat capacity. White Star's management could even be forgiven for considering *Norge*, a twenty-three-year-old vessel, vastly inferior to the design of *Titanic* when taking form on Harland & Wolff's drawing boards in 1907–8. Ismay's logic in limiting the number of lifeboats for *Titanic* may not necessarily be as outrageous as it initially appears. It is plausible that Ismay even believed *Norge* had vindicated his point. By making his Olympic Class more resilient to damage – each carrying fifteen bulkheads and the most extensive double keels on the sea – increased their ability to contain flooding and remain afloat for longer periods, if not indefinitely. Juxtaposed, *Norge* was not intended to remain afloat with more than one of her compartments compromised, whereas *Titanic* could withstand the breaching of four times as many.

The forty occupants of the last boat to leave *Norge* were never recovered. Ismay was well aware lifeboats laden with occupants were unlikely to be found after several days aimlessly and helplessly adrift, if ever found at all. He was fervently of the opinion the North Atlantic was no place for flotillas of lifeboats, a viewpoint arguably bolstered by the loss of *Norge* six years prior to his discourse with Carlisle over the very issue of increasing lifeboats on the Olympic Class. The time the survivors in the six boats that left *Norge* waited before they were discovered by passing ships ranged from one to eight tortuous days. Exposed to the most appalling gales, the occupants were able only to sustain themselves on meagre rations of biscuits and drinking water. Of the eight lifeboats carried by *Norge*, two could not be deployed at all and only five had their occupants rescued.

Ismay was not alone in this view. Indeed it echoed across the shipping community that although they played a seminal role to safety at sea lifeboats received lower priority to the alternatives at their disposal. The opinion did not lack official endorsement either. When questioned at Lord Beresford's committee of 1887 whether bulkheads or lifeboats were 'most desirable' for ensuring safety, the answer given by the Board's principal officer for Liverpool was indicative: 'boats and rafts can be of but little avail … owing to the absence of efficient bulkheads'. Beresford equally concurred, endorsing in his findings 'that the proper placing of bulkheads, so as to enable a ship to keep afloat … is most important for saving life at sea … upon which the full efficiency of life-saving appliances largely depends'.

It may even be argued that Ismay had credible reason to believe lifeboats may one day be rendered obsolete aboard ships possessing sufficient bulkheads and a powerful wireless. *Titanic* bore the most powerful set of her day. Moreover, recently defined shipping lanes in the North Atlantic diminished the possibility of collision with opposing craft. Disasters were uncommon. Should disaster befall one, it was universally accepted, due to the sheer number of ships traversing the Atlantic, that there were plenty of others in the vicinity able to provide assistance. Ismay genuinely believed Carlisle's notion to install more lifeboats on *Titanic* wholly unnecessary, and equipped *Titanic* with twenty lifeboats – sixteen provisioned with a compass, tow-rope and packet of long-lasting biscuits. With the Merchant Shipping Act requiring that all vessels grossing over 10,000 tons carry a minimum of sixteen sets of boats, operatively so 'under davits', Ismay rejected Carlisle's recommendations and met the British Board's requirements by installing the minimum number the law required *Titanic* to carry: sixteen. Ismay installed the four Engelhardts in concession since *Titanic* already exceeded the mandatory amount for Rule D of the Act to apply.

Following the loss of *Titanic*, Ismay would deny all knowledge of his impasse with Carlisle and twice dismissing proposals to stow multiple boats per davit. But in its wake the official responsible for advising the British government on regulations for lifeboats and with the power to increase its controversial cap was called to Mersey's court to state the case for the Board of Trade.

Sir Alfred John Chalmers was the professional advisor to the Marine Department of the Board of Trade between 1896 and his retirement in August 1911, services for which he was knighted. Prior to joining the Board in 1877 Sir Alfred had spent sixteen years in the merchant service and was approached in 1904 by Sir Walter Jack Howell, chief of the Marine Department, to consider revising the boat scale of the contentious Act of 1894.

Sir Alfred more than appreciated that existing regulations had grown antiquated at the turn of the twentieth century, but he too believed safety at sea had already made exponential improvements without government meddling with the Rules. Seeing no desire to revise them he advised Sir Walter of a host of reasons opposing any increase to the cap. Chiefly, safety had improved across an assortment of areas. Hulls, particularly post-1880 with the transition from tall ships to iron steamships, had become more durable, bulkheads too. The introduction of defined shipping lanes had not only reduced the likelihood of collision but avoided regions notorious for ice and fog. Wireless radio was also growing in use. But most crucial of all, year-upon-year fatalities on Atlantic routes was consistently falling and the quantity of lifeboats carried at sea increasing voluntarily. Sir Alfred was adamant shipping operators 'should not be interfered with' by imposing on them further regulations or impulsive modifications to existing requirements. Raising the tonnage limit, he argued, may even reverse the improvements already made by the shipping industry advancing the durability of their fleets and the quantity of lifeboats carried by them without the need of state intervention. Steamers rarely, if fever, carried their full complement of passengers anyway – throughout 1911 *Olympic* was only booked at half capacity herself. Sir Alfred preferred to allow operators to deal with the matter themselves, feeling them burdened with far too much red-tape to contend with already.

The guiding principle for Sir Alfred's reticence to legislate for more lifeboats would also, he predicted, impose logistical nightmares upon the operators. Believing that sixteen lifeboats, the upper limit required under existing rules, was the most even the largest ships could safely stow and deploy during an emergency, Sir Alfred harboured concern that revising the regulations would adversely encumber decks

if laden with too many boats. Carrying more, he reasoned, ran the risk of potentially impeding evacuation. Any extra boat not nested within its own set of davits
would, he argued, need to wait for and then be heaved into a vacant set. In consequence, not all boats aboard could be lowered swiftly which would thereby
heighten panic because the crew would have to perform this additional task – an
extra burden. Calculating that each lifeboat would require at least three crewmembers to operate, increasing their number would require additional seamen
trained and signed for the voyage under the sole pretext that they may be needed
to man one of these boats.

Defending the regulations to the hilt, during the British inquiry Sir Alfred
even impressed the point that *Titanic* herself carried too many lifeboats, contest-
ing that 'there would have been a probability of just as many [lives] saved' had
she fewer boats than the amount actually carried. It was an all too perfunctory
remark that hinged on the fact that only 705 (60 per cent) of the 1,178 lifeboat
seats available on *Titanic* were filled: 473 remained empty including 'two boats
being still on deck when the ship sank ... what would it have availed them to
have had boats to accommodate all on board?' Having fewer boats, he reasoned,
would have induced officers to ensure each was filled both with alacrity and
to capacity – achieving less in actuality even when blessed with an unch, characteristically flat sea. His logic, although strictly true, was entirely incidental: Sir
Alfred overlooked the fact that a supply of more boats would invariably allow the
escape of more occupants even with 40 per cent of seats remaining unfilled. If her
twenty lifeboats had been filled to capacity, pressed Sir Alfred, this would have
lessened the time to launch all the boats she carried. It was a standpoint on which
he pinned the traditional argument, going to the heart of the issue: watertight
compartmentalisation. If that was improved evacuation may not even be necessary in the first place.

The civil servant in charge of the Board of Trade between 1907 and 1919 was Sir
Hubert Llewellyn Smith, with Sir Alfred serving as chief advisor to Sir Hubert's
deputy, Marine Secretary Sir Walter Howell. Sir Walter too was an experienced
official who had tenured the position since 1899. However, he was himself dead
within ten months of the loss of *Titanic* while the Board's regulatory process was
undergoing its most significant overhaul for two decades.

The attitude of regulators, as well as the wider industry, was placated by vast
improvements in mortality at sea. The number of recorded deaths of passengers
travelling between North American and British ports aboard British-registered
vessels was not only low but consistently falling. Between 1892 and 1901 just
seventy-three deaths occurred among the 3.25 million passengers that crossed
the Atlantic; fatalities on British ships travelling those same routes falling to just
nine over the ensuing decade (1902–11). This declining trend was experienced
by other nations also. Indeed, the total number of deaths recorded on ships of
all nationalities traversing between Britain and North America between 1871

and 1881 was 822. Finally, of the 6 million passengers who journeyed across the Atlantic from 1901 to 1911 just fifty-seven of these were lost at sea. The industry was enjoying an impeccable record at a time when vessels were becoming larger and faster and with the stakes in safety growing furtively in tandem. Disaster loomed ever present, and with the loss of *Titanic* the Rules of 1894 were finally updated, at the expense of 1,523 lives.

Complacency in transportation ruled the day, dogged by bureaucratic lethargy unwilling to align governance to a rapidly evolving technology. Ensnared by a deceptively optimistic record of safety, owner and regulator cultivated a false confidence in their fleets' infallibility at sea. Their saving grace indeed being the bulkheads installed in *Titanic*. Affording crew the window to deploy all her main lifeboats, albeit in meagre supply, recent assessments have born testament to this bulkhead design and have proven it possible that the two hours and forty minutes *Titanic* took to succumb was sufficient time to fill all 1,178 seats available among her twenty lifeboats. Oh, the wonder of hindsight – a point that survivor Lawrence Beesley eulogised so eloquently in his own experience of the disaster:

> A few more boats, a few more planks of wood nailed together … and all those men and women whom the world can so ill afford to lose would be with us today, where there would be no mourning in thousands of homes which now are desolate, and these words need not have been written.

Overconfidence in sea travel spawned a contagion of arrogance between regulator and operator, crewmember to passenger. The process of evacuating and regulating *Titanic* exposed as a muddle, resulted in a needless loss of life for which no one had the temerity to accept responsibility.

CHAPTER 9

THE SILENT WITNESS

'I was not paying a great deal of attention to her.'

Captain Stanley Lord, 14 May 1912

An unremarkable vessel ploughing through an equally innocuous voyage saw within a single evening both it and its senior crew enter maritime lore and become the most contested aspect of the whole *Titanic* yarn. This is the story of the *Californian* and her unsuspecting encounter with the world's most famous ocean liner one fateful April evening.

Californian, an inconspicuous 447ft-long cargo carrier grossing a modest 6,223 tons, was launched in Dundee on 26 November 1901 by Caledon Shipbuilding as hull number 159. Operated by the Leyland Line, her maiden voyage began on 31 January 1902. Harking back to 1850, at the turn of the twentieth century Leyland had become the largest cargo haulier on the North Atlantic and because of its success was purchased by Morgan's IMM in 1902 for a highly respectable $11 million. Featuring as an integral part of IMM's strategy to conquer both North Atlantic freight and passenger markets, *Californian,* along with others from Leyland's fleet, were adapted to also provide accommodation for fee-paying passengers. Although primarily a cargo liner, by 1912 *Californian* was licensed to carry forty-seven passengers in addition to her crew of fifty-five.

Her commander, Stanley Lord, in the employ of Leyland since 1900, qualified as master in February 1901, having previously turned down a position with White Star. Gaining his Extra Master's Certificate a few months later, in 1906, aged twenty-eight, Lord received his first command – covering the illness of the regular master of Leyland's 5,608-ton *Antillian*. Receiving his own full-time captaincy straight afterwards, on 27 March 1911, the now thirty-five-year-old began his fourth stint as master: his auspicious posting on *Californian*. His twenty-eighth voyage as master would bring him infamy as the captain who stood idly by while *Titanic* sank. Even the notion of it proved sufficient to see him fired and his name tarnished for the remainder of his life; he dedicated his retirement to seeking ears

sympathetic to his version of events, even if to only afford him the slightest benefit of some insurmountable doubt. His efforts were in vain.

Departing berth 24 of Liverpool's Royal Albert Dock at 1.30a.m. 5 April 1912
Californian, its cargo of cotton, Stanley Lord and a crew of forty-seven, began a
roundtrip to Boston of what all believed to be just another humdrum winter's
Atlantic crossing.

Joining Lord on this particular voyage was a senior crew comprising: Chief
Officer George Stewart, Second Officer Herbert Stone, Third Officer Charles
Groves and twenty-year-old apprentice officer James Gibson. Because of the
shortage of coal resulting from the recently concluded miners' dispute, to conserve her fuel, cruising speed would be reduced from 13.5 knots to 11. Indeed,
the voyage progressed as any other until at 6.30p.m. on the 14th when crew
sighted three icebergs drifting closely by. At 7.30p.m. Lord radioed the sighting
to Captain Japha, his colleague on _Antillian_: 'Lat 42.3N Long 49.9W three large
bergs five miles to southward of us, regards, Lord.'

Californian had just one operator manning her wireless, twenty-year-old Cyril
Furmston Evans, who had qualified from the Marconi training school just six
months previously and was relatively fresh to the position. The radio call sign
assigned them was MWL. Evans had radioed Lord's message to a nearby ship,
Titanic, to have them forward the warning to _Antillian_. The limited range of the
wireless aboard _Californian_ required the message to be relayed, an accepted and
necessary practice at sea. Evans had been listening to the outbound traffic from
Titanic most of that evening and had sent Lord's message to _Titanic_ to take advantage of her more powerful signal. _Titanic_ obliged and Japha duly received his
message – replying again via _Titanic_: 'thanks for information, seen no ice.'

Californian, meanwhile, had been heading deeper into a 400-mile stretch of ice
which, by 8p.m., Lord noticed, had become discernibly denser. To support the
sole lookout in the crow's nest, Lord posted another to the Forecastle to watch
for ice. Then, at 10.18p.m., after sighting what he believed to be 'a brightening' –
light refraction from ice – Lord considered the risk too great to continue in the
dark and had _Californian_ pulled to a halt: 'one quarter, to half a mile, from the edge
of a low ice field'. At 10.21p.m. on the 14th he logged _Californian_ at a standstill.
Intending to allow her to drift until daybreak, Lord calculated their stopped position as 42°5'N, 50°7'W, 124 miles further west of the previous reading that noon.
As a safeguard Lord asked Mr Mahan, his chief engineer 'to keep the main-steam
handy' in the ship's two boilers throughout the evening, maintaining pressure in
the engines to move her from harm's way should any ice drift undesirably close.

Californian was clearly not alone in the bustling North Atlantic shipping lanes
and Lord had inadvertently brought his ship to a halt within a few miles of the
stricken _Titanic_. The events of that evening are detailed here, taken from the
words of its own crew gleaned from the testimonies presented soon afterwards
at the British court of inquiry. They detail a chain of events that would turn the

captain and crew of *Californian* into the scapegoats for the unprecedented loss of life incurred by the *Titanic* disaster.

The evening continued.

With *Californian* at a standstill, at around 11p.m. to his south-east, Captain Lord presently identified a light 'approaching me from the eastward', from what he believed to be a steamer bearing 'one masthead light'. Soon afterwards he then 'saw a green light' – a starboard bridge sidelight. Heading from that direction was indeed *Titanic*: the bearing of the two ships pointing the starboard and the mast-lights of *Titanic* toward the south-east horizon and starboard quarter of *Californian*. As the minutes passed, the presence of this ship drew the attention of Lord and his crew:

[Question 6729] 'Did you see any deck lights?' asked the Attorney-General. 'A few,' answered Lord.

[6730] 'It was sufficiently close for that?' – 'Oh yes, she was getting closer all the time.'

[6761] 'At what distance do you think she was from you when you could see the lights?' – 'About five miles.'

At that moment Lord had no indication that the ship to the south-west was in any form of distress. Indeed, at that time *Titanic* was not. Her first CQD was not transmitted until 12.15a.m. However, Lord and his crew were aware *Titanic* was with them in the vicinity. On seeing the lights from the ship to their south-east Lord visited Evans in the wireless shack to enquire which vessels he had contacted that evening. Recalling the messages exchanging the ice warning to *Antillian*, Evans replied: 'I think the *Titanic* is near us, I have got [in contact with] her.' Yet Lord remained convinced the lights he had seen came from 'a medium size steamer' or cargo vessel since it was insufficiently lit in his view to be a passenger liner, particularly one of any real size like *Titanic*. Lord requested Evans 'let the *Titanic* know we are stopped and surrounded by ice', which at 10.55p.m. Evans does.

The man commanding the watch on *Californian* since 8p.m. that evening was Lord's third officer, Charles Groves. At 11.25p.m. Groves had also spotted 'two white masthead lights' of a ship 'about 10 or 12 miles away', emerging from the south-east. He informed the captain of the sighting who asked if Groves could 'make anything out of her lights?' Groves replied, 'She is evidently a passenger steamer', because it emanated 'a lot of light. There was absolutely no doubt her being a passenger steamer,' he insisted. Confused which type the distant ship was, Lord had Groves 'Call her up on the Morse Lamp' to ask her to identify herself. Groves does so at 11.30p.m., sending the standard request: 'what'. He received no reply. While he was signalling Captain Lord returned to the bridge, Groves pointing the distant ship out to him as he arrived.

As Lord peered in its direction he found the same dull lights that he had seen previously, reiterating, 'That does not look like a passenger steamer', since to him it was too poorly lit, like a cargo ship. Groves, however, stood by his observation: 'It is, sir. When she stopped her lights seemed to go out.'

The time this conversation took place was 11.40p.m., the very moment *Titanic* was turning to port to avoid the iceberg. At the British inquiry Groves recounted why he was so adamant of the precise time the lights seemed to disappear suddenly from this remote craft:

[8217] 'Because that is the time we struck one bell to call the Middle watch' [midnight to 4am].
[8218] 'Do you remember that bell was struck at the time?' – 'Most certainly,' asserts Groves.

Groves was not overtly concerned, however. He believed the distant ship had stopped and extinguished its lights for the night, a similar practice observed on his previous posting where it 'was the custom to put all the deck lights out' around midnight. Adding, 'when I saw the ice I came to the conclusion that she had starboarded to escape some ice'. Still the perception of this distant ship being in danger had not occurred to Groves as he handed over the watch at midnight to the second officer, Herbert Stone. 'She is a passenger steamer,' Groves pointed out as he departed the bridge at 12.08a.m.

Shortly afterwards Stone, the new watch commander, was also drawn to the mystery steamer's lights: 'One masthead light, and a red side light [port bridge light] and two or three small indistinct lights … approximately about five miles' to the south-east. Joining Stone on the watch that midnight was Gibson, the apprentice officer, who too noticed this 'glare of lights', as well as a red port light and flickering mast-light, 'four to seven miles' away when examining it with binoculars. At 12.12a.m. Gibson attempted to contact it by Morse Lamp, to no avail.

Captain Lord retired for the night at 12.15a.m., choosing to bed down fully clothed on the Chart Room sofa, directly beneath the wheelhouse. Opting for the Chart Room instead of the warmth and bed of his own cabin next door is a seemingly odd decision considering the bitter evening. But Lord had done this to keep himself close at hand should his ship, adrift in the busy shipping lane and precarious ice field, come suddenly into trouble.

Evans had sent Lord's message to *Titanic* at 10.55p.m., the only other ship he knew within the locality. The message was to inform her *Californian* was 'stopped and surrounded by ice'. Unfortunately while sending this message Evans had interrupted a transmission from Jack Phillips, his Marconi opposite on *Titanic*. Phillips had spent a long day at the transmission key, clearing his tedious backlog of passenger messages. It had been a particularly demanding day for Phillips. His wireless had been bought down earlier by a malfunction and by the time he and his colleague Harold Bride managed to have the set running again the messages had mounted up. Taking advantage of a strong signal with Cape Race, Phillips was working vigorously through his pile of messages. Frustrated with the interruption he famously interposed Evans' transmission: 'Keep out, Shut up. I am busy. I am working Cape Race'. Already receiving an ice warning from *Californian* at 7.30 that evening, Phillips was vexed to receive a similar message from the same ship just a couple of hours later.

The famous 'shut up' portion of Phillip's reproach was not transmitted literally but as 'DDD' – Marconi shorthand for an abrupt request for other users to keep the sender's airwaves free. Being the ship's only operator, Evans had likewise endured a long day. On duty since 7a.m., upon seeing the clock approach midnight Evans decided to turn off his wireless and go to bed, shortly after his rebuff from *Titanic*. At 11.35p.m. the ears of *Californian* were deaf.

At 12.15a.m., on returning to his cabin after completing his watch, Third Officer Groves decided to call by the wireless room. Groves was an amateur wireless enthusiast and partial to listening to Evans' set, but as he walked into the darkened room he found Evans in bed, almost asleep. Groves quickly enquired, with which ships had he been in contact? Evans drearily responded: 'Only the *Titanic*, you know, the new boat on its maiden voyage.' Evans slipped off to sleep, but Groves sat quietly down at the wireless and donned the earphones. Evans, now unaware of Groves, was unable to inform him that the clockwork drive for the set's magnetic signal detector needed winding. Groves, too inexperienced to realise this himself, was unable to tune it. Not wishing to disturb Evans again, he slipped quietly out of the shack and on to his own cabin. Had Groves managed to tune the set he would have been one of the first to hear *Titanic* transmit her calls for help.

Elsewhere on ship, Ernest Gill, an assistant donkeyman (a mechanic maintaining a type of coal-injection engine so named due to its nodding motion), had just completed a torrid four-hour shift in the engine room. Stepping out on deck at 12.35a.m. to savour a quiet cigarette in the still and cool evening air, Gill soon noticed a light from a ship 'too large' to 'have been anything but a passenger boat'. Estimating it 'not more than 10 miles' away, after lingering for about ten minutes he saw a white rocket explode above it, followed eight minutes later by another. Although he was convinced that the vessel was in some form of distress, Gill simply turned to his bunk, believing he 'had no business to report' what he had just seen, and assuming that someone on the bridge had seen the rockets also.

The rockets supplied to *Titanic* were intended to propel, like a firework, to a height of 800ft then explode into several small bright-white stars. However, these exploded too low to be effective over a particularly wide area. To those aboard *Californian* their luminescence would appear only to reach the height of the distant ship's mast-light, or at best masquerade as low-level twinkling stars.

The crew of *Californian* would later report these rockets made no sound as they exploded. This would indeed be true. There was no wind in that area of the Atlantic that evening, muting sound which would have otherwise carried further under normal conditions. Had the sound of their explosions even reached

Californian, distance would have left them barely discernible. Despite being at a standstill in a flat calm, the noise of *Californian* creaking and the ice tapping against her hull was enough on its own to disguise any sound made by distant explosions.

Donkeyman Gill may have neglected his duty by not informing the bridge, but he had assumed correctly. Stone, alone in the wheelhouse, had seen the rockets too. Both were witness to the first of a series of eight launched by Fourth Officer Boxhall to signal the distress of *Titanic*. Launching the first from a socket mortar tube at 12.45a.m., he fired seven other rockets each separated by eight-minute (comparatively long) intervals.

Believing that the rockets had been fired from the same ship he had observed to the east, Stone would later protest that they had not originated from *Titanic* but from another ship further in the distance. On seeing the first rocket spewing its white stars so low on the horizon his first thought was that 'it might be a shooting star'. Appearing well behind the ship bearing the lights, he assumed that even if the apparition had indeed been a rocket its source was from another craft further distant out of sight. He continued to look on, seeing four more 'white rockets bursting in the sky'. At 1.15a.m., using the speaking tube, he reported the event to the captain.

Lord, awoken, sought principally to determine from Stone if the rocket was 'a company's signal'. Uncertain, Stone began speculating: 'Possibly she was signalling to us to tell us she had big icebergs around her,' adding, 'they possibly might have been distress signals' or 'possibly they might have come from another ship'. Lying restively on the Chart Room sofa Lord tells Stone to 'go on Morsing' the ship in the distance and ask it what the rockets meant.

Stone was uncertain of the purpose of the rockets. He believed white was not the usual colour customarily employed as distress signals at sea, subsequently dismissing any significance to their meaning, later maintaining: 'I just thought they were white rockets, that is all.' But following his conversation with Lord, Stone had Gibson – who was on the quartermaster's deck below the wheelhouse readying the Patent Log – return to the bridge and attempt to raise the ship by Morse Lamp as requested. Stone and Gibson attempted in vain on three occasions to contact the ship, the two consequently deducing the lights as private company signals – launched either to warn of icebergs in that area or for some other inexplicable reason such as a celebration.

By 1.20a.m. Stone had counted eight rockets: the precise number fired by Boxhall from *Titanic*. Stone and Gibson then conversed about the distant ship. Stone remarked it 'looks very queer, out of water' and 'that the lights looked peculiar, unnatural' as if it were 'porting for some iceberg close at hand and was coming back on her course again, showing her other lights, the original light'. Gibson corroborated: 'her lights seemed to be higher out of the water'. Stone suppositioned, 'a ship was not going to fire rockets at sea for nothing' and at 2a.m. sent Gibson below to wake the captain and 'tell him that altogether we had seen eight of these white lights like white rockets in the direction of this other steamer'. Gibson and Lord discuss the rockets' colour and again put conjecture as to their meaning, yet Lord remained on the sofa – denying at the British inquiry that his discourse with Gibson had ever taken place.

The bridge of *Californian* elevated its occupants 49ft above sea level, putting the range of its viewing horizon at 8 miles under clear conditions. That on *Titanic* was 60ft above sea level, affording its crew in clear conditions a horizon of 9.8 miles. Whatever lights Lord, Stone, Groves and Gibson had seen must therefore have fallen within the 8-mile viewing horizon of *Californian*. The rockets exploding 800ft in the sky would naturally increase this range, although not significantly. Was this incontrovertible proof that *Californian* was in close proximity and observing the dying moments of *Titanic*?

The crew aboard *Californian* were not the only witnesses to lights this evening. To the despair and frustration of those stranded aboard *Titanic*, they too saw lights from a nearby ship, or something they to be believed a ship. Did these sightings confirm that *Titanic* and *Californian* were close enough to see each other? Prayers for a miracle rescue seemed answered as some aboard *Titanic* watched the flickering of lights seemingly from a ship tantalisingly close and ostensibly able to assist:

[15401] 'I saw her green light and the red. She was end-on to us. Afterwards I saw the ship's red light ... and the two masthead lights. I judged her to be, a four-masted steamer,' Fifth Officer Boxhall would recall at the British inquiry. [15394] 'I was sending rockets off and watching this steamer.'

Boxhall had sighted the two white mast-lights of a steamer 22.5 degrees off the port bow of *Titanic* and attempted to raise contact by Morse Lamp towards the source, receiving no reply.

[15409] 'I judged her to be between 5 and 6 miles when I Morsed to her, and then she turned round, she was turning very, very slowly until at last I only saw her stern light.'

Third Officer Pitman too saw what he thought was a stern light of a ship in the distance:

[15061] 'I saw a white light which I took to be the stern light of a sailing ship.' [15062] 'How far away did you judge it to be?' – 'about five miles.' [15064] 'Was it a good night for seeing a light?' – 'An excellent night.'

These were joined by an abundance of corroborating sightings aboard *Titanic*. Second Officer Lightoller, having ordered Robert Hichens whom he placed in charge of lifeboat 6, 'pull for that light ... steer for that light' [1161] he had seen 'about two points on the port bow, about five miles away' [1162], but 'the light was moving, gradually disappearing' [1183].

'I could see a steamer's lights a couple of miles away on our port bow. If I could get the women and children into the boats, they would be perfectly safe in that smooth sea until the other ship picked them up,' recalled a convinced Lightoller in 1935.

Frederick Fleet, also in boat 6, was also instructed by Lightoller to row for the bright light seen from the ship's portside. They did so, but it eluded them:

[17428] 'There was a light on the port bow.'
[17429] 'Did you see this light on the port bow before you left the crow's nest?'
– 'No, it must have been about 1 o'clock.'
[US inquiry] 'We pulled for it, but we did not seem to get any nearer to it.'

George Symons, in charge of lifeboat 1, spotted a stern light on a ship believed to be moving westwards, and directed the boat towards it:

[11468] 'that steamer's light was in sight about a point and-a-half on the port bow, roughly between five and ten miles away when they fired the rockets.'
[11712] 'We were rowing for the light.'

From the Boat Deck, Captain Smith had Able Seaman Thomas Jones, placed in charge of lifeboat 8, 'row for the light and land the passengers and return to the ship … I could not get near … that was the light everybody saw in the distance' [US inquiry].

Other survivors would sight these distant lights and believe them to be from a ship travelling towards them. Thinking rescue was at hand, boat 8 pulled continuously towards this light but was unable to reach it – making the furthest endeavour to reach the source. Jones would recall, 'I had to carry out the captain's orders and pull for the light; so I did so.' Only at dawn did he turn the boat round and join the remaining flotilla.

Walter Wynn, in charge of lifeboat 9, saw in the distance 'a red light first, and then the red light disappeared, and I saw a white one' [13337]. All were convinced this ship in the distance was coming to their aid. A total of sixteen witness accounts described the movements of one unidentifiable ship nearby; 'something' evidentially was out there.

Prior to stopping for the night *Californian* had been following a westbound heading of S89°W. At a standstill since 10.21p.m. on the 14th, her bow was left facing east-north-east. Throughout the course of the evening the current would slowly swing her bow 225 degrees clockwise – a rotation no faster than half a knot. By 1.15a.m., although now pointing west-south-west, the crew, disoriented, would believe her bow was still facing its original horizon. To the crew on *Californian* the rockets would always appear to the south and this unidentified ship in the distance would seem to be travelling eastward, when in fact they were not. Believing also that the lights seen after 1a.m. were stern lights, the crew falsely deduced that the ship in the distance was heading safely away.

Abruptly, at 2.20a.m. Stone and Gibson noticed the lights from the distant ship had vanished. This was the exact time that *Titanic* sank. Stone and Gibson, convinced it had merely slinked out of view, at 2.40a.m. once more called the captain on the speaking tube to inform him the mystery ship had disappeared. Again, Lord denied having this conversation, maintaining that he slept peacefully until woken by his chief officer at 4.30a.m. No one aboard *Californian* later refuted they had seen any rockets – they were simply confused by their purpose. They had tried on several occasions to contact this ship by Morse Lamp. But instead of waking Evans, their sole wireless operator, and have him raise contact and enquire what the rockets meant, the watch left him unstirred till sunrise.

When, at 4a.m., Chief Officer George Stewart took over the watch from Stone he was informed of the night's events. Stewart picked up the binoculars and presently sighted 'a steamer to the southward' in the same direction that Stone had seen the ship firing the rockets. Asking if this ship was the source of the rockets Stone confirmed that it was. Stewart then sent for Captain Lord at 4.30a.m. to tell him of the rockets discovered earlier by Stone. Lord arrived on the bridge and informed Stewart that he already knew of the sightings. Lord too located the distant ship and assumed, as Stewart had, that this was the same craft that Stone had identified as the source of the rockets. The captain, dismissing any doubt of its wellbeing, proclaimed, 'She looks all right, she is not making any signals now'. However, this ship sighted by Lord and Stewart was in fact *Carpathia* racing to rescue the survivors from *Titanic* adrift in her lifeboats. Lord sent Stewart to wake Evans and check the airwaves to ascertain if 'there is anything the matter'.

Evans 'took up the phones at once', tuning in his set at 5.40a.m., and was greeted with a terse message from *Mount Temple*: 'Do you know the *Titanic* has struck an iceberg and she is sinking?' It had still not dawned on the crew that, during the night, they might well have casually witnessed a disaster unfold beneath their very noses. Interestingly, when Evans received notice of the sinking, Captain Lord then set course for the CQD given to them by *Virginian*, not to the spot at which the ship firing rockets in the distance had been observed by his crew just hours earlier. Lord was absolutely convinced the ship he and his crew had seen that evening was not the one that had signalled its distress.

Later, upon later arriving at the CQD, they joined the search for wreckage, finding *Carpathia* 6 miles to their distance taking aboard the final survivors from the lifeboats: 'Arrived scene of *Titanic* disaster half-past eight AM 15th. All survivors then aboard the *Carpathia*. Have not and did not see any survivors,' radioed Captain Lord to an expectant media on 18 April – believing their interest in him was to end there.

Finding only a small amount of drift wreckage and six empty lifeboats abandoned by *Carpathia*, at 11.20a.m. *Californian* resumed the remaining 1,000-mile leg of her journey to Boston. Heavy, lingering fog cast a veil over *Californian* and the closing stages of her journey, which terminated 4a.m. on the 19th at Leyland's Clyde Street pier. Meanwhile, a revelation had come to light. If *Californian* was close enough to see the deck lights of *Titanic* as well as her distress rockets, could she have been within easy reach of rescuing everyone trapped on board? Instead it was *Carpathia* – travelling 58 miles from the south-east – that facilitated a rescue – albeit too late for 1,500 souls in their hour of desperate need. Recriminations focussed on the Leyland crew; had *Californian* been an idle bystander at the most emotive maritime disaster of modern times?

Strangers in their Midst

The sightings from *Californian* undoubtedly intimate that her crew had seen a nearby ship approach, pull to a stop and fire several white rockets. Yet the descriptions of their sightings diverge from a craft bearing one mast-light (Lord), two mast-lights (Stone), and being brilliantly (Groves), or poorly lit (Lord).

At the British inquiry Second Officer Stone would remind the court 'a steamer that is in distress does not steam away from you'. Indeed so. However, were Lord and his men steadfast liars, or did they genuinely believe the ship in the distance was really under no form of distress, or were they actually describing more than one ship? Until his dying day Captain Lord would strenuously attest that the vessel observed by both him and his crew was not *Titanic* but another nestling between them, with the true *Titanic* firing rockets beyond this nearer unidentified craft. The plausibility of this gave rise to speculation about a mysterious 'third ship' traversing the vicinity that evening.

Lord maintained his rationale to not wake his wireless operator hinged on the basis that Evans had specifically named the one ship he had been in contact with that evening as *Titanic*. In a written statement dated 25 June 1959 Stanley Lord insisted the lights seen in the distance were from a 'vessel of no great size', certainly one neither portly nor bright enough to mistake for the largest steamer in the world. He recalled remarking to Evans that this nearby ship 'isn't the *Titanic*'. With Evans that evening able only to contact one ship – *Titanic* – Lord deduced that the craft he had seen appear from the south-east must therefore bear no radio, for surely Evans would otherwise have been able to contact it, mentally eliminating *Titanic* thenceforth as the candidate for the distant ship.

With wireless inactive Lord's crew were left that evening with just one method with which to communicate with this unidentified ship – the Morse Lamp. With it they attempted on three occasions to raise contact, all to no avail. When learning later of a rocket fired from that same ship Lord 'thought it was acknowledging our signals [from] our Morse Lamp'. Testifying in court to what he believed the rockets denoted, he deduced that the ship must be 'communicating with some other steamer at greater distance to ourselves' and attributed the observations as those of a different ship with another far out of view firing rockets beyond it. To Second Officer Stone these rockets appeared to reach 'only about half the height of the steamer's masthead light … I thought rockets would go much higher than that'. If there was indeed a third ship between *Californian* and *Titanic*, who could this mystery interloper have been?

The Senatorial inquest would hear Captain Lord testify: 'at daylight we saw a yellow-funnel steamer on the south-west of us', a sighting he reiterated at the subsequent British investigation. A ship named *Mount Temple* soon found its name pulled into the fray. Apart from *Californian* she was logged second nearest the CQD position at the time the distress signals were broadcast that evening.

The main distinguishing characteristics of *Mount Temple* were her four masts and single funnel painted in the company colours: yellow, topped by a black soot rim. Was this the mysterious 'third' ship?

The 8,790-ton *Mount Temple*, operated since 1903 by the Canadian Pacific Line as an emigrant transport, was on this particular crossing under the command of fifty-one-year-old James Henry Moore. Laden with 1,609 passengers and crew she departed Antwerp on the 3rd, westbound for St John, New Brunswick. At 12.11a.m. her Marconi operator, John Durrant, received the CQD from *Titanic*. He relayed it instantly to the captain who, after a quick calculation, charted the position of *Mount Temple* at 41°25'N, 51°14'W, 49 miles to its south-west, placing his ship second nearest to the distress location of *Titanic* (41°46'N, 50°14'W).

Course set to N65°E, the ship headed to the CQD at 11.5 knots. Increasing the lookouts to two, *Mount Temple*, encountering a dense ice field, was brought to a stop at 3.25a.m., 14 miles from the CQD. It was shortly before then that Moore had noticed what he believed to be a 'green light of a sailing vessel' to the north-west, just 1 mile from his port bow. Could this light have come from the same craft that had been stirring interest aboard *Californian*? If it was then Stanley Lord's name could be cleared.

Captain Moore had spotted the craft shortly after 3a.m. and although unable to determine its size he attributed it as being akin to a schooner. Almost simultaneously he then sighted another ship, this time a steamer, a tramp, heading east and bearing a black funnel. *Mount Temple* arrived at the CQD position at 4.30a.m. and again saw the tramp nearby. Pulled alongside *Californian* at 7.30a.m., the crew joined the search for survivors. Finding nothing, at 9a.m. Moore resumed the voyage to St John where *Mount Temple* docked on the 19th, met by a sole reporter. By then the candidates for this mysterious ship had increased still. The name *Almerian*, for one, was thrown into the ring.

Almerian, a fellow Leyland hauler of 2,984 tons, had left Mobile, Alabama, at 10a.m. on 3 April under the command of Captain Richard Thomas. Her single

284hp engine, able to muster only 11 knots, found *Almerian* by the 15th still just a third of the way into her long trudge to Liverpool. Thomas' course intended to take her, at best, within 80 miles of the area in which *Titanic* struck the iceberg. *Almerian*, however, was not equipped with a wireless, and her crew was consequently unaware of the disaster until making port on the 25th. Conceivably straying north and toward the CQD position to skirt the western edge of the 2-mile-wide ice barrier that had brought *Californian* to a halt on its eastern edge that same evening, eastbound *Almerian* was soon accompanied on the western face of the barrier by *Mount Temple*. Thomas, bringing his ship to a halt at 3a.m. to await daybreak before negotiating the ice field logged through dead reckoning this position as 41°20'N, 50°24'W. Discovering shortly that a nearby ship had likewise pulled to a standstill because of ice they signalled it by Morse Lamp – receiving a reply, albeit partial: 'ount'. Resuming the journey at sunrise, Thomas pulled close enough to read its nameplates, *Mount Temple*. Clearing the field by 10.30a.m., *Almerian* continued east – sighting then a four-masted steamer (*Carpathia* collecting the lifeboats) – still unaware of the tragedy that had taken place nearby.

Aboard *Mount Temple* Captain Moore was adamant that the ship he spotted featured 'a black funnel with a white band'. Captain Lord, on the other hand, testified to two sightings at 7.30a.m. on the 15th: *Mount Temple*, followed by a 'two-masted steamer [bearing a] pink funnel [and] black top' – insinuating that a fellow Leyland liner was in this locale.

Like *Californian*, *Almerian* too was operated by the Leyland Line: their funnel livery was salmon pink, with the top quarter sheathed by a black soot rim and no white markings whatsoever. Although adorning a different-coloured funnel to that seen on the vessel sighted by Captain Moore, *Almerian* (sporting two masts) was nevertheless named in Lord's statement of 1959 as the ship he had seen at 7.30a.m. on the 15th bearing the pink funnel – *Californian*, which by time was through the western extent of the ice barrier. With Lord seemingly positive in his identification of both *Mount Temple* and *Almerian*, what then of Moore's sighting of the tramp sporting the black and white funnel?

Speculation about the owner of this funnel soon focussed on *Saturnia*, an 8,611-ton passenger steamer belonging to the Anchor-Donaldson Line, a company whose funnel livery was indeed totally black save for a white band encircling its upper third. *Saturnia* was westbound from Glasgow to St John, New Brunswick, when receiving the distress call from *Titanic* at 1a.m. Turning straight for the CQD, her master, Captain Taylor, even managed to get her within 6 miles of it by 4.30a.m. However, after sighting a vast quantity of icebergs Taylor believed that the risk too great to continue, pulling his ship to a standstill at the eastern rim of the barrier; *Mount Temple* lodged on its opposite border.

Another name embroiled in the intrigue, albeit hastily eliminated, was *Trautenfels*, a 2,932-ton petroleum tanker operated by the Hansa Line of Bremen. Headed westward from Hamburg to Boston under Captain Hupers, *Trautenfels* sported two masts and one funnel – painted in the company livery: black, with white band bordered by two red rings. On 14 April Hupers had radioed a warning reporting 'heavy field ice for 30 miles' on sighting two '200ft' icebergs at 42°01'N, 49°53'W at 5.05a.m. Rerouting his ship 25 miles further to the southwest *Trautenfels* cleared this region at 8a.m. that day, arriving in Boston on the 18th. The whereabouts of *Saturnia*, on the other hand, remained less clear. All that is known is that she was on the same eastern edge of the barrier as *Titanic* and *Californian* during the time of the collision. Within 6 miles of the CQD by 4.30a.m., *Saturnia* was, however, much further to the east and beyond viewing range of *Titanic* and *Californian* when the distress flares were fired. None of her passengers or crew reported any flares that evening, and her black and white livery also failed to fit Lord's description of the ship bearing the pink funnel.

It was all too much scrabbling in the dark for the Board of Trade's liking, and they dismissed derisively Lord's suggestion of *Mount Temple* as the mystery ship. 'It would have been utterly impossible for the *Mount Temple* at any time while the *Californian* had in sight the vessel she saw sending up rockets, to have been between the *Californian* and that vessel,' scathed the Board's lawyer, Sir Robert Ellis Cunliffe, on 6 November 1912, meeting Lord's attempt to deflect attention onto Captain Moore with utmost incredulity to even 'suggest that someone else may also have been guilty of conduct that was blameworthy'.

Our search for the mystery lights, however, must not cease there. The final and most intriguing suspect worthy of examination as their source is Saefaenger Company's *Samson*. A small wooden Norwegian sail-craft dating from 1885, *Samson* grossed a modest 506 tons and, measuring 148ft in length, was able to muster a pedestrian rate of only 7 knots. Unequipped with wireless and under the command of Captain Carl Johann Ring, this decrepit craft was illegally hunting seals off the Canadian coast. In 1912 *Samson* was not a strong candidate as the third ship but in 1962 a startling revelation from her former chief officer, Henrik Naess, saw her name shoot to the fore. Naess was belatedly admitting that he too had seen white distress rockets on the evening of the disaster, although at the time he construed them as instructions from the coastguard for *Samson* to come alongside for investigation.

The confession hints that *Samson* gave *Titanic* the slip that evening and this is why its crew kept their silence until Naess' crisis of conscience half a century later. Unfortunately for Lord she proved a red herring. Although Isafjördur Harbour record *Samson* departing and returning to the Icelandic port on 6 and 20 April, sheer distance proved it highly improbable for *Samson* to have been anywhere near *Titanic* and *Californian* by the 15th. Doing so would have required the dilapidated sail-powered relic to assail 3,000 miles in fourteen days, an unlikely feat considering the craft's meandering 7-knot ability. Naess' potential benefit to Lord's claim was to waiver further under scrutiny of the detail. Because of its illegal activity Naess confirmed all lights on *Samson* had been doused so not to draw attention, inadvertently ruling out the possibility of these being the deck lights seen by either *Californian* or *Mount Temple* – even if by chance *Samson* was within the locality at that precise moment.

Moore, who in his deposition at the Senatorial inquiry placed much emphasis on his schooner sighting, would at the British hearings markedly minimise its significance in his account. The captain's inconsistency and contradiction between the two hearings betrayed Moore's fears of risking his own reputation falling foul to an opinion that was already tarnishing Captain Lord. Luckily for Moore his testimony was largely overlooked, to Lord's detriment.

The true identity of the 'mystery ship' is of course unanswerable. However the possibility of there being one cannot be easily discounted. A total of twenty-five ships were known to be within the general locale of *Titanic* at the time on the evening of her CQD, highlighting the fact that the North Atlantic teemed with traffic. Harbour records also indicate that there were at least thirty-six vessels accompanying *Titanic* on the North Atlantic at the time of her collision – of these, eight belonged to Morgan's combine. That is, if the ship between *Californian* and *Titanic* existed at all. It was, if anything, an intriguing conspiracy to fill newspaper columns in hot pursuit of attention-grabbing headlines unravelling this unprecedented calamity concerning the world's safest and most lauded craft. The debatable potential rescue by *Californian* remains even today the haziest aspect of the *Titanic* saga. Tired of the 'contradictions and inconsistencies' in the testimonies of Stanley Lord and his crew, inquiry chairman Lord Mersey would deliver them his damming and forever-lasting verdict: 'the truth of the matter is plain … the ship seen by the *Californian* was the *Titanic* … not more than eight to ten miles … apart at the time of the disaster'. Yet, despite any assertion to the contrary, the myth of the 'third ship' refuses to fade away.

Unfinished Business

The British investigation examining the loss of *Titanic* would declare, somewhat vindictively, that 'not more than eight to ten miles' of water separated *Titanic* from *Californian*. It was a crucial assertion from the report's author, Lord Mersey, undoubtedly quick to apportion the lion's share of blame for the disaster on shoulders outside of Government. His barbed indictment of Captain Lord had no bounds:

> When she first saw the rockets the *Californian* could have pushed through the ice to the open water without any risk and so have come to the assistance of the *Titanic*. Had she done she might have saved many if not all of the lives that were lost.

Ruling out the 'third ship' theory the British establishment had found its scapegoat in the guise of Stanley Lord. Attributing in all but name the loss of 1,500 lives to the inactions of the *Californian*, the stale regulations of the British Board of Trade were not the ones remiss. Lord Mersey was steadfast – *Californian* was close enough to have rendered assistance to *Titanic*.

When stopped for the night at 10.21p.m. that fateful day, Captain Lord determined his position for the log by process of dead reckoning. The location he recorded was 42°5'N, 50°7'W, logging *Californian* 19.5 miles north of 41°46'N, 50°14'W; Boxhall's CQD – likewise arrived at by the imperfect art of dead reckoning. This distance was vehemently refuted by Lord: '19 miles away is not, in my opinion, where the *Titanic* hit the berg'. The British investigation heard Stanley Lord argue that the overnight position of *Californian* was instead '32 miles' to the north of the location where he discovered floating wreckage at 11.20a.m. the following morning: 41°33'N, 50°1'W. Lord noted the find as 'not a great deal' of wreckage, just 'several boats, deckchairs, cushions, planks', appearing more like drift wreckage than a field of debris marking the detritus of a major catastrophe just hours before. This, felt Lord, was clearly not a substantive enough marker for his detractors to base their case. Naturally, should Lord have wanted to reduce his exposure he would hope to place as much distance between *Californian* and *Titanic* as possible, unfortunately for him neither inquiry believed him.

The Senate inquiry put *Californian* a mere 5 miles from *Titanic*, the British court insisting the two were between 8 and 10 miles apart. The actual distance still remains hotly contested in countless peripheral investigations by government bodies, authors and judicious proponents of both camps who all place *Californian* anywhere between 5 and 32 miles away from the foundering position of *Titanic*. The nail in Lord's coffin came in the evidence presented at the Washington hearings by Captain John Knapp, deputy hydrographer for the US Navy. It remained a crucial obstacle for Lord's supporters to surmount:

> …a radius of 16 miles, which is approximately the farthest distance at which the curvature of the earth would have permitted the sidelights of the *Titanic* to be seen by a person at the height of the sidelights of the *Californian*.

In order for anyone aboard *Californian* to have seen the deck lights of *Titanic*, Knapp was convincing in setting the maximum range of visibility for the two ships at no further than 16 miles apart. His evidence established for *Californian* a 'hypothetical position', a midway location between this extremity and a 7-mile radius in which he calculated that anyone aboard *Titanic* could have seen the sidelights of *Californian*. Disparity still rages, and the true whereabouts of *Californian* in relation to *Titanic* will never be known; however, there are plenty of facts of which one can be certain.

When *Californian* finally arrived at the CQD position her crew were only in time to witness the occupants of the final lifeboat, number 12, clamber aboard the rescue ship *Carpathia*. *Californian* joined the search from 8.30a.m. until 11.20a.m., finding no bodies or survivors but a miniscule amount of floating debris.

Nothing concerning *Titanic* over 14 and 15 April was reported either by Lord or his officers in the logbook of *Californian*. Indeed, the log was neither altered nor had Lord intended to omit the events of that evening. He was doggedly convinced that the ship spotted firing rockets simply warranted no mention. To him it was just another matter of ships passing in a not so entirely unusual Western Ocean winter's evening.

When *Californian* arrived at Leyland's pier at Boston's Albany Docks at 7a.m. on 19 April only a handful of reporters were present; quite unlike the throng of tugboats filled with media surrounding *Carpathia* when it landed the survivors at New York the previous evening. At this time the press in Boston had wanted only to interview Lord since his ship had been mentioned as one of those first to arrive at the scene.

Once the gravity of his potential involvement in the disaster unfurled, on 18 April, Lord allegedly gathered statements from officers Stone and Gibson, instructing them to behave as nothing untoward had happened when ashore. Unfortunately for them Donkeyman Ernest Gill and his colleagues could not contain themselves. Gossip began filtering through Boston's dockside bars. Then, on the 20th, local newspaper *The Daily Item* exposed the revelation that the crew of *Californian* was close enough to see the distress rockets of *Titanic*. On the 24th Captain Lord was stating his case in his first newspaper interview. Headlines shimmied from praise: 'Leyland liner rushes to scene', to sordid condemnation: 'All might have been saved'. Rumours now placed Lord's ship just 5 miles from the scene of *Titanic*'s foundering. The naming and shaming of Stanley Lord had begun, literally 'in Ernest'.

Paid a handsome $500, Ernest Gill gave his exclusive written statement to the *Boston American* newspaper on 25 April, publishing his full, damning account of the rockets, sightings, and the fact that his captain 'refused to respond to her signals of distress … and refused to risk his ship by sending her through the ice at night to the rescue'. Unable to restrain himself, Gill candidly announced that 'no captain who refuses or neglects to give aid to a vessel in distress should be able to hush up the men'. The account proved unpalatable not only for Lord but also for Leyland's management, IMM – owners also of White Star Line.

Lord soon found himself heading to Capitol Hill to present evidence at an official inquiry, his first attempt in a lifelong battle to clear his name – harangued for making no endeavour to respond to a ship's mid-ocean distress and rescue those trapped aboard it. It was a grievous charge. Lord's ship was not only close enough to see the flares from *Titanic*, but it took no action. Robert Ballard, who would discover the wreck of *Titanic* in 1985, would in later years lament that the one task Lord needed to do was simply to ask his wireless operator to tune in the set once these rockets were first sighted. Had Evans done so he would have heard some fifty vessels responding to her distress calls. Instead, after the event, all Lord could do was fight his case, putting *Californian* distant enough to have rendered no use to the souls trapped aboard *Titanic*.

With many government papers dating up to 1914 summarily concealed from public scrutiny until their declassification in 1964, only then was it possible to scrutinise the record of events surrounding *Californian*. Public interest grew and the content of the unearthed files was to spark a fresh investigation.

The Merchant Shipping Act of 1970 empowered the secretary of state for transport to reopen cases whose original investigations had previously closed. On 20 June 1990 Cecil Parkinson MP, then transport secretary, finally commissioned a report to re-evaluate the matter concerning *Californian*. The research was tasked to the Southampton-based Marine Accidents Investigation Branch (MAIB), a unit created by the Department of Transport in 1989. The newly formed MAIB was in want of a case to rouse publicity and *Californian* was an expectantly con-troversial case study. Their investigation was the first formal study to assess her position in relation to *Titanic* since Ballard's discovery of the wreck. It was also the first occasion that the issue had been appraised using modern navigation equip-ment and satellite technology. The report, compiled by an inspector at the MAIB, Captain Thomas Barnett, was eventually filed on 12 March 1992 – one month shy of the eightieth anniversary of the disaster.

The report determined that *Titanic* had most likely struck the iceberg in posi-tion 41°47'N, 49°55'W, with her wreck coming to a rest at 41°43.6'N, 49°56.9'W, 13.5 miles north-east of Boxhall's CQD. It presumed the location of *Californian* at the time of collision as 41°49'N, 50°06'W, 13 miles closer to *Titanic* than origi-nally recorded by Captain Lord (42°05'N, 50°07'W); Barnett divining *Californian* between '17 and 20 miles' from her ultimate foundering position.

Captain Lord's estimation that he needed at least two hours to reach the CQD position became a point the MAIB reappraisal expended some effort to atone. The report made key summations in Lord's favour, widening the maximum possible viewing range by 'abnormal refraction permitting sight beyond the ordi-nary visible horizon' caused by air reacting to a cooler than normal temperature near the water surface allowing the crew of *Californian* to see *Titanic* beyond the 16-mile limit normally possible. Also giving credence to Lord's indifference to the urgency of the rockets, Naess' own admission had underlined an indicative view among seafarers that the use of flares at sea was all too common in 1912.

Although the report far from exonerated Stanley Lord, it concluded that had he responded immediately at the moment of the first CQD call no 'reasonably probable action by Captain Lord could have led to a different outcome to the tragedy', refuting Mersey's findings to the contrary. Lord, the reappraisal ascer-tained, would have been unable to rescue any more survivors than those already in the lifeboats, although it berated him for not making the effort. The establish-ment's case against Lord was finally showing signs of clemency.

In a letter written to his MP, dated 17 October 1912, Lord acknowledged: 'I admit there was a certain amount of slackness on board the *Californian* [during] the night in question.' Yet he was unable to answer why a rational man – who had served at sea since 1891 and as a captain since 1906 – was suddenly in 1912 purporting 'slackness'. By ignoring a succession of 'confusing rocket signals' Lord was not denying his crew had seen the flares but simply electing not to respond to them. Lord's apparent lassitude toward the ship firing these rockets in the middle of the Atlantic was rooted in the fact that he believed them to be 'company sig-nals' – ones that did not indicate distress. Indeed, to clarify such likely confusion, definitions and the appearance of distress signals were outlined in Article 31 of the internationally recognised code in force at the time of the disaster: 'Regulations for the Prevention of Collisions at Sea':

> When a vessel is in distress and requires assistance from other vessels or from the shore, the following shall be the signals used or displayed by her, either together or separately:
>
> At Night: Rocket or shells, throwing stars of any colour or description, fired one at a time, at short intervals.

The regulations were explicit: a 'rocket ... of any colour' fired at night denoted distress. Typically the reality proved more ambiguous as not all flares at sea were fired in distress. Shipping companies supplied them on their vessels to identify themselves with others at night. Wireless was still in its infancy. To distinguish these so called 'company' or 'private' signals from distress flares, the 1894 Merchant Shipping Act required every shipping operator register a full description of these non-emergency signals and detail the locations in which they were to be used so not to indicate the ship as being in any form of distress. The entry for White Star, registered on 20 November 1903, was as follows:

> Two green pyrotechnic lights exhibited simultaneously; used anywhere within the British jurisdiction and on the high seas.

Colour was used to identify the shipping line. To further differentiate rockets not signifying distress, company signals exploded into balls of light, often launched from Roman Candles. By virtue of the fact that they were not rocket-propelled these exploded at a much lower level and were thus intended for use within coastal waters.

Titanic was supplied with twelve white rockets, fired from a socket mortar offset to 20 degrees. In addition she carried thirty-six others in varying colours plus twelve blue Roman Candles. All manufactured by Cotton Powder Co. Ltd. of London, the main rockets were launched from a tube that propelled them high into the firmament before exploding into twelve balls of small luminous white stars: another example of White Star's penchant for corporate branding.

When informed of the first white rocket Captain Lord asked his second officer, Herbert Stone, to clarify what he had seen:

[6910] 'I asked the Second Officer … Is that a company's signal? And he said he did not know,' answered Lord.

[7846] 'What was she communicating?' – 'I do not know,' replied Stone.

[6912] 'It did not satisfy you that it was a company's signal?' – 'It did not, but I had no reason to think it was anything else.' returned Lord.

Stone's rationale to dismiss these as company signals was founded on the fact that they exploded too low on the horizon: 'only about half the height of the steamer's masthead light' – the type fired from Roman Candles, the norm for non-emergency signals. To him it indicated the source of the rockets was either further in the distance or from the nearby ship firing these low-level non-emergency signals. As for the deck lights, Lord had his hopes pinned on these being from an unidentified third ship lying between them and *Titanic*.

With both the captain and the officer in charge of the watch believing that the signals denoted something other than a distress signal, they kept the ship in the distance under observation, seeing no urgency to satisfy their curiosity or to enquire about its motive for discharging the rockets. Having 'no reason to think it was anything else', Lord returned to sleep on the Chart Room sofa; reasoning smarting in the face of diligence. His peers, intuitively knowing that rockets or flares launched at sea – regardless of colour – just may indicate distress, would certainly have argued against disregarding them. Captain Lord's confusion had highlighted seafaring's regular misinterpretation of the government regulations of the period; clarity over the colour of distress signals continued unresolved until 1948 – henceforth only red flares would denote distress.

For his failure to assist a vessel in distress, proceedings against Lord, although considered, never saw fruition. It was impossible to prove in his case that 'loss of life has been caused by his wrongful act', so indictment under the provisions of the Merchant Shipping Act was not possible. Clause 4 of the Maritime Conventions Act of 1911 too made captains negligent 'where the master has failed to stand by after a collision … even though such failure may not have contributed to an accident'. Again prosecutors would be pressed to prove beyond doubt that Lord knowingly believed the ship discharging rockets was at that time in distress and 'failed to stand by'. Despite its initial benevolence the MAIB report of 1992 also criticised Lord for taking no remedial action when seeing the rockets from *Titanic*. Their conclusions went on to affirm that although Lord's crew was unlikely to have seen *Titanic* herself, they had seen her distress rockets and failed to recourse this sighting with appropriate measures. Their officers stood by on watch counting a succession of rockets, one after another, a total of eight times.

Although no investigation could find Lord to be the cause of the disaster, he was unable to refute his inaction. Had he responded to the CQD calls earlier *Californian* would undoubtedly have beaten *Carpathia* to the rescue of the lifeboats' occupants. But the death toll from *Titanic* still remains at 1,523, and as we know only too well, history followed another course.

Stanley Lord was dismissed from the Leyland Line on 13 August 1912. Retiring from the sea in 1927, he would maintain until his death on 24 January 1962 that the ship launching rockets in the distance was not *Titanic*. Regardless of the truth, one fact will always remain. Lord not once acknowledged his failure to respond to a phenomenon most commanders in his position would action instinctively: to simply check all was okay.

Although the true distance between *Californian* and *Titanic* will never be known, *Californian* was, and always will have been, the closest ship to the stricken *Titanic*. Unless proven otherwise, the spectacle the crew of *Californian* observed that fateful evening was indeed the rockets from a certain ship: *Titanic*. An association for which Captain Lord and the SS *Californian* shall forever be recorded by history as 'the ship that stood still'.

CHAPTER 10

'FURTHER PARTICULARS LATER'

'When day broke, I saw the ice I had steamed through during the night. I
shuddered, and could only think that some other hand than mine was on that
helm during the night.'

Captain Arthur Henry Rostron

Every story has its dashing hero and ours arrives in the guise of the SS *Carpathia*,
a 541ft-long, 13,564-ton passenger steamer operated by the Cunard Line. Built
by C.S. Swan & Hunter Ltd of Newcastle, *Carpathia* was launched on 6 August
1902 and embarked on her maiden voyage, Liverpool to Boston, on 5 May the
following year. When Cunard added Hungary to their schedules in 1903, transporting emigrants to New York, the ship – originally built for the Liverpool,
Queenstown, New York run – was withdrawn in 1905 to undergo a refit to adapt
her to service Hungary as well as an array of additional Mediterranean ports.
Carpathia, able to accommodate 2,550 passengers, comprised an occupancy of
100 in first class, 200 in second and, since the refit, 2,250 in steerage – originally
1,704 – after sacrificing a portion of cargo space.

By 1912 *Carpathia* had become the popular choice among Cunard's holiday
travellers. Bound first for Gibraltar, then calling at the Mediterranean ports of
Genoa, Naples and Trieste, then terminating at Fiume, Hungary, *Carpathia*
departed Cunard's pier 54 at New York on the stroke of noon, Thursday 11 April.
Bearing 128 occupants in first class, fifty in second, 565 in steerage and a crew
numbering 325. Guiding them on what would seem as yet another run-of-the-
mill eastbound crossing was their commander, Arthur Henry Rostron.

A highly experienced seafarer, having first gone to sea as a cadet in 1882, Rostron
had joined Cunard in 1895 as fourth officer, one year after achieving his Extra
Master's Certificate. Attaining the rank of captain in 1907, traversing the busy, often
treacherous lanes of the North Atlantic saw Rostron on 18 January 1912 receiving
his sixth command, *Carpathia*.

The senior crew joining him were Thomas Hankinson, the chief officer, Horace Dean as the first, James Bisset (later commodore of the Cunard fleet 1944–7) as second officer, with Eric Rees as third and Geoffrey Barnish serving as fourth. Assigned the call sign MPA, the onboard Marconi wireless provided *Carpathia* with a range of 150 miles, half that of *Titanic*. Operating the set on this crossing was twenty-one-year-old Harold Cottam; serving at sea for the Marconi Company since the age of seventeen he was the youngest qualified wireless operator of the time.

As the voyage progressed, the day of the 14th arrived fairly innocuously for the occupants of *Carpathia*. Being the sole operator aboard, Cottam had been bound to his set's transmission key since 7a.m. It had proven a particularly hectic day, one that found him clearing a backlog of messages well into the night. As the clock turned midnight it marked the end to his usual routine, but that evening Cottam remained at the set awaiting a reply to a message he had earlier sent Captain William Hains of *Parisian* – MZN. As soon as he received this message Cottam hoped to call it a night. But all of a sudden at 12.25a.m. a transmission instead blurted through from MGY: 'Come at once. We have struck a berg. It's a CQD old man' – *Titanic* in mortal danger in position 41°46'N, 50°14'W.

Cottam responded immediately; 'Do you require assistance?'

'Yes, come quick,' entreated the terse reply. Cottam, rising in an instant from his chair, darted to the bridge to alert the watch commander, First Officer Dean. Dean in turn marched the news to Rostron's cabin – finding the captain close to falling asleep.

Rostron, sprinting to the Chart Room, calculated the distance from the distress position. They were 58 miles away. He set a course, N52°W, straight for the CQD, ordering his chief engineer: 'pile every ounce of steam into the boilers'. They raced at the full speed *Carpathia* could muster – 17.5 knots – outstretching her normal 14.5 knot pace. They headed directly for the ice field. Rostron doubled his lookouts to eight as a precaution, and at 2.45a.m. they encountered the first of many icebergs.

Aboard, all routine work was cancelled: First Officer Dean superintended preparations to receive survivors; the bosun had twelve of the eighteen lifeboats swung out in readiness to rapidly heave anyone from the frigid water; stewards set about converting the first-, second- and third-class dining saloons into medical centres; hot food and drinks were prepared. Blankets were gathered; passengers were organised; ladders flung over the side – strewn along the hull. By 2.30a.m. preparations were complete, but at 1.45a.m. Cottam lost radio contact with *Titanic*. Time was racing.

With a green flare sighted at 2.40a.m., Rostron believed that *Titanic* was still afloat: it was a false dawn. The glare had come from one of her lifeboats: *Titanic* was lost. At 3.50a.m. Rostron brought the engines to a standstill; a lifeboat was spotted 300 yards ahead.

The boat they had discovered was lifeboat number 2. Its commander, Fourth Officer Boxhall, ignited the flares to beacon *Carpathia* toward them. He was the first survivor to board *Carpathia* – reporting the loss of *Titanic* to Rostron as he arrived. At 4.10a.m. the boat's remaining occupants followed. As daybreak arrived the scene revealed a dispersed flotilla of lifeboats. Salvation, amid the inauspicious gaze and close proximity of twenty-five icebergs towering out of the water some 150–200ft, was now underway, 7 miles from Boxhall's CQD calculation, 16 miles from where *Titanic* would eventually be discovered seventy-three years later.

A requisite since the Mercantile Marine Acts of 1850 and 1854 to record every fatality at sea, Rostron ensured protocol was followed to the letter. The crew began compiling lists of survivors as well as those known or believed to have perished with *Titanic*. Next to the names of survivors the chief purser and his deputy scribed, 'Arrived Titan-Carpath, 18th April 1912'. Those who were known to have boarded *Titanic* though had not been rescued received the notation 'Died at sea, 15th April 1912'. All deaths from *Titanic* were subsequently officially recorded in Britain as caused by drowning. At 8.10a.m. Second Officer Lightoller, climbing aboard via a ladder from lifeboat 12, became the 705th and final survivor rescued. Instead of rejoicing, Lightoller tasked himself with compiling a list of surviving crew. All lists were complete by 17 April.

Once all had transferred safely aboard from the lifeboats, Rostron asked Reverend Father Roger Anderson to conduct a brief service in the first-class saloon to mark the passing of those left behind. At 4p.m. *Carpathia*, brought to a standstill, allowed him to administer the burial of four bodies, of which three had succumbed to exposure post rescue: the fourth, a third-class passenger, expired in collapsible boat A prior to rescue. *Carpathia* departed the scene at 8.50a.m., the same time that *Californian* began relaying its wireless messages of the evening's events. Soon after boarding, Bruce Ismay and Captain Rostron agreed to return *Carpathia* to New York and to land the survivors there. Shortly after the reverend's service, Ismay composed a telegram to officially inform his New York office of the terrible loss of the line's cherished standard-bearer.

Deeply regret advise you *Titanic* sank this morning, after collision iceberg, resulting serious loss life. Further particulars later. Bruce Ismay.

Addressed to Phillip Franklin, White Star's senior official in New York, headquartered at 9 Broadway, the message remained unsent for two days until 5.50a.m. on the 17th – overlooked by the operators dispatching those from survivors to anxious relatives back home. Despite suffering severely frostbitten ankles, the surviving operator from *Titanic*, Harold Bride, set to work at the transmission key to allow Cottam a much appreciated rest. Cottam had been awake for twenty-four hours. The rescue had proved particularly poignant for Cottam, a friend of Jack Phillips, Bride's colleague, who lost his life on *Titanic*. Cottam and Bride tirelessly worked the key, transmitting survivor's messages via *Olympic* and the Newfoundland station at Cape Race. The operators were, however, given direct orders from Rostron to shirk any communication with the press, a censorship for which the captain was later criticised by the subsequent US inquiry as telegrams from government officials, even one from President Taft himself, had been brushed aside in the foray. The scramble on land for news of the sinking had driven the airwaves to frenzy.

Ismay's communiqué finally arrived at White Star's offices around 9a.m. on the 17th. He had written seven others, signing off each with his codename YAMSI – his surname reversed. The messages were all for the attention of Franklin, five urging to delay the 18 April departure of *Cedric* so as to race the crew, along with himself, immediately back to Britain. Franklin instead dispatched *Cedric* as scheduled, redeploying IMM's 18,565-ton Red Star liner *Lapland* to await the surviving crew and fulfil Ismay's request. Spending much of his time alone in the doctor's cabin, at 8.23a.m. on the 18th Ismay then sent a further telegram, this time requesting that the lifeboats recovered by *Carpathia* be collected as hastily as possible upon their arrival in New York.

In London on the 16th White Star's office officially confirmed the disaster in a letter to Sir Walter Howell of the Board of Trade, a message that he in turn relayed to the Prime Minister.

As the recipient of Ismay's messages from *Carpathia*, Franklin became White Star's impromptu spokesman, announcing the unfolding developments of the rescue to the world's press. The comments he made during Monday 15 April at their offices on Broadway's Bowling Green Park echo the confusion they reported:

1.58a.m.   In his home at 41 East 61st Street Franklin is woken by a call from a journalist asking to confirm reports from Montreal that SS *Virginian* received a message from *Titanic* saying she was sinking. Franklin telephones the Associated Press to seek verification himself, they too could only substantiate *Virginian* had picked up such message.

2.20a.m.   Franklin receives confirmation *Titanic* had indeed been involved in a serious incident, but still afloat.

3.00a.m.   Sends a telegram to *Olympic* insisting they 'make every effort to communicate' with *Titanic*.

6.05a.m.   Captain Haddock on *Olympic* responds to Franklin's request, reporting they were 310 miles from the CQD but had been unable to communicate with *Titanic* themselves.

8.00a.m.   Crowds start to besiege White Star's offices and piers, to whom Franklin assures, 'We place absolute confidence in *Titanic*, we believe the boat is unsinkable.'

2.00p.m.   Captain Haddock messages confirmation that *Titanic* had sunk at 2.20a.m. that morning and that *Carpathia* had recovered all her lifeboats whose survivors numbered just 675.

6.16p.m. Haddock's transmission finally arrives at Franklin's desk: he withholds the news.

7.00p.m. Franklin at long last confirms to the assembled press: 'Gentlemen, I regret to say that the *Titanic* sank at 2:20 this morning'.

8.00p.m. In the attempt to instil confidence he adds that the message from *Olympic* 'neglected to say that all the crew had been saved'.

8.15p.m. Soon admitting: 'probably a number of lives had been lost.'

8.45p.m. 'We very much fear there has been a great loss of life'.

9.00p.m. Confirming ultimately a 'horrible loss of life'.

11.00p.m. Lists of known survivors begin appearing on walls outside White Star's premises on both sides of the Atlantic.

In Britain large crowds gathered outside Oceanic House, just off London's Trafalgar Square, White Star's capital base since 1 May 1905. Similar crowds flocked to Canute Road, Southampton, and 30 James Street, Liverpool – their global headquarters since 1897. Throngs grew as desperation intensified for the names of survivors and known casualties, of friends and loved ones. There was scant information; newspapers on the 15th published reports founded on assimilated transmissions and hearsay, heightening uncertainty and the angst of relatives. Early editions had run headlines that morning stating *Titanic* was not only still afloat but under tow to Halifax, and that three ships had aided in her rescue, safely transferring every passenger. On the 16th the terrible truth began sobering this false hope: only one ship, *Carpathia*, had rescued the survivors, who numbered only 800: 1,400 lives had been lost. By the 17th the actual toll was confirmed, with lists of names trickling slowly over the airwaves. The rolls were displayed on hoardings outside White Star's offices. Anguish intensified through Captain Rostron's strictly imposed news blackout from *Carpathia*.

To chaperone *Carpathia* to New York President Taft dispatched cruisers USS *Chester* and USS *Salem* to shield her from boats swarming around her brimmed with pressmen and purposefully 'paralysing' all communication to and from *Carpathia*. Adding to the frustration of the media, Rostron had merely confirmed the sinking in a telegram sent to Cunard's New York offices. Received at 10a.m. on the 15th it advised negligibly: '*Titanic* struck iceberg sunk Monday 3am 41°46'N, 50°15'W *Carpathia* picked up many passengers in boats will wire further particulars later proceeding back to New York'. Rostron then sent a similar message to the Associated Press, although volunteering no further detail. The number of survivors aboard was confirmed at 6.10a.m. on the 17th in a telegram issued at the approach into New York Harbour, stating simply that *Carpathia* was '498 miles East of Ambrose Channel … saved total 705'. His censoring of all outbound transmissions yielding any detail of the disaster left press concocting stories from collages and snippets of accounts gleaned from messages between other ships and land stations. The world grew hungry for news – any news – on a possible catastrophe. The airwaves filled with speculation.

Shrouded with fog, *Carpathia* reached the Ambrose Lightship at 6p.m., Thursday 18th. Heavy rain ensued, delaying her arrival into New York Harbour by thirty minutes – the weather mirroring the sobriety of the occasion. At 7.45p.m. *Carpathia* passed the Battery at Manhattan; teeming with 10,000 onlookers who witnessed in deference the city's most morose arrival.

Flanked by boats laden with reporters *Carpathia* proceeded along the North River, pausing briefly at White Star's piers 59 and 60, opposite West 20th Street, where at 8.37p.m. crew unloaded the thirteen reclaimed lifeboats of *Titanic*. The survivors' journey, however, was still incomplete. *Carpathia* turned to Cunard's pier number 54, West 14th Street. Here she moored at 9.30p.m. to disembark the survivors. Upon arrival Captain Roberts, Cunard's marine superintendent, boarded *Carpathia* with White Star's Philip Franklin, the spectacle witnessed by an estimated 30,000 spectators lining the quayside; the piers themselves were cordoned by 175 police officers, allowing through the relatives of survivors only.

First- and second-class survivors led the dismal procession ashore: Ismay was immediately hustled to the Ritz-Carlton Hotel. Of the walking wounded, 106 were hospitalised at St Vincent's – although half were discharged within two days. Of the 705 rescued, the only item of luggage with them was a single brown holdall. As a gesture to the survivors all usual border formalities for first- and second-class passengers were tactfully waived. At 11p.m. the third-class survivors left *Carpathia*, with the former crewmembers the last to disembark. The four surviving officers and 206 crew of *Titanic* were transferred by the tender *George Starr* and ferried to IMM's pier 61 to board *Lapland* where they would spend the following nights in isolation from reporters.

On 20 April *Carpathia*, replenished with food and linen, departed New York with her full crew and 743 passengers to resume their detoured voyage to the Mediterranean. Prior to stepping ashore, survivors had meanwhile raised $4,360 in donations for the crew of *Carpathia*. Upon her return to New York on 29 May a delegation of seven first-class passengers from *Titanic* presented Rostron and his officers with an engraved loving-cup, along with commemorative medals struck especially for each of his crew in gratuity from their fellow survivors. The sinking was in no doubt to impart an indelible imprint upon the lives of all involved.

At 10a.m. on the 20th *Lapland* too departed New York, bearing 167 of the surviving crew. They arrived to a hero's welcome in Plymouth at 7a.m. on the 29th. Of the crew not aboard, forty-seven remained in New York, twenty-nine under summons to appear at a Senatorial inquest sanctioned by the president himself, eager to root out the causes of such an unforeseen event. Once this investigation was complete *Celtic* returned a further forty-three of the surviving crew to Britain, arriving in Liverpool on 6 May. Many of the surviving crew returned destitute, diminished to living on shipwreck payments from the National Sailors and Firemen's Union since their normal pay had ceased the moment *Titanic* sank: 2.20a.m., the time Captain Smith relinquished them of their duty.

With their involvement at the American investigation concluded, Ismay and his four surviving officers finally departed New York on 2 May. Aboard *Adriatic* – the former flagship of White Star Line – they arrived at Liverpool at 7.30a.m. on the 11th, greeted by a large jubilant crowd. But for many there was far less cause for celebration. On 9 May White Star had published their list of the passengers known to have died or survived. The weeks since the disaster had passed agonisingly slowly for the relatives still awaiting the fate of the missing crew.

Wireless Operator Harold Bride returned to England on *Baltic*, arriving on 18 May, the same day that the body of *Titanic*'s bandleader, Wallace Hartley, received a lavish burial in his hometown of Colne, Lancashire: one of a small proportion of the victims whose remains had been recovered.

Hastily arranged by Franklin, White Star had dispatched Commercial Cable Company's *Mackay-Bennett* to retrieve bodies from the wreck site. Departing Halifax, Nova Scotia on 17 April, its crew recovered fifty-one on their first day at the scene, 20 April. Returning on the 25th the two missions of *Mackay-Bennett* would find a total of 306 bodies around 42°N, 49°20'W. White Star commissioned further ships to work the area in shifts to recover the anticipated stockpile of remains. On 25 April, Anglo-American Telegraph Company's *Minia* began its duty, finding seventeen bodies. On 3 May Canadian Ministry of Marine and Fisheries' *Montmagny*, hampered by fog, recovered four. After leaving for the scene again on the 13th they returned empty-handed. *Algerine*, operated by Browning Brothers, found on 16 May only a single body. Collectively, all missions retrieved 328 victims.

Impossible to identify 128 of the bodies, 119 were buried at sea. The remaining 209 were brought to Halifax, Canada. Being the only facility large enough, the Mayflower Curling Rink served as a makeshift morgue to allow relatives to identify the remains of victims returned ashore. Fifty-nine were taken by their families for private burial, the remaining were interred among three cemeteries throughout the city: Fairview (for Protestant victims), Mount Olivet (Roman Catholic) and Baron de Hirsch (Jewish) – the funerals lasting from 3 May to 12 June. Since the merger with White Star in 1945 the upkeep of these gravestones continues to be funded by Cunard to this day. However, 1,194 bodies remained unaccounted for. Passing steamers stumbled upon others until 8 June when the last, the body of a crewmember, was recovered by *Ilford* en route to Hamburg.

Some of the dead were found 130 miles from the CQD position: *Oceanic* stumbled upon collapsible boat A on 13 May. Still containing the bodies of three victims, abandoned weeks earlier by *Carpathia*, so as not to distress passengers the ship's doctor officiated their burial from a lifeboat, returning to *Oceanic* with the collapsible in tow. Once hauled aboard, *Oceanic* resumed her voyage to New York. The fourteen boats recovered from *Titanic* were deemed her sole items of salvage and collectively valued at £930 ($4,972), their fate remaining unknown. After being stripped of their insignia it is believed that the thirteen boats delivered by *Carpathia* were returned to Britain aboard *Olympic* on her departure of 25 April.

Upon arrival these were either destroyed or refurbished for clandestine redistribution among other vessels.

The immediate aftershock of the disaster had witnessed the emergence of bold statements in some newspapers, claiming 'all' had been saved, not by *Carpathia* but a ship named *Virginian*. Unlike Lord and *Californian*, who stood accused of failing to aid *Titanic*, the press in their haste to report the disaster ran early editions that instead named *Virginian* the star of a remarkable role she never even performed.

Launched in 1904 for the Allan Steamship Line, the 10,757-ton *Virginian* was highly advanced for her day – being the first liner on the North Atlantic fitted with triple propellers driven solely by turbine engines. The wireless call sign assigned *Virginian* was MGN. Commanded by G.J. Gambell, she departed Halifax on 14 April bound for Liverpool where she arrived safely on the 21st.

At the time MGN received the distress call directly from *Titanic*, *Virginian* was 170 miles north of the distress position and entirely out of hope of rescuing any survivors. However, the name *Virginian* was to be embroiled across newspaper headlines around the globe as the heroic saviour of *Titanic* herself.

It all began at 1.02a.m. with William James Cotter, the ship's Marconi operator, receiving the distress call from MGY. After a chain of events Wall Street's *The Evening Sun* famously rushed the first in a series of befuddled headlines, declaring on the 15th 'All saved from *Titanic* after collision'. Adding not only that *Carpathia* and *Parisian* had rescued the survivors from *Titanic*, the newspaper also claimed that *Titanic* was still afloat and under tow to Halifax: underwriters scrambled to reinsure the ship and sent prices soaring. The practice of reinsurance – transferring risk from the originating insurer to another – was commonplace for any ship delayed en route.

On the 16th the story broke that *Virginian* was towing *Titanic* to Canada where it was planned to beach the wounded liner. The account went on to purport that another Allan Line vessel, *Parisian*, had rescued all the survivors and *Carpathia* had been only a standby to the incident and transferred 800 passengers from *Titanic*. The story even alluded that all three ships had arrived at the CQD position around the same time and clearly stated that *Titanic* was not only still under her own steam but that most, if not all, of her occupants were safe and well. A day later a confused press realised that the story was erroneous: only 800 lives in total had been saved and *Virginian* had arrived too late to rescue any whatsoever. Both the facts and the names of survivors and known victims soon vanquished any false optimism. The worst had been confirmed.

The roots of this fantastical revelation had stemmed from Gambell sending a message to his head office in Montreal reporting that *Virginian* was altering course to aid *Titanic*. On hearing this, their marine superintendent, George Hannah, telephoned Harold Strange, reporter for the *Montreal Gazette*. Around midnight on the 15th Strange passed the report to Carr Van Anda, editor of the *New York Times*. Knowing a potentially momentous story was in the making the newspapermen took to the

airwaves. Meanwhile, aboard *Olympic*, Captain Haddock received news of the sinking from White Star's *Celtic*, the same time as a message from a concerned woman
in New York was also sent to *Olympic* enquiring 'are all passengers safe?' Unable to
answer, Haddock messaged the Leyland liner *Asian* to assist the enquiry and ask if
they too could go and help *Titanic*. *Asian* replied they were unable to assist as were
towing an oil tanker to Halifax – Deutsch-Amerika Petroleum's *Deutschland*.

The tanker, travelling to Philadelphia from Stettin, Germany, had run out of fuel
and sought tow to Halifax: it was the very ship whose request for assistance had
earlier been relayed to *Titanic* by *Baltic*. The reply *Asian* gave was 'towing steamer to
Halifax'. *Olympic* then forwarded a message from *Parisian* confirming that *Carpathia*
had rescued all those found in the lifeboats. *Carpathia* in turn radioed *Virginian* and
Baltic to say that they had taken aboard 'about 800 passengers' and to tell them to
stand down. The press pieced the messages together and put out perhaps the most
erroneous headlines in history. The errors were not exposed until 1.45a.m. on the
16th upon Haddock's confirmation to White Star that *Carpathia* was carrying the
sole survivors.

Captain Gambell was just as confused about how his ship had become entangled in the headlines. It is unsurprising however: hundreds of messages frantically
transmitted at the same time, overcrowding the airwaves, found transmissions fused
together. Officials, friends, families, reporters, indeed the entire civilised world, were
desperate for news, any news, on the fate of *Titanic*. With Rostron's censorship the
press grew ever charged to glean any information as was possible from the mire. The
messages concerning *Virginian* led to the *Wall Street Journal's* sensational declaration
of 'All Saved': its rather belated retraction was printed in 1998.

Community of Grief

The days following the sinking impassioned the world to share universal con-
dolences for the victims and bereaved families. Both sides of the Atlantic saw
people, rich and poor, coming to terms with a disaster unequalled in scale and so
indiscriminate of class and gender. On 16 April, King George V led the tributes,
sending a telegram to Bruce Ismay addressed to his headquarters at Liverpool:

> The Queen and I are horrified at the appalling disaster which has happened
> to the *Titanic* and at the terrible loss of life. We deeply sympathise with the
> bereaved relatives, and feel for them in their great sorrow with all our hearts.
> GEORGE R and I.

In the House of Commons that same day Prime Minister Asquith echoed this
sentiment, expressing also his pride for the men who gave their lives on *Titanic* so
that women and children were able to survive:

We cannot say more at this moment than to give necessarily imperfect expression to our sense of admiration that the best traditions of the sea seem to have been observed in the willing sacrifices which were offered to give first chance of safety to those least able to help themselves.

President Taft, who authorised a Senate investigation into the sinking on 17 April – much to the disgust of the British government – likewise condoled:

In presence of the appalling disaster to the *Titanic*, the people of the two countries are brought into community of grief through their common bereavement. The American people share in the sorrow of their kinsmen beyond the sea.

Announced to the stunned disbelief of their underwriters by a single strike of their famous Lutine Bell, Lloyd's of London, insurers of *Titanic*, noted the sinking in their Casualty Returns; the book remaining open at this most infamous entry even today:

Titanic, British Mail: Southampton for New York, foundered April 15 about 2:20am in lat. 41.16 north long. 50.14 west after collision with ice. Reported by wireless from *Olympic* to the Cape Race wireless station. Further reports state that loss of life is very serious.

The sinking had struck the global insurance industry an unprecedented blow – writing off $10 million through private policies on life and property, the largest ever from a single disaster, stock markets plunged into charged confusion. White Star, however, was ultimately denied a settlement since the line had failed to satisfy the official inquiry of their absolution from blame against the loss incurred. White Star had no alternative but to forego the entire insurance. But this disaster would extend far beyond financial losses: it had wreaked an eternity of bereavement on the families of the 1,500 victims it claimed; death was indiscriminate. The loss of *Titanic* also spawned an instant cultural tragedy. Ordinary people taking the voyage in the hope of forging themselves a more prosperous future had perished side-by-side with millionaires. So rarely had disaster transcended the social pyramid. No Edwardian platitude was able to stem the sorrow left in its wake. A cross section of humanity had been lost.

Daniel Marvin, nineteen, returning to New York with his wife upon the conclusion of their honeymoon in Europe, was just one of the dead. As was Hudson Allison, aged thirty, returning to Canada with his wife Bess following a business meeting in England. William Stead, sixty-two, from Wimbledon, South London, was on his way to address a peace conference at New York's Carnegie Hall. Victor Giglio, twenty-four, valet of Benjamin Guggenheim, was returning to New York with his master. Alfred Whitford, thirty-seven, from Guernsey, was employed as a steward in second class. Father Robert Bateman, fifty-one, was returning to

Florida after visiting family in Bristol. Reginald Coleridge, twenty-nine, from Devon, was heading to Detroit on business, after which he planned to holiday in Canada. Frank Parkes, eighteen, was travelling with Thomas Andrews as a member of Harland & Wolff's nine-man guarantee team, all of whom died. Leonard Hickman, twenty-four, from Hampshire, was emigrating to Canada with his two brothers, Stanley, twenty, and Lewis, thirty: all also lost. Thomas McCawley, thirty-six, from Southampton, was employed as gym instructor on *Titanic*. Sinai Kantor, aged thirty-four, from Russia, was uprooting to New York. Henry Morley, thirty-eight, from Worcester, was eloping to Los Angeles with his girlfriend. George Swane, aged eighteen, was travelling as chauffeur to Hudson Allison. Frederick Goodwin, forty-two, from Fulham, London, was emigrating to America with his wife Augusta, forty-three, and their six children (the youngest was one-year-old Sidney) the family hoping to settle in Niagara Falls: all perished. John and Anne Sage, both forty-four, from Hackney in London, were emigrating to Florida with their nine children to establish a farm: all were lost. Wilhelm and Anna Skoog from Sweden were emigrating to Michigan with their four children: all were lost. Charles Turvey, sixteen, from Bayswater, London, was pageboy to the first-class restaurant. Gerios Yousseff, aged twenty-six, from Lebanon, was emigrating to Ohio to work at a steel foundry. Leo Zimmermann, aged twenty-nine, from Germany, was emigrating to Saskatoon, Canada. Bertram Crosby, forty-two, from Croydon, was attendant of the Turkish Baths. Ivan Stankovic, thirty-three, from Croatia, was heading to New York in search of employment. Owen Allum, eighteen, from London, was travelling to join his father. William Mackie, thirty-two, from West Ham, London, was a junior engineer on *Titanic*: he and all his colleagues perished. Arthur William May, sixty, and son Arthur, twenty-one, both from Southampton, served as stokers on *Titanic*: between them they left two widows and nine children. Oscar Woody from Virginia was a mail room assistant; on what was his forty-fourth birthday he drowned along with his four postal colleagues after trying desperately to save 200 sacks of mail.

Then there is of course the captain, 'EJ' Smith, who after a lifetime of dutiful service was one roundtrip from beginning a well-earned retirement with his wife Sarah. Lives ended, families were lost and separated. *Titanic* was a classless and thoroughly human tragedy reaching across society like never before.

A memorial service held at St Paul's Cathedral in London, at the stroke of noon on 19 April, drew an attendance of 10,000 mourners. A similar mass held at Westminster Cathedral on the 22nd preceded a special concert at the Albert Hall on Empire Day, 24 May. On 17 April the lord mayor of London, Councillor Sir Thomas Boor Crosby, founded the Mansion House Fund to support the families of the 535 lost crewmembers resident in Southampton. Raising a total of £413,000 within its first year, the fund continued until 1958 making payments to families of the 673 perished crewmembers. Similar funds also sprang up in Liverpool and Southampton.

The world was coming to terms with the disaster, which left in its wake two contrasting reactions. The lines owned by International Mercantile Marine operating on the Atlantic – Red Star Line and White Star – changed their courses to a more southerly pattern to avoid this fatal region of ice, as well as increasing their life-raft capacity to accommodate every passenger and crewmember aboard their fleets. A temporary, albeit improvised, amelioration to the shortfall of life-saving appliances the law had hitherto failed to demand that ships carry.

On the other side of the spectrum the New York Stock Exchange saw Marconi's market value soar. 17 April also found *Majestic* formally reassigned to fill the departures originally timetabled for *Titanic*, maintaining White Star's trio servicing their Southampton/New York route alongside *Oceanic* and *Olympic*. The world was responding. Unrest, however, was stirring.

Ending a crossing during which she received her stricken sister's distress call, Captain Haddock docked a shell-shocked *Olympic* at Plymouth on the 21st. On the 24th, moments before she was due to depart again for New York, 284 stokers walked off the ship amid concern over the durability of her two dozen hastily installed collapsible lifeboats. Although *Olympic* was now furnished with forty-four boats, which had also received the seal of approval from Captain Maurice Clarke of the Board of Trade, a leak was discovered in one of the new boats during a test specifically intended to assure the crew of their safety. Unwilling to travel on this twin of *Titanic* the stokehold crew downed shovels and refused to continue the voyage. A replacement crew was signed the following evening, but, deeming them to be insufficiently trained, fifty-three sailing crew also left the ship in protest – and were subsequently arrested for desertion. Although all were acquitted on 5 May, the action had pressed its point. *Olympic*'s much-delayed voyage was ultimately cancelled in the early hours of 26 April. White Star had to refund the passengers and *Olympic* was withdrawn from service that autumn to undergo an extensive overhaul to improve her watertight subdivision.

Elsewhere, disquiet with White Star was growing, precariously. In Britain, a frank and lively House of Commons debate on 21 May berated 'the absolute neglect and unconcern' that the Board of Trade had shown through their unkempt regulations. Furthermore, under American law the Harter Act of 1893 allowed aggrieved relatives to file damages for loss of life and luggage should the operating company responsible be proven negligent for their loss. Claims seeking compensation against American-owned White Star were growing and were being filed in a deluge. The amount sought by survivors and families of victims came to an eye-watering $16,804,112, and found White Star filing limited liability at the Southern District Court of New York on 8 October. The ensuing judgement accepted for the limitation to be set to the formula as used in British law, and ruled that White Star pay a maximum of $3,450,000 (£690,000) in recompense for the loss of life and luggage incurred in the disaster. The floodgates opened. Suits against the line mounted and were heard at Judge Julius Mayer's court between 22 and 29 June 1915, for earlier, over in Britain, a modest but potentially devastating case had come before the Commercial Court, West London. The verdict for *Ryan v. Oceanic Steam Navigation Company Ltd* had disastrous consequences for the shipping operator.

Thomas Ryan from County Cork had lost his cattle-trader son, Patrick, in the disaster and was suing for damages against White Star's owners for the loss of the family's sole breadwinner. On 26 June 1913, presiding judge Sir Clement Bailhache ruled that both Captain Smith and his watch commanders – by virtue of their concerns, fully aware of the prospect of encountering ice during the evening of the disaster – had neglected their duty by maintaining the excessive pace of the ship. Ryan was awarded £100 compensation. The judgement had not only given legitimacy to Lord Mersey's critics but exposed White Star's culpability. In what became the first serious appraisal into the sinking since the widely considered whitewash of the British inquiry, the line's attempt the following February to overturn the verdict only added to their woes.

Appeal judge Lord Justice Vaughan Williams upheld the Commercial Court's verdict and was unabashed in placing White Star at fault: 'the knowledge or apprehension of danger which Lightoller certainly had, and Captain Smith possibly had … can give to the charge of negligent navigation in proceeding in the circumstances' and because of this prior awareness of ice and failure to take remedial action to avoid it, 'danger … was neither unforeseen nor unforeseeable'. Smith travelling his ship apace through this region, ultimately resulted in a disaster that Williams, to the dismay of White Star, surmised 'might not have happened if he had slowed down'.

Facing the prospect of a barrage of similar claims, on 17 December 1915 White Star conceded to foot the bill for compensation, albeit limited to a token $664,000 (£136,701). The cap was set on the proviso that all suits on both sides of the Atlantic were dropped. The settlement, formalised on 28 July 1916, saw White Star paying just 4 per cent of the original total lodged against them. In his dictum Judge Mayer set the formula of compensation for each loss of life at £7,294, and £1,390 for lost property or £8,371 for loss of life and property, plus £2,234 for each instance of injury and loss of property.

The aftermath of *Titanic* was not completely a tale of litigation, however. Rostron's gallant entry into the disaster was marked by a slew of commendations: the Congressional Medal of Honour in 1913; the Freedom to the City of New York in 1926 and in Britain a knighthood (a KBE); then to Cherbourg in 1929 to receive the French Legion of Honour. Feted equally by his employer, Rostron was elevated to more salubrious postings for Cunard: as master of *Lusitania* and in 1915 a stint on *Mauretania* where, after the war, he remained as her captain until 1926. Appointed commodore of the Cunard fleet in 1928, as captain of their flagship *Berengaria* he served with her until his retirement in 1931, publishing his autobiography *Home From the Sea* that year. Rostron died of pneumonia on 4 November 1940 – internationally lauded for his role in the disaster.

Carpathia herself came to a less celebrated end than her much elevated former master. On 17 July 1918, 120 miles west of Fastnet Rock on the southern Irish coast, she was sunk by a torpedo from the U-55 submarine: five lives were lost, fifty-seven saved. The wreck of *Carpathia* was discovered on 27 May 2000, lying at a depth of 500ft. Its discovery received little fanfare, although it was hardly necessary. Her name was already enshrined for its glorious entry into history on that bitter April evening.

CHAPTER 11

DEVIL IN THE DETAIL

'The Board of Trade had passed that ship as in all respects fit for sea in every sense of the word, with sufficient margin of safety for everyone on board. Now the Board of Trade was holding an inquiry in to the loss of that ship … when one had known, full well, and for many years, the ever-present possibility of just such a disaster.'

Charles Lightoller, *Titanic and Other Ships*, 1935

With the loss of the world's largest, most high-profile and 'safest' liner, which claimed more than 1,500 lives, two officially sanctioned inquiries, one on either side of the Atlantic, were quickly put into motion to root out the causes of such an unprecedented disaster.

Courtesy of *Carpathia* all surviving passengers and crew were first landed on American soil, giving the US government the impetus to have its investigation underway first. Doing so did not, however, have Britain's blessing. The eagerness of the American authorities affronted British sensibilities. For not only were all the surviving witnesses brought first to America, but so was Bruce Ismay, managing director of a British-registered company, the operator of *Titanic* – a much prized and sunken British-registered vessel. Nevertheless a British inquiry had to wait its turn.

Authorisation to conduct a hearing to investigate the disaster was granted by President Taft on 17 April – the day prior to the anticipated arrival of *Carpathia* bearing the survivors along the New York approach. Employing Senate Resolution 283, President Taft summoned his Commerce Committee to form an investigatory panel with the purview to call witnesses and give particular scrutiny to the British Board of Trade's regulatory process and inspection practices. Mindful that they were about to become the lightning rod for accusation, Britain was outraged. Moreover the appointment of William Alden Smith as chair of the subcommittee sparked equal trepidation from IMM.

Smith, an outspoken Republican senator for Michigan, was known for his personal loathing of rail operators, that exerted, in his view, a considerable sway over the fortunes of the economy. Opposed to the owners, who in his eyes monopolised transportation and unscrupulously held the public purse to ransom for the betterment of their personal wealth, the senator harboured no benevolence toward the railroad tycoons – Morgan for one – feeling that IMM were freely wielding similar impunity in shipping. Being an American entity, should Smith therefore find IMM culpable for the disaster, the provisions of the Harter Act would see them liable for all lost goods and cargo carried in *Titanic*, opening the floodgates to a torrent of claims demanding compensation. The Act, effective since 1 July 1893, would only limit this liability as long as the shipping operator was not held to be at fault for the 'damage or loss resulting from faults or errors in navigation or in the management' of the vessel concerned.

Smith assembled a panel of fellow senators chosen to provide a balanced, thus naturalised, sphere of political persuasions. Francis Newlands (Nevada) became its vice-chairman and was joined by fellow Democrats Duncan Fletcher (Florida) and Furnifold Simmons (North Carolina). Jonathan Bourne (Oregon), Theodore Burton (Ohio) and George Perkins (California) formed Smith's Republican contingent. To assist the panel with the more technical aspects of marine matters George Uhler sat as the committee's sole non-political member: Uhler hailed from the Steamboat Inspection Service, a body set up by Act of Congress in 1871 to monitor standards and safety at sea.

Aware from intercepted messages that Ismay was seeking a swift return to Britain, Smith and his entire investigatory panel, travelling from Washington with two marshals, marched aboard *Carpathia* at 3.30p.m. on the 18th to personally subpoena Ismay and the surviving senior crew. Witnesses gathered, the committee opened its hearings at 10.30a.m. the following morning in the opulent East Room of New York's plush Waldorf-Astoria hotel. The choice of venue provided a poignant backdrop. The hotel, opened in 1897 as the world's largest, was owned by a celebrity victim of the disaster, John Jacob Astor. The city as location for the inquiry added yet more poignancy for it boasted the world's tallest structure at the time: the yet unfinished 750ft Woolworth Building. This very building had featured in a White Star Line promotional montage to tantalise passengers through highlighting the gargantuan sizes of *Titanic* and *Olympic* by comparing them alongside world-famous landmarks. The level of interest in the investigation, however, saw the committee decamp to Washington DC on its third day, 22 April, in favour of the Caucus Room of the Russell Senate Office at Capitol Hill. Classically themed and opulent, the room provided an aptly theatrical backdrop to the throng of press and spectators vying for seats at this, the hottest draw in town.

The hearings summoned eighty-two witnesses, among them eighteen surviving passengers, thirty-eight crewmembers and twelve experts of telegraphy. Of those called, twenty-nine were American, but fifty-three were British citizens, prompting diplomatic outcry back home that an inquiry involving a British ship and British subjects should under no circumstances be held in America and accusing Senator Smith's committee of having no jurisdiction to do so. The claims were dismissed on the grounds that *Titanic* had been carrying American fee-paying customers and was owned by an American entity, IMM – enough justification in its eyes to licence investigation. After seventeen days of wading through testimony from its succession of witnesses, the investigation closed its doors on 25 May. Taking leave to compose his impassioned statement on the 28th, Smith then addressed his conclusions to a packed Senate; it was delivered with prose and piety carefully targeted at the reporters filling its galleries:

> We went to the side of the hospital ship with purpose and pity and saw the almost lifeless survivors in their garments of woe – joy and sorrow so inter-mingled that it was difficult to discern light from shadow, the sad scene was only varied by the cry of reunited loved ones whose mutual grief was written in the language of creation.

There were no holds barred for America's British cousin in Smith's nineteen-page report, which levied the full weight of criticism at the Board of Trade: 'whose laxity of regulation and hasty inspection the world is largely indebted for this awful tragedy'. The British establishment was incensed, more so with the report's omission to place any responsibility of the sinking on the actual owner of IMM and *Titanic*, John Pierpont Morgan – a motivation most certainly influenced by the financier's unofficial capacity as the country's central banker. Realising it imprudent to apportion Morgan liability over the loss of the ship, Senator Smith was in no mind to baulk at deflecting fault onto the malpractice of a British government department. There was criticism in abundance: fellow British operator Leyland Line suffered his wrath also. *Californian*, blasted the senator, was 'nearer to the *Titanic* than the 19 miles reported by her captain', Lord, who 'failed to respond' to her calls for help was 'most reprehensible' for his inaction. Smith did, however, seek national recognition for Captain Rostron. But crucially, the sena-tor's focus was to set in stone his own improvements to maritime safety.

Calling to remedy existing legislation on the supply and use of lifeboats Smith demanded that boat assignments for both passengers and crew be displayed in every room at sea. As well as requesting twice-monthly lifeboat drills conducted with all crew in attendance (stokehold crew often refused to participate), during which four members would be pre-assigned each boat, he insisted that every vessel using American ports arrive with enough lifeboats to 'accommodate every passenger and every member of the crew' on board. Turning his attention to wire-less, he acknowledged that the disaster had shown the 'glaringly apparent' need to man the equipment round the clock and that communication between operator and bridge officer should exponentially improve.

The recommendations continued: rockets fired at sea should only denote distress; ships bearing more than 100 passengers should carry at least two search-lights; the heights of double hulls should clear a ship's load-line by at least 10 per cent and bulkhead walls should do so by at least 25 per cent. Smith also called for every bulkhead to reach a single watertight deck and for regular reviews to ensure that regulations remain conversant with technological developments and that standards of safety should continually evolve.

Unsurprisingly, the criticism expressed in the report was distilled scornfully in Britain, where the foreign secretary, Sir Edward Grey, expressed utter contempt for the senator's 'denunciatory' apportioning of blame for the disaster at the Board of Trade. James Bryce, Grey's ambassador in Washington, refused to recognise the legitimacy of Senator Smith's jurisdiction, demanding from the outset that the president dissolve the committee. The protests, however, fell upon deaf ears.

Fielding such questions as 'Do you know what an iceberg is composed of?' and 'Did the *Titanic* go down by the head or the bow', Senator Smith freely acknowl-edged that he inferred no 'pretension to experience or special knowledge of nautical affairs'. Nor had he made any secret of the fact that the investigation would enhance his own political stature. Yet despite its sensationalism and histri-onic intent, Smith's report laid bare key flaws in maritime regulation. But with it now satisfied and the principal witnesses free to return home, Britain expended no less energy on having their own investigation swiftly underway.

On both sides of the Atlantic a growing army of commentators were acrimo-niously concerned that a British government body had formulated rules that, if applied, would have reduced an already deficient number of lifeboats carried by *Titanic*. The shipping operator also stood accused of their 'speed mania' and conceited refusal to equip *Titanic* with the additional boats she so sorely needed and was perfectly able to carry. Foreseeing the firestorm ahead, both the Board of Trade and White Star Line began securing their defences. But quarters outside government smelt a rat, pondering volubly whether a government-sanctioned investigation really would indict a fellow body of neglecting its duty. The entire establishment was now under scrutiny, feeding a fear among some observers that the government would covertly induce its investigators to deflect blame else-where. Speculation of a whitewash, even today, remains rife.

In Britain the loss of *Titanic* was formally announced by Sydney Buxton, presi-dent of the Board of Trade, during the Downing Street Cabinet meeting on 16 April. On the 19th he asked the Lord Chancellor to form a special Court of Inquiry to investigate the sinking, which on the 22nd the Prime Minister con-firmed would indeed be established to examine the circumstances of the disaster.

The court was formed by the Board's Marine Department under the provisions of the controversial Merchant Shipping Act, the very edict that undermined the quota of boats for *Titanic*. With the key witnesses still in America and giving evi-dence at the Senate inquiry, the 'Order for Formal Investigation' remained unsigned

The Scottish Drill Hall during the Court of Inquiry hearings in London, Sir Cosmo Duff Gordon occupying the witness stand in front of a 1:48th scale model of *Olympic*. Its chairman, Lord Mersey of Toxteth, is seated behind the raised desk, flanked by five technical assessors. The 21ft ½-ton model of *Olympic*, built by Harland & Wolff in 1910 to adorn the entrance hall of White Star's offices in New York, was on 2 May 1912 returned to Britain aboard *Adriatic* to aid the inquiry. To its left stands a large map of the North Atlantic in full view of banks of seats thronged with reporters, legal advisors and curious spectators. (TopFoto)

by the Lord Chancellor until the 30th. Only then, when procedure was satisfied, did protocol permit the British investigation into the disaster to commence.

Opening its doors on 2 May at the 300-capacity Scottish Regiment Drill Hall on London's Buckingham Gate, however a repeat of the immense media interest seen in America found the court uprooting to the larger Caxton Hall on its sixteenth day, 4 June. The hall on Caxton Road accommodated a greater number of seats as well as affording occupants improved acoustics to the Drill Hall.

Heading the inquiry was Baron John Charles Bingham – Lord Mersey of Toxteth. Grandee of the legal establishment, he was appointed commissioner of wrecks on 23 April by the Lord Chancellor, especially to head the investigation. Unlike his American counterpart, who relied on a single expert to advise its panel on technical matters, the British court appointed a team of five experts – assessors – to sift painstakingly through nautical intricacies and exchanges from the witness box. The assessors, all experienced maritime professionals, were nominated by various organisations to provide the court with a broad range of expertise. Its shortlist was subsequently approved on the 29th by the home secretary, Reginald McKenna, and those appointed were Professor John Harvard Biles (chair of naval architecture at the University of Glasgow), Captain Arthur Wellesley Clarke (retired elder brother of Trinity House), Edward Catmore Chaston (senior engineer at the Board of Trade), and the retired Royal Navy veterans Rear-Admiral The Hon. Somerset Arthur Gough-Calthorpe and Commander Fitzhugh Lyon.

Leading the counsel for the Board of Trade was the government's rather implacable chief lawyer, Rt Hon. Sir Rufus Daniel Isaacs KC MP, attorney-general 1910–13. Fielding the nation's foremost lawyer highlighted the ramifications should the government's regulatory processes be found to be the decisive factor for the high loss of life on *Titanic*. The government wielded an impressive legal team for the hearings: assisting Sir Rufus was the solicitor-general, his ministerial deputy, Sir John Allsebrook Simon – the pair were aided by Butler Aspinall KC and the Prime Minister's son, Raymond Asquith.

Fearing its own sword of Damocles, White Star too assembled formidable representation. Headed by the influential Sir Robert Bannatyne Finlay KC MP – formerly attorney-general between 1900 and 1906 and who later held the position of lord chancellor as Viscount Finlay of Nairn – he was joined by high-flyers Maurice Hill KC, Frederick Laing KC, and Norman Raeburn.

Representing the officers of *Titanic* was L.S. Holmes of the Imperial Merchant Service Guild and standing for the surviving and deceased crew was Thomas Scanlan MP of the National Sailors & Firemen's Union. Thomas Lewis for the British Seafarers Union represented the widows and surviving crew residing in Southampton. W.D. Harbinson represented third-class passenger interests and, finally, Charles Robertson Dunlop, counsel to the Lord's Commissioners of the Admiralty, appeared for the Leyland Line and the much maligned officers of *Californian*, arguing the case for their dubious role in the affair.

As her interiors and manoeuvrability were identical to *Titanic*, on 6 and 13 May the court transferred to Southampton to view the layouts of *Olympic* and oversee running tests recreating the same avoiding manoeuvre performed so unsuccessfully by her ill-fortuned sister. Then, on 11 May, *Adriatic* arrived at Liverpool, following a brief call at Queenstown; she was returning home the material witnesses – Ismay and the surviving officers – all now at liberty to present their testimony at the Board of Trade's investigation.

The thirty-six days of hearings, which became the longest inquest in British legal history, saw a total of 25,622 questions put to ninety-seven witnesses: forty-four crewmembers, nine Board of Trade officials, two design representatives from Harland & Wolff and two passengers, all represented by some fifty lawyers. The principal witnesses heard were Bruce Ismay, Edward Wilding (newly appointed chief designer at Harland & Wolff), Captain Stanley Lord, the surviving officers of *Titanic*, and an array of experts, including luminaries such as wireless inventor Guglielmo Marconi and Major Sir Ernest Shackleton.

Sir Ernest, the renowned polar explorer, was called for his knowledge on icebergs and navigation of ice regions. A member of Captain Scott's first expedition to Antarctica between 1901 and 1903 aboard *Discovery*, Shackleton returned with his own team in January 1909, which became at the time the first to venture within 100 miles of the South Pole – an achievement for which he was knighted. During the hearings he criticised the speed *Titanic* was navigated at, insisting that a captain of Edward Smith's wisdom should have anticipated the presence of ice in environs boasting little wind and lower than average temperatures for that time of year.

Also giving depositions were Captain Rostron of *Carpathia* and Board of Trade mandarin, Sir Walter Howell. Unlike the American investigation, which also sought testimony from twenty-one passengers, only two were called throughout the entire session of the British hearings: Sir Cosmo Duff Gordon and his wife Lady Lucile. Their evidence, however, was not to provide the court with insight from a passenger's perspective: they stood accused of bribing the seven crewmembers of their lifeboat – boat number 1 – £5 each to row away from the ship and abandon intentions to turn back to save potential survivors from the water. There were a total of twelve occupants in boat 1. Despite room for twenty-eight more it was alleged that the Duff Gordons bribed its crew amid fears that the boat would be overwhelmed by others clambering aboard it should they return to the site. Their representation, Henry Edward Duke KC MP, argued that the money was instead a token of gratitude to reimburse the crewmembers for replacement uniforms upon their return to England. With lack of evidence to the contrary the Duff Gordons were exonerated of any wrongdoing by the inquiry.

Lord Mersey elected against calling other passengers to testify, in order to – as he put it – curtail repetition. The decision, however, fuelled speculation of conspiracy. He parried these accusations as clear vindication of his discretion: considering that the information most passengers had presented to both the American investigation and the press was either distorted, fallacious or embellished, occasionally to the point of being blatant. Fully aware that it is a human trait to unintentionally misjudge facets pertaining to timings, facts and specifics, Mersey was predisposed against inexpert testimony, which he felt would mislead the inquiry. There were after all literally hundreds of eyewitnesses who survived the disaster, and saw its events firsthand and from every conceivable angle. Sifting through their testimony, in Mersey's mind, added only to data already collected from surviving crew. Mersey considered that his remit was to establish how the disaster occurred, and that technical information from crewmembers and professionals was all he needed to obtain. Having to put on record inaccurate observations and numerous and potentially mistaken assumptions, plus a fair amount of repetition, would prove not only capricious but counterproductive to the court. Potentially unwilling to court controversy by receiving passenger testimony it was an aversion that he would retain when chairing the tribunal for the loss of the *Empress of Ireland* in 1914, during which he retorted: 'I do not myself think that to multiply evidence will be to increase our knowledge of the facts.'

The inquiry closed on 3 July, the investigations in Washington and London tallying between them 2,111 pages of first-hand testimony: but of what? One was faced with claims of a whitewash, the other overshadowed by its technical naivety. The two inquiries certainly contrasted in style. The British investigation was chaired by an esteemed member of the judiciary, the American headed by a career politician. Their differences were broad, moulded by the two men leading them.

The Rt Hon. Sir John Charles Bingham QC, holder of the dubious position of commissioner of wrecks for the United Kingdom, was specifically chosen to head the British investigation. Born in 1840 to a merchant in Liverpool he moved to London to study law, graduating in 1870. A Queen's Counsel in 1883, he formed his own practice in 1885, political aspirations seeing him run for Parliament in 1892 as a Liberal Unionist. Although the attempt was unsuccessful he was elected in 1895 for the division of Liverpool Exchange. His appointment to judge in 1897 had him relinquishing the seat to return to law to serve on the King's Bench Division of the High Court, where he received a knighthood. In 1909 Sir John became president of the Probate, Divorce and Admiralty Division of the High Court, a tenure during which he forged a reputation for leniency. During this time he was appointed privy councillor but in 1910 was forced into early retirement by a heart condition. Ennobled as Baron Mersey of Toxteth that year, he came to the fore in 1912 to serve as wreck commissioner for the *Titanic* hearings – joined by his son, Charles Clive Bingham, as its official secretary.

Mersey was criticised for purportedly contorting the questioning to divert blame of any sort away from the Board of Trade, no matter how compelling the evidence against them, engineering his court to ensure that he delivered the establishment a desirable verdict. Accusations of whitewash would resurface in a similar inquiry during which he again adopted an apparent show of compassion toward the British-based Canadian Pacific Line when chairing the investigation into the loss of the *Empress of Ireland*. Others, however, experienced a different side of him; he was known for his abrasiveness and unapologetic refusal to suffer fools when cross-examining witnesses. Mersey was remunerated 1,000 guineas for his work in the *Titanic* inquiry, after which he retained the position of wreck commissioner: he later presided over the SOLAS conventions of 1913–14 as well as the investigations into the politically sensitive disasters of the *Falaba* and *Lusitania*. Appointed member of the Admiralty Transport Arbitration Board in 1914, he was raised to viscount in 1916 for his prowess at the Admiralty Court during the First World War. He died aged eighty-nine on 3 September 1929.

Notwithstanding any lack of ambition, Mersey's equally distinguished counterpart was Senator William Alden Smith. Born in 1859, Smith at an early age garnered entrepreneurial zeal and a passion for journalism. Qualifying as a lawyer in 1882, he became a specialist in transport law; ultimately founding two railroads of his own as well as a newspaper, the *Grand Rapids Herald*. Venturing into politics in 1888 upon taking his seat at the Michigan State Central Committee (until 1892), he was elected Republican senator for Michigan in 1895. Retaining the seat until his resignation in 1907 he was returned both that year and again in 1913, yet vested interests in shipping found him at odds with the apparent self-regulation he felt was keenly exhibited by the major operators – thus at the first opportunity he petitioned President Taft to establish a Senate committee to investigate the loss of *Titanic*. Its sessions, to which he summoned her senior surviving crew and company chairman, prompted speculation that he had entered the fray to enhance his own profile through the intensity of interest the investigation would likely attract. Furthermore, Senator Smith held a known personal dislike of J.P. Morgan despite, like many of his contemporaries, benefitting from funding provided by IMM. He no doubt salivated at the opportunity to chair the inquest. Smith retired from the Senate on 3 March 1919 and died in his hometown on 11 October 1932.

Root and Branch

Of the two investigations of 1912 examining the loss of *Titanic*, by drawing a wider pool of expert opinion and immersing in more labyrinthine detail, the British inquiry is regarded as offering more credibility than the American. It was considered that the American investigation had been set up too brashly, turning out ill-prepared as a result and drawing upon too little expertise. The American investigation was also undermined by its determination to apportion someone (namely captains Smith and Lord) or something (IMM) with negligence, as well as enhancing the profiles of its inquisitors in the process. Even its legitimacy was called into question. In addition, Smith's investigation was blinkered by its eagerness to accuse British sailors and organisations and apportion blame for the disaster.

Mersey's court, albeit not a 'trial' in the strict sense, in contrast established clear objectives from the outset. With a detachment as insipidly as that with which an accountant views his ledger, Lord Mersey, unruffled by the excitement surrounding the disaster, trawled vast technical input to dispassionately identify deficiencies and to avoid these causing disaster again. Blame was never its objective. Yet it too was marred for seemingly making every endeavour not to censure or discredit the British Board of Trade, British shipping or the British government, for doing so would have caused its mercantile marine untold reputable and financial havoc. Mersey was also criticised for dismissing the significance of passenger testimony. The two investigations raised more questions than were answered; however, their findings were far reaching and, based on first-hand accounts, form the bedrock of all future study of the disaster. Mersey's much-awaited seventy-four-page report detailing his all-encompassing findings was presented amid much interest on 30 July 1912.

Beginning with navigation, the report saw the most compelling evidence heard against Captain Smith. Its author acknowledged Smith's resistance to alter the course of *Titanic* or reduce her speed while knowingly heading into an area infested with ice. Mersey, however, was satisfied that Smith's actions were not reckless since he was following an accepted 'precautionary' and widely used practice employed by North Atlantic commanders: maintaining the speed and course of a vessel when among ice while relying on the attentiveness of the lookouts to sight it in time. Calling for an end to this custom, Mersey insisted that captains were no longer to place such undue reliance on their lookouts. Finding also that issuing them binoculars would hinder their ability to sight ice at night, Mersey shirked controversy by favouring the industry's preferred ice-seeking method: the naked eye.

Corroborating with his American counterparts, Mersey deemed claims of the mistreatment of third-class passengers to be unfounded. Although not a single third-class passenger had been called to testify, Mersey's report stated that those in third class were simply less willing to leave *Titanic*, because doing so required the abandonment of all their worldly belongings on the ship. Mersey also vindicated Bruce Ismay's own actions for abandoning the sinking ship. He believed that the chairman's escape had not prevented anyone else from being saved since 473 seats in the lifeboats went unfilled: the boat that Ismay boarded, collapsible C, left *Titanic* with eight seats empty. In dealing with Ismay's purported sway over Captain Smith, Mersey – heeding the view supported by a slew of White Star captains – accepted that Ismay had never previously interfered in the navigation of any vessel he travelled on, even as chairman of the line.

Mersey then appraised the conduct of others. Applauding Arthur Rostron and the crew of *Carpathia* for their speedy rescue of the survivors, the report also dealt with behaviour of the crew of *Titanic*. Praising them for overseeing the evacuation gallantly and without regard for their own personal safety, he found that during the disaster the crew had acted courageously and that their actions were exemplary under the intense circumstances. He did, however, call for police-style officers to serve as part of the crew, trained in crowd management and how to respond during an emergency. Deciding also that the sinking was caused by abnormal weather conditions not hitherto experienced by her officers, Mersey concluded that with the damage *Titanic* sustained from the iceberg her crew could have done no more to prevent her loss. The inquiry was also keen to stress that *Titanic* suffered no underlying defect from her design: carelessness was the overriding cause of her demise.

What then of her commander? During a career spanning almost forty years Captain Smith had commanded more than 150 westbound crossings to North America. The experienced master incontrovertibly understood his duty of care to those aboard his ship, but the 'excessive speed' with which it steamed through an ice field that he knew was present was not found to compromise this duty. Smith had followed an unwritten though widely accepted protocol of maintaining speed amid icy conditions because of, as Lord Mersey put it, 'competition and in the desire of the public for quick passages rather than in the judgement of navigators. But unfortunately experience appeared to justify it.' Mersey would not castigate Smith for following protocol, albeit a tacit one. The captain was merely 'exercising his own discretion in the way he thought best':

> He made a mistake, a very grievous mistake, but one in which, in face of the practice and of past experience, negligence cannot be said to have had any part; and in the absence of negligence it is, in my opinion, impossible to fix Captain Smith with blame.

Mersey firmly believed that English law harboured no precedence with which to apportion a charge of negligence upon a deceased individual: 'I feel the greatest reluctance in finding negligence against a man who cannot be heard', unless 'there is a fixed practice which binds me'. There was none. He conceded that the incident could not have been unforeseen by either Smith or his hand-picked senior crew. Unwittingly laying grounds for counter claims of negligence, Mersey's absolution of Smith was successfully challenged at the Commercial Court in a landmark ruling the following year – resurfacing calls claiming that his inquiry was a whitewash. However, in Mersey's view the collision was by no means the result of inept leadership. Smith had followed a widely accepted maritime convention that meant therefore that neither he, White Star or the crew could be to blame if following it resulted in disaster. Mersey would, however, outlaw the practice of racing relentlessly through ice, ruling it a breach of duty for any captain doing so in future. He recommended that during night if the presence of ice was reported to the captain, he should be obliged to either reduce speed or alter course and avoid the area completely. Although Smith had committed an error of judgement by applying the practice, doing so in the eyes of the court had not left him culpable.

Although cleared of any wrongdoing, Bruce Ismay bore the brunt of public condemnation, considering his survival contemptible while so many of his passengers and crew were left to their deaths on *Titanic*. Ismay was always going to be instrumental in the impending investigation bound to take place after the loss of an insured and registered vessel on its maiden voyage, incurring also considerable loss of life. Strangely though, until reaching New York aboard *Carpathia* Ismay somewhat naively maintained that he 'had not the slightest idea that any inquiry was contemplated'. Crucially he found sympathetic ears at Mersey's court: had Ismay remained on *Titanic*, Mersey asserted, he would only have achieved adding himself to the death toll. Indeed, had Ismay perished he would most likely have been hailed a classic British hero. Captain Smith, who died at his post, was instantly championed in death, honoured in songs for keeping imperturbable in the face of adversity, and stoically going down with his ship. Yet it was the captain, not Ismay, whose actions were instrumental in provoking disaster.

The report then turned to the contentious issue of the Board of Trade. Prior to the disaster the record of safety on Anglo-American routes had improved significantly over the three previous decades. But despite that fact Mersey ruled that pure common sense should dictate that the quantity of lifeboats carried at sea should no longer be based on tonnage or cubic capacity as it had been since 1854. He demanded a more simplified rule: one that divined lifeboat allocation based on the total number of occupants the vessel was able to carry.

Although branding the Board's regulations outmoded, Mersey went on to attest that all boats that left *Titanic* had not been filled to capacity because the organisation behind the evacuation, although disciplined, was poorly facilitated by the crew. He also argued that Smith's order 'women and children first' was actually to the detriment of saving life since it had been translated too literally by his officers, namely Charles Lightoller, who would rather leave seats empty than fill them with men. Mersey attributed the main reason for the vacant seats to the general apathy among passengers to abandon *Titanic* because they believed her infallible, or because the reassurance of lights, which some believed came from a distant ship – *Californian* – fed a false sense of imminent rescue.

Mersey called for compulsory lifeboat drills to be conducted once a week on every Atlantic voyage. The drills would not only test the crew's handling of the boats but also their operation of bulkhead doors: a ruling devoutly enforced to this day. Mersey also suggested the load capacity of each lifeboat be clearly marked on its hull to allay fears of overloading and that watertight compartments and double hull walls on ocean-going craft should be extended to provide greater clearance above the waterline. The report would also require all vessels to carry a wireless and have it manned at all times, day and night, and for the eye testing of lookouts to be both mandatory and regularly conducted.

Crucially, the court did not find White Star negligent on the grounds that they had not only complied with, but exceeded, every active stipulation of the Board regarding safety – particularly those pertaining to the supply of lifeboats. Although Mersey expressed disappointment that none of the boats lowered from *Titanic* returned to rescue others from the sea after she had sunk, he called for all lifeboats to be fitted with an onboard motor as well as routinely being supplied with signal flares.

Mersey's clean-up of the regulations ensued. Criticising the Board's laxity in testing the strength of bulkheads, he urged them to recall their regulatory committee to report improvements in their protective measures. He panned the Board's lethargy to update regulations on lifeboat capacity, although pulled short of naming these inadequacies as the cause of the high loss of life. Warning them instead to keep the regulations conversant in the future, he had been placated by reviews by the Board between February 1911 and March 1912, which produced several proposals to extend the upper limit of existing regulations governing lifeboat capacities for ships grossing beyond the 10,000-ton scope of the Act of 1894. However, he was unconvinced that had any of the proposals been implemented prior to the disaster the recommended provisions would have provided enough capacity to save everybody aboard *Titanic*. Controversially his criticism ceased there, and he lessened the blow for the Board of Trade by insisting that their 'officials had discharged their duties carefully and well' – a statement that led the entire investigation to be dismissed as a whitewash.

The system, still needing something to blame for the disaster, found this in *Californian*. Her officers the most ideal scapegoats, Sir Rufus' persistent, if irreverent, questioning of Stanley Lord saw the captain vilified in Mersey's report for failing make any attempt to answer the distress rockets his crew had seen launched by *Titanic*. Surmising that *Titanic* and *Californian* were 'about 5 miles apart … though not more than 8 to 10 miles', he insisted *Californian* 'could have pushed through the ice to the open water without any risk and so have come to the assistance of the *Titanic*. Had she done she might have saved many if not all of the lives that were lost'. Mindful of Stanley Lord's inaction over the sighting of the distress rockets, Mersey ruled all future occurrences to warrant indictable offence for any captain failing to aid another vessel whose crew could perceive in any form of distress.

As for the matter of compensation the Merchant Shipping Act limited liability to £15 per ton for loss of life, and £8 per ton for loss or damage to goods (being £690,000 for 46,000-ton *Titanic*) as long as the operating company (White Star Line) was not proven negligent. Mersey was wary not to place Captain Smith, and therefore White Star Line, at fault, for doing so would remove the ceiling set in the Act and give way to compensatory claims. Such claims would most certainly cause the ruination of a well-established company and with equal certainty forsake its trade to rivals overseas. Mersey was equally cautious not to point the finger at the Board of Trade for approving a ship bereft of life-saving appliances. Blaming either party, he feared, would signal an avalanche of claims that would inevitably for years swamp the legal system just as they were starting to in America; an outcome the British government, still reeling from burgeoning welfare and military expenditure, could ill afford.

Mersey's inquiry sought to correct, not berate, a struggling shipping industry. It established the first ever multinational conference to study and monitor safety of life at sea: SOLAS. Having set SOLAS the remit of creating internationally aligned standards – watertight compartmentalisation, lifeboat supply, navigation and the application of wireless – its first session took place in London on 12 November 1913. Attended by thirteen governments, it too was presided over by the august Lord Mersey. The British delegation at the conference, nominated by various maritime organisations, comprised Sir John Biles (an assessor at the *Titanic* inquiry), Sir Arthur Norman Hill (chair of the Board's twenty-member Advisory Committee on Merchant Shipping between 1907–37 – the very panel that in 1911 rejected Alexander Carlisle's proposals for extra lifeboats for the Olympic Class), Commander Frederick George Lording (nominated by the Board of Trade) and Captain Sir Herbert Acton Blake

(Trinity House). More widely known as the Titanic Conference, its findings were presented on 20 January 1914 and came into legal effect from 1 July 1915.

SOLAS agreed guidelines for sending and receiving wireless distress signals. Stipulating also that all lifeboats be strong enough to be lowered safely with 'its full complement of persons and equipment' to avoid repetition of being sent away half filled because of fears of their being unable to bear a full load. Fundamentally, the conference had established the International Ice Patrol, dispatching two vessels to mount permanent watch 'for the study and observation of ice conditions' in the North Atlantic. Since 1923 the International Ice Patrol (now part of the US Coast Guard) has without fail deposited wreaths at the CQD position of *Titanic* each 15 April; in more recent years they have been dropped to the site by plane.

Public outcry saw a chastened Board of Trade implement Mersey's recommendations in full – acutely aware of the greater urgency to review legislation. Nonetheless, the publication of Mersey's report found much of the media convinced of an establishment cover-up. Dissatisfied with its scope and apparent reticence to confront the actions of the Board of Trade and White Star's Edward Smith, *The Daily Telegraph* echoed the consensus verdict of the time: 'The report having in effect acquitted them of all blame, it is not likely that any attempt will be made hereafter to establish the contrary'. Maybe deflection was indeed Mersey's goal, but his and Senator Smith's reports both provide unparalleled insight that may one day lead to a final universally accepted conclusion establishing who or exactly what was responsible for the greatest maritime disaster of the modern age.

CHAPTER 12

A REPUTATION FOR SAFETY

> 'I cannot imagine any condition which would cause the ship to founder. I cannot conceive of any vital disaster happening to this vessel. Modern ship-building has gone beyond that.'
> Captain Edward Smith speaking of *Adriatic*, May 1907

Upon the birth of White Star Line, founder Thomas Henry Ismay penned a book of 'General Rules', issued since 1870 to each of his captains, with which to set out the standard of management and safety that each was to enforce on their vessels. After its first rule, reminding them in no uncertain terms to follow all the rules, the book moved to its second decree, spelling out the company's paramount concern – the responsibility of their captains:

> The commanders must distinctly understand that … whilst they are expected to use every diligence to secure a speedy voyage, they must run no risk which might by any possibility result in accident to their ships. It is to be hoped that they will ever bear in mind that the safety of lives and property entrusted to their care is the ruling principle that should govern them in the navigation of their ships and no supposed gain in expedition, or saving of time on the voyage, is to be purchased at the risk of accident. The Company desires to establish and maintain for its vessels a reputation for safety, and only looks for such speed on various voyages as is consistent with safe and prudent navigation.

The *Titanic* disaster exposed a wealth of deficiencies with White Star's persistence for 'safe and prudent navigation' – deficiencies that toppled like dominoes to doom *Titanic*. The unheeded iceberg warnings; lookouts unequipped with binoculars; the captain sallying forth his ship through a region in which he expected to encounter ice; the first officer whose reactions compounded the ship's injury; the ship whose rudder was unable to skirt her round the iceberg, nor whose bulkheads reached high enough to contain the flood she sustained; and more crucially, the appalling shortfall in lifeboats it carried: resolving any of these may have sufficed to avert disaster. But what exactly had allowed this series of failings to occur, considering that from the outset White Star was so assiduous that 'a reputation for safety' was accorded as their 'ruling principle'. Here we shall explore the causes of the disaster and determine point-by-point how inevitable catastrophe loomed over *Titanic* that fateful evening of April 1912.

The Lookouts

Both official inquiries of 1912 raised into question the actions of the crew, particularly of Reginald Lee and Frederick Fleet, the two lookouts on duty in the crow's nest at the moment of the iceberg's first sighting. The fact that none of the six lookouts aboard *Titanic* were equipped with binoculars at any stage during the maiden voyage, despite even twice requesting the use of a pair, remains the nucleus to the ship's subsequent failure to avoid the iceberg. Lookout George Symons represented his colleagues' first request, put to Chief Officer Henry Wilde shortly after departure from Southampton: 'There are none,' Wilde would dismiss. The lookout's second request came from George Hogg who approached Second Officer Lightoller moments after *Titanic* left her Queenstown anchorage – now non-stop to New York. Lightoller informed Hogg that they would be supplied with a pair later.

Officers were not legally obliged to provide their lookouts with binoculars. Ceasing their mandatory supply in 1895, White Star passed the onus to individual captains to make such provisions on their ships. For *Titanic* a pair was indeed assigned to her lookouts and the crow's nest even boasted a container specifically to store them. Yet, during her maiden voyage this pair remained locked within a container to which no one aboard had any access.

Hogg knew exactly who to ask for the binoculars. The crewmember responsible for supervising the lookouts was the second officer, who, just hours before *Titanic* departed Southampton, was David Blair. During the preparations for departure, Blair had secured the binoculars inside a lockbox in his cabin for safekeeping. When Captain Smith transferred him from the roster a day prior to cast-off to clear the way for Henry Wilde, Blair mistakenly walked ashore carrying the key to this container with him. His replacement, Charles Lightoller, subsequently occupied the cabin containing the lockbox, to which he had no access. As a consequence no binoculars were made available to the lookouts for the duration of the voyage, these being the only pair aboard *Titanic* that lookouts could borrow. Although each of the eight officers carried their own binoculars, an additional pair was also left on the bridge for piloting; none of these however could be 'loaned' to lookouts.

White Star paid their lookouts an additional 5s a month above the pay level of ordinary seamen and specifically recruited lookouts who were fully aware of the importance of their job, subjecting them to regular and stringent eye examinations. After the disaster Fleet and Lee had their eyesight re-tested – both passed.

Because of growing concern over the location of ice reported in a wireless message received from *Caronia* on the morning of 14 April, upon nearing the area reported in this region that evening the then watch commander, Charles Lightoller, had Sixth Officer Moody alert the crow's nest to 'keep a sharp lookout for ice, particularly small ice and growlers, until daylight'. Fleet, however, would later maintain that the bridge ignored three sightings of ice reported during the thirty minutes prior to the collision, during which he and his colleague Lee noticed an increase to the amount of fuzziness – mistaking it as haze – forming round *Titanic*. This increased in the final ten minutes before sighting the iceberg, but because his earlier reports elicited no response from the bridge, alleged Fleet, he and Lee decided against passing on this latest observation, which, had the officers checked for themselves, would most likely have identified the haze as ice.

Earlier, at 7.15p.m., First Officer Murdoch had Samuel Hemming, a lamp trimmer, seal the cargo hatch below the crow's nest to prevent the light emanating from the forward holds impairing the lookouts' vision. Concern had grown among senior crew in the hours leading to collision over the lookout's visibility amid the strong likelihood of encountering ice due to the falling air temperature. This awareness of ice among the watch crew sparked further controversy during the Thomas Ryan case of 1913, which sued against the officers' failure to equip the lookouts with binoculars. Ryan argued that had they been given binoculars to locate icebergs at greater distance from *Titanic*, their discovery may have provided sufficient notice for the bridge to take evasive action. The revelation had earlier been refuted by Lord Mersey's investigation, deeming to the contrary that at night the naked eye was far superior to binocular lenses in limited ambient light. Indeed, a moonless evening with no natural light present to reflect from nearby icebergs vanquished any hope of sighting them in adequate time. The 'blink' theory bandied at the time equated the magnitude of reflected light to the size of the iceberg; the greater the blink the larger the berg, however every method available to sight ice was still entirely dependent on at least some source of light.

Binoculars manufactured prior to 1914 (the Zeiss type) had not the ability of succeeding models to gather enough light into their lenses to enhance visibility at night. Those on *Titanic* were technically less effective than the naked eye and their use – successfully argued at Mersey's court through the convincing testimony of celebrity witness Sir Ernest Shackleton – sufficed only to enable the bearer to identify and examine objects only once already discovered.

Aboard other ships of the period, although lookouts were supplied with binoculars they were not actually used as part of the routine of their watch. Preferring to trust unaided vision, they believed the naked eye far more effective at discovering objects day or night: an opinion that was shared by each lookout on

Titanic. Mindful also that binoculars required some seconds for the user to focus on their target, there was concern that using them to detect objects delayed the lookout reporting the sighting to the bridge. In 1912 the role of the lookout was plain: sight an object, light, or other ships in their vicinity and report that sighting immediately to the bridge by sounding a warning bell with three sharp strikes. Lookouts were not to identify what they had seen, but merely to report that they had seen 'something'. The actual identification of the object in question was for the officers on the bridge and was why each carried their own pair of binoculars, to evaluate the hazard.

The shipping industry's aversion to providing lookouts with binoculars was also fuelled by the constrained view of the horizon the glasses afforded opposed to the peripheral scope of the naked eye. By not providing binoculars, shipping lines removed the lookout's temptation to rely on them. With the lookout high aloft in a crow's nest and in a facing headwind, the industry felt the use of glasses was more a hindrance to the ability to sight objects day or night, believing the lenses in such conditions being particularly susceptible to fog and smear. Nonetheless, after the disaster the stance was given a negative press, White Star finally made binoculars available to every lookout who wanted use of them.

Perched 95ft above sea level, the lookouts on *Titanic* stood in an unshielded crow's nest fixed to her forward mast. At this height clear conditions afforded its occupants a viewing horizon of 11.2 miles. Yet by 11.40p.m. on the evening of the collision Fleet and Lee had already endured freezing headwinds of 25mph for one hour and forty minutes. With unprotected eyes the cold and moonless sky was not only hampering their vision but sapping concentration: hardly conducive for sighting distant objects when running *Titanic* at full speed.

In this age of fledgling technologies, shipping in 1912 still leaned heavily upon traditional methods of detection. Both official investigations strove to ascertain why this most modern liner had been left bereft of searchlights, arguably invaluable tools for discovering icebergs at night; Senator Smith's report called for their subsequent compulsory supply. The reason why the shipping community had previously been less receptive to adopting the lights proved typically convoluted.

Despite their use already widely endorsed by the Royal Navy at the time, practice was still averse to supplying mercantile vessels such as *Titanic* with searchlights. To the navy a 24in searchlight had proven highly effective for sighting even the smallest icebergs within a 2,000–yard circumference. But their merchant cousins were far less convinced, believing the nuisance of the lights outweighed all the advantages. Principally they felt the reflection produced by the beam hindered the vision of not only the lookouts but the crew on the bridge too, potentially also diffusing the ship's own navigation lighting and interfering with lookouts on other liners. Secondly, it was reasoned that reduced visibility in coastal waters ran the risk of searchlights from other ships becoming misconstrued as lighthouses. Merchant shipping considered the alternative too dangerous to employ in the bustling lanes of the North Atlantic and this became a view shared by the surviving officers of *Titanic*, who, even in hindsight, testified that had the lights been available to them they would still not have employed them on *Titanic* to look for ice. Like their colleagues across the industry navigation was considered far safer without them. This was a resistance formed on experience.

In 1889 White Star had fitted a searchlight to *Teutonic*, with the American Line also installing them on *City of Paris* and *City of New York*. Yet within months all three saw them removed because the lights were deemed too dangerous to use on the Atlantic and often found that icebergs reflected their beam, making all but their edges almost invisible. It was thus decided that not having searchlights removed the temptation of placing too much reliance on them to influence the naviga-tion of a vessel. The British inquiry would accept such lights salutary nonetheless to illuminate ice ahead of the ship, but agreed a solution could be a non-pivotal forward-facing light fixed above the wheelhouse that could be switched on from the bridge, a type already commonplace for vessels navigating the Suez Canal.

On 28 May 1912 the Senate committee published its recommendations into the disaster. These included the mandatory provision of a minimum of two searchlights on every vessel carrying more than 100 passengers. Yet even in the aftermath of *Titanic* their application was deemed largely ineffective. HAPAG, who launched their 52,117-ton *Imperator* on 23 May, had during her fitting-out hastily installed a searchlight to boost public confidence in her safety. However, throughout her career this searchlight was not used once to search for ice, purely because crew still considered it too dangerous for the North Atlantic.

The practice, however, to rely upon lookouts to find ice both at night and with-out aid of binoculars or lights, had been unwittingly bolstered by Captain Rostron. While heading *Carpathia* to the CQD position at full speed he doubled her lookouts to eight. Navigating *Carpathia* for over three hours through the same ice field that ensnared *Titanic*, Rostron had demonstrated that the disaster had occurred due to Captain Smith's inadequate lookout complement for the speed his ship was main-taining, traversing that same area – binoculars therefore may not have availed *Titanic*.

Despite all the hypotheses, practice and technologies in use in 1912, until the emergence of Radar in 1937 these provided negligible improvement to the ability of crew to discover an iceberg in the path of a ship on a calm, moonless evening, until she had virtually stumbled upon it. In clear conditions, with no waves to break against or natural light to reflect, the stealthy iceberg rightly remains the true nemesis of the mariner.

Navigation

As with air travel today ocean-going vessels in 1912 were likewise required to follow designated lanes to avoid collision with other craft. Westbound vessels travel-ling from Queenstown to New York would follow a 3,000-mile 'track' forming an arc known as the Great Circle, a route taking full advantage of the curvature of the earth by reducing the mileage between European and North American ports.

Originally devised by the US Navy, transatlantic shipping lanes were adopted by the major merchant operators – HAPAG, Norddeutscher Lloyd, French Line, Cunard and White Star – following a conference chaired in London by Bruce Ismay on 15 November 1898. The lanes came formally into operation on 15 January 1899, their designation, however, was not permanently static. During summer months – 15 August to 14 January – all westbound traffic traversing the North Atlantic followed a route named the Outward Northern Track. In these months the Labrador Current rarely carried the Arctic ice floes much south of the 43rd Meridian. Cooled in winter months, the current drifts ice further south, encroaching on this northern shipping lane and it was not uncommon for it to reach as far south as the 42nd Meridian and to 45°W to the east. Therefore, as a precaution, this westbound lane was moved 200 miles further to the south during wintertime: 15 January to 14 August. This winter route was named the Outward Southern Track and required vessels to perform a crucial change of course at a location referred to as the 'Corner'.

The point marking the Corner was set at 42°N, 47°W – due south of the Grand Banks area off Canada's Newfoundland. This detour, adding 220 miles to the voyage, avoided the south and easterly extent of the winter ice floes, as well as the notorious Newfoundland fog. Westbound vessels 'rounding the Corner' would perform a 24-degree turn to change tack from the lightship off Fastnet – marking the southernmost tip of Ireland – to the lightship off Nantucket, Massachusetts, thereby maintaining the most direct route to New York Harbour. This change also applied to the two Homeward (eastbound) lanes running to the south of their respective Outward winter/summer companions.

As a further precaution at the height of winter – April to June – the position of the Corner was moved to 41°N, 47°W, an additional 60 miles to the south. Relocating the Corner for the Outward Southern Track during these high winter months was introduced as a result of abnormally colder winters experienced in 1898, 1903 and 1905. Cooler than usual conditions in those years saw icebergs drifting further south of their usual extremity, in fact so far south that they withstood the warmer waters of the Gulf Stream, the point at which icebergs traditionally melted away. These more atypical seasons found the Gulf Stream carrying ice eastward and, until a point, their incursion even breached the revised winter tracks. On these occasions between April and June the extent of ice reached as far south as 39°N and 38°30'W to the east. As a consequence the extremity of ice encountered during these years was marked on all charts for the North Atlantic – the Western Ocean – along with the notation, 'Ice has been seen in this area in April, May and June'. As a further precaution a general ice alert was also observed between April and August. Such details were made available in 1909 by the US Hydrographic Office in their publication *Sailing Directions*, which gave navigational advice for east coast American shipping. This information was also distributed by the British Admiralty on all charts for the North Atlantic, complete with dotted line marking the extent of ice during specified months. The chart aboard *Titanic*, number 2058, bore this same information. In only the fourth occasion for fifteen years, the winter of April 1912 transpired to be equally as cold.

It is assumed the iceberg that struck *Titanic* had likely been adrift in the Arctic since 1910. Caught in the Labrador Current it continued into the Atlantic and by April 1912 ventured as far south as the Grand Banks. The cooler conditions allowed this and hundreds of other icebergs to drift further south than usual and into the Gulf Stream, itself chilled by abnormal temperatures. Showing little sign of fatigue, this Armada of icebergs continued until they eventually not only breached the standard shipping lanes but peppered the winter Outward Southern Track also – the route followed by *Titanic* along with every other westbound vessel at that time of year. As a result of the previous winter's anomalies a temporary Corner was in effect in April 1912 at a position an even further (240 miles) to the south-east, 38°N, 45°W. On the 14th Captain Smith had requested in the night-order book that the crew postpone making this turn at this revised location by thirty minutes, rousing speculation that he had done so in response to becoming aware of an incident that had taken place 100 miles to the north of the revised Corner.

Travelling westbound from Le Havre with 1,000 passengers, French Line's 8,590-ton *Niagara* had collided violently with an iceberg on the evening of 11 April, puncturing two openings into her hull. The incident potentially induced Smith to delay the Corner for *Titanic* in order to avoid the ice now known to be obstructing the winter Outward Southern Track. Indeed, its presence in that region was reported to him in warnings that were received via the wireless earlier that day. As it emerged, however, Smith had only detoured *Titanic* less than 10 miles further south of her intended point, an insufficient amount to be anywhere near circumnavigating the southern extent of the ice field through which *Titanic* was rapidly traversing. Even just ten minutes prior to the collision with the iceberg, *Titanic* was still 2 miles within the standard path of the winter Outward Southern Track.

Captains were afforded leeway to deviate outside the prescribed lanes. White Star's own General Rules stressed they 'be left to their own judgement … and be guided by circumstances' in the navigation of their vessels. After the disaster however, the location of the Corner of the Outward Southern Track was pushed 180 miles even further to the south. If his delay seemed so insignificant, why had Smith not kept this heading and continued further south?

The coalminers' strike had seen even the precious supply aboard *Titanic* a prevalent factor during her maiden voyage. *Titanic* carried just slightly more coal than the minimum stock she needed for the outward trip. Clocking up additional mileage would run her the risk to running out of fuel mid-ocean. It proved a conundrum for Smith, and the presence of ice was causing the sea veteran much concern. Throughout the night of the 14th Smith had grown increasingly troubled by the worsening conditions. Rapidly falling air temperature had him acutely aware that the possibility of encountering ice at some stage of the voyage was increasingly likely. Smith was particularly wary of the mischief of a calm sea, which created harder viewing conditions for his lookouts, who were denied the whiteness of waves breaking against nearby icebergs. At 8.55p.m. he articulated these concerns to the then watch commander, Second Officer Lightoller:

'There is not much wind,' said Smith to Lightoller.

'No it is a flat calm,' agreed he and continued to echo his captain's unease that it was 'rather a pity the breeze had not kept up whilst we were going through the ice region', referring to the lack of wind to produce discernible waves against the bases of nearby icebergs.

Lightoller remained upbeat however: 'of course there will be a certain amount of reflected light from the bergs'. The captain agreed and remarked they should at the very least see the pallid outlines of any nearby. With that the conversation ended.

Smith left Lightoller in command of the bridge at 9.20p.m. and went off to his cabin, famously asking to be woken 'if it becomes at all doubtful'. With this, Smith withdrew to his suite directly behind the bridge, remaining there until the collision. Yet despite this conversation the speed of *Titanic* remained at 75rpm, 22.25 knots – her full speed – unabated for more than a day. Hope of finding exactly why the captain was so intent on steaming *Titanic* at full tilt through an ice field he knew to be present disappeared with Smith and his ship's logbooks to their watery grave. However, the days following the disaster saw the notion emerge that his rationale for delaying turning the Corner was in an attempt to steal time by shortening the voyage. Was Smith in a hurry?

Even for years after the disaster Smith's Western Ocean peers continued shaving away voyage time by literally cutting 'the Corner', slicing as close to Newfoundland as they could. Time was everything, and *Titanic* was scheduled to arrive at her New York pier at 5a.m. on Wednesday 17 April. To achieve this Smith needed to keep her at 20 knots. The stokers in her six boiler rooms were also given advance notice that the ship would require extra steam to make a spurt on the 15th to arrive in New York one day ahead of schedule. This detail is known since specific authority was given for stokers to use coal stored in the reserve bunkers set aside for emergencies. Also, in the *New York Times* edition of 15 April Bruce Ismay printed the announcement confirming the arrival of *Titanic* revised to 4p.m., Tuesday the 16th – a clear margin ahead of her scheduled slot eleven hours later. Who was deciding the speed of the ship became the overriding controversy in the wake of the disaster with speculation that the company chairman was overruling the captain in eagerness to race to New York and an overture of glory. Ismay was undeniably keen to see how his new ship could perform and was equally bent to make an impression on New York's expectant media.

Both *Olympic* and *Titanic* boasted a service speed of 21 knots. The engines in *Olympic* afforded her a maximum speed of 22.75 knots, and those in *Titanic*, slightly more powerful, were able to achieve 23.25. Ismay had a perfect reason to expect *Titanic* to better the time of five days, sixteen hours and forty-five minutes that *Olympic* took to complete her maiden voyage, during which she averaged a speed of 21.17 knots.

Table 4: Daily mileage and average speeds of Titanic *and* Olympic *during their maiden voyages*

	Titanic		Olympic	
Full day travelled	Distance (nautical miles)	Av. speed (knots)	Distance (nautical miles)	Av. speed (knots)
Day 1	484	20.98	428	20.1
Day 2	519	20.91	534	21.6
Day 3	546	22.06	542	21.9
Day 4	258	22.11	525	21.2
Day 5	–	–	548	22.2
Day 6		–	317	19.3
Total/Average	1,807	21.44	2,894	21.17

With the average speed on the Atlantic 15.16 knots, only nine ships in 1911 were fast enough to exceed 20 knots, and one of those, *Olympic*, was specifically designed without high speed in mind. Her engines able to produce 46,000hp, even 55,000hp at a push, *Olympic* paled in comparison to the 68,000hp and 26 knots that *Mauretania* could muster. *Mauretania* was built with the explicit purpose to recapture the Blue Riband for Britain and Cunard, which she achieved in her first year of service, completing the crossing in four days, ten hours and fifty-one minutes, putting any chance of a speed attempt beyond the grasp of Ismay's 21/22-knot Olympians.

Although clearly above average Atlantic pace, like her sister the engines within *Titanic* were not intended to attempt a transatlantic speed record, let alone conjure any hope to attain it. Her engines were designed to carry passengers on a comparatively quick voyage that also afforded them the opportunity to sit back and admire her splendour. Those in a rush to cross the Atlantic chose Cunard. White Star's Olympic Class were so comfortable that the line believed their cabin classes were prepared to concede a little speed in return for more time aboard the most prestigious ships afloat. Ismay was well aware of the limitations of *Titanic*, although he also appreciated a mileage record for a single day's journeying was not entirely out of the question. After all, arriving on the Tuesday afternoon would allow an extra day to victual *Titanic* for her return to Southampton – scheduled for Saturday the 20th – and maybe leverage more publicity in the process. Doing so, however, would disrupt the raft of arrangements already made by his jealously coveted elite: hotel bookings and ongoing travel connections would all have to be altered at considerable, but not unforgivable, inconvenience. But would that risk outweigh the benefit of publicity to showboat this inaugural crossing?

On departure from Southampton on Wednesday 10 April the engines on *Titanic* were driven at 68rpm, increasing to 70rpm on leaving Cherbourg. Upon leaving Queenstown and heading into Wide Ocean they wound up to 72rpm. Rising further to 75rpm on the 13th, it was intended to maintain the engines at this speed (between 21.75 and 22.25 knots) until the 15th, but controversy had sparked while *Titanic* was anchored at Queenstown that Ismay had prearranged this with the chief engineer, Joseph Bell. Conventionally any increase in speed needed to be cleared by the chief engineer; even captains had to heed his opinion. Ismay and Bell conversed about intentions to drive the engines at 78rpm, their almost maximum speed, 'if we had fine weather', on either the 15th or 16th so to, as Ismay put it, 'economise our coal'.

Being a steamship, any increase in speed required advance notice. In preparation for the spurt planned for the 15th two unlit double-ended boilers inside room 2 were lighted on the morning of Sunday the 14th to allow the twenty-four hours necessary to raise a serviceable head of steam. All single-ended boilers in room 1 remained unfired to preserve fuel due to the recently concluded miners' strike – the very reason the speed of *Titanic* was kept to 75rpm between the 13th and 15th was to conserve this supply. Ismay's plan was, as long as they had the weather, to open the reserve bunkers for a final sprint over the 15th and 16th and to bring *Titanic* into port slightly but decisively ahead of schedule.

At the time of collision *Titanic* was travelling at 22.25 knots, her engines turning at 75rpm. Although her logbook was lost in the disaster this actuality is determined through averaging the 260 knots registered on the Patent Log between the time it was last reset – noon on the 14th – and the moment of collision with the iceberg. The Patent Log, a tiny propeller towed behind a ship to record its speed over set periods of time, was reset every two hours in the case of *Titanic*. Between noon and the collision that evening it had counted 45.5 knots over two hours, averaging *Titanic* a speed of 22.25 knots per hour.

Captain Smith too was known for his flamboyance in navigation, in fact this was a quintessential characteristic for captains of the era. It was also a trait that appealed to both shipping companies and passengers alike, who adored commanders exhibiting verve for showmanship, and considered it proof of ability as well as a desire to keep to the schedules. Having the chairman of his company aboard would certainly provide Smith with an enticement to have *Titanic* better the time he set with *Olympic* during her maiden voyage the previous year. Yet would Smith, this seasoned veteran, readily steam his own craft full speed into a known ice field just for the sake of putting on a good show?

The fact that the whereabouts of ice were reported via the ship's wireless, in locations straddling her path, suggests a captain brazenly imprudent. With Lightoller also paying particular care in the hours leading up to the collision to caution the lookouts to watch specifically for ice, credence grows towards Smith's heedlessness with pace though this region. It would be Smith and Lightoller's very conversation that formed the basis of a legal challenge in 1913 that successfully established their negligence for maintaining this speed.

At the ensuing inquiries Ismay was at pains to distance himself from accusations of exerting his influence over Smith. He argued that his captain had kept the engines at full speed to clear the region as quickly as possible in case the weather turned to fog, itself a more hazardous alternative.

Despite its commercial advantages, travelling ships at speed was not officially endorsed by the shipping companies. White Star's own regulations, unchanged since 1870, forbade captains to speed for the 'saving of time ... at the risk of accident'. Unofficially, however, operators preferred commanders who kept to the timetables, because simply, those ships sold more tickets. In addition, White Star employed a lengthy exempting clause printed on the reverse of their tickets to pre-empt claims for negligence against hazardous navigation: a waiver subsequently ruled unlawful by the Thomas Ryan case of 1913. Yet few people today would continually choose an airline that habitually ran late and the matter was no different with sea travel in 1912 – particularly with the number of lines vying for business.

Was Smith then no less than complacent in steaming *Titanic* into an ice field at full speed? Slowing such a prestigious liner on its maiden outing would certainly be a decision that he wanted to avoid. But in 1912 it had been customary for a quarter of a century hitherto the disaster that as long as conditions were fair in areas in which ice was present, captains would put their lookouts on high alert and maintain normal speed day or night, and preserve that speed until ice was spotted. This methodology avoided the ship delaying arrival at destination by not slowing down in the precautionary pretext that it may encounter ice. As long as schedules were being met, the custom went tacitly endorsed by the shipping operators themselves, commanders only slowing their ships if the sea about them was visibly formed of pack ice or worse. Until April 1912 no one had died as a result, and the logic was consequently deemed by the wider shipping community to be a safe and effective navigational protocol and passed unchallenged by regulatory bodies for twenty-five years. By 1912 its unblemished application for a quarter century and official endorsement through a conspicuous silence found the practice etched into the consciousness of North Atlantic commanders who viewed it as an all-but formalised procedure.

With sailing conditions for *Titanic* on the evening of 14 April so favourably calm for winter, Captain Smith was induced to draw on this unblemished and universally employed convention. He ploughed his ship onward. Because of this technique, the irrefutable factor that caused the sinking, Smith was pardoned of negligence by the two ensuing formal investigations on the basis that past 'experience appeared to justify it'.

Even with his awareness of ice, Smith steamed his ship unabated. At the US inquiry the surviving wireless operator, Harold Bride, recalled the captain had 'personally acknowledged' the iceberg warning received from *Baltic* and handed to him by Bride. In a telling display of master and subordinate, Smith later surrendered this message to his travelling chairman, Bruce Ismay. The captain had not done so to seek advice regarding their speed or about the whereabouts of ice; the message contained an appeal for *Titanic* to deviate course to assist a fellow liner in difficulty.

Apart from the message *Baltic* had sent containing an ice warning it also forwarded a request from an oil tanker of the Deutsch-Amerika Petroleum Co., *Deutschland*: 'Last night we spoke Oil Tank *Deutschland* Stettin to Philadelphia not under control short of coal'. The tanker, all but bereft of fuel, was dangerously adrift in position 42°42N, 55°11'W in the middle of the main shipping lane. *Deutschland* had radioed for a tow to port, which *Baltic* received and forwarded to *Titanic*. Ismay purportedly dismissed the request under the premise that their assistance would delay his hoped early arrival at New York. The chairman instead slipped this message into his pocket. It was the only occasion on which Captain Smith approached Ismay regarding the navigation of *Titanic*; however, the gesture clearly inferred that Ismay was exercising sway over his captain. Disastrously for *Titanic*, this message giving the location of ice now lay in Ismay's pocket, instead of the Chart Room table.

This particular trip was Ismay's third such crossing on a maiden voyage, *Adriatic* and *Olympic* being the other two. Shortly after the disaster Ismay asserted that his motive for taking the maiden voyage of *Titanic* was 'merely to observe the new vessel, as I had done in the case of other vessels of our lines … I was a passenger and exercised no greater right or privileges'. Continuing, 'I was not consulted about the ship, her course, speed, navigation, or her conduct at sea … the only information I ever received on the ship that other vessels had sighted ice was by a wireless message received from the *Baltic* … handed to me by Captain Smith without any remark'.

If the truth be known, despite his status as chairman, Ismay purveyed no knowledge of seafaring nor at any point made pretence otherwise. Bruce's awareness of seafaring was the antithesis of his father's exceptional brilliance. He had not interfered with the navigation of his two previous maiden crossings nor during his trips aboard other White Star vessels. Ismay's utmost concern was with his fleet, styling their features and improving their first-class areas. It was its opulence that earned White Star distinction as the line of choice for the wealthy. Ismay believed unashamedly that he employed captains to manage the workings of their ships. He would instead absorb himself with the running and marketing of the business. For Ismay was a man with meticulous eye for detail, not mechanics, and this was exactly why he commanded so little respect amongst his peers in the shipping community.

Had Ismay been advising Captain Smith regarding the speed *Titanic* should travel, being the concerted type Smith was, he would have neither heeded nor solicited advice from any non-seafarer such as Ismay. Nor was Smith obliged to. As master and commander of his craft, whether the chairman of the company was aboard or not, all decisions regarding its navigation was to be made by and solely by the captain; few enforced this standpoint more than Edward Smith. At the British inquiry Bruce Ismay relayed the high regard that the captain harboured at White Star: 'He was a man in whom we had entire and absolute confidence.' Smith's officers likewise viewed him with utmost deference, as did many others who longed to serve under him at some point in their career. When writing of Smith in 1935 Lightoller too recalled him with kindred fondness:

> He was a great favourite and a man any officer would give his ears to sail under ... he had a pleasant quiet voice and invariable smile. A voice he rarely raised above a conversational tone; not to say he couldn't. In fact I have often heard him bark an order that made a man come to himself with a bump.

In the wake of the disaster the main shipping lines would hire designated 'assistant captains' tasked to coordinate lifeboat drills and even assume command should the primary master become unable to do so. Yet none who worked with Smith could find a single doubt in his faculties as master-mariner. Although he was a popular, benevolent, sometimes even daring man, Commodore Edward John Smith was a true stickler to the rulebook, upholding supreme pride in fulfilling a duty that had garnered him unconditional trust throughout the industry. Not once was he ambivalent in his own authority or how to apply it. His warmth of heart always inspired the devotion and respect of his crew. Smith was not a man who would allow any landsmen or junior seafarers to undermine the authority and reputation that he had toiled for more than forty years to establish. In his report of 28 May 1912, inquiry chairman Senator Smith could cast no aspersion against the incontestable experience of the Atlantic's most highly remunerated mariner:

> Captain Smith knew the sea and his clear eye and steady hand had often guided his ship through dangerous paths. For forty years storms sought in vain to vex him or menace his craft. Each new advancing type of ship built by his company was handed over to him as a reward for faithful services and as evidence of confidence in his skill.

Be it occasion or his impending retirement, his own subconscious, just possibly, becalmed the venerable captain's tenacity towards his eager chairman.

Iceberg Warnings

As history has recorded, the two wireless operators on *Titanic*, Jack Phillips and Harold Bride, famously neglected to deliver to the bridge four of the seven ice warnings received on the day of the disaster. Of the three that were delivered only the ice sighting in one of them, the message from *Caronia*, would ever be marked on the ship's navigation chart. Of the remaining two messages delivered to the bridge, Bruce Ismay pocketed that from *Baltic* given to him earlier by Captain Smith – later waving the paper at two prominent female passengers before returning it to Smith that evening. The third was the first warning received from *Californian*. The location of ice given in both these sightings remained uncharted, and when the watch commander looked at this chart, the sighting by *Caronia* was all the information he had at hand; consequently he would believe the only region to avoid was 42°N, 49° to 51°W.

Indeed, rather than White Star it was the Marconi Company that employed the ship's wireless operators. They did however remain answerable to the captain, since they were also deemed to be an aid to the ship's navigation. The operators would send and receive messages regarding navigation but their attention often became diluted with the fee-paying transmissions from passengers. Ranging from hotel reservations and customary postcard greetings the growing backlog of messages found Bride and Phillips devoting priority to commercial signals over those germane to ice sightings and navigation. Such pressure was showcased in the instance in which Phillips brusquely interjected through an inbound transmission from *Californian* repeating its earlier report of ice. 'Keep out, shut up. I am busy', Phillips retorted famously, since it interrupted an outbound message of his own. Most lines employed just one operator per ship, who manned the set for as long as they could then terminated communication at the flick of a switch when unable to stay awake longer. *Titanic* sported two operators, maintaining twenty-four-hour coverage as both the workload and the status of the ship was deemed such to warrant it.

Cape Race was a major receiving station on the south-eastern tip of Newfoundland, bearing the call sign MCE. Phillips had been transmitting MCE passenger messages to have them relayed to onward stations overland. Because of the limited range of early equipment messages were relayed ship-to-ship in order to reach their intended destinations. As *Titanic* neared the Grand Banks, the station at Newfoundland became Phillips' first opportunity to communicate directly with the mainland. Airwaves often became cluttered and it could be extremely confusing, especially for novices, to decipher its growing cacophony of signals. The muddle added stress on Bride and Phillips, both of whom were busy earning their keep for Marconi; the sending of commercial messages was, after all, the primary reason luxury liners were carrying their sets.

Although principally a private enterprise, wireless operators did appreciate the importance of transferring navigational information to the bridge. To secure this commitment a proportion of the operator's salary was paid by the shipping line to cover the expense of using the equipment as a navigational tool. Contributing toward the salaries in this manner also ensured the radio operators were never independent of their formal place among the crew – securing their awareness and responsibility toward the safe navigation of the ship. Being a recent innovation, the bridge, however, would not always treat the warnings contained in their messages with the urgency they deserved.

Despite Captain Smith being personally handed two messages containing ice sightings – those from *Baltic* and *Caronia* – only one of the messages delivered to the bridge by the operators on the day of the disaster actually found its way to the chart. Four other messages reporting the whereabouts of ice – those from *Noordam, Amerika, Mesaba* and the second message from *Californian* – would all fail to leave the wireless operator's tray.

An eighth message received by *Titanic* that fateful day had been Morsed by lamp from the passing steamer, *Rappahannock*. Despite the report being received directly by the bridge (either by Murdoch or Moody) this sighting too remained neither recorded on the chart nor drawn to the captain's attention. Had all warnings received the day of disaster been charted, a pattern outlining a barrier of ice 400 miles long by several miles wide would have materialised directly in the path *Titanic* was headed. The unmarked warnings left the commander of the bridge with no indication of the obstruction straddling his path unless he collated, read, then calculated the positions from each warning, whether they lay in the wireless shack or were tucked into the frame of the Chart Room table.

The wireless may have revolutionised communication and the ease with which to exchange information at sea, however the two official investigations into the sinking admonished the lack of cohesion between wireless operator and bridge house as a major factor causing the loss of *Titanic*. Ruling it in consequence, mandatory for wireless operators to communicate all information relating to navigation immediately and directly to the bridge, watch officers were also obliged to mark the positions of reported ice upon the chart. No longer were ice warnings to be handled so nonchalantly as operator and crewmember often regarded them in April 1912.

Officer of the Watch

Commanding the bridge at the moment of the sighting and impact with the iceberg was First Officer William Murdoch. Conspicuously having *Titanic* perform a series of manoeuvres in the seconds up to and after her collision with the iceberg, it had been alleged that this exacerbated the damage and ultimately sealed the ship's fate. These actions purportedly filled Murdoch with such guilt that – if Hollywood is to be believed – it culminated in his apparent suicide with a revolver on the bridge shortly before *Titanic* vanished towards the seabed.

Murdoch's command of the bridge began at 10p.m. on the evening of the disaster. Crucially, in the seconds prior to Fleet's sighting, the bridge itself was surprisingly devoid of officers. Murdoch was outside in vigil in the starboard navigation wing, his second-in-command, Fifth Officer Joseph Boxhall, had been ensconced in the Chart Room since 8p.m. writing up the stellar observations taken at 7.30p.m. Quartermaster Alfred Olliver too was outside, returning to the bridge house after checking the compass platform behind the officers' quarters. This left just two crewmembers in the wheelhouse at the moment Fleet sighted the iceberg: James Moody, the most junior officer on ship, and Quartermaster Robert Hichens who was manning the helm.

When seeing the iceberg Fleet sounded the crow's nest bell with three hard strikes, simultaneously telephoning the bridge. Moody received his call, relaying the news to Murdoch outside: 'Iceberg, right ahead'. Running back to the wheelhouse Murdoch ordered the engines slammed into full speed reverse and for Hichens to spin the helm hard-over to port. At the time of the sighting just 500 yards of water separated *Titanic*, heading at full speed, from this towering, lumbering and indestructible wall of ice. During her sea trials less than a fortnight hence it had been calculated that *Titanic* required 850 yards to pull to a halt from a speed of 20.5 knots, and needed some minutes to complete it. But Murdoch had no intention of stopping *Titanic* before ramming the iceberg. He instead hoped to swing her bow, then stern, away from the berg to skirt round it using the tiller commands 'hard-a-starboard' followed by 'hard-a-port'.

Murdoch's reversing of the engines has often given the impression that he squandered valuable seconds that otherwise could have been spent keeping the ship 'full ahead' and taking advantage of her momentum while turning to port, possibly even averting collision. It is this claim that forms the crux of the criticism against the first officer. However, his split-second thinking was neither out of panic nor confusion, but a canny display of inspired seamanship.

Ordering the helm 'hard-a-starboard' (a sharp turn to port) achieved swinging the bow away from the iceberg but the stern towards it. By then reversing the helm 'hard-a-port' returned the bow towards the berg again, but the stern away, a sequence known as 'porting-around'. Murdoch slowing the engines was an attempt to steal the ship time to complete this manoeuvre. When Captain Smith entered the bridge from his connecting suite behind, Murdoch articulated his plan to 'port-around' the iceberg but had insufficient time to execute it. Nonetheless, his intent to do so had not strictly been in vain. The idea to 'port-around' the iceberg had saved *Titanic* from far greater damage.

Known to average 200,000 tons, icebergs do not recoil or alter course when struck by even the largest of ships. Had Murdoch kept the bow veering port it would have smashed the iceberg along the entire hull of *Titanic*, killing in the process hundreds of passengers accommodated along her starboard flank and potentially forcing the ship to capsize. Instead Murdoch's manoeuvre pivoted *Titanic* sufficiently to bump her away from the iceberg as they met. It is why most passengers barely noticed the collision at all, recalling *Titanic* quivering gently upon a dulled impact which, after all, had seen thousands of tons of ice and metal collide. Although fatal, the resulting damage was confined to the bow, keeping *Titanic* afloat long enough for her crew to launch all of the main lifeboats she carried.

Prior to the disaster Murdoch had honed an aptitude to avoid objects in his vessel's path. At night and en route to New York in 1903, while leading the watch as first officer of White Star's brand new 15,801-ton *Arabic*, he averted collision with a sail-ship. By taking over the wheel of *Arabic* himself he deftly performed the same manoeuvre he would later order aboard *Titanic*. Swinging the stern then bow of *Arabic* round the approaching ship, the two vessels missed by matter of feet. The incident would provide Murdoch with the schooling to attempt avoiding the iceberg in 1912. However, with *Titanic* he made two significant errors. Firstly, he was not in the wheelhouse the moment the iceberg slid into view of the bridge. He was instead on the starboard navigation wing, decamped to improve his forward view. Unlike the unshielded and ill-equipped crow's nest the bridge house was undoubtedly the best place on *Titanic* to sight objects in their path. Each night in open sea the wheelhouse was maintained in complete obscurity to ensure the eyes of its occupants were kept dark-adapted and unimpaired. Each officer was equipped with binoculars and their experience and indoctrination in seafaring imbued within them an acute awareness for sensing and preparing for danger. Lookouts did not possess such aptitude. This instinct had Second Officer Lightoller rooted to position in the wheelhouse throughout his entire watch, between 6p.m. and 9p.m. on the night of the disaster.

'I took the precaution of taking up a position on the bridge in which everything ahead was clearly in view and maintaining that position for the remainder of the watch,' recollected Lightoller at the British inquiry, 21 May.

In his testimony Lightoller was adamant. Had the iceberg appeared during his watch that evening, 'I should have seen it in sufficient time to clear it quite sufficient'. Murdoch instead abandoned the wheelhouse in favour of the unshielded navigation wing in the hope of achieving a clearer vantage of the ship's path opposed to that offered by the wheelhouse itself – incidentally, he still did not see the iceberg until it was reported by the lookouts.

Murdoch's much-contested second mistake was ordering the bulkhead doors closed to seal shut the ship's sixteen watertight compartments. Although it was a purely instinctive and perfectly sound reaction to employ a new safety feature, particularly when following a collision likely to have breached the hull, the consequences of Murdoch's closure of the doors proved fatal.

With ice damage that extended through the first five compartments, water entering the hull was confined within this area, making it extremely heavy at the bow. Its assimilated weight began pulling the bow lower, tilting the deck to flow water over one bulkhead wall into the next, filling each compartment as the ship's angle became further accentuated.

It is argued that had Murdoch left these doors open, water would have set-tled and flooded compartments more evenly, maintaining buoyancy of the ship – widening the window for a potential rescue: assuming water moving freely around compartments would not develop the ship a serious list. Spurred by instinct, Murdoch activated the one safety feature specifically intended to isolate such damage, with a simple flick of a switch.

In the seconds that followed, Captain Smith marched into the wheelhouse from his suite immediately aft, upon doing so automatically taking command from Murdoch. Smith too requested the watertight doors closed – at which Murdoch confirmed that they already were. Possibly with the intention of head-ing the ship northwards and to Halifax, their nearest port, Smith – the extent of damage unknown to him – ordered engines 'slow ahead'. *Titanic*, with her hull open to the sea, limped onward at 8 knots for a further twenty minutes after sustaining a fatal impact with an iceberg. The damage soon proved far from superficial, and at 12.09a.m. Smith finally pulled her engines to a halt. Yet this resumption to the ship's forward motion had inadvertently driven further water into the hull, augmenting pressure against the forward bulkheads and the weight already within the bow; their subsequent failure dooming *Titanic*. With all its empiric wisdom of the sea, by 1912 technology had advanced bountifully for the maritime architect to incorporate an ever increasing arsenal of contraptions to counteract human error. To Edwardians *Titanic* had come to be synonymous with this progress, which on paper had finally delivered the 'unsinkable' ship.

Design of ship

Despite what many depictions suggest, *Titanic* was an exceptionally well-made vessel, White Star employing the best materials, artisans and designers of the era with which to construct her. Yet features in her design significantly hindered her chances of survival, even sealing her fate at the extent of damage sustained from the iceberg.

Titanic was famously lost due to her bulkhead design. She, the 'unsinkable' ship, transpired to be perfectly sinkable after all. Her configuration of bulkheads instilled a belief of infallibility within *Titanic*. Upon striking the iceberg, passen-gers and crew alike greeted the occasion with equal complacency. Nothing, they believed, could overwhelm the safest ship in the world.

Imbued suspiciousness to everything around us today finds modern society far less convinced of bold assurances of safety, but where did the overbearing confidence among Edwardians in this so-called 'unsinkable' ship stem from? It is perhaps the greatest untruth concerning *Titanic*, but prior to the disaster neither White Star nor Harland & Wolff once intimated that she or her sisters were in any way unsinkable; albeit both were conspicuous by their silence to rebuke the

A watertight door within
Olympic, photographed
prior to the installation
of the stokehold flooring
that will be level to the
height of the white line,
the cylinder to the left
houses the float-triggered
closing mechanism.
(*The Shipbuilder*)

claim. The marriage between *Titanic* and 'unsinkable' was in fact the fruits of an article from the quarterly magazine, *The Shipbuilder*. Their summer special edition of 1911 was devoted to dissecting every feature and fitting of *Olympic* and *Titanic*. Filling its 130 pages, it arrived on the newsstands the day *Olympic* embarked Southampton for her maiden crossing.

Surpassing all others in both scale and opulence the two leviathans were causing a stir in the media, inducing the scramble to glean every shred of detail one could on these new oceanic marvels. Being a technical journal, *The Shipbuilder* divulged to its readership all the intricacies that they craved. Every Edwardian obsessed with distilling as many facts about ships as they were able to gather marvelled at the indulgence and cutting-edge technology White Star was now retailing. In this edition the journal made reference to the type of watertight door featured on *Olympic*, the same type also shortly to be installed in *Titanic*. Able to completely seal every bulkhead compartment at the flick of a switch from the bridge, the journal rhapsodised the simplicity with which disaster could be avoided:

> In the event of accident, or at any time when it may be considered advisable, the captain can, by simply moving an electric switch, instantly close the doors throughout and make the vessel practically unsinkable.

And there it was, 'practically unsinkable', the phrase newspaper journalists craved to embody the advancement of British technological achievement as the nation that had proven shipbuilding had finally outwitted catastrophe. Hot on the heels of the launch of Cunard's *Lusitania* and *Mauretania* the Olympic Class under-scored a momentum in British innovation that had finally brought an end to a decade of German triumph. Britannia was once again ruling the waves. The faith was infectious: Bruce Ismay himself acknowledged after the disaster that 'in building the *Titanic* it was the hope of my associates and myself that we had built a vessel which could not be destroyed by the perils of the sea', yet even this was a claim not lacking foundation. White Star was one of the few lines that employed full-time trained lookouts, but since the early days of steam the real safeguard against collision lay neither with alert eyes or the lifeboats carried, but in the specially designed bulkhead crumple zones dividing the hull.

As with car frames today, crumple zones were installed into hulls to allow the bow to concertina on impact and hold water from spreading aft and overwhelm-ing the rest of the ship. *Titanic* was fitted with such a crumple zone. Her forward bulkhead extended to the base of C Deck, rising clear of the waterline by 58ft. But despite her forward fortification *Titanic* was not equipped to sustain a side-ways glancing collision as received from the iceberg. Opinion soon mounted to wish Murdoch had piled *Titanic* into the iceberg head-on. Perhaps had he done, all the books and films about her may have never needed to materialise.

Titanic has not been the only ship to strike an iceberg. Collision with ice was by no means uncommon hitherto the arrival of Radar. Because methods for sighting objects out at sea had evolved so little, if at all, most collisions still had a propensity to occur head-on. Victorian engineers knew better than to count on the attentiveness of lookouts, heightening instead the ability of forward bulkheads to absorb a blow to the bow and confine water in the damaged part of the hull, as far forward as possible. The forward-most wall on a ship thus became named, as is to this day, the collision bulkhead. As rule of thumb this bulkhead lay aft of the bow at a distance exactly one-twentieth of the ship's total length; as it was for *Titanic* – the walls rising likewise again toward the stern to ensure similar protec-tion at both extremities.

The effectiveness of the collision bulkhead was proven in November 1879 when the bow of Guion Line's 5,164-ton *Arizona* – Blue Riband holder at the time – met with an iceberg and lived to tell the tale. Travelling at high speed on a dark and mist-hazed evening, *Arizona* rammed headlong into a 60ft iceberg off the Newfoundland coast. Disintegrating 30ft of her hull, the forward bulkhead not only held but allowed *Arizona* to continue under her own steam the 220 miles to St. John, New Brunswick, where she underwent repair, needing one month to extract the 200 tons of embedded ice from her bow. Even as late as 11 April 1912 the bow of French Line's *Niagara* held after colliding with a large iceberg in the same region *Titanic* met her doom on the 14th. *Niagara* successfully reached

New York under her own steam; her bow repaired, she remained in service until 1931. In the dead of night of 8 July 1907, 75 miles north of the distress position of *Titanic*, Norddeutscher Lloyd's *Kronprinz Wilhelm* hit her bow upon a 50ft iceberg while at 16 knots, yet she too made port without assistance. On 4 August 1911 Anchor Line's *Columbia* struck an iceberg in fog just off Cape Race, again damage was confined to the bow and the ship continued to New York. On 9 May 1909, British liner *Volturno*, en route to Halifax, sat encircled by icebergs near Newfoundland for forty-eight hours. Indeed the last collision with an iceberg incurring serious loss of life was as recent as 1959: *Hans Hedtoft* sunk with all ninety-five hands off the Greenland coast during the return leg of her maiden voyage. Ice was a deadly menace, causing six noted collisions on the North Atlantic in 1912 alone.

Head-on collision was likewise given careful consideration when designing the Olympic Class, kitting them out with crumple zones also. Recent simulations at Harland & Wolff, which ploughed a computerised model of *Titanic* into an iceberg, demonstrated that she too would have remained afloat had she struck head-on. Crumple zones were that effective.

We know *Titanic* had been steaming at 22.25 knots through the ice field for two hours and ten minutes prior to collision, her bulkhead doors remaining open until impact. Physics suggests that had Murdoch rammed *Titanic* into the iceberg he may have saved the ship, but at what expense? The entire contingent of off-duty stokers and firemen as well as hundreds of third-class passengers asleep in their bunks were accommodated in the bow. After the disaster, Edward Wilding, Harland & Wolff's newly promoted chief designer, estimated that around 200 occupants would have been killed had Murdoch done this. With split-second thinking Murdoch's instinct as a seasoned mariner left him just one option: avoid.

Both *Olympic* and *Titanic* were designed using contemporary methods of the era, including the installation of remotely operated electronic bulkhead doors, a thoroughly modern innovation of their day. Similar doors aboard other ships had to be cranked shut manually with a tool. In order for manual doors to be effective this communication between bridge and the crewmember operating them in the belly of the ship relied wholly on their synchronised dash to seal the affected compartments in time. A most difficult task with a heavy door – assuming, that is, someone was there or able to close it. Drills were therefore part of the regime during voyages to ensure crewmembers involved rehearsed the entire procedure; one such drill took place during the maiden voyage of *Titanic* on 11 April.

The bulkhead configuration installed within *Olympic* and *Titanic* was intended to keep them afloat even with all four of the forward compartments flooded. Unfortunately for *Titanic* the glancing blow from the iceberg breached her first five compartments, as well as the double hull beneath. Within twenty minutes of collision the second, third, fourth and fifth compartments were overwhelmed, with the first and sixth filling rapidly also.

As *Titanic* ground her keel across the iceberg's sunken precipice the damage was sufficient to reach an area occupied by the fireman's tunnel, exposing it to the sea. This 100ft-long passageway afforded stokers direct access from their living quarters above to the boiler rooms below. Running directly abaft bulkhead B, the forward end of this tunnel lay just 3½ft from the hull's outer plating, and despite housing suction pumps, the impact with the iceberg found these rapidly overcame by the surge of water in this tunnel. Once breached, water had unhindered access through the bulkhead separating compartments three and four: wall C.

For stokers to access this tunnel a dual set of narrow spiral stairwells sited at its forward end gave direct communication between their living quarters on D Deck in the Forecastle above. Once water entered this tunnel its sole and unrestricted path was up these stairwells, which penetrated the overhang of the bulkhead wall dividing the second and third compartments. The breach of this tunnel turned it and the connecting stairwells into arteries, hastening the inflow of water within these compartments. Having absorbed 14ft of water within the first ten minutes, the level in the hull rose to 24ft over the next ten minutes, at which point an estimated 7,450 tons had entered the bow; a rapidity sealing the fate of *Titanic*.

Harland & Wolff's major oversight for *Titanic* had been crucially neglecting to extend her bulkheads to a single – thereby 'watertight' – deck. As her bow grew heavier the angle of decks increased, and once water had filled one compartment its only escape was over the top of an adjoining compartment via the corridors of the deck above (some of which were 9ft broad). Brunel's *Great Eastern* offered no such openings penetrating its bulkhead walls. Those on *Titanic*, however, were compromised by a total of thirty-one doors, of which only twelve could be closed automatically from the bridge. Fundamentally, all bulkheads on *Great Eastern* reached the same watertight deck, 30ft above the waterline. In stark contrast, the walls on *Titanic* varied wildly – the shortest amidships clearing her waterline by little more than 2ft – denying her a uniformly watertight height.

With no major shipping incident to influence design in the years preceding the launch of *Titanic*, White Star leveraged keen advantage of the cavernous 'Olympics', promoting their first-class areas as the largest afloat, unhindered with bulkhead divisions. Extending every compartment wall high above the waterline was, at that time, deemed less of a necessity. To the operators the pitfalls of bisecting first-class passenger areas outweighed any commercial benefit. Disasters were becoming rare.

Nevertheless, in the wake of *Titanic* the regulations governing bulkheads were revised, increasing the minimum heights of the walls to clear the ship's maximum load-line and for improved durability to withstand greater pressures: those on *Titanic* collapsed one-by-one against the hydrostatic weight crushing them. Crucially, the new regulations demanded compartments become completely watertight by reaching the same – unbroken – level.

The iceberg buckled plating along the starboard hull, and further injury was sustained as *Titanic* ground her keel across its submerged ice shelf, breaching the outer hull guarding her Tank Top. The double keel on *Titanic* measured 5ft 3in deep and subdivided into forty-four watertight tanks: six were filled with drinking water, with six others storing a further 1,000 tons of water to feed the cooling systems of the immense boilers. The remaining tanks contained water purely for use as ballast. In effect all forty-four tanks offered *Titanic* a secondary watertight barrier in the base of her hull and an additional safeguard in the event of running aground.

Aside from the seventeen transverse walls in the double bottom, fifteen continued through the Tank Top flooring to form the bulkhead divisions. The double bottom also contained three longitudinal girders: one ran 670ft along the centreline, winged by two companions extending 447ft beneath the engine and boiler rooms – the heaviest section of the ship – to provide extra strength to the flooring above. The area surrounding the boiler and engine rooms themselves was in turn shielded by dual watertight walls, which protectively encased these compartments either side. These, rising clear of the waterline by 2½ft, theoretically gave *Titanic* a total of sixty-two isolated watertight compartments: sixteen clearing the waterline. However, as *Titanic* ran over the ice ledge it tore open the forward five tanks along the starboard flank of her double bottom. The force distorted her starboard longitudinal girder and also unseated the bulkhead walls fixed above. This rupture caused further tanks to flood, compromising the Tank Top, and granting water access to a seventh compartment: boiler room 4. Whereas the double starboard wall shielding boiler room 5 was breached by no more than 2ft, this sixth compartment was also compromised through its flooring. Its failure doomed *Titanic*.

Unlike the attention that designers lavished on bulkheads, the advances in rudders and their ability to handle enormous craft evolved little over the ages. Indeed, the rudders on the Olympic Class were designed to appear more decorative than functional. To endow their leviathans a graceful profile, Harland & Wolff had based their rudders on the same elliptical variation that harked from the tall ships of old. White Star did not wish their huge Olympians to look ungainly, so focussed as much attention on forming chic exteriors in accompaniment to their sumptuous interiors. However, in practice, the type of rudder chosen would prove disastrously ineffective for *Titanic*.

It is known that when sighting the iceberg, Murdoch intended, albeit unsuccessfully, to pirouette *Titanic* round it. Her speed (22.25 knots; equal to 38ft per second) and distance from the iceberg when initially sighted (500 yards; 4.4 lengths of the ship) provided just thirty-seven seconds for the rudder to swerve the 46,000-ton liner and allow Murdoch to complete his avoiding manoeuvre.

As modern and state-of-the-art as the Olympic-Class ships were, the shape of their sterns was based on that of a schooner – a design dating from the 1700s –Harland & Wolff's 'D' design. White Star and Harland & Wolff opted for a more traditional profile, befitting the stateliness of the Olympic Class. Fitting them with this smaller rudder was a willing compromise since the vessels were intended for more sedate crossings in contrast to their speedier Cunard adversaries.

The 'Olympics' were each fitted with a single-bladed elliptical 'plate' rudder formed of six steel panels, which when assembled amassed a combined weight of 101.25 tons. To steer a ship of this scale, incidentally the largest man-made object of its day, the rudder of *Titanic* had to be huge. At a lofty 78ft 8in tall by 15ft 3in deep and by 1ft 11.5in broad, her rudder was mounted to the hull by seven 11in-wide hinges. Because of the sheer bulk of *Titanic*, however, even this vast rudder represented a mere 1.37 per cent of the total surface area of hull beneath the waterline.

Although the turning circles of *Olympic* and *Titanic* still compared favourably to more modern liners, elliptical rudders were more effective at slow speeds due to their reduced surface area in contact with water. Vessels, in contrast, carrying the larger, squarer type of rudder – such as the one installed on the Blue Riband holder, *Mauretania* – were not only larger in volume but immersed entirely beneath the waterline, maximising controllability at high speed. *Mauretania*, even at full speed, was able to change course within just ten seconds. Whereas one third of the elliptical rudder on *Titanic* stood clear of the water's surface, unlike the fully immersed squarer alternative, elliptical types provided the benefit of less drag.

During *Titanic's* sea trials, various turning manoeuvres were conducted, predominantly when travelling her at 18 knots. Her 3,850-yard turning circle had been measured while driven at 20.5 knots; all tests to her rudder that day were undertaken below her intended 21-knot service speed. The size of this rudder proved cruelly ineffective at successfully controlling the liner turning sharply at speed when avoiding the iceberg two weeks later.

Her weighty 101-ton rudder required dedicated engines with which to steer it. Connected to the bridge by a pipe filled with a mixture of hydraulic fluid and anti-freeze, these engines were triggered by pistons controlled by a Brown Telemotor commanded directly by the helm. The time for an adjustment on the helm to register through the chain of telemotors, valves and hydraulics and onto the steering engines themselves, required approximately four seconds. Turning the wheel at velocity widened this response even further. Waiting a number of seconds for this assortment of mechanisms to even begin taking effect would have felt like a lifetime to Hichens clutching the wheel, watching the iceberg draw nearer. Had Captain Smith been more mindful of this delay he could have reduced speed knowing *Titanic* would turn more effectively should the need arise.

The effectiveness of the rudder on *Titanic* when measured during her sea trials was performed with engines driven only in forward. Her rudder, mounted directly abaft the ship's central propeller – exiting the hull 12ft 3in above the keel – aided the rudder's efficiency by the immediate backwash. This was flanked by two larger screws in close proximity on protruding wings, 16ft 3in either side of the centreline. In the seconds prior to collision Murdoch ordered these outer propellers reversed to slow *Titanic*: the turbine-powered central propeller itself was unable to operate in reverse, and its sole purpose was to give the ship forward thrust at times when the telegraph was set to either 'half' or 'full speed ahead'. It was the work of the outer propellers to give the ship dexterity, and, driving these, were two vast 15,000hp reciprocating engines which, in order to avoid the iceberg, had slammed from 'full speed ahead' to 'full speed astern' within seconds,.

The two outer propellers boasted a surface area 160sq.ft each and were spaced on protrusions wide enough apart to dissipate their squall so not to unsettle the flow of water around the central screw. The thrust from the propellers changing direction at high speed created a vortex of turbulence around the rudder, churning and agitating the water at the precise time the rudder was hard-over at full torque. This, and the reducing speed of *Titanic*, severely hampered the effectiveness of this all too diminutive rudder.

Over-steering such a rudder hard-over to port, together with the sliding motion in which Murdoch's manoeuvre had forced *Titanic*, swung her stern toward the path of the iceberg while gliding the bow away. After 'hard-a-starboard', Murdoch then put the helm hard-over to starboard to 'port-around' it. To do this he turned the rudder from full-lock to port, to full-lock starboard, against the force of water, further compromising its effectiveness by increasing the resistance against it. *Titanic* was certainly no swan.

But what of the key question: how was this, the world's mightiest ship, not impervious against six relatively small 'slits' to her hull?

Steel, favoured for its cheaper production and comparable lightness to iron, is also a weaker alternative to lining ships. Harland & Wolff had been plating ships with steel since the 1880s; *Garfield* was their first, completed in 1882. By the emergence of *Titanic* the yard had perfected the mass production of steel, forging her plates from a mild-steel compound known as Siemens-Martin – the process created by Sir William Siemens and later improved by Pierre-Émile Martin in 1868 for the manufacture of large quantities of rolled steel. By 1878 the method had become the universal standard, for it not only produced steel in high volume but maintained a higher and consistent quality.

Employed first for *Teutonic* and *Majestic*, the particular compound of steel used on *Titanic* dated from 1910 and was considered to be top-notch – as one would expect of White Star. It was a type renowned for its toughness, and was widely referred to as 'battleship quality' since the Admiralty endorsed its use for their fleet. Its strength was attributed to the compound's high quantities of sulphur and slag – an impurity – forgiven in merchant liners since the resilience of their plating was intended to withstand the rigours and pressures of seawater against the hull, not inbound artillery. Favoured for its low levels of carbon – the 'mild-steel' component – it increased strength to produce discernibly rigid plating for the hull, which by 1910 commonly averaged a tensile strength of between 28 to 32 tons per square inch. To counter this, the upper hulls of the Olympic Class featured two leather-filled expansion joints to afford their superstructures the necessary malleability to absorb the motions of undulating seas and alleviate its stresses on the less-flexible hull. Unlike her plating, however, they were fastened with rivets fashioned from two varieties of metal: steel – employed along the side of the hull because of their strength – and wrought-iron for elsewhere.

Since all types of forged metal contain elements of slag (crystallised sulphur) – a deposit from the smelting of ore – the quantity used in Edwardian vessels typically varied between 2 and 2.5 per cent. Its presence in the steel recovered from the wreck of *Titanic*, however, was found to exceed 9 per cent and in some instances was as high as 13. The higher the content of slag, the more the metal is susceptible to fatigue. The inflexibility of this particular compound found the plating and rivets encasing *Titanic* prone to brittleness when exposed to freezing point: the very temperature of the sea where she would founder on 14 April. Whereas freshwater freezes at 28°F (-2°C), its levels of salt gives seawater a far lower freezing point, determined only by its salinity. Sea temperatures of 28°F were considered low, even for winter, and as a result the level of slag within her steel when forged was believed not to pose too much concern for *Titanic*. This steel compound, however, was used to forge not only her plating but many of the 3 million rivets fastening it to her frame. These steel rivets were each set hydraulically at a pressure of 800psi by a 3-ton machine hoisted into position by crane. Handled by squads of workers, it drove home the rivet heads one at a time along three-fifths of her hull or as far as its curvature would dictate: 'as far forward and aft as possible'. Harland & Wolff had been practicing portable hydraulic riveters since 1871, preferring these as a cheaper and more consistent alternative to hand riveting. But in areas too tight for the machine to reach, the remainder were hammered into place by hand using smaller, softer wrought-iron rivets.

Unlike its depiction in movies, the damage inflicted by the iceberg was not a savage tearing of plates, but in reality was a bursting of rivet seams causing plates to separate. Prolonged exposure to temperatures below freezing found both the hull and its rivets deceptively prone to distress. The impact of the iceberg was calculated by the US Navy's Hydrographic Office for the ensuing Senate investigation, which estimated it to be a force of energy equal to 1,173,200 foot tons; the impact sheared the heads off these extremely embrittled rivets, six sections in total. Whereas Cunard's *Mauretania* contained a million more rivets to reinforce such weakness, White Star uncharacteristically chose to line *Olympic* and *Titanic* with a surprisingly low-grade supply. Ultimately, after the disaster extra banks of rivets were applied to *Britannic* to avoid a similar failure to her hull, correcting a weakness that had not triggered any alarm bells even when following the almost identical failure suffered by *Olympic* during her collision with HMS *Hawke* in 1911. This key incident demonstrated the rivets used in Ismay's new class to be prone to bursting even within Britain's comparatively warm coastal waters.

Design, confidence and abnormal sailing conditions for the winter of 1912 had lulled Captain Smith into a lower state of prudence than his experience would have normally allowed for this regent but deceptively flawed class. Indeed, the report of the British inquiry would later only conclude of human error: 'that the loss of the said ship [*Titanic*] was due to collision with an iceberg, brought about by excessive speed at which the ship was being navigated'. It became as close as Mersey's court would venture to accusing either Captain Smith or White Star of negligence – also deflecting culpability from their regulators, the British Board of Trade. The captain was exonerated for a string of failings that heightened his ship's exposure to disaster and the Board of Trade, disarmed by decades of steadily improving safety records, was exonerated for slackening its grip and allowing unsafe practices to continue because, by chance, adopting them had avoided disaster. Their aversion to meddling resulted in a virtual abdication of safety policy to the individual shipping companies, whose own motives was prejudiced by profit.

Prior to the loss of *Titanic*, mortality at sea was indeed at its all-time safest. Between 1891 and 1911 British-registered liners had transported 9 million passengers across the North Atlantic in some 24,000 voyages. Of these passengers just 118 lives had been lost, and only one had been the result of a collision. Conventional shipping lanes of 1912 were by no means unsafe. However, utmost consideration was to have *Titanic* not only as safe as possible but to become the safest vessel of her era. Yet even she would succumb to the sea on her first voyage, because of a captain's determination to travel his ship apace toward a ubiquitous hazard, which culminated in a collision that bought all the factors explored here into play. The consummate 'EJ' had made a grievous misjudgement, ultimately costing the lives of 1,523, including his own. With them went the fate of the world's greatest, if unluckiest, liner, ingloriously undone by its own advances in safety.

CHAPTER 13

A CLASS DIVIDED

'Wealth rubbed elbows with poverty and democracy in the crowd which
besieged the steamship line officials, and both classes were in deep grief.'
The Boston Globe, 16 April 1912

Much is written of the Edwardians and their heady 'gilded era' but skulking
beneath its milk and honey resided a country at the heart of the greatest Empire
the world had ever known, which was unable to feed swathes of subjects within
its own towns and cities. The turn of the twentieth century saw Britain overtaken
by America as the world's wealthiest nation. No longer could Britannia claim the
role of world leader that she had enjoyed so autonomously under Queen Victoria.
Her death in 1901 heralded with it the end to Britain's once unrivalled prosperity.
On every level its fortunes began to change, and dramatically so. Near defeat in
the Boer War against a tiny republic in the Transvaal found the superpower nurs-
ing an unfamiliarly bloodied nose. With costs amounting to £200 million, the
close of the war in May 1902 left Britain's economy in turmoil.

A study in 1905 exploring Britain's distribution of wealth was to reveal that
38 million of its populous lived either on or below the accepted poverty line
and that the suffrage of the poor had been keenly ignored and forsaken to the
workhouses. Rising food prices saw the General Election of 1906 sweep aside
two decades of Conservative rule in a monumental swing to the Liberal Party.
A progressive-thinking but tempestuous Britain was dawning. Despite their new
agenda to reform, the Liberals found even their tenure convulsed with simmering
unrest between social classes, drawing the country perilously close to full-scale
constitutional crisis. It was David Lloyd George's introduction of welfare reforms
in his 'People's Budget' of November 1909 that proved to be the powder keg for
a historic backlash from the landed classes, whose taxes were raised to fund them.
Inevitably it was the poor who bore the brunt of the increases. Landlords raised
rents on their properties to retrench the burden for themselves, yet never before

had the rich been so indulgent with their spending. The divide separating the rich from the poor had grown to alarming proportions.

'We are not concerned with the very poor,' wrote E.M. Forster in his 1910 novel, *Howard's End*. The frivolity of the rich in the new century was indeed masking the hopeless drudgery of the working classes. Blighted by squalid living conditions and spiralling unemployment, the lucky ones who could afford a ticket flocked to the booking halls of the shipping lines. En masse they embarked with little more than hope and fortitude in exchange to begin anew on the opposite side of the Atlantic in a land free of the shroud of poverty back home.

The arrival of *Titanic* came at a time when social upheaval was at its zenith. Sterling was devalued by a quarter due to spiralling welfare introductions and the government's unrelenting arms race with Germany upgrading the entire Royal Navy. Trade Union membership had risen to an all-time high of 3.4 million: a national workforce ill at ease. The summer of 1911 saw industrial action almost close down the rail and dockyard industries amid increasingly violent protests over pay and working conditions. The most stoppages were experienced in 1912: 834 separate actions amassing the equivalent of 41 million working days, more than the combined amount lost through stoppages in the entire eight years previous. With a quarter of Britain's workforce engaged in shipping, the opening months of 1912 were beset with embittered disputes in mining, docksides and railways, severely disrupting shipping and the recovery of Britain's stuttering economy.

Tired of earning £1 for every sixty hour week worked, 1 million coalminers joined the campaign for minimum wage that those working in construction and manufacturing had already been granted in 1909. Stokers, greasers and trimmers did not have the benefits of a permanent sailing crew, earning erratic wages as a result, signing on afresh voyage to voyage. The coalminers' dispute led to the formation of the Southampton-headquartered British Seafarers' Union in October 1911, but as ships lay idle by March 1912 the strike had hit Southampton's stokehold crews particularly hard. Unable to timetable their own fuel-starved craft the characteristically opportunist operators – particularly Cunard – returned their fleets to the shipyards to undergo unscheduled repairs. Dockyards fell silent. Of its total population of 120,000 the dispute found unemployment in Southampton soar to 17,000, with its Northam Girls School noting that in their children 'distress is daily becoming more acute owing to stagnation caused by the coal strike'. The arrival of *Titanic* that April heralded a welcome inoculation to the town's fortunes.

The politic of the era had given the emergence of *Olympic* and *Titanic* unique significance. This was a sentiment mirrored keenly in the press, which lionised the duo as marvels of engineering, symbols of Britain's technical savvy and the vanguards of its long-awaited revitalisation and prosperity. Their timing, albeit coincidental, was impeccable. Britain's countenance and sense of fortuity had finally but palpably returned.

To the wealthy, however, the period was their halcyon era. To them, the poor, the wretched recipients of the fortunate's philanthropy, seemed all too distant to matter. It was their playful, innocent age, one ultimately bought into check by global warfare. But this and the loss of *Titanic* had seen family members of the rich perish alongside society's poorest.

The mid-1890s had seen the volume of migrants crossing the North Atlantic average 370,000 a year. By the early 1900s numbers swelled to 1 million per year, an exodus recording its peak in 1907 at 1.3 million. New York was the most popular destination, receiving 12 million through its halls between 1892 and 1920. A tide of humanity was on the move and shipping operators struggled to meet demand.

At sea, immigration class was third class, the lowest class. Their travelling accommodation aboard was often worse than the conditions they were escaping from at home. As more travelled, their conditions at sea deteriorated. Overcrowding in third class grew to such extremes that sometimes voyages proved fatal.

Until 1870 the traditional location of first-class cabins had always been at the stern of the ship, a custom that changed when White Star's first *Oceanic* marked a new epoch – the first liner to axis its design purely on comfort. Because of its extremities, accommodation in the bow and stern meant for a far less comfortable journey than others berthed amidships. For *Oceanic* Harland & Wolff substituted the traditional location for third class, the centre of the ship, in favour of first-class staterooms. Accommodation for her 1,102 passengers in third was ousted to the bows and the areas above and around the rudder in the stern, an arrangement subsequently adopted by all emigrant-carrying liners since. Shoehorned within the bow and very stern, *Oceanic* heralded a new age for third-class travel: steerage.

The average migrant, absconding from life in either remote farmland or insanitary urban tenements saw in consequence their expectations of accommodation at sea as unassumingly modest, fortunately for shipping operators. Yet so luxurious was accommodation on *Titanic* that her steerage areas set a standard unmatched for that class on land or sea. In fact her third-class accommodation was so good that it rivalled second class on other ships.

No longer bunked in dormitories, steerage aboard the Olympic Class offered its passengers actual cabins, albeit shared by as many as eight occupants. Their public rooms were alluringly pictured in White Star brochures with the line: 'the interval between the old life and the new is spent under the happiest possible conditions'. Indeed, to an impoverished migrant, crossing the Atlantic on *Titanic* was a holiday lodged in comparative luxuriance and a delightful preclude before the hardened reality of finding employment and starting anew in a distant far-flung land.

Titanic was designed to accommodate 1,134 passengers in third class, housed within 222 rooms and sharing just two bathtubs among her entire contingent. Their allocation was stark in contrast to the remaining 540 rooms put aside for her 1,469 occupants travelling in first and second class – the most splendid rooms afloat. Despite constituting the smaller proportion of passengers, first-class accommodation on Cunard's *Aquitania* would account for 75 per cent of the ship's net volume, yet until the 1920s the real money in Atlantic shipping was still earned from third class.

Third class comprised of migrants, seeking any next available westbound ship. They were among society's poorest, so tickets were priced conspicuously low and competitively. Steerage on *Titanic* of £7 10s was no insignificant sum in 1912 when skilled workers' earnings averaged 40s a week. Still, even that was a fare worth paying for a new and better life, for they were not intending to procure return tickets. Their accommodation, squeezed in the bow and stern, saw cargo holds similarly located in these parts of the ship, and out of a further drive to utilise every available inch of space aboard, open congregational spaces occupied by third-class passengers on westbound voyages were transformed into additional storage areas, even for cattle, on eastbound journeys when no migrants were carried.

And so, April 1912 witnessed 709 emigrants board the maiden voyage of *Titanic*. Entire families bearing all their worldly possessions arrived quayside wide-eyed and high-spirited having secured their berth on the world's most prestigious liner, in awe of the largeness of the fabled 'Ship of Dreams'. Of them just 183 were actually British; the remainder comprised Austrians, French, Italians, Scandinavians, even Chinese. Yet despite this hodgepodge of cultures, Edwardian standards of civility were as stringently adhered to as if they were on land. On land the working classes rarely had the opportunity to interact with the gentry, and aboard ship hierarchy was just as vigorously observed. First-class passengers would occupy the upper decks while those in third resided deep downstairs, bunked and sandwiched near working areas and engine space. The full microcosm of society was transplanted into the confines of the ship, and the two extremes were separated as if on land, by the inhabitants of society's new mediocrity: second class. Steerage passengers would not, in fact could not, venture into the realms of first class – breaking exception only in an emergency. Interaction undesirable, third- and second-class passengers would board *Titanic* two hours before first-class. Furthermore, to purge the temptation of fraternisation during the voyage, third-class berths put single travelling males in the bow, and families, married couples and single women in cabins in the stern.

Apart from hierarchical preference, class segregation was also imposed to prevent the spread of disease, and for this reason each steerage passenger was subjected to three medical examinations. The first, conducted by doctors hired by the shipping lines, was performed at the quayside prior to boarding. Upon arrival at New York, officials would board to conduct the second examination in the ship's own hospital facility. Those who passed disembarked at Ellis Island for a final screening and to formalise their entry. Each was required to pass a plethora of examinations for common diseases, such as trachoma – a highly contagious eye infection – only after which would they then be interviewed to rubberstamp their suitability for citizenship. Anyone failing was returned to their originating port without the remainder of their family, their passage home at the expense of the shipping operator.

At sea aboard *Titanic* the Well Deck cargo areas transformed into open promenades for third-class passengers once a day, a spectacle observed to the amusement
of first-class, whose own open areas looked upon them. It was not unknown, on
occasions, for first-class passengers to toss food and coins to the migrants corralled
in the Well Decks below. But other than singing and promenading, sea life had
little to offer third-class passengers, pensively whiling away this week-long journey.
There were no squash courts, Turkish baths, modern amenities nor ablutions available to them, just busy communal areas in which to amuse themselves, fuse cultures
and rumbustiously capitalise on the longest break from reality many had experienced in a lifetime.

Aboard *Titanic* an army of 100 stewards was assigned to attend the 190 families
comprising first class on her maiden voyage. Travelling with them were twenty-
three maids and eight valets housed in separate accommodation to save their
first-class masters the indignity of having to converse with their servant in public.
This, the last vestiges of Victorian class order, would maintain social structure
even in disaster, during which it was not uncommon for crews to keep third-class
passengers from the Boat Deck until all the women and children, followed by
first- then second-class males had each taken their seats in the lifeboats. Written
evacuation procedure often omitted them, even for *Titanic*; every passenger's
chance of survival hinged almost entirely on the class of their ticket. While *Titanic*
sank, only women and children were allowed into her lifeboats, although the
edict largely applied if they were from first or second class. The odds were stacked
firmly against third class: on *Titanic* they were twice as likely to die than patrons
ticketed first or second class.

A previous incident at sea that threatened lives would showcase the extent
of this distinction even amid the grip of disaster: the evacuation of White Star's
Republic in 1909. Her crew had first ordered all women and children into the
lifeboats, followed afterwards by first-class men and then those in second, before
finally third-class 'foreigners' – one of her officers later haughtily vaunting that
even in adversity 'the privilege of class [was proudly] upheld'.

The lives of women claimed in the *Titanic* disaster amounted to 139 from
first class and fifteen from second, but of the 179 women travelling in third only
eighty-one survived. The statistic was no kinder for children. All twenty-nine
travelling in first and second class was saved whereas just twenty-three of the sev-
enty-six third-class children aboard were rescued. In fact, the most controversial
aspect of the disaster is that it claimed the lives of more third-class children than
first-class men; figures seen from the safety of the twenty-first century purvey a
disaster almost incomprehensible to observers today.

Table 5: Survivals and deaths resulting from the Titanic *disaster*

	Total on voyage		Survived		Died	
First class	337	15%	201	29%	136	9%
Second class	271	12%	118	17%	153	10%
Third class	712	32%	179	25%	533	35%
Crew	908	41%	207	29%	701	46%
Total	2,228	100%	705	100%	1,523	100%

Of the total complement of passengers and crew aboard *Titanic* just 32 per cent were saved. Aboard the maiden voyage third-class passengers represented one-third of the total travelling occupancy on *Titanic*, yet they accounted for just one-quarter of the 705 subsequently rescued: a figure that would no doubt have been far greater had *Titanic* been booked to capacity.

The Olympic Class was designed to meet the individual requirements of the three travelling classes, allowing for as many berths as possible to satisfy both profit and demand. Pooling the upper, middle and lower social classes in the confines of a ship involved keeping the classes physically segregated to preclude against interaction, no matter how incidental. The design of *Titanic* made it virtually impossible for any third class passenger to interlope into a first- or second-class domain: in particular the Boat Deck, home to the lifeboats. Even as she sank, crew purportedly kept these – Bostwick – gates locked to bar third-class access to this area. Pleas from passengers to be allowed through the gates were repeatedly rejected by crewmembers under the premise that lifeboats spe cifically for third class would be provided later. In only a few instances were steerage passengers led up to the lifeboats. The remainder were left to fend for their lives, abandoned to hopelessness or the mercy of a kindly steward's charity.

When the collision with the iceberg occurred at 11.40p.m., lifeboats were uncovered twenty-five minutes later, yet third-class males were kept below deck until 1.15a.m., one and a half hours later. Eventually allowing them up proved a pointless gesture; only six boats remained at that time, all of which were thronged by other passengers and were leaving full. The last was lowered from *Titanic* at 2.05a.m. Even when finally given access to other parts of the ship, some third-class passengers chuckled at the privilege of being allowed the heresy of intruding into first class, despite the knowledge that the ship was doomed. White Star would be later criticised for bolting the gates barring access to saloon-class areas, and more so for failing to open them during the emergency. Some passengers had resorted to breaking down these gates while the water surged at their ankles, although even at this stage anyone caught damaging White Star property was charged for the infraction by the witnessing crewmember. The line would later maintain that no preferential treatment was afforded to first- or second-class passengers. The statistics tell a different story.

Britain's official investigation into the disaster would later corroborate that the gates denying third-class access to the Boat Deck should have been opened by crew the moment it was apparent that *Titanic* was going to sink. Crucially, however, the inquiry's conclusions made no acknowledgement that third-class passengers were afforded lower priority than saloon-ticketed passengers. Although, even after rescue by Cunard's *Carpathia*, the 179 surviving third-class passengers were accommodated according to class. Upon their arrival at New York at 9.30p.m. on the 18th, surviving third-class passengers were withheld from disembarking until 11p.m., well after survivors from first, followed by second class, had all trooped ashore. The press too paid little attention to the plight of third class throughout its coverage of the disaster. Of the forty-three interviews given by survivors upon the arrival of *Carpathia*, just two were with third-class passengers. Newspapers proudly roll called of names of first-class victims across their front pages with 'others were also lost' trailing behind in small type.

At the arrival of *Carpathia* the surviving third-class passengers were still subjected to the bureaucracy applied to regular emigrants, although the procedures had been tactfully waived for first- and second-class survivors who were whisked to Manhattan. The third-class passengers who had survived the greatest sea tragedy of modern times and were newly bereft of their worldly possessions, were abandoned and destitute in a distant land utterly alien to their culture.

Even in death little compassion was afforded the relatives of third-class victims – in some cases the disaster had claimed entire families. When the body of a third-class passenger had been recovered, their relations were unable to afford the cost of its repatriation; that is, if it were brought to land at all. The majority of the 119 bodies were buried at sea by the ensuing recovery missions were of those of third-class passengers and stokehold crew.

Nor would they find justice at the British investigation. W.D. Harbinson, the lawyer representing third-class interests at the British hearings, would himself admit finding 'no evidence' of 'any discrimination practised either by the officers or the sailors in putting them into the boats'. Its chairman Lord Mersey would likewise record 'no truth' in allegations of any third-class passenger on *Titanic* having been obstructed maliciously or 'unfairly treated [nor] that their access to the Boat Deck had been impeded, and that when at last they reached that deck the first- and second-class passengers were given precedence in getting into the boats'. His verdict, therefore, was unsurprising, albeit not a single surviving third-class passenger had been asked to testify otherwise at the inquiry.

Mersey attributed the disproportionate toll on third class to the 'greater reluctance of the third-class passengers to leave the ship, by their unwillingness to part with their baggage'. He asserted: 'They were not unfairly treated'; the opinion was echoed by his American counterpart, likewise reporting that 'no distinction was made between first-, second- and third-class passengers' during the evacuation.

The treatment of crewmembers was also to mirror their social status. At 2.20a.m. on the 15th, all pay was ceased the very minute *Titanic* sank. Southampton bore the brunt of the disaster, as 699 of *Titanic's* crew, employed as stokers, greasers and trimmers, resided there. In some communities in the town, Northam in particular where the majority lived, not a single family was untouched by the disaster, directly or otherwise knowing somebody who perished. In many cases their widows and children had lost the family's breadwinner – spurring the city's mayor, Councillor Henry Bowyer, to introduce a special fund to save them from destitution. 'Nothing approaching this appalling blow has ever fallen upon the port,' wrote a solemn *Daily Mirror* on 18 April, describing the impact the disaster exerted throughout Southampton. Over the following months the fund kept 600 families clothed and fed. Supplied by charity and support from various unions, food banks were also seen across Southampton for the families of lost crew whose wellbeing was now wholly reliant upon them. The ensuing litany of social research waxed enthusiastic about how the sinking became a tragedy that affected all classes, but as is typical with disasters, clearly none suffered more than the poorest.

Improvements did follow in the disaster's wake. *Britannic*, when entering service in 1915, sported six lifeboats on her Poop Deck specifically for the sole use of third-class passengers. However, looking back at the evacuation of *Titanic* though the eyes of today provides an abrasive insight into the estranged classes of Edwardian Britain. The very fact that the wealthiest passengers perished shoulder-to-shoulder with the poorest had for the first time in 1912 hammered home the stark realisation that within any strata of society, mortality is the equaliser of humanity. The inequality of death on *Titanic* heralded a thawing of society's rigid established order. So unjust was the scale of preferential treatment of first-class passengers, that their unrequited right to survival over a lower class traveller was not to pass so devoutly again. The splendid *Titanic* became the unwitting stage to the unforeseen finale of distinction between class during evacuation, and first-class infallibility was her surprise casualty – albeit under magnanimous duress. Society was awakened by the poised and conformist lower class whose deaths brought with them an end to a period of history that had proven not to be so 'golden' after all.

CHAPTER 14

LARGER THAN LIFE

Titanic [ti-tan-ik] *adjective*:
a) having great stature or enormous strength; huge or colossal,
b) of enormous scope, power, or influence.

Upon forging himself a name for building expansive bridges and developing the modern railway, the 1840s found Isambard Kingdom Brunel devoting his engineering genius to shipbuilding. Consecutively producing three of the world's largest ships, Brunel – arguably the most accomplished engineer of modern history – advanced the progress of maritime design through pioneering what became the true 'longship'. The size of vessels had evolved little until 1838 when the launch of his first ship, the 1,320-ton, 235ft wooden paddle steamer *Great Western*, heralded a new era of shipbuilding.

Great Western was so named as she was deemed to be the extension of Britain's Great Western Railway, a network that now had America itself as the new destination of the line. To produce even longer hulls, however, wooden hulls had finally to make way for a stronger alternative. When completed in 1843, his second ship featured the first hull lined solely with metal – iron. At 322ft long and with a tonnage of 2,936 she was by far the largest craft of her day. Intentions to christen her *Mammoth* yielded to a more patriotic moniker during construction and she became SS *Great Britain*. Launched by Prince Albert on 19 July 1843 she was able to carry 360 passengers and a crew of 130. Capable of mustering 1,800hp her engine was the first to power a vessel across the Atlantic using a screw propeller in lieu of paddle-wheels or sails. The immensity of *Great Britain* enabled her holds to carry enough coal (1,200 tons) to sustain her engines for an entire transatlantic crossing – entering her into the record books as the template of the modern ocean liner.

Apart from being able to carry more passengers, cargo and machinery, Brunel had proven that ships with longer hulls required less exertion to propel them through water. Aided by the design of celebrated marine engineer John Scott Russell, the final ship of Brunel's trio, whose construction began in 1854, was finished in 1858:

hugely over budget. The 693ft-long iron-hulled *Great Eastern* dwarfed her sisters. Grossing a tonnage of 18,915 the bewildering scale of *Great Eastern* housed within her enough coal to steam non-stop to India and Sri Lanka and carry as many as 4,000 passengers. With *Great Eastern*, more than twice the length of the world's previous largest vessel – his own *Great Britain* – Brunel had overcome his biggest hurdle: how to prevent her hull snapping and twisting through tempestuous seas, a problem that had never been more incumbent on shipbuilding till now.

As a wave reaches the centre of a hull the water around it becomes too low to support the bow and stern, thereby bending it downward at the extremities, a phenomenon referred to by the industry as 'hogging'. Conversely, with waves primarily supporting the bow and stern, the weight of water amidships forces the hull to bend upward – 'sagging'. Hogging and sagging – exaggerated on a longer hull – has the potential to snap it in two. To counteract this, Brunel installed ten longitudinal beams, each 3ft 3in deep, into the keel of *Great Britain*, giving rise to the concept of the double hull and paving the way for the possibility of even larger ships.

With *Great Eastern* out-measuring *Great Britain* by 371ft, Brunel estimated that if using conventional techniques, giving her hull the necessary support would require it to be lined with iron plating 4in thick. This supply of iron would not only prove too costly to manufacture, but would leave the ship far too heavy to be commercially viable. Brunel instead devised a modified version of the dual hull he had previously employed on *Great Britain*. The new design comprised of two iron plates, each 1in thick and spaced 2ft 10in apart, in the base of the ship to form a honeycomb of cellular box-shaped compartments. This cellular arrangement was inspired by a concept used in Robert Stevenson's Britannia Bridge of 1850. Strong enough to run trains across its 472ft expanse through a square iron tube, the bridge required no additional support other than the two towers that raised it into position. Brunel realised that by flattening the hull, he would be able to incorporate the 'box bridge' model within *Great Eastern*.

The double-layered hull earlier installed in *Great Britain* had not been made watertight, with Brunel only intending to provide it with the necessary rigidity. However, after she ran aground on 22 September 1846 he decided to give the double hull for *Great Eastern* a dual purpose. Making both the inner and outer hulls watertight was more in response to a logistical challenge than a concern over safety. Should she require maintenance, no dry-dock in the world was large enough to accommodate *Great Eastern*. She had after all been constructed along the banks of the Thames at Millwall as no yard's slipways were large enough to build her. She would also unorthodoxly be nudged directly into the river, but her launch would almost ruin even Brunel's reputation. Amid the full glare of the assembled press, *Great Eastern* was unceremoniously shoved by hydraulic rams across silt and mud of riverbank to get her afloat in the deeper channel. Inch by inch, the process took three months to accomplish. But this was exactly the point. Because of her sheer scale, *Great Eastern* was given a completely flattened hull to sit her upright on land since she would routinely be beached throughout her career to undergo repair. Brunel was well aware that a hull of this magnitude would undoubtedly sustain damage during such processes, so the double hull was to afford her the strength and protection to survive this relatively unscathed.

Harland & Wolff became the first yard to adopt Brunel's double hull concept, incorporating it into their vessels from 1861. By the time *Titanic* appeared on their drawing boards they had perfected the principles of the cellular hull to an art form. Their launch of White Star's 704ft *Oceanic* in 1899 marked the first occasion that a vessel surpassed the length of the epochal *Great Eastern*. Technology had taken forty-one years to transcend Brunel's leviathan, but once this milestone had been reached, ships began growing in size, rapidly: *Oceanic* surpassed the size of *Kaiser Wilhelm der Grosse*, launched just two years earlier, by 42 per cent.

White Star's quest to develop the ultimate gargantuan continued apace with their Big Four liners: the 20,904-ton *Celtic* of 1901 became the first to out-gross *Great Eastern*, and with each of White Star's Big Four the limits of marine engineering edged to ever higher plateaus. *Celtic* was outsized by her sister *Cedric* in 1903, and in turn was overtaken by *Baltic* in 1904 – itself outdone in May 1907 by the 24,541-ton *Adriatic*. Cunard too held the trend, putting the 31,550-ton *Lusitania* into service in August 1907, which by November that year was surpassed by her own sister, *Mauretania*. In 1907 alone, the title of 'world's largest vessel' would change hands on no less than four occasions, the very year Ismay and Pirrie conceptualised the even larger Olympic Class. Soon mutterings were circulating, questioning now whether ships had really become just too large too soon.

Measuring 786ft long, *Mauretania* amassed 31,938 tons. Able to carry 2,165 passengers, she too would be eclipsed by White Star's 882ft *Olympic*. Boasting a carrying capacity for 2,764 passengers as well as a crew of 900 the 45,324-ton *Olympic* out-grossed the mass of *Mauretania* by 30 per cent. It mirrored a tempo that saw the average weight of a North Atlantic express liner double from 5,784 tons in 1895 to 11,722 tons by 1911. With well over 3,000 people travelling aboard a single crossing, far more than competitive superiority was in jeopardy.

This size war of ocean liners became a marketing novelty, and at the turn of the century the maxim in shipbuilding was 'the bigger, the better'. The newly emerging Edwardian era relished its statements of bravado and might. To them it was crucial to associate achievement and power with size: the larger the vessel, the more indestructible it was therefore perceived to be. Nothing would demonstrate engineering prowess more plainly than to bestow the ships with Classical personas: the monikers *Olympic*, *Titanic*, *Gigantic* originated from Grecian mythology; *Lusitania*, *Mauretania*, *Aquitania* and *Laconia* recalled ancient provinces. A ship worthy of the deities instilled confidence among its impressionable fee-paying mortals.

As competition intensified, operators pressured their naval architects to outdo the dimensions of their rivals: *Titanic* weighed 62 per cent more than *Oceanic*, which had been completed ten years previously, when she reigned supreme as largest on the seas. White Star chose their most experienced master, Edward J. Smith, to command their Olympic Class. Yet even his commands were previously served on far more diminutive craft: *Republic (I)* 420ft, *Coptic* 430ft, *Germanic* 455ft, *Cufic* 475ft, *Runic* 550ft, *Majestic* 566ft, *Baltic (II)* 709ft and the 725ft *Adriatic (II)*, before setting foot on the 882ft *Olympic*. Neither Smith nor his crew had the experience or technology at their disposal to handle a ship the size of White Star's 'Olympics'. The rate liners were growing at had completely outpaced the acumen of any serving crew.

Held together by half a million rivets amounting to 270 tons, and fixing plating to her steel frame in quadruple rows, the hull gave *Titanic* unprecedented might. But despite these attributes the very demise of *Titanic* stemmed from her famously oversized mass; a problem not unique to her. *Olympic* would suffer her share of misfortune too. The extraordinary scale of the White Star Olympians exposed a hydrographical force never previously experienced to such perilous extent.

While towing *Olympic* to the outfitting basin following her launch on 20 October 1910, 'a gale of wind, not strong, blew [her] against the side of a buttress' in the yard's wharf, an incident Harland & Wolff later confirmed had left her hull scratched and dented. The 24,600-ton hull of *Olympic* had been possessed by a mere gust of wind. The event raised wider concerns about the unknown forces that ships of this scale now seemed suddenly and easily prone.

From the outset *Olympic* was haunted by this new hydrodynamic spectre. The 198-ton tugboat *O.L. Hallenbeck*, one of eleven tugs guiding *Olympic* into New York's pier 59, fell victim to the force in the closing stages of her maiden voyage on 21 June 1911. Captain Smith was present on the bridge with Harbour Pilot Julius Adler commanding: the docking had caught the tugboat in the backwash of *Olympic*, drawing the 200-ton tug beneath her stern. The tug was crushed, inflicting upon it $10,000 of damage. The ensuing legal challenge was later dismissed in White Star's favour, although only through lack of evidence to the contrary.

The second and most serious incident involving *Olympic* occurred within sight of the Isle of Wight, on 20 September 1911. *Olympic* had departed Southampton at 11.25a.m. that morning bearing 1,313 passengers and a crew of 885, beginning what was her fifth outward crossing to New York. Captain Smith in attendance, she was again at the time under the command of the harbour pilot, Trinity House's Captain George William Bowyer. Known affectionately by White Star as Uncle George, he had piloted all of their ships in and out of Southampton since 1906.

Navigating around Southampton even today remains a treacherous affair and requires considerable skill, as its bustling waters are beset by shallows. The role of the pilot therefore is to manoeuvre the ship though the narrow deepwater channel of Southampton Water and out to open sea; its safe limits marked by the Nab Lightship (replaced in 1920 with a fixed lighthouse).

On this occasion Bowyer had set the speed of *Olympic* to 11 knots, heading her out of Southampton Water to then perform a sharp turn port at West

Bramble buoy to bring her into Spithead, a stretch separating the mainland from the north-eastern shore of the Isle of Wight, an area notorious for its shallows. Meanwhile, at 12.39p.m., HMS *Hawke*, a 360ft Edgar-Class cruiser captained by Commander William Frederick Blunt, was rounding the isle's Egypt Point and heading eastward along the Solent at 16 knots.

By 12.43p.m. completing her manoeuvre at Bramble Bank, and skirting the vast jutting sandbanks marked on the surface by buoys identifying the deepwater channel, *Olympic* headed into Spithead. Increasing speed to 14 knots, Bowyer had mistakenly cut this turn too short, narrowing the channel for the rapidly approaching *Hawke*. The two vessels continuing east steamed parallel at 16 knots, *Hawke* converging upon the starboard wing of *Olympic*. With little more than 100ft of water separating them Blunt attempted to turn *Hawke* starboard to widen the gap but her steering mechanism seized momentarily, locking the rudder 15 degrees to port. On *Olympic* Bowyer told Captain Smith of his intention to 'port-around' *Hawke*. Smith, watching from the starboard navigation wing, was asked by Bowyer 'If she [*Hawke*] is going to strike, sir, let me know in time so I can put the helm hard over to port, is she going to strike?'

'Yes, she is going to strike us in the stern,' he answered.

The 7,350-ton battlecruiser continued toward *Olympic*, pulled ever closer by the forward momentum of the liner's precipitous hull. At 12.46p.m., they collided. The bow of *Hawke* struck deep into the starboard quarter of *Olympic*, decimating the warship's 5in-thick armour-plated prow. Reinforced with concrete and designed specifically for ramming, the bow's impact had forced *Olympic* to swing 34 degrees to port, punching an 85ft hole into her stern. The damage penetrated 8ft deep into her starboard quarter beneath her Well Deck, a point 86ft forward of her rudder, leaving exposed a bank of unoccupied second-class cabins straddling decks D to G.

Despite the severity of the damage, *Hawke* limped into Portsmouth under her own steam. *Olympic*, however, with two compartments flooded and her starboard propeller inoperable, anchored off the Isle of Wight's Osborne Bay. Patched and temporarily seaworthy, *Olympic* returned to Southampton the following day. The rivets holding her plating in the area struck by *Hawke* had burst under the impact, highlighting a weakness in their durability that would ultimately prove fatal to her sister less than a year later.

The incident was heard at a Royal Navy Court of Inquiry on 22 September 1911. Chaired by Captain Henry Grant, it ruled the civilian operator (White Star) the negligent party. The line subsequently elevated the matter to the County Court on the 29th, likewise deferring onward to the Admiralty Court. The case *Olympic v. Hawke*, presided by Sir Samuel Adams, was finally underway on 16 November. To restage the collision it commissioned tests conducted at the National Physics Laboratory by Professor John Biles LLD DSc – who within a year would become an assessor for the *Titanic* inquiry. Through floating models in its vast experimentation tank, Biles discovered that the displacement caused by the forward motion of a ship of equal size to *Olympic* produced a force around its stern that imposed a suction effect on any craft that happened to be nearby.

The hearings closed on 19 December, again ruling navigational error by the pilot for bringing *Olympic* too far south of her intended path and trapping *Hawke*. Culpable for the costs, White Star appealed, albeit unsuccessfully, on 5 April 1913, but persevered, having the case finally brought before the House of Lords in 1914. White Star was represented by Sir Robert Finlay, the very lawyer who had led their earlier defence at the *Titanic* hearings; opposite was Attorney-General Sir John Simon, appearing on behalf of the British Admiralty. Presided by the Lord Chancellor himself, the case was again dismissed on 9 November, once more ruling the pilot to be at fault. As Trinity pilots enjoy immunity from prosecution, both the Royal Navy and White Star ended up footing the bill for the repair of their own vessel.

Olympic was re-patched and taken at a sedate 10 knots to Belfast on 4 October 1911 to undergo repairs that were to take six and a half weeks, costing White Star to the tune of £250,000: the original agreement with Harland & Wolff left the line responsible for the cost of ongoing repairs to their vessels. She resumed service on 20 November. Her size would continue to prove problematic for the crew, but by 1912 they were considered to be adequately experienced, and many of them transferred to her sister, *Titanic*. Yet even prior to striking the iceberg *Titanic* was involved in a precluding incident that occurred on 10 April, a stone's throw from her custom-built berth at Southampton, moments after casting off for her doomed maiden voyage.

The extent of the modifications that had taken place in Belfast to construct the Olympic Class heralded similar adaptations at Southampton to accommodate the trio in service. The existing facilities at Britain's largest port underwent an extensive upgrade to house the dimensions of White Star's record-breaking leviathans.

Work on an entirely new dock specially to accommodate the 35ft draughts of *Olympic* and *Titanic* began in 1908. Finished at a cost of half a million pounds it was completed in time for the maiden voyage of *Olympic*. Its huge three-sided quay housed a mooring frontage of 1,600ft along its two sides separated as a parallelogram 600ft apart enclosed 15½ acres of water. Dug to provide a draught of 53ft at high water and 40ft at low tide, even its lowest ebb would grant 5ft of water beneath the Olympic Class. Funded by the London and South Western Railway as part of a consortium with Southampton Dock Company and various other shipping lines it was named the White Star Dock as it had been dug to the specifications of the Olympic-Class liners: *Olympic* became the first occupant of the facility on 3 June 1911. Rather than always returning them to Belfast for repair, Harland & Wolff's nearby Trafalgar dry-dock was likewise lengthened to maintain them shore-side.

White Star Dock, containing berths 43 to 47, formed the hub of White Star's express services to New York – an operation that had transferred from Liverpool in 1907 in preparation for the Olympic Class. Renamed Ocean Dock in 1922 its immensity still sees it playing host to the world's largest liners today. From here *Titanic* cast from berth number 44 at the stroke of noon on 10 April.

Heaved from the quayside by two tugboats of the Red Funnel Line – *Albert Edward* and *Ajax* – the pair was soon joined by four others – *Neptune, Hector, Vulcan* and *Hercules* – guiding *Titanic* along the narrow river Test and to Southampton Water. Versed in handling *Olympic*, two tugs pushed *Titanic* from the stern as the remaining four guided her starboard flank, the docks passing along their portside. To head her into Southampton Water the flotilla proceeded past unoccupied berth 43. Keeping *Titanic* steady at 6 knots the group continued by vacant berths 42 and 41 and onward to the refrigerated cargo facility at number 40, which was occupied by the 370ft cargo hauler *Beacon Grange*. They then came parallel to berths 39 and 38.

All officers on *Titanic* were on duty, supervising the key cast-off points. Captain Smith and Harbour Pilot George Bowyer were joined on the bridge by Fourth Officer Boxhall and Fifth Officer Lowe. Chief Officer Wilde and Second Officer Lightoller occupied the Forecastle. Overseeing matters from the stern was First Officer Murdoch. Manning the Docking Bridge nearby was Third Officer Pitman, with Sixth Officer Moody at the gangway entrance sealing the main passenger doorway.

Southampton had become littered with craft due to the strike action of coalminers. The resulting scarcity of fuel saw many voyages cancelled and April 1912 found many vessels idle at Britain's main port, 'rafted' side by side in columns along Southampton's berths to accommodate their idled fuel-starved residents, as well as to leave others free for the few ships still in operation. One such column was moored along berths 39 and 38. Here, secured against the quay, sat White Star's *Oceanic*, and, tied to her since the 6th, *New York* of IMM's American Line.

Under normal circumstances the deepwater channel of the river Test, down which *Titanic* was guided, afforded a clearance of 500ft between the dockside and the rim of its perilous shallows. With *New York* moored along the offshore flank of *Oceanic* the two liners narrowed this channel by 150ft. Separated by only 30 yards of water, as *Titanic* passed, the force from the wave she generated caused the 10,798-ton *New York* to rise and fall so violently that it snapped all six mooring ropes fastening her to *Oceanic* and the dockside.

The wave had been triggered by the water drawing only 2ft above low tide at noon. Even at slow speed the thrust from her propellers sitting close to the riverbed exacerbated the surge of displacement from her hull. Travelling *Titanic* too fast produced a vast squall beneath *New York*. Crowds witnessing the departure shrieked as the stern of the 517ft *New York* swung loose towards *Titanic*. Her straining tethers forced *Oceanic* to a list of 'several degrees' while still attached to her moorings dockside, not righting herself until *Titanic* passed fully by. Realising the danger, the pilot powered the portside propeller of *Titanic* in a bid to shove *New York* away in its backwash. At this same moment Captain Gale on the tugboat *Vulcan* got a line onto the stern of *New York* and began to heave her away from *Titanic*.

As *Titanic* passes along the quayside at Southampton at midday on 10 April 1912, her surge of displacement wrenches the liner *New York* from her moorings aside *Oceanic* [far left], veering her stern towards *Titanic*. The tugboat *Vulcan* [centre] heaves *New York* away from *Titanic*, narrowly averting collision. (Mary Evans Picture Library)

Bowyer then slowed *Titanic* to a standstill, but *New York*, now drifting freely along the port flank of *Titanic*, dragged *Vulcan* helplessly behind it. As *New York* slid downstream her stern then swung into the path of *Titanic*. Bowyer slammed the great engines into reverse. Aided by tugs *Neptune* and *Hector*, *Titanic* eased away from *New York*. The crew of *Hercules* managed to control the bow of *New York* and with *Vulcan* still attached to her stern, the trio heaved the wayward liner out of harm's way and secured her to vacant berth 37. Once the all-clear was given, at 1p.m., *Titanic* resumed her voyage. The two vessels had avoided collision by 4ft. With a collective exhale of breath the maiden voyage continued out of Southampton and safely to open sea without further incident: a portent of the disaster to come.

A further mishap, this time concerning *Olympic*, would occur at the twilight of her illustrious career: a collision involving the Nantucket Lightship *117* which marked the infamous shoals 42 miles south-east of Nantucket Island. On 15 May 1934, veiled in fog and en route to New York, Captain John Binks of *Olympic* had lost radio contact with the lightship, and reduced *Olympic*'s speed from 20 to 3 knots as a precaution. Unable to determine the distance to the lightship's fog signals, *117* loomed out of the mire directly ahead of *Olympic*. Binks spun her helm hard-to-port but the lightship, caught in the 52,000-ton displacement, was pulled beneath the bow of *Olympic* and was sent to the seabed along with three of its crew. Until the collision the venerable Binks held an unblemished record in his forty-five years at sea.

Each incident had been caused by the vast displacements of *Olympic* and *Titanic* generating a hydrodynamic force, known as the Canal Effect, and drawing nearby objects toward them – 'pull-in'. The captain of *Mauretania*, John Pritchard, recalled in 1911 never experiencing such pull-in with his ship, but the Olympic Class had revealed a new and serious concern. Coupled with the dearth of knowledge of how to counteract it, pull-in on the 'Olympics' proved particularly challenging. The largest ships that White Star had produced before them, the self-proclaimed Big Four, grossed 50 per cent less volume than *Olympic*. Captain Smith had chosen key senior crew from *Olympic* to transfer with him to the maiden voyage of *Titanic* in order to pool their collective experience, already in want of supply in April 1912.

The lengths of other liners of the period had shown no significant leap in those such as Cunard's 790ft *Mauretania* and White Star's 725.5ft *Adriatic* of 1909, nor the 882.5ft *Olympic*. Liners topping 700ft had been in existence since 1899. To a crew an increase of 157ft was no great concern. Their inexperience however lay with the additional displacement the length created. Grossing 31,938 tons, *Mauretania* was 14,390 tons shy when usurped by *Olympic* as the world's largest liner. The displacement of the Olympic-Class hulls, able to draw sizeable craft toward them with considerable ease, prophesied the futility of trying to dodge the 46,000-ton *Titanic* round an approaching iceberg. Steaming into the ice region at full tilt, her crew had exposed the depth to which seafaring had miscalculated the dynamics of their charge. Yet industry's preoccupation with the tonnage race to produce the next ship to surpass *Titanic* was already in hot pursuit while the debris of disaster still rained upon her seabed grave.

When plans for the belated addition to the Lusitania class, the 45,647-ton *Aquitania*, were approved by Cunard in January 1911 they billed her as the world's largest ship. The 909ft *Aquitania* measured 1ft over her German rival, HAPAG's 52,117-ton *Imperator*, whose construction had begun on 18 July 1910. Launched on 23 May 1912, five weeks after the sinking of *Titanic*, *Imperator*, almost 6,000 tons heavier than *Titanic*, was likewise advertised as the world's largest when entering service on 10 June 1913; she sported forty wooden and forty-three collapsible lifeboats to placate the confidence of her passengers. Determined to retain her title as 'longest ship' HAPAG fitted to her bow a 10ft outstretched bronze eagle to inflate her overall length to 919ft, out-measuring *Aquitania* when she finally entered service that May. *Imperator* too was followed by her even-longer sister, the 948ft *Vaterland* on 3 April 1913: 65ft longer and 7,954 tons heavier than *Titanic* sunken just months before.

The main operators still avidly competing with the Olympic Class were not, however, doing so in flagrant disregard for safety following the disaster. All were to some degree undergoing construction at the time that *Titanic* struck the iceberg. 'Bigger' however, was still deemed 'better'. Though in the aftermath of *Titanic* the travelling public would no longer share the exuberant marketing of invincibility that the shipping operators encouraged. The next British-owned liner commissioned after the disaster that was actually larger than *Titanic* would not appear until 1936: RMS *Queen Mary*. Had scruples finally infiltrated a wildly cavalier shipping industry and its collective responsibility to exercise greater care, or was the decaying state of the global economy the influencing factor that would finally prevail to stay their hand.

CHAPTER 15

LOST PROPERTY

'I had expected people to be excited about our finding the *Titanic*, but never in
my wildest dreams had I anticipated this level of excitement.'
Robert D. Ballard, 1987

At 3.30p.m., 8 November 1929, an earthquake rocked the bed of the North
Atlantic Ocean, spewing thousands of tons of sediment across the shelf of the
Grand Banks, the area in which *Titanic* was known to have sunk. Rumours spread
that the wreck of the missing liner was either destroyed or buried by silt, ending
with it the possibility of anyone ever finding her. Above on the surface, at the
epicentre of this earthquake at the very moment it struck, was none other than
Olympic. Her captain, Walter Parker, noted in position 42°12'N, 56°56'W that the
vibration from its shockwave had engulfed his ship for two minutes, a shaking so
acute that crew feared she had struck an underwater object, possibly a wreck. The
ghost of *Titanic* had come to haunt the Atlantic once more.

The days following the loss of the *Titanic* saw numerous suggestions emerge in
newspapers contriving schemes with which to recover her wreck. All involved
inflating it to the surface using anything from balloons to ping-pong balls.
However, there was one overriding problem still to overcome: *Titanic* had yet
to be found. Logically, the resting place of *Titanic* was always anticipated to be
within a few miles of Boxhall's CQD position. But with the sea in that area of the
Atlantic averaging a depth exceeding 2 miles, finding her wreck would be looking for a needle in one enormously dispersed haystack.

The first serious attempt to locate *Titanic* took place in 1953. Coordinated by
British salvage company Risdon Beazley Ltd, it employed echo search methods
through use of explosives. The expedition, however, ended just as the succession of similar attempts that ensued over the following three decades – fruitless.
Locating *Titanic* turned into the maritime quest for the Holy Grail and seventy-three years would pass until the first searchlights would finally illuminate
the lost liner.

The successful search for *Titanic* was conducted by a joint French–American venture. Starting on 5 July 1985 the first stage of the hunt was supervised by Jean-Louis Michel of the French research institute, IFREMER (Institut Français de Recherche pour l'Exploration des Mers). Aboard *Le Suroit* they scoured a predefined 150 square-mile zone using SONAR. After covering 70 per cent of the region, which yielded no trace of *Titanic* whatsoever, they were joined on 22 August by their American colleagues. Arriving with the research vessel *Knorr* and twenty-four scientists and researchers was Dr Robert Ballard.

Ballard was a lead scientist in Massachusetts for Woods Hole Oceanographic, a renowned research institute founded in 1930. At the time Ballard was also a US Navy reservist commander. Leveraging his high-ranking contacts he forged a deal with the US Navy to loan him use of their deep-ocean submarine. The agreement was struck on the condition that he use it to experiment deep-sea exploration on their behalf. Being the height of the Cold War the exercise would prove to the Russians the technological advances of America's capabilities in deepwater search. Ballard was granted use of their small three-man submersible over a limited timeframe to allow him to secretly photograph the wreck of the USS *Scorpion*. The *Scorpion*, armed with nuclear torpedoes, had sunk in mysterious circumstances on 22 May 1968, 400 miles from the Azores, taking with it all ninety-nine crewmembers. Resting at a depth of 11,500ft the US government wanted Ballard to record the condition of the wreck to assess possible radiation leakage. In return Ballard would be allowed use of the craft to photograph the wreck of *Titanic* for the remaining duration of the agreed period.

The submarine loaned to Ballard was named *Alvin*. Dating from 1964 *Alvin* was upgraded with a titanium alloy encasement in 1974 to give the 18-ton submersible the ability to dive to 13,000ft for up to ten hours at a time: ideal for visiting *Titanic*. At the time *Alvin* was one of two submersibles in existence able to reach such depths. The other was *Mir I* of the Russian Navy.

Taking over the search from his French companions, Ballard arrived at the site with only eleven days remaining before *Alvin* was to be returned to the navy. Suspended from the 2,500-ton *Knorr* hung two specially designed sledges laden with underwater cameras, which scanned the seabed with ROVs (Remotely Operated Vehicles) *Argo* and *ANGUS*. *Argo* shot moving images, while *ANGUS* (acronym for Acoustically Navigated Geological Underwater Survey) snapped still photographs.

The days passed monotonously by as monitors surveyed nothing but endless footage of barren seabed. With 510 square miles already searched and only four days of the expedition remaining, at 1.05a.m. on 1 September 1985 the cameras finally brought something into view – something man-made. The object stumbled upon was quickly identified as a boiler, a Scotch cylindrical boiler, the very same as that belonging to their target. Ballard had discovered *Titanic*: 314 miles from the epicentre of the tremor that in 1929 was feared to have destroyed it.

Back up on *Knorr*, their encounter with the world's most famed wreck evoked from its discoverers mixed emotions of jubilation and reflection. Rather than rejoice the find that would no doubt secure his name in the history books, Ballard remained sensitive to its dignity and marked this truly momentous occasion with all the sobriety that it deserved.

The position of the wreck was fixed at 41°43'N, 49°57'W, approximately 13.5 miles from the CQD position (41°46'N, 50°14'W) derived at by Boxhall on the night of the disaster. Lying at a depth of 12,460ft amid the Newfoundland Ridge of the Grand Banks – 325 miles south-east of Cape Race – it rests upright and close to the edge of a crevice, since daubed Titanic Canyon.

As the first images of *Titanic* for almost three quarters of a century were emblazoned across TV screens and the front pages of tabloids, journals and magazines throughout the world, Ballard kept her exact location a closely guarded secret. The expedition had run out of time and *Knorr* was turning home to Woods Hole and a rapturous welcome.

Ballard next returned to the site on 13 July 1986. Instead of guiding cameras from the surface, this time he intended to see the wreck for himself. Squeezing into *Alvin* he became the first human since 1912 to set eyes on *Titanic* without aid of a lens. His first view was of the prow of the wreck looming toward him from the murky abyss. Immediately beginning to take images, still and moving, he was soon weaving the specially adapted ROV *Jason Jr* inside the hull to capture footage from the wreck itself.

Jason Jr had been developed in 1984 to explore the interiors of the *Scorpion*. Piloted by a joystick from *Alvin*, its camera, housed in a blue watertight protective encasement, was steered by small thrust propellers linked by a cable that allowed its operator to explore up to 250ft inside *Titanic*. It was far too dangerous, even impossible, to send in a manned sub. Perching *Alvin* on a lip of the Boat Deck, Ballard guided the tiny robot deep into the forward stairwell, once the grandest area of the ship.

Respectfully leaving every artefact in situ, Ballard only took images from *Titanic*, but lowered a memorial plaque on a capstan on the stern, the spot most of the victims perished on the night of disaster, gravitating toward the Poop Deck to await their end.

The revelation Ballard had stumbled upon in 1985 was, of course, *Titanic*, lying broken in two sections. This finally confirmed survivor accounts that reported the ship to have appeared to splinter just below the water's surface. The fracture was largely concealed from view, and for seventy-three years this fuelled a widely believed misconception that *Titanic* lay intact on the seabed.

Up on the surface *Titanic* had broken between funnels 3 and 4, the weakest part of her hull – the area straddled by her cavernous reciprocating engine room. With the waterline at her second funnel, and 39,000 tons of floodwater inside the hull, the weight within her bow heaved the stern clear of the surface culminating in an incline of 45 degrees. Bearing a now considerable load within her bow, the over-whelming pressure concentrated on the mid-section of her frame. With one third of her hull elevated and completely airborne of the water, an exertion of 35,000 pounds per square inch focussed upon this axis. Its intensity forced the hull to snap at its weakest point, the shaft of the after grand stairwell and the area beneath, which spanned the largest cavity of the ship – an expanse largely unsupported by longitudinal decks.

The accepted theory of what happened below the waterline as *Titanic* sank has her bow section falling stem-first, at which moment the two sections were con-nected only by the 3in-thick keelbar. As the bow sank, this umbilical link hoisted the stern perpendicular to the sea. Wrenching free of the keelbar, the descending bow pulled the stern to a near-vertical position to the water surface, the sleek hydrodynamic shape of the bow sheering its way to the seabed with steadily increasing velocity.

The bow section measures 470ft long and sits gracefully upright on the seabed save for a slight list to port. Despite its age, this section of the wreck has maintained its shape comparatively well, although today it is in the advanced stages of decay. The impact of the bow as it slammed to the seafloor was met with such magni-tude that its stem piled 60ft deep into the silt. In consequence it concealed forever the damage sustained by the iceberg itself. The force of this impact buckled the hull downward by 6 degrees at a point directly below the forward Well Deck – caused by the rear of this section coming to rest on a higher level of seabed. Using satellites to fix its location, Ballard recorded the bow at 49°56'49"W, 41°43'57"N.

As for its less streamlined companion, once free of the bow, the air trapped inside maintained the stern at a near-vertical position on the surface. Hanging momentar-ily like a frozen pendulum, reportedly for thirty seconds, it too slipped beneath the surface, leaving behind its occupants fighting for their lives in the icy water and flailing wildly for floating wreckage. Unlike the bow, whose lines sheered its way to the seabed, the heavy vertical stern plummeted; landing upright with an almighty force, it pummelled the rudder 45ft into the ocean floor. The official position of the stern sits at 49°56'54"W, 41°43'35"N, the two halves of hull resting 800 yards (1,970ft) apart, with the rudder in opposite orientation to the bow.

The stern section begins at the point of the interior once occupied by funnel 4. The areas between funnels 3 and 4 are completely lost, obliterated by the force of the splintering hull. Paused at an upright position on the surface, objects in the compartments at the point of fracture – the five single-ended boilers of room 1 – dislodged from the stern section, spilling its heavy contents vertically to the seabed along with the full spectrum of engine-room paraphernalia. The boilers thus mark the spot *Titanic* foundered (41°43'N, 49°56'W) and, coincidently, the first parts of the wreck discovered by Ballard in 1985. The other boilers remain in situ in the bow, as do the huge reciprocating engines that still rest on their com-partment fixings, draped by the mangled form of what now remains of the stern.

The planking of the Poop Deck is torn backward over the sides of the stern, it drapes the hull plating, which was crumpled outward by its considerable impact with the seabed, which slammed its keel 50ft into the silt. Today, the twin outermost propellers are partially visible; buried to their steel hubs they remain attached to their fixings. The after Well Deck too suffered greatly from its fall, with its walls splaying away from the keel, transforming this once slender stern into chaotic victim of gravity.

The bow section has fared more favourably than the stern. Upon striking the iceberg the bow began a gradual process which, over the two and-a-half hours prior to descent, steadily exchanged all air inside with water. With the bow fully exhausted of air, water inside counterbalanced the pressure outside, giving its plating internal support. In contrast the stern remained largely devoid of water, rising slowly airborne of the surface as the bow was pulled downward. Once broken free of the bow, the stern, laden with machinery from the two engine rooms and thus far heavier than its forward companion, tumbled too sharply to expunge the air trapped inside, collapsing against the pressure of water outside its unsupported shell on striking the seabed. The fall of the two hull sections aptly parodied the diverging living standards of their former occupants. The elegant hydrodynamic bow filled with first-class cabins glided gracefully to the seabed, whereas the stern crammed with engines and third-class berths freefell into the abyss with an almighty thump.

Despite over 1,500 people going down with *Titanic* there are neither skeletons nor clothing to be seen. Due to the vast concentration of bacteria in the depths of the Atlantic, all such organisms have been consumed throughout the ensuing decades. The only personal items remaining are those impervious to bacteria: leather shoes, eyeglasses and combs – stark reminders of the human tragedy the finality of *Titanic* was.

The breakage formed two fields of debris spilled by the fissured hull. The fields overlap each other. That nearest the stern measures between 2,000ft and 2,600ft and mostly contains items of engine-room machinery. The other, fanning outward from the bow section and extending for 1 mile, comprises articles principally from the ship's passenger areas.

All four funnels from *Titanic* were torn away during her descent to the ocean floor, their shards strewn among the debris fields comprise the priceless cache of miscellany that ranges from boilers to bottles, bedpans to bulwarks: rich pickings for any would-be salvors seeking keepsakes from this, the most famous wreck of all.

After Ballard's visits the French team returned to the site in 1987. With *Nautile*, a newly built 19-ton submersible capable of diving up to 20,000ft, throughout their thirty-two dives they retrieved 1,800 artefacts from the two debris fields of fragments littering the ocean floor. The site was not visited again until 30 June 1991, this time by a joint Russian-Canadian venture aboard the *Akadomik*. Armed with the deep sea submersible *Mir 1*, they began removing artefacts close to the areas surrounding the hull.

'Loved to Death'

When first examined by Ballard during his dives of 1986, the ship's two masts, their lower steel sections only, sat connected to the wreck lying horizontal on the deck, flattened during descent. He found the steel crow's nest still on its fixings on the forward mast. He also discovered three of the eight cargo cranes still in situ, and four lifeboat davits in their original positions standing as they were left the night of disaster. Much of the wooden decking had also survived. As for the bridge, only the stand for the brass telemotor remained on its original mounting. The wreck's remaining rudiments were strewn among the debris fields. After visiting *Titanic* on his second expedition since his famous discovery it would be almost another twenty years before Ballard returned and set eyes on the wreck once more. In June 2004 he explored the site, this time to specifically compare its rate of deterioration since 1985. He was saddened by what he saw – noticing a multitude of significant changes. Most poignantly he found the crow's nest had since disappeared from its foremast fixings, not through pilfering but through accelerated decay. He also noticed an entire deck had since collapsed in the stern, and that the roofs over the reading and writing rooms, as well as that of the gymnasium, had also caved in. The walls of the officers' quarters had collapsed too. Disturbingly, he found that two decades of visiting submersibles perching upon the Boat Deck in order to lower cameras down into the hull had left it permanent damaged. He found signs of intentional damage too. Comparing his latest images with those taken during his expeditions of 1985–6 Ballard discovered much of the wreck had now ceded its shape and rigidity, the Promenade Deck particularly. His study confirmed that since discovery *Titanic* was decaying demonstrably faster than anyone had feared.

No longer revealing its painted hue of 1985 the hull today is completely encrusted and blistered by rusticles: living micro-organisms that feed on wrought-iron and cause it to corrode. Once bacteria has consumed its fill it falls free and dies only to be replaced by another and for the process to start over again, repeating the cycle until the iron itself has been eaten away. Activity stirred by countless visiting submersibles has hastened its regeneration. Over time the rusticles will devour and degenerate the strength of wrought-iron into the consistency of pulp.

Today, as it has since 1912, the wreck of *Titanic* endures water pressure of over 6,000lb (2 tons) per square inch. With the steel calloused by rust, bacteria and barnacles that now consume its entire hulk, the pressure will eventually overwhelm and collapse whatever remains of *Titanic*. It will forever be too dangerous for manned explorations to venture inside the wreck itself. Any remaining rigidity in the two hull sections will most certainly succumb in the not too distant future. Yet, with all the technology at our disposal today do we not have a moral duty to try and preserve it? Here we come to this contentious issue: the future of *Titanic*.

Resting more than 12 miles from any coastline, no single nation can lay claim to the wreck of *Titanic*, lying far beyond the protection of any national boundary. The sinking endowed her with unprecedented fame, so much so that any artefacts salvaged from her wreck inexorably become priceless treasures. With over 1,000 items already recovered from her two debris fields, opinion is divided as to how to protect the resting place of history's most beguiling disaster.

The first measure to protect the wreck was put in place on its discovery in 1985: Robert Ballard withheld the release of its coordinates until 1986 to stave off a rush of would-be treasure hunters flocking to the site in the hope of recovering its bounty. Such fervour led the US government to instigate the first legal step to safeguard *Titanic*. Their RMS Titanic Maritime Memorial Act came into law with some immediacy on 21 October 1986. Calling for international recognition of the wreck for its 'cultural and historical significance', the Act fundamentally designated it a formal gravesite – prohibiting salvage:

Section 2(b1): 'To encourage international efforts to designate the RMS *Titanic* as an international maritime memorial to those who lost their lives aboard her in 1912.'

Section 2(b4): '…no person should physically alter, disturb, or salvage the RMS *Titanic* in any research or exploratory activities which are conducted.'

Further measures ensued, namely under the guise of Senator Lowell Weicker of Connecticut. Calling for an outright ban on any artefacts from *Titanic* imported to America for sale his bill was also passed:

Notwithstanding any other provision of law, no object from the RMS *Titanic* may be imported into the customs territory of the United States for the purpose of commercial gain after the date of enactment of this Act.

– 3 August 1987.

Although well intentioned, the Act bore one essential flaw. Artefacts are still raised and in large quantity, and are still brought to American soil. They are not sold of course, but exhibited – for a fee. The proceeds from their tickets and merchandising fund yet more dives to salvage yet more artefacts from the wreck to supply yet more exhibitions – all drawing record attendance.

In Britain the Protection of Wrecks Act of 1973 enjoys jurisdiction within only British territorial waters. New legislation to agree more universal protection was therefore required. Article 303 of the United Nations' 1982 'Convention on the Law of the Sea' grants protection to vessels of archaeological significance on the proviso that they lie within 200 miles of the national coastline of a signatory state. *Titanic* indeed rests within 200 miles of Canadian coastal waters, however, UNESCO's

'Convention on the Protection of Underwater Cultural Heritage' (2001) only safe-guards wrecks that are over 100 years old; applicable for *Titanic* from 2012. For younger wrecks, new individual international accords are needed to cater for those likewise coveted dearly by salvors: *Andrea Doria, Empress of Ireland, Lusitania*, to name but a few. Its manifestation, however, would not be the first occasion of such an arrangement.

Precedence for a wreck lying in international waters that was accorded both multinational and legally binding protection was first granted to Estline's 15,566-ton passenger ferry *Estonia*. Sunk in international waters in the Baltic Sea during the early hours of 28 September 1994 while en route from Tallinn to Stockholm, rough seas capsized and claimed the ferry in a mere thirty-five minutes, taking with it 852 lives, of which all but ninety-two remain inside her wreck to this day. A multinational agreement initiated by Sweden was jointly signed by Estonia and Finland along with four other nations on 23 February 1995. The agreement granted the wreck the status of an internationally recognised unconsecrated underwater tomb, criminalising 'any disturbing activities' for perpetuity.

Known as the Gravesite Treaty, Article 2 of the agreement set four coordinates marking out a 1.5-mile exclusion zone around the wreck. The sensitivity of the tragedy saw the treaty brought into force within five months of the disaster, and even afforded round-the-clock surveillance from the Swedish Navy and Finnish Coast Guard; there was even scope for encasing her beneath a protective concrete shroud. More crucially the accord set a benchmark for other wrecks in interna-tional waters to also enjoy legally recognised and enforceable protection. Similar arrangements are now adopting the Gravesite Treaty to allow further covenants to extend to other wrecks that likewise warrant sanctity.

Like *Estonia*, *Titanic* offers no archaeological importance. Both date from extensively documented periods of history. Any agreement for *Titanic* would need therefore to justify her protection as a gravesite for the 1,523 passengers and crew whose lives she claimed; in particular the unrecovered victims still techni-cally resting within her wreck despite any physical forms no longer remaining. Setting such exclusion zones is already long-standing practice for sunken military vessels granted war-grave status regardless of where they lie. However, in Britain the Department of Transport laid the foundations to extend similar protection also to British-registered merchant vessels wrecked in international waters. Its Merchant Shipping and Maritime Security Act became law in 1997, Section 24 permitting the initiation of proceedings to establish statutory arrangements to protect the wrecks of merchant vessels lying beyond its territorial waters.

The Act empowers the secretary of state by legally binding international agree-ment to prohibit access to that wreck, and the area surrounding it, and to restrict anyone disturbing both it and its artefacts. In acknowledgment to her 'symbolic importance' Britain duly inaugurated diplomatic efforts to formulate a multi-national arrangement seeking the 'in-situ preservation' of *Titanic* and her artefacts both in and surrounding her wreck, and to set that protection in stone.

After six years of consultation Britain put forward its signature on 6 November 2003, with America following suit at a ceremony in London 18 June 2004. The agreement called for measures from the four nations identified by America's Titanic Maritime Memorial Act – France, Canada, Britain and America – to afford the site worthwhile protection.

The four nations are required to agree, recognise and enforce the sanctity of the final resting place of *Titanic*. All of them share vested interests: Canada, whose coastline lies closest to the wreck; Britain, whose flag she flew and was her nation of inception and registry; America, discoverers of the wreck and whose citizen – J.P. Morgan – originally owned *Titanic*. These three nations all agree the resting place of *Titanic* should indeed be protected, not for archaeological significance, but as a site of intrinsic cultural heritage. The fourth signatory, however, France, has a more unilateral interest; salvaging the site through their oceanographers, IFREMER. Opposed to leaving its artefacts in immersion and at the mercy of the sea, France has performed more excavations of the site than any other nation. Although agreeing in principle to recognise *Titanic* as a maritime memorial, France also believes any agreement should permit its preservation by the best means at their disposal – salvaging: preserving the artefacts so they can exist forever.

To be valid, Britain's agreement requires the signatures of at least two of the proposed four party nations: despite signing America has yet to ratify since beginning the process in 2007. As with the protection given to *Estonia*, the treaty can only criminalise offending activity from citizens of those nations privy to it. Consequently Britain intends to expand signatories to include Russia and Japan and other nations technologically proficient to mount their own dives. Although it will not prohibit exploration for 'non-intrusive surveys', the agreement seeks to enforce a regime of licensed access and provide a more permanent solution to the existing arrangement, which awarded a sole company salvage rights of the site – RMS Titanic Incorporated, a firm set up by former car salesman, George Tulloch, in 1987 – acknowledging that this situation may not enjoy longevity.

After recovering 800 artefacts from the site in July 1993 the company filed for exclusive salvage rights at the Admiralty Court in the District Court of Norfolk, Virginia. Granting them 'salvor-in-possession' on 7 June 1994, the court awarded the corporation exclusivity to retrieve artefacts from around the wreck of *Titanic*, except from within the hull itself. Their justification: to preserve artefacts associated with *Titanic* because of their symbolism to cultural heritage, which makes them worthy of preservation. The alternative: observe the virtues, but allow these artefacts to corrode to nothingness if left on the seabed.

The signing period of Britain's international agreement has since closed. Other signatures were withheld, because cordoning off the wreck would be detrimental to their interests. However, need to accelerate the protection of *Titanic* was highlighted when satellite footage of what was believed to be a private French vessel making an unauthorised dive to the site was taken in 2002. When Hollywood visited the wreck in 1995 using the Russian *Mir II* to take footage for the film *Titanic* it awakened a renaissance in interest. Since the film's release in 1997 a marked increase has been seen in the number of dives retrieving artefacts from the site – supplying growing numbers of exhibitions – spurring the diplomatic push to complete the drafting of the quad-national agreement.

Assigning protection to a wreck in international waters does, however, raise more moral and wider objections on the virtues of ring-fencing portions of the high seas. Establishing such exclusion zones is not only politically inflammable but also potentially unenforceable. Fundamentally, any international agreement defining no-go areas beyond national boundaries, such as the Gravesite Treaty, would only apply to nations that were party to it. Any citizen of any country not privy to such a treaty could quite legally flout its terms by visiting the site and doing as they wished while there. Naturally, the treaty nations would protest, but that individual may only risk prosecution should they ever set foot in any nation bound by that treaty. Such a scenario certainly presents the potential for diplomatic consternation, for in international waters any military or official of a treaty nation that threatened or forcibly removed that same individual from the 'protected area' may in the process of doing so arguably be committing an illegal act itself. Thereby any treaty sectioning off expanses of international waters may be technically unenforceable as no group of nations can decide claim to no-man's-land. However, by virtue of their existence such arrangements do signify mutual understanding between nations to actively prohibit citizens from disturbing and profiteering from its bounty, and internationally convey this intent.

With any agreement affording legal protection to *Titanic*, universally or otherwise, it will of course be virtually impossible to enforce or eliminate unauthorised salvage of the wreck itself. The logistics would require round-the-clock surveillance of the site either by manned vessels or submerged listening posts. Impracticalities aside, poor structural condition, enhanced decay and depth of two miles has inadvertently saved the artefacts entombed inside *Titanic* from salvage – not moral intervention.

General salvage from other wrecked vessels of the twentieth century has failed to ignite the level of interest *Titanic* draws. Her artefacts bring with them huge commercial value by their mere association alone, but changing the law is not all just for *Titanic*. With provisions in place, such protection will likely extend to other notable wrecks also leveraging commercial notoriety, or lying in shallower waters vulnerable to hobby divers in wet suits. As currently for others in national waters, salvaging within defined areas of protection may be performed under licence – controlled access – managed by an organisation identified by international agreement administered by an internationally recognised and independent authority. The British agreement identifies the International Council of Monuments and Sites, a non-governmental conservation body founded by the United Nations' International Restoration Charter of 1964. Alternatively there is the International Maritime Organisation (IMO). Likewise established by the UN (1948), although the IMO's membership is voluntary the four key nations in the matter of *Titanic* are each bound by its authority: Britain, member since 1949; Canada since 1948; France since 1952; and America since 1950. The early incarnation of the IMO – the then Intergovernmental Marine Consultative Organisation – was formed to update the findings of the SOLAS conventions; itself a derivative of the *Titanic* disaster. Achieving its original remit in 1960 the IMO's modern concerns include the monitoring of traffic, load–lines, dangerous cargoes, water pollution and, still, maritime safety.

The case of 'why bother' was answered by Dr Ballard shortly after his return to the site in 2004. Recording the noticeable decay that had taken place since his last visit in 1986 he lamented: '*Titanic* is literally in danger of being loved to death.' So just maybe the final chapter for *Titanic* is indeed still yet to be written.

CHAPTER 16

ECHOES OF TRAGEDY

'God himself could not sink this ship.'
Titanic deckhand's remark to passenger Sylvia Caldwell, 10 April 1912

Few of us need to be told that prevention is better than cure and in the days before Radar none appreciated the adage more than those engaged in shipbuilding, whose drive to localise flooding in the hull became the best form of protection the architect could bestow upon their craft.

The 617-ton paddle steamer *Royal William* was in 1838 the first hull subdivided into watertight compartments, beginning a concept that was soon to become the hallmark of Isambard Kingdom Brunel. When finished in 1843, his SS *Great Britain* was the first metal-hulled vessel to bear them. Although being the world's longest ship – by some considerable margin – her five bulkheads were installed more to provide strength to her hull than to curtail flooding. However, after two separate incidents in 1854 – the losses of the *Arctic* and *City of Glasgow*, between which claimed 830 lives – safety became the prevailing motive for their presence in passenger liners henceforth. A resulting new law was introduced to oblige all British vessels exceeding 100 tons to be internally subdivided with watertight compartments. They soon proved their worth.

When on 26 January 1856 Cunard's first iron ship, *Persia*, began her maiden voyage, at 398ft in length and housing seven transverse and two longitudinal bulkheads the 3,300-ton liner was the largest of her day. During this voyage while steaming at 11 knots she collided headlong into an iceberg, decimating 16ft of starboard hull. Sustaining damage that would have sunk any lesser vessel, her forward bulkhead not only confined the ensuing flood to the damaged compartment but she was able to continue to New York under her own steam. *Persia* was repaired and eight months later even managed to set a new Atlantic speed record. Two years afterwards Brunel launched his masterpiece – SS *Great Eastern*.

Containing ten transverse bulkheads spaced 60ft apart and towering 30ft clear of her waterline, the compartments on *Great Eastern* were bisected by two longitudinal walls. Spaced 36ft apart, the walls ran parallel for 360ft to form an inner layer of iron encircling her engine and boiler rooms. *Great Eastern* was also the first craft to incorporate a new safety feature: a watertight double keel that was 2ft 10in deep. They made her remarkably resilient. Her bulkheads held after striking a rock off Montauk Point, Long Island, on 27 August 1863, inflicting a lesion 83ft long and 9ft wide to her port bow. Of the 820 people aboard just twenty died, all of whom from the initial impact. The bulkheads held and allowed *Great Eastern* to reach New York under her own steam. She was repaired and remained in service for a further twenty-two years.

The two incidents showcased the value of bulkheads and their application was adopted worldwide. The Steam Navigation Act of 1846 had set the first legal requirement for the installation of compartmenting walls, demanding that all British steamships carry two – one fore and one aft – to encase the engine room. The regulation was further updated as part of the Merchant Shipping Act of 1854, which called for all vessels over 100 tons to fit a minimum of four bulkheads: one fore and one aft the engine room plus two others protecting each of the peak tanks at the bow and stern. Unfortunately in practice the directive proved indicatively vague. Only intended to shield the engine room and the hull's extremities, the lack of clarity created a fog of confusion. Maritime architects interpreted the edict to require ships over 100 tons to carry 'only' four bulkheads. The decree was consequently withdrawn in 1862 leaving no legal requirement in its stead to govern the quantity and quality of internal subdivision. Alarmed by this new dearth of regulatory stewardship, in 1867 the Institution of Naval Architects called for all ships to be fitted with watertight bulkheads and for them to be able to keep the vessel afloat should any two adjoining compartments become breached. As so few craft met this benchmark, as since 1862 it was not compulsory to do so, the Board of Trade made it a legal stipulation, albeit eventually in 1890. During this period however, an unregulated shipping industry began voluntarily increasing the quantity of bulkheads within their vessels – albeit only to placate their insurers. Lloyd's demanded a minimum of five be installed in the larger steamers of the day. Not wanting to buck this improving trend the Board concluded against legislating for an increased minimum in bulkhead supply.

With standards improving so wilfully, by the time *Olympic* and *Titanic* appeared on the drawing boards in 1907 the installation of bulkheads had evolved tremendously. Bearing fifteen apiece, the architects of White Star's new 'Olympics' based the heights of their bulkheads on a concept that would not allow water to rise above the ship's natural waterline should the undamaged compartments adjoining them counterbalance the weight by dispersing the inflow. Transverse divisions were believed to be better suited for this. *Titanic* contained fifteen. Each was stiffened and sealed by a vast network of supporting beams, yet midway through her first voyage they famously succumbed to her glancing blow with an iceberg.

It is universally known *Titanic* perished as the result of overconfidence in her design, but how safe was she really, and had Harland & Wolff's draughtsmen failed her? To better assess the effectiveness of her compartmentalisation it is vital to compare the structural integrities of other notable liners of the period. The findings draw insightful parallels with *Titanic*, and of the selection explored here are comparable in both scale and notoriety as each were equally revered in their heyday as being among the 'safest afloat'. No matter how improved upon they were, not only did their subdivision fail to save them but it compounded their demise. Despite the ensuing connotations proclaiming *Titanic* as unsafe, in the light of the evidence reviewed here her compartmentalising may in the end prove to have been among the soundest of all.

Republic, 1909

Originally built by Harland & Wolff for IMM's Dominion Line, hull 345 was launched on 26 February 1903 as *Columbus*. Embarked upon her maiden voyage on 1 October that year – Liverpool to Boston – by 17 December she, along with three others, was transferred to the White Star fleet to allow the line to expand their routes to the Mediterranean. Renaming her *Republic*, White Star would leave her on the Liverpool to Boston run for the summer, then in winter flit her between New York and the Mediterranean.

The richly furnished *Republic* proved herself extremely worthy of White Star's unremitting standards of design. Her yawning classically inspired Saloon Deck dining room formed the centrepiece of the ship, sporting a tall ornate stained-glass domed ceiling. This, and her generously spacious staterooms and lounges proved *Columbus* highly popular and, with little need of conversion, as *Republic* she became her new owner's standard-bearer on these routes. Her twin quadruple-expansion engines and their 16-knot output found her over several years routinely completing the fastest crossings between Queenstown and Boston. The 570ft long and 67ft wide 15,378-ton liner was able to accommodate 280 passengers in first class, 250 in second, 2,300 in steerage and a crew of 300. Encasing five decks and subdivided with twelve transverse watertight bulkheads capped by an advanced cellular keel, her hull was intended to meet existing regulations by remaining afloat should any two compartments become flooded. Indeed in her prime it was acknowledged that she was even able to remain afloat with as many as five or six compartments breached. As a result, *Republic* was widely reported to be 'practically unsinkable by collision'.

With her irrepressible captain, William Inman Sealby, she was considered to be in safe hands. Born in 1862 he had served with White Star Line since beginning his apprenticeship in 1877. Climbing swiftly through the ranks, his doughty aptitude saw him rewarded with his first command – *Coptic* – in 1896, and by 1908 his seventh, *Republic*.

Departing New York at 3p.m. on 22 January 1909, *Republic* was bound for Gibraltar – thence onwards ultimately to Genoa – with 525 passengers and a crew of 297. Later that evening however, sailing conditions manifested to a thickening fog. With visibility deteriorating, the following morning Sealby's lookouts detected the blasts of a nearby whistle; the source was Lloyd Italiano line's 5,118-ton *Florida* heading to New York from Naples with 824 emigrants. At midnight, Sealby, out of precaution, ordered the bulkhead doors closed, also sounding her whistle in two-minute intervals to announce their presence. Meanwhile, seeking the Nantucket Lightship, Captain Angelo Ruspini aboard *Florida* – unequipped with wireless – strayed her into the eastbound lane in which *Republic* was travelling. At 5.47a.m. Sealby's lookouts sighted through the mire the bow of the 381ft *Florida* bearing upon them. Both craft took evasive action simultaneously. It was too late. Minutes later *Florida* rammed headfirst into the port hull of *Republic* and into the compartment housing her engines and electric dynamos. Three of her passengers were killed instantly, another succumbing to injuries later in hospital. Despite a resulting power failure, the wireless operator of *Republic* managed to keep his set working and dispatch a historic plea for help: it had become the first transmission of CQD mid-ocean.

Undamaged, save for 30ft of her bow, at 7a.m. *Florida* began receiving the transference of passengers and crew from the mortally stricken *Republic*, Sealby and forty-six crewmembers remaining behind in an attempt to keep their charge afloat. In answer to the CQD White Star's *Baltic*, the first of three ships to arrive at the scene, from 7.30p.m. facilitated a second transfer of passengers, this time from the now dangerously overcrowded and crippled *Florida*.

Florida gingerly continued to New York. But despite attempts to tow *Republic* to the island of Martha's Vineyard where Sealby intended to beach her, the following day floodwater within her stern gradually overwhelmed their compartment walls and *Republic* was cut loose from the assisting tugboat. She sank at 8.30p.m. that evening – thirty-six hours post collision. Sinking to a depth of 270ft, 50 miles from the Nantucket shoreline, *Republic* had become the largest and most structurally advanced vessel to sink by collision to that date. Never before had a vessel so coherently subdivided been lost, albeit until dubiously bettered by *Titanic* three years later. Yet most likely due to the success and unprecedented scale of the rescue no official inquest would be held to assess this incident, and regulations on bulkhead integrity remained fatefully unaltered.

Empress of Ireland, 1914

Construction on hull 433 began at Fairfields shipyards in Govan, Glasgow, on 10 April 1905. The £375,000 project, *Empress of Ireland*, was launched on 27 January the following year. Measuring 569ft long by 65ft wide the eight-deck *Empress* grossed 14,191 tons and was operated by the Canadian Pacific Line to service their routes between Liverpool and Quebec. Designed to accommodate

1,536 passengers comprising 310 in first, 468 in second, 488 in third and an additional contingent of 270 in steerage, she also boasted a crew numbering 420. For
safety she was fitted with ten transverse bulkheads sealed by twenty-two lateral-
sliding doors, plus two others that closed vertically. Unlike on *Titanic*, these doors
relied on manual operation, each requiring one minute for its specially designated
steward to crank the door fully closed with a large key. Adhering to the Board of
Trade's criteria, she was designed to remain afloat in the event that any two of her
eleven compartments became flooded. Also, like *Titanic*, she too featured a double
hull. Containing 1,500 tons of water ballast, the double bottom was 5ft deep at
its centre, tapering to 3½ft either side; the entire hull was held together with 1.1
million hydraulically driven rivets.

Originally equipped with sixteen 2.5-ton steel lifeboats and four Berthon collapsibles affording aggregate seating capacity for just 940 of her potential 1,956
passengers, the redress in requirements resulting from the *Titanic* disaster saw capacity increased by twenty collapsible boats to provision 1,860 ancillary seats. As a
further precaution in light of the disaster, crew would muster at 10a.m. each day of
the voyage to conduct a lifeboat drill as well as test her watertight doors. By 1914
she was thereby deemed to be a safe and consequently highly popular vessel.

Under the command of Captain Henry George Kendall – her regular master
since 1908 and whose experience of the sea spanned twenty-five years – *Empress
of Ireland* slipped out of Quebec 4.27p.m. on 28 May 1914 to begin what was
her ninety-sixth voyage. Bound for Liverpool on this particular crossing were
1,057 passengers and a crew of 420. Continuing down the Saint Lawrence
River at 15 knots the following day, shrouded in fog, a collier vessel 8 miles
ahead was travelling towards them from the opposing direction. This other craft
steaming at 10 knots was the 6,028-ton, 440ft-long Norwegian *Storstad*, laden
with cargo comprising 10,400 tons of coal. Commanded by Captain Thomas
Andersen, being a Scandinavian vessel *Storstad* sported the region's customary
necessity: a strengthened ice-breaking bow.

Upon learning of the collier's presence Kendall began evasive action. Not
seeing them, however, Andersen maintained course. Soon crew on the *Empress*
too lost visibility of *Storstad* in the fog. In precaution the engines of the *Empress*
were slammed into reverse, but *Storstad* continued unabated. Two minutes later,
now at a standstill, Kendall's crew discovered the lights of *Storstad*, whose crew
by which time had likewise spotted the *Empress*. Reversing his own engines
Andersen pivoted *Storstad* to avoid the liner, which was now barely a few feet
away. Minutes later the reinforced bow of *Storstad* careered into the starboard
side of the *Empress*, impaling itself 25ft into her hull. The collision punched an
opening 350sq.ft directly amidships of the *Empress*, right upon the area braced
by her fifth bulkhead – the wall separating her two boiler room compartments
– opening 175ft of floor space to the sea. The watertight doors were ordered
closed – the captain defying company regulations to keep the doors permanently

manned during fog while travelling the Saint Lawrence – although because of their manual operation two on the starboard side were forgotten and remained open. Designed to remain afloat with exactly these compartments (her two largest) breached, the demise of the *Empress* was instead owed to a sudden and irreversible list created by her longitudinally arranged coalbunkers.

Along her hull's centreline, three compartments forming the two boiler rooms and engine room were separated port and starboard by a protective, but non-watertight, 246ft longitudinal wall. Upon the bunkers on its starboard flank becoming awash with seawater this longitudinal division confined the flood to the damaged side of the *Empress*. The weight of the sodden fuel in her affected bunkers overbalanced the *Empress* into an immediate 18-degree lunge to starboard, pulling her Main Deck under and allowing yet more water over the tops of the remaining compartments as well as through any of her 12in portholes left open. With water cascading aboard at a rate of 1,000 gallons per second, she was unable to counterbalance the ensuing influx. Remaining afloat for just fourteen minutes, she succumbed so suddenly that crew could launch only five of her hoard of forty lifeboats. Of the 1,477 people aboard only 465 survived; 840 passengers and 172 crewmembers were lost – it was a disaster second only in scale to *Titanic*.

The resulting investigation was conducted in Quebec at the King's Bench Courthouse on 16 and 17 June, headed by *Titanic* inquiry stalwart, Lord Mersey. Declaring his findings on 11 July Mersey cited the high death toll to the sudden and severe starboard list the *Empress* had developed. Undone by her longitudinally bunkered coal this arrangement very soon became a contributory factor to the loss of the most revered liner of the day – Cunard's stately innovator: RMS *Lusitania*.

Lusitania, 1915

Lusitania, the very ship that prompted the creation of White Star's 'Olympic' trio, was the product of Cunard's naval architects Leonard Peskett and William Luke. Launched upon the smashing of a champagne bottle at 12.30p.m. on 7 June 1906, job 367 – *Lusitania* – was waterborne at the Clydebank yard of John Brown & Co. eighty-six seconds later as the world's newest largest liner. Intensive preliminary testing with a substantial 47ft scale prototype, allowed Cunard to hone her impressive dimensions. Her 787ft-long, 88ft-wide hull housing its nine decks was by some clear margin the largest of the day and her completed 31,550-ton bulk required a draught of almost 32ft. Yet she was certainly no turtle. Installed within were four powerful turbine engines, their combined output of 68,000hp among four propellers gave a cruising speed of 25.5 knots. *Lusitania* was the innovation of her day.

During her maiden voyage, Liverpool to New York, which began on 7 September 1907, her quadruple turbines attained Cunard the coveted Blue Riband. Although unlike other racers of the era attention to her lavish interiors was afforded equal measure to her record-breaking enginery. Her perfect fusion of style and speed heralded a new epoch in travel and directly spurred White Star's famous retaliation, *Olympic* and *Titanic*.

The British government had funded her construction on the proviso that she could be requisitioned as a supply vessel in times of war: Admiralty officials monitored every stage of her development with interest. Within weeks of Britain declaring war on Germany, Cunard on 17 September 1914 cordially delivered *Lusitania* to the Admiralty to serve as an auxiliary cruiser. As agreed in the terms of their loan granted in 1902 the British Admiralty also conscripted her younger sister, *Mauretania*, reimbursing Cunard £1,300 a day for her services as a troopship. *Lusitania* would remain in commercial servitude as an auxiliary transport.

On 1 May 1915, laden with 1,265 passengers and a crew of 694, she departed Cunard's pier 54 at New York to begin her 202nd Atlantic crossing. In command was fifty-eight-year-old Captain William Thomas Turner, widely respected and serving with the line since 1883.

With Britain and Germany embroiled in conflict the Imperial Navy considered the prospect of maiming such a high-profile liner to be an immense prize. All identifying markings were thus removed. *Lusitania* flew no national flag. Her name lettering and funnel livery were blackened out. She was, however, demonstrably easy to identify as only four other British liners bore four funnels: *Aquitania*, *Britannic*, *Mauretania* and *Olympic* – all as equally revered by German U-boats.

Heading east on this voyage to Liverpool, *Lusitania* was bearing a cargo that the Admiralty had requisitioned her third-class passenger areas to stow: war provisions. This type of cargo – typically comprising of food – had on this occasion been stowed poorly by a crew bereft of experienced trimmers. Its uneven distribution would impede her handling, but controversially *Lusitania* was also carrying munitions, albeit in quantities sufficiently low to pass the restrictions imposed by America, a neutral government. *Lusitania* also happened to be returning paperwork relating to the *Titanic* disaster following lengthy hearings for compensation still wending their way through British and American courts.

While nearing the end of the voyage, at 7.52p.m. on the 6th, her wireless operators received a message from Queenstown. The sender, the vice-admiral in charge of the Irish coastal shipping region, warned of U-boat activity in the area, for patrolling the Irish Sea and the bay of Liverpool in his submarine, U-20, thirty-year-old Kapitanleutnant Walther Schwieger had on that very day sunk two British-owned cargo haulers in the St George Channel: *Candidate* and *Centurion*. Upon receipt of this message, Captain Turner ordered the bulkhead doors closed, the lookouts doubled and all lifeboats swung overboard in readiness for hasty deployment.

Heavy fog early the following morning forced Turner to slow *Lusitania's* engines from 21 knots to 15. Lifting by 11a.m., improving visibility allowed them to wind up to 18 knots in a bid to catch the high water at Liverpool for 7a.m. on the 8th. But by 1.40p.m., now within eyesight of the Irish coastline, Schwieger had *Lusitania* sighted though the rangefinder of U-20. Identifying a liner with four blackened funnels, the U-boat converged upon its target until just 550m of sea lay between them.

Unsure exactly which of the four-funnelled bounties his target was, at 12.15p.m. Schwieger loosed a single torpedo. Packed with 300lb of explosives it streaked towards *Lusitania* at 22 knots, striking her starboard bow. The explosion imparted a 200sq.ft opening directly upon the bulkhead wall, separating her forward stokehold cross-bunker with boiler room 1, the two compartments taking in water at 100 tons a second. *Lusitania* lurched immediately into a 15-degree roll to starboard. Her angle, rapidly developing to 22 degrees, rendered all portside boats beyond use. Critically, the damage had also lacerated the pipes supplying the hydraulics for her watertight doors. With the electricity also failed, crew were unable to seal her compartments.

The force from the torpedo triggered a sudden secondary explosion, which, it was later argued, was the detonating consignment of munitions and aluminium powder carried within her disputed cargo. However, the more likely cause of this second explosion is something far less dramatic, though equally devastating. A boiler in room 1 whose damaged cooling system let its temperature soar unregulated until it ruptured, caused an explosion so devastating that it hastened the ship's demise. *Lusitania* lasted just eighteen minutes. She sank to a depth of 295ft, 8 miles off Ireland's Old Head of Kinsale. Just 764 people survived: 1,198 died.

Following the loss of *Titanic* the original lifeboat capacity for *Lusitania* had been increased from sixteen wooden boats to twenty-two and by a further twenty-four collapsibles, ample room for her licensed occupancy: 563 in first class, 464 in second, 1,138 in third and a crew of 827. Yet in echo of the evacuation of *Titanic*, no boat assignments had been circulated. The ensuing confusion piqued desperation, squandering precious minutes before *Lusitania* could remain afloat no more. But why had she heeled so violently, so suddenly?

Segmented by thirteen transverse and two longitudinal bulkheads, *Lusitania* housed 175 watertight compartments sealed by sixty-one electrically operated doors, which required thirty seconds to close. On paper she was comprehensively subdivided: 'with the most stringent regard to making the vessel unsinkable' exalted *The Shipbuilder* magazine in 1906. Yet, lasting a mere eighteen minutes it was a fraction of the almost three hours that *Titanic*, sporting just sixty-two compartments, remained afloat and upright for after striking the iceberg.

Adapting the trail blazed by *Great Eastern*, many designers incorporated bulkheads to encase the coalbunkers arranged longitudinally along their outboard walls in order to afford them greater shielding against fire. By 1907 such configurations were commonplace in the Royal Navy's Dreadnoughts since it also provided an additional layer of armament to the hull and magazine, as well as encasing any side-on impact to a transverse dividing wall. The system was based on the premise that, should the hull sustain damage along its side, the inboard bulkhead would curtail the free-flow across the expanse of the largest compartments and avoid water overwhelming the opposite side of the hull: this was the theory.

Unlike their German and Cunard counterparts, White Star in 1889 began to disfavour incorporating longitudinal formations within their vessels; *Teutonic* and *Majestic*, their last to feature longitudinal bulkheads, very soon had them removed. Their motive for doing so was guided by practice, for when longitudinal compartments flooded they confined the inflow to the damaged side of the hull. Although honeycombing the side of the ship to meticulous extent offered clear benefit to battleships, doing so was not considered abundantly necessary for passenger vessels. When designing the Olympic Class Harland & Wolff understood that confining the settlement of water to one side of the hull drastically increased the burden on that side. As was proven later with notable causalities of Dreadnoughts during battle, longitudinally divided vessels were more susceptible to capsizing than others exclusively compartmented transversely. Furthermore, as with any steamship, for the benefit of stokehold crew the coalbunkers on *Lusitania* were located as close as was feasible to the boilers. With her furnaces consuming 1,000 tons of coal daily, any bulkhead door adjoining a bunker and boiler room had to remain open to allow this constant access for crew – thwarting the effectiveness of the compartments since because of the explosion the doors were jammed open due to the malfunction of their closing mechanisms and the lodged remnants of strewn coal.

Absorbency too was a key danger for storing coal, which becomes heavier once in contact with water. Saturated coal thus augmented the weight in an already waterlogged hull, which could be fatal if the ship suffered a severe breach. In the case of *Lusitania* the torpedo's breach of the cross-bunker granted water access to her starboard flank bunkers. The contents housed within her 16ft bunkers sandwiched between the inner hull and longitudinal bulkhead catastrophically undermined her stability.

When commenting on the loss of the *Titanic*, *The Shipbuilder* magazine would report in 1912 that the longitudinal configuration inside *Lusitania* was a more effective solution to the transverse arrangement aboard *Titanic*. The magazine also proposed enhancements to the longitudinal system to arrest the signature list that eventually led to the demise of their example in 1915. To curb the list the journal proposed linking the compartments to their opposite twin through a series of trimming valves to transfer water from the distressed side to the undamaged compartments opposite to counterbalance this weight: improving the builders' own remedy, which advised crew to intentionally flood the adjacent larger compartment.

As a safeguard, all bunkers on *Lusitania* were encased by a protective skin, so to in theory retard the likelihood, should one become flooded, of the coal housed in the adjacent bunkers becoming immersed by water. These inboard longitudinal bulkheads extended to the floor of her Lower Deck, G; this was not the case for *Titanic*.

Only *Titanic*'s double bottom was longitudinally subdivided, leaving the transverse walls above permitting water to foul all coal bunkered in each affected boiler room, introducing with it a far greater hull space into direct contact with water at the same time. The damage sustained from the iceberg immediately swamped all coal stored within her forward boiler room (number 6), quickly soaking all the supply in room 5, adding to an already overbearing weight inside her bow. Filling symmetrically, however, the transverse system held *Titanic* upright and afloat two hours and twenty-two minutes longer than the less amenable longitudinal configuration was able to provide *Lusitania* – indeed, it would have held almost indefinitely on *Republic* had her compartment walls been stronger. By permitting water to flow the full breadth of the deck *Titanic* kept evenly balanced, filling steadily and providing adequate time for crew to launch every regular lifeboat successfully. In the aftermath of the loss of the *Lusitania* a rethink was instigated to the application of longitudinal configurations, acknowledging their shortcomings to the transverse alternative.

Britannic, 1916

Owing to the loss of *Titanic*, extensive safety modifications were applied to her belated sister, *Britannic*, not only to improve her safety but to restore public confidence in both White Star and their fleet. To forestall a carbon copy of her sister's fate, Harland & Wolff extended five of her sixteen bulkhead walls to reach the base of B Deck rising generously clear of her deepest load-line by 40ft. Fitted with an additional bulkhead in her stern, this configuration of sixteen newly strengthened walls, all protruding a minimum of 21ft above her waterline, intended to keep *Britannic* afloat should any six become compromised; as opposed to the limit of four on *Titanic*. Giving access between compartments were sixty-three vertically closing watertight doors of the same type featured on *Titanic*.

A further upgrade incorporated into *Britannic* involved raising the extent of her double hull sidewalls to clear the load-line by 6½ft – being just 2½ft on *Titanic* and the subsequently modified *Olympic*. Consequently, additional plating was installed to line this now taller inner skin of *Britannic*. To bear this extra weight her designers widened her hull to maintain the overall buoyancy of the superstructure above the waterline.

The heavier parts of the ship, such as the boilers, engines and ballast tanks, necessitated a position as low as was feasible in the hull to frustrate capsizing. However, with all these structural alterations applied, as well as her eight vast and newly added lifeboat gantries, *Britannic* had become far heavier above the waterline than originally envisioned. To correct this undermining of stability, Harland & Wolff widened her beam by 18in to push the axis of buoyancy within her hull as low as was viable.

The purpose of double walls was to afford additional protection to the side of the hull along its most vulnerable areas: the two engine and six boiler compartments. At

31in deep (1in more than her sisters) the double walls on *Britannic* spanned 447ft along each flank of hull providing it with a dual protective layer encasing 52 per cent of surface area beneath the load-line. In addition, the freshwater tanks along the outboard sides of the newly segregated compartments housing the electricity generators also served as a continuation of double hull in this section of the ship, thereby increasing the overall below-surface area of encasement by inner layer to 62 per cent.

Beneath this sat a further encasement, the double keel. That on *Britannic* contained six longitudinal bulkheads – as opposed to three on her sisters – dividing the bilges beneath her Tank Top into twice as many compartments. The combined safety upgrades on *Britannic* were explicitly intended to withstand the exact damage which had claimed *Titanic*, but for *Britannic* her double keel and sidewalls were complicit to her own downfall.

On 21 November 1916 while traversing waters patrolled by German U-boats *Britannic* struck a mine on her starboard bow, blasting a hole just feet forward of the area unprotected by the most expansive double-lined hull afloat. The mine, packed with 150kg of explosives, ruptured her first and second bulkhead walls, also filling the fireman's tunnel, channelling it – as happened with *Titanic* – through the wall separating the fourth compartment. To make matters worse, at 8a.m. her watertight doors had been left open to allow stokers to change shift. The explosion, rupturing the closing mechanisms of the door connecting the fireman's tunnel with boiler room 6 gave water unrestricted access to a fifth consecutive compartment. The explosion had also jammed open the bulkhead door separating boiler rooms 5 and 6. Within just two minutes all six forward compartments were compromised, the maximum her designers catered to keep *Britannic* afloat.

In a desperate attempt to beach her upon the nearby island of Kea, Captain Bartlett ordered the engines 'full speed ahead'. This accelerated motion inadvertently drove yet more water into the rent portion of hull, and consequently forced *Britannic* to an irreversible list starboard – spilling yet more seawater through the portholes left open along her lower decks. Although opened for airing the wards in preparation to receive patients, warzone dictums required all portholes to remain closed. As the list progressed, water began encroaching the starboard cavity of her double-hull walls, affording it unhindered access along two thirds of the ship's length.

Concern about this arrangement of sidewalls had earlier featured in the American Senate's report of the *Titanic* disaster, calling for future transverse systems to both reach and attach the outer plating to curtail the channelling of water between the inner and outer layers. As a further complication for *Britannic* the extra longitudinal divisions within her double keel also confined the weight of water inside her double wall open to the sea. Nullifying the effectiveness of her transverse compartments, these compounded a list from which *Britannic* could not recover. She rolled to her side and sank fifty-five minutes after striking the mine, afloat barely long enough to evacuate all but thirty of the 1,065 occupants she carried.

The parallels with *Titanic* explored here corroborate that no matter how sophisticated or 'stringent' their designs appeared on paper, the effectiveness of bulkheads proved highly erratic when maintaining buoyancy. The transverse systems within *Titanic* and *Republic* saw measured, deliberate, intakes of water. Unconfined to the damaged side of the hull, floodwater within transverse configurations maintained an even keel, taking, in consequence, longer to fill. Confined within the afflicted area, the accumulated water proved insurmountable for the hull to counterbalance, a feat fiendishly elusive for the naval architect to neutralise within a longitudinally subdivided hull.

The effectiveness of bulkheads of the last century erred more on the side of hope than exacting science. With no two incidents ever truly identical, the naval architect was faced with a daunting array of eventualities to consider. He would space compartments to ensure that those breached would distribute the inflow in a manner that allowed water to settle and maintain the ship's stability and through longitudinal division he hoped to frustrate the water's ability to flood. His intransigence from the longitudinal method, primarily the consequence of navy sponsorship, was revived by shipping's next antagonists, *Imperator* and *Aquitania*. But along with his inquisitive delight to eradicate the unpredictability of error by employing the most trusted means available, was to give his creations the greatest durability – the means by which White Star's first *Britannic* owed its survival. When completed on 6 June 1874 as Harland & Wolff's 83rd hull, the £200,000 *Britannic (I)* housed eight transverse bulkheads. On 19 May 1887 she collided with her running mate, *Celtic*, in fog at their midway points between Liverpool and New York. The bow of *Celtic* ploughed hard into the port hull of *Britannic*, punching a 4ft vertical opening below her waterline and filling the compartment aft of the engine room. *Britannic* developed a worrying list to starboard and, amid considerable concern that she was going to sink, her 470 passengers were transferred to *Celtic*. Her carpenters, however, stemmed the flood and *Britannic* returned to New York under her own steam. She was back in service three weeks later.

Coupled with its fair share of luck, pre-emption remains the true friend of the shipbuilder and his fraught bond with the sea. Though by the hand of Harland & Wolff, the industry's incessant pursuit of invincibility had, just maybe, come closer to achieving this than hindsight suggests we believe.

CHAPTER 17

FOREVER YOUNG

'*Titanic*, name and thing, will stand as a monument and warning to human presumption.'

The Bishop of Winchester, 21 April 1912

Ask anyone what they know of *Titanic* and their response will be unsurprisingly detailed: that she sank 100 years ago on her maiden voyage after striking an iceberg and carried too few lifeboats to save everybody aboard. Awareness of these facts is almost pre-programmed into us at birth. Everyone knows the existence of *Titanic* and her iconic demise. Such is the intrigue of tragedy.

The stately ship, its dinner-jacketed millionaires and flat-capped stokers together sliding unruffled into a serenely calm Atlantic emblazoned *Titanic* across headlines around the world at such unprecedented velocity that the magnitude of the event became arguably history's first truly global media sensation and particularly its first 'modern' disaster. Marconi's wireless had news of the sinking resonating across both sides of the Atlantic almost simultaneously, concurrently striking the desks of news editors in London and New York with previously unimaginable speed. Never before were the media able to report the drama of a sea tragedy as its events were still unfolding. Yet due to this speed, the story's circulation cultivated an abundance of inaccuracies surrounding the disaster, some eventually becoming willingly accepted as fact in the succeeding years.

Every regional and national newspaper clamoured for a scoop on the sinking, halting print runs to become the first to engorge their readership with every horrifying detail. Any account relating to *Titanic* printed, be it version, hearsay or opinion, was glorified and distributed as fact by editors too time-pressured to verify authenticity. Fact became romanticised and over the ensuing decades much of the actual events on the night of the disaster were disseminated amid a haze of nostalgia. Numerous eyewitness accounts of *Titanic* and her final hours formed a legacy to the somewhat discombobulated view of the disaster we know today. Witnesses keen to recite opinion or sightings of events they had merely heard, or they believed they heard, than had actually seen for themselves. Survivors too young to recall its detail would in later years regale to ever-growing audiences the intricacies of mere proximity to disaster – their embellishment indulged by dwelling more on the serenity of an event than of the terror of disaster. There are many traces of their disparity of fact.

According to eyewitnesses the accounts of the final sighting of Captain Smith extend from him shooting himself, swimming to a lifeboat to lift a baby to its occupants, belligerently jumping into the frigid ocean vowing to follow his ship to the seabed, and exalting 'don't mind me, men', to standing temperately on the bridge refusing to leave his post. Some accounts were to canonise Smith as a hero, whereas others consigned to history a withdrawn sullen captain racked with guilt for imprudence and inexcusable pomposity to duty of care.

Disputes over the how and why of disaster stir equally impassioned views over the most trivial of aspects, most notably the final tune performed by the eight-member ensemble serenading passengers while *Titanic* slid slowly to the icy deep. The five-verse hymn 'Nearer My God to Thee' is the most touted candidate, but even were this not the final tune that evening it was immortalised in ensuing memorial services around the world. Yet a point would be proven: anything associated with *Titanic* is hotly contestable. One theory in circulation even expounds the notion that the iceberg may not have struck *Titanic* at all, and that her wreck is instead *Olympic*, duplicitously swapped to masquerade as her famous twin. Questions over these simplest of details highlight the inconsistency and contradiction of survivor contribution and the motivation for allowing their evidence to be widely overlooked at the original inquiries. Beguiled by their plight, reporters far and wide were only too keen to proffer even the poorest survivors handsome sums for their version of disaster; embellishment induced, engineered to transcend the sinking into an event far greater than a mere misfortune of navigation.

Seven hundred people survived the disaster, arriving in New York shocked, disorientated, and physically and emotionally fatigued. Formal interviewing did not occur until four days post rescue, affording survivors the opportunity to dwell, deliberate and distil events and rumours with fellow survivors and passengers aboard *Carpathia*. By their arrival in New York, observations were tainted. The building of a more tenacious legacy was already begun.

The sinking inspired a slew of celebratory culture. Poetry, ephemera, triumphant songs, all reprised a glorious disaster; this would be unthinkable to imagine in the wake of disasters today, but in 1912, although grieving, the Edwardians were supremely proud that a grand British ship had met a very Britannic end. Valour and convention in the face of abject adversity had shined righteously through.

The legend of *Titanic* had of course benefited immensely from her goading and temptation of fate: her woefully brief sea trials; overconfidence in durability; the ignored ice warnings; meagre ration of lifeboats; overzealous ambitions; public sector dithering; and of course, that ignominious affiliation with the word 'unsinkable'. Even her registration number, 390904, which, with a modicum of imagination, when transposed was interpreted to read the hex NOPOPE, dissuaded many of Harland & Wolff's Catholic employees from wanting to work on the project (although the majority of the yard's workers were Protestant). Yet it is crucial not to understate the loss of *Titanic* as history's most noteworthy tragedy at sea; its outcome was absorbed into the lives not only of those affected, but wider society also. The glorification of her life and death was to engrain *Titanic* deep into world culture. This now leads to the most vital question — that of her future, the physical remnants of this great all-prevailing cautionary tale.

The salvage of the wreck and its artefacts stirs much passion. Ingrained to unparalleled depth within our psyche, opinion on the motives of visiting it and salvaging artefacts are staunchly entrenched, be it for the public interest, monetary gain or indeed both. Some view *Titanic* as a grave, not to be flaunted but sanctified and observed with reverence for perpetuity. Others embrace her as celebrity, desiring that her artefacts are saved for curation because their intrinsic symbolism to global heritage demands it. Both camps raise valid arguments, yet ultimately only time will decide the outcome of this quarrel. Indeed, *Titanic* may wilt to nothingness within our lifetime, but the fortitude of her legend will prevail without need for relics; surely this is the greatest gift of preservation. *Titanic* will endure in culture, gathering with it curious momentum long after the tides of sea and time have withered her physical presence from existence.

Consensus supports that items within her hull be left and observed as a maritime tomb — and so far this has been respected — but if her structure was sounder and more able to withstand manned submersibles, or if she lay in shallower waters, one can only wonder if such principle of morality would be honoured then. We remember *Andrea Doria*, resting within reach of hobby divers who hoist souvenirs from her hull each year despite the entombment of the forty-six souls claimed in her sinking. The loss of *Titanic* is unquestionably the most significant and infamous transportation disaster of modern history, with a death toll surpassed only as recently as 20 December 1987 with the collision of the Philippine passenger ferry *Dona Paz* with the oil tanker *Vector*. The overcrowded ferry took with it 4,749 lives, yet few of us recall this tragedy, let alone are compelled enough to delve into the stories of the lives lost there. How many people could name ships of the Edwardian period other than *Titanic* or *Lusitania*; they are infamous by tragedy. Even fewer are aware that *Titanic* had two sisters. But why has the story of maritime shipping become condensed to just one ship?

Much has been written and produced about *Titanic*, yet had she not been smote by an iceberg her name may be remembered for entirely less auspicious reasons than is known for today — albeit considerably less documented. Had the iceberg passed her by, *Titanic* would no doubt have entered service as a hospital or auxiliary transport in the First World War. Should she have survived the war she may have continued a lengthy but otherwise uneventful career in forgotten normality. Proving vastly economical for White Star, *Titanic* would eventually have become obsolete, politely retired, before unceremoniously being scrapped, playing out a parallel existence alongside twins *Olympic* and *Britannic*. Her name would not even venture into conversation or fill yards of bookshelves. But if it was not *Titanic* that caused the regulations on lifeboats and radio use to be modified and tightened, ending the systemic complacency with safety, it would have been a different liner. Had it not been for the disaster however, *Titanic* could have synonymised achievement instead of being a metaphor for calamity. Would Marconi have gained the universal recognition of his invention so soon after the birth of wireless telegraphy had *Titanic* not struck that iceberg? Would *Queen Mary 2* be carrying enough lifeboats today? There will be disasters as long as there is development, for without failure there can be no learning. Without learning, there is no progression. The cycle of trial and error is ordained, and the justly superstitious maritime world will forevermore evade use of 'Titan' even as part of a craft's name; a moniker that now shall always synonymise catastrophe. Who today would sail on a ship named *Titanic* other than in morbid curiosity to tempt fate?

For over thirty-six months *Titanic* rose skyward aloft Belfast's Queen's Island. Proudly delivered to White Star Line in April 1912, her arrival was universally trumpeted as the greatest marvel of maritime engineering. In her first voyage, however, she would instead become the Atlantic's greatest casualty and an enduring moral to humankind's obsession with 'fortune favours the bold'. Ismay's resplendent poisoned chalice was stricken at its sparkling best. But unbeknownst then, another tragedy to British vivacity had just unfolded at the foot of the world.

When Captain Robert Falcon Scott famously raced to the South Pole he discovered that Norway's Roald Amundsen had arrived one month before him. Scott perished on 29 March 1912 while returning to base camp. Along with the sinking of *Titanic* the two events harbingered the end of Britain's envied hubris. To those who perished aboard *Titanic* Prime Minister Asquith extolled the 'willing sacrifices which were offered to give the first chance of safety to those least able to help themselves' – there was no shelter for cowards. Both Scott and Smith yielded great personal qualities as well as faults, despite their misjudgments that effectively perpetrated their own deaths and those of others. Their dutiful demises left them beyond criticism – and national heroes. To Edwardians it was un-British to censure the dead. Someone instead who survived was singled out for blame for *Titanic*, the man who abandoned her in one of the canvas boats installed in concession to placate concerns with his ship's safety: company chairman Bruce Ismay. The captain was solely responsible for the speed and navigation of *Titanic*, but he was not branded the 'Brute'.

Instead, in death Edward Smith found eternal honour. His £740 statue, carved by the hand of Scott's mourning widow, was unveiled near his village green, its inscription, memorialising his duty and heroism, makes no mention at all of *Titanic*. The public would instead point its rancour at Bruce Ismay, the man who had given creation to one of the greatest achievements of maritime architecture, consigning him to history as petulant and lily-livered.

The disaster heralded in its wake a new era of transformation. The loss of the *Titanic*, arguably a political event, foreshadowed an unimaginable downturn in prosperity and a watershed for social change: the First World War, the republican uprising in Ireland, revolution in Russia, and a deepening economic crisis that was soon to paralyse the civilised world. The scale and virtues that *Titanic* implanted upon society was unprecedented, even inspiring Nazi propaganda minister Josef Goebbels to have director Herbert Selpin, the finest director of his day, craft a film chronicling the sinking. Entitled *Titanic* it was completed in 1943, adopting a slightly amended plot that would be deployed as anti-British propaganda. A complete failure in its intention to denounce unscrupulous British capitalism, the film, however, is said to offer the greatest portrayal of the sinking. Its skilful depiction and tormented reality has it hailed as one of the greatest German films of the era.

The plight of *Titanic* and her occupants continues in a still-growing repertoire of poems, scores, websites, memorabilia, books and appreciation societies – fruits of the insatiable hunger for her story today.

Maintaining notes to document his voyage and anticipated trip of a lifetime, science teacher Lawrence Beesley, incumbent of second-class cabin D56, escaped *Titanic* in lifeboat 13. Beesley's account, which was subsequently regarded as the most accurate of the disaster from a passenger's perspective, was published just two months following the sinking, entitled *The Loss of the S.S. Titanic*. It became the first in a long line of tomes recounting the disaster – and remains in print to this day. But today we know *Titanic* the celluloid star. The first film retelling her story was as early as June 1912, Germany's *In Night and Ice*, which was hotly followed in 1913 by *Saved from the Titanic* and by *Atlantic* in 1929, and Goebbels' rendition in 1943 – perpetuating a rapidly inflating public fascination. White Star, who scornfully appealed to the Board of Trade to cease the marketing of the 'deplorable' *Atlantic* under the premise that it revived prejudicial and reputable damage to British shipping, was brushed aside by Hollywood's love affair with *Titanic*.

Her story's endurance truly took flight in 1953 with *Titanic*, followed in 1958 by *A Night to Remember* and 1979's *SOS Titanic*, and culminated with James Cameron's memorable *Titanic*, which premiered on 19 December 1997. Costing $200 million to produce, the epic remained until 2010 the most commercially successful film of all time. Although its characterisation was superficial, *Titanic* humanised the tragedy and caused the resurgence of a still-expanding interest in the ship; one minute's silence was observed at the request of its director during the 1998 Oscar ceremony, during which his opus won eleven categories. *Titanic* has since been the subject of three television mini-series, a successful Broadway musical and countless well-attended artefact tours. Even with a canon of films in tow recounting her loss, more shall undoubtedly follow regardless of audiences' familiarity with the outcome of her story. Her legacy and uniqueness as an historical event transcends modern folklore, a story shedding not one ounce of potency for a century. This folklore has even ascended spaceward: capsule Gemini 3 of 1965, *The Molly Brown*, was named in reference to the fortitude of an 'unsinkable' first-class passenger, Margaret Brown.

Titanic, name and soul, extends far beyond her mouldering metal hulk lying mangled on the ocean floor. Who on earth does not or will not know of *Titanic* within their lifetime? Which single event will in equal measure remain for a century analysed with such X-ray intensity? Humanity is now more likely to associate the word 'titanic' as the name of a ship that sank nearly 100 years ago than with the dictionary definition for large. Everyday objects that our great-grandparents would remember are today routinely auctioned for sums vastly beyond their material worth simply due to merest provenance with *Titanic*.

Captains Scott and Smith had not only sacrificed their own lives to duty but had done so with dignity intact. Alongside engine room stokers, passengers rich and poor, millionaires and migrants, all shoulder-to-shoulder faced death nobly. The gap separating the social classes had, and for the first time in camera, discovered a new plateau. The upper and lower classes of society learned that their kin had stoically accompanied each other in death regardless of position on the social spectrum. The fact that this honour in death went beyond material wealth caused a change in society's regard for those in other classes, and this now forms the foundation of *Titanic*'s enduring legacy.

The blasé Edwardians announced their 'unsinkable' ship to the world, yet it was unable to remain afloat for its inaugural voyage. Its famously inadequate supply of lifeboats were because it was genuinely believed that larger quantities would not be needed. Its captain steamed full-speed into an ice-infested area he knew existed because it was deemed acceptable to do so. Wireless operators discarded warnings of ice, and the band serenaded passengers through the night with no regard for their own wellbeing. Passengers were so reticent to escape that they had to be ordered into the lifeboats, many of which were lowered half empty while scores of people remained obediently behind. There were those who were prepared to die for the sake of saving a stranger – to be gentlemen, to be noble. Loved ones bade farewells, faithfully adhering to 'women and children first' to the bitter end. Dignity was upheld in the pall of doom. There was uncertainty about how and why the disaster occurred to *Titanic* – even of what occurred in her dying hours. This was a disaster that was as farcical as it is edifying: horrific, yet regal. The story of the hapless ship will forever remain firmly in our consciousness. We will forever rediscover *Titanic*.

When artefacts retrieved from *Titanic* were displayed at a temporary exhibition at London's Science Museum in 2003 it completed an extended and record-breaking run. Snaking though galleries of artefacts and generous reproductions of the ship's grandiose interiors, the exhibition focussed visitors to experience the personal effects and stories of those who had journeyed and died on the ill-fated voyage. Its centrepiece was a 2.5-ton section of hull and a touchable 'iceberg', the event was the biggest draw in town. Box office demand for a rerun of the exhibition in 2010/11 demonstrated that the lines of attendees had no intention of dwindling yet. Global fascination, however, is not proliferated through glass cases alone. Proposals to build a replica of *Titanic* followed during a recent renaissance in the popularity of cruising due to the ever-growing ranks of holidaymakers who prefer travel without flying; the romance of 1912 wins through even if it means booking a cabin on a ship named *Titanic*. Astounding are the outlets mankind contrives from tragedy. But *Titanic* was no ordinary tragedy. She is entwined within our psyche, for she enriches the greatness of humanity. *Titanic* is no inanimate name.

From time immemorial celebrity has mirrored society's innermost desires, be it fame, infamy or fortune, but what does our ongoing fascination with *Titanic* tell of the society in which we live today? Her sinking was the last great act of chivalry, the curtain-call to Old World pluck. She was never just another ship. In her one voyage she transgressed into culture through passengers rich and poor willing to forsake themselves for the survival of others, because doing so was simply the natural and correct thing to do. Such altruism is unthinkable in the world of survival of the fittest that embroils us today. *Titanic* underlines how removed we are from her bygone age of graciousness.

So now we reach the end of our exploration of a ship whose physical loss has become the eternal emblem of both the power and fallibility of mankind's attempts to achieve technical perfection, yet proving to be of no avail against the power of nature. Her legend is unfettered. Her grace and beauty, terror and catastrophe, her name is the very paradigm of success and disaster and its profound presence in our culture serves to time honour the needless destruction of life and thwarted ambitions that resonate still from the loss of the RMS *Titanic* on 15 April 1912.

APPENDIX ONE

WITHOUT PREJUDICE

Who Owned Who

The interconnected roles and relationships of the owners, builders and regulators of *Titanic*:

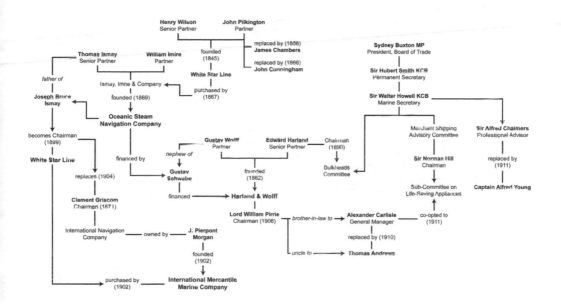

© Allen Gibson

THEATRE OF WAR

The Great Atlantic Routes

The flow and extent of ice in the North Atlantic; how it encroached on the summer shipping lanes causing their relocation southward during winter to avoid it.

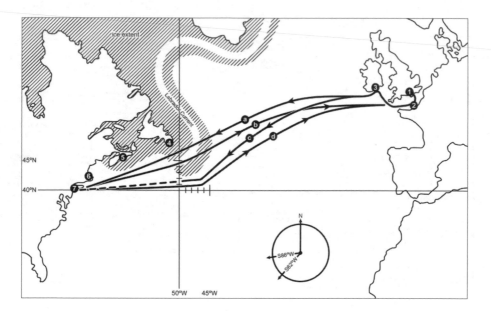

© Allen Gibson

Key to locations:
1) Southampton
2) Cherbourg
3) Queenstown
4) Cape Race
5) Halifax
6) Boston
7) New York

Key to routes:
a) Outward Northern Track
b) Homeward Northern Track
c) Outward Southern Track [followed by *Titanic*]
d) Homeward Southern Track

PROTECTION FOR PERPETUITY

Estonia *Accord*
The full text of the agreement awarding internationally recognised protection to the wreck of the passenger ferry *Estonia*, which laid the groundwork for similar measures for *Titanic*. Known also as the Gravesite Treaty it was the first arrangement to grant perpetual sanctity to a civilian vessel wrecked in international waters. With the exception of Germany all nations along the Baltic coastline are signatories. The agreement was distributed by the International Maritime Organisation and thereby is observed by its entire membership.

AGREEMENT BETWEEN THE REPUBLIC OF ESTONIA, THE REPUBLIC OF FINLAND AND THE KINGDOM OF SWEDEN REGARDING THE MS *ESTONIA*

THE REPUBLIC OF ESTONIA, THE REPUBLIC OF FINLAND AND THE KINGDOM OF SWEDEN, hereinafter referred to as the Contracting Parties.

RECALLING the disaster on the night of 28 September 1994 when the MS *ESTONIA* sank in the Baltic Sea on her way from Tallinn to Stockholm.

WISHING TO protect the MS *ESTONIA*, as a final place of rest for victims of the disaster, from any disturbing activities.

URGING the public and all other States to afford appropriate respect to the site of the MS *ESTONIA* for all time.

HAVE AGREED AS FOLLOWS:

Article 1
The wreck of the MS *ESTONIA* and the surrounding area, as defined in Article 2, shall be regarded as a final place of rest for the victims of the disaster, and as such shall be afforded appropriate respect.

Article 2
The area constituting the final place of rest shall for the purpose of the Agreement be delimited by straight line from point number 1 through points 2, 3, 4 and back to point 1:

Point number 1 (Upper Left) 59°23,500'N, 21°40,000'E
Point number 2 (Upper Right) 59°23,500'N, 21°42,000'E
Point number 3 (Lower Right) 59°22,500'N, 21°42,000'E
Point number 4 (Lower Left) 59°22,500'N, 21°40,000'E

all positions defined by geographical coordinates in World Geodetic System 1984 (WGS 84).

Article 3
The Contracting Parties hereby agree that the MS *ESTONIA* shall not be raised.

Article 4
1. The Contracting Parties undertake to institute legislation, in accordance with their national procedures, aiming at the criminalization of any activities disturbing the peace of the final place of rest in particular any diving or other activities with the purpose of recovering victims or property from the wreck or the seabed.

2. The Contracting Parties undertake to make it possible to punish the commission of an offence, established in accordance with paragraph 1 of this Article, by imprisonment.

3. Notwithstanding the above provisions, a Contracting Party may take measures to cover the wreck or to prevent pollution of the marine environment from the wreck.

Article 5
Each Contracting Party undertakes to submit information to another Contracting Party on pending or ongoing activities having been criminalized in conformity with Article 4 and involving a vessel flying the flag of that Contracting Party.

Article 6
This Agreement shall enter into force thirty days after the date when the Contracting Parties have notified the other Contracting Parties in writing that the necessary constitutional procedures for its entry into force have been completed.

Done at Tallinn on 23 February 1995 in three originals, each in the English language.

IN WITNESS WHEREOF the undersigned, duly authorise thereto, have signed this Agreement:

For the Republic of Estonia *[signed: Jüri Luik]*
For the Republic of Finland *[signed: Jaakko Kaurinkoski]*
For the Kingdom of Sweden *[signed: Lars Grundberg]*

Effective from 26 August 1995 30 days following ratification among Contracting Parties

Distributed by the IMO, 16 November 1995

National Archives, Kew: FO 949/974

APPENDIX FOUR

AN UNDUE ENCUMBRANCE

The Letter of Law

Following the loss of *Titanic* the regulations governing lifeboats and their supply at sea fell subject to intense scrutiny. Detailed here are extracts from the Merchant Shipping Act of 1894 which, still by 1912, directed the provision of lifeboats 'life-saving appliances' for Britain's mercantile marine. The Act applied to all types of vessels and in light of the disaster saw controversy for under-regulating the supply of lifeboats for the larger liners of the day.

4(a): Operation

Section 427 of the Act granted the Board of Trade authority to issue Rules with which to prescribe the minimum quantity and quality of safety apparatus each type of craft (other than fishing boats) was required to carry.

> 427(1): The Board of Trade may make Rules (in this Act called Rules for life-saving appliances) with respect to all or any of the following matters, namely:
> (a)   the arranging of British ships into classes, having regard to the services in which they are employed, to the nature and duration of the voyage, and to the number of persons carried;
> (b)   the number and description of the boats, lifeboats, life-rafts, life-jackets, and life-buoys to be carried by British ships, according to the class in which they are arranged, and the mode of their construction, and also the equipments to be carried by the boats and rafts, and the methods to be provided to get the boats and other life-saving appliances into the water which methods may include oil for use in stormy weather; and
> (c)   the quantity, quality, and description of buoyant apparatus to be carried on board British ships carrying passengers, either in addition to or in substitution for boats, lifeboats, life-rafts, life-jackets, and life-buoys.

A forty-day period before the Rules and their revisions were implemented is outlined in Section 427(2). This includes the time frame for which the validity of the amended Rules could not be challenged in court until their enactment into law:

> 427(2): All such Rules shall be laid before Parliament so soon as may be after they are made, and shall not come into operation until they have lain for forty days before both houses of Parliament during the session of Parliament; and on coming into operation shall have effect as if enacted in this Act.

The obligation for all shipping owners and captains to ensure their vessels complied with the Rules is established in Section 428:

> 428: It shall be the duty of the owner and master of every British ship to see that his ship is provided, in accordance with the Rules for life-saving appliances, with such of those appliances as, having regard to the nature of the service on which the ship is employed, and the avoidance of undue encumbrance of the ship's deck, are best adapted for securing the safety of her crew and passengers.

The appointment and composition of a Committee on Life-Saving Appliances to advise the Board of Trade on compiling, monitoring and amending the Rules of Section 427 is outlined in Section 429:

> 429(1): For the purpose of preparing and advising on the Rules for life-saving appliances, the Board of Trade may appoint a committee, the members of which shall be nominated by the Board in accordance with the Seventeenth Schedule to this Act.

The Seventeenth Schedule detailed how that membership was to be constituted:

> (1)   Three ship-owners selected by the council of the Chamber of Shipping of the United Kingdom.
> (2)   One ship-owner selected by the ship-owners' associations of Glasgow and one ship-owner selected by the Liverpool steamship owner's association and the Liverpool ship-owners association conjointly.
> (3)   Two shipbuilders selected by the council of the Institution of Naval Architects.
> (4)   Three persons practically acquainted with the navigation of vessels selected by the shipmaster's societies recognised by the Board of Trade for this purpose.
> (5)   Three persons being or having been able-bodied seamen selected by seamen's societies recognised by the Board of Trade for this purpose.
> (6)   Two persons selected conjointly by the committee of Lloyd's, the committee of Lloyd's Register society, and the committee of the Institute of London Underwriters.

The penalty for non-compliance, ill-repair, and non-readiness of life-saving appliances was enforced in Section 430:

> 430(1): In the case of any ship:
> (a)   if a ship is required by the Rules for life-saving appliances to be provided with such appliances, and proceeds on any voyage or excursion without being so provided in accordance with the Rules applicable to the ship; or
> (b)   if any of the appliances with which the ship is so provided are lost or rendered unfit for service in the course of the voyage or excursion through the wilful fault or negligence of the owner or master; or
> (c)   if the master wilfully neglects to replace or repair on the first opportunity any such appliances lost or injured in the course of the voyage or excursion; or
> (d)   if such appliances are not kept so as to be at all times fit and ready for use;
> then the owner of the ship (if in fault) shall for each offence be liable to a fine not exceeding one hundred pounds, and the master of the ship (if in fault) shall for each offence be liable for to a fine not exceeding fifty pounds.

Finally, the Board's inspections to ensure compliance with the Rules are established under Section 431; being that the ship was not permitted to embark until the correction of all deficiencies identified by the inspector:

431:

(1)   A surveyor of ships may inspect any ship for the purposes of seeing that she is properly provided with life-saving appliances in conformity with this Act, and for the purpose of that inspection shall have all the powers of a Board of Trade inspector under this Act.

(2)   If the said surveyor finds that the ship is not so provided, he shall give to the master or owner notice in writing pointing out the deficiency and also pointing out what in his opinion is requisite to remedy the same.

(3)   Every notice so given shall be communicated in the manner directed by the Board of Trade to the chief officer of Customs of any port at which the ship may seek to obtain a clearance or transire, and the ship shall be detained until a certificate under the hand of any such surveyor is produced to the effect that the ship is properly provided with life-saving appliances in conformity with this Act.

To ensure the safety and seaworthiness of emigrant-carrying ships was maintained, the master of that ship was required to obtain a certificate for clearance from the embarkation port's emigration officer approving both that it and her passengers and crew were medically fit and sufficiently provisioned for the voyage:

314 (1): A ship fitted or intended for the carriage of steerage passengers as an emigrant ship shall not clear outwards or proceed to sea until the master has obtained from the emigration officer at the port of clearance a certificate for clearance, that is to say, a certificate that all the requirements of this part of this Act, so far as the same can be complied with before the departure of the ship, have been duly complied with, and that the ship is in his opinion seaworthy, in safe trim, and in all respects fit for her intended voyage, and that the steerage passengers and crew are in a fit state to proceed, and that the master's bond has been duly executed.

4(b): Division A − Class 1

Authorised by Section 427 of the Act the Board of Trade issued a set of Rules to clarify the provisions of Sections 427/31. Originally put into practice on 31 March 1890 the Rules were brought into legal effect on 1 November that year under existing legislation − the Merchant Shipping (Life-Saving Appliances) Act, dated 1888. Receiving minor revision on 9 March 1894 their amendments became effective on 1 June under a new Merchant Shipping Act, itself created to consolidate all existing legislation for shipping into a single Act of Parliament. The Rules were once more updated on 10 February 1902 and enforced from 31 March that year; those applying to ships of similar size to *Titanic* remaining unaltered since the revision of 1894.

Under these Rules *Titanic* was classified a craft of Division A − Class 1; a British-registered emigrant-carrying steamship accommodating more than fifty persons in steerage. The Rules pertaining to life-saving appliances for this class of vessel were as follows:

(a)   Ships of Division A − Class 1, shall carry boats placed under davits, fit and ready for use, and having proper appliances for getting them into the water, in number and capacity as prescribed by the Table in the Appendix to these Rules *[Appendix 4(d)]*; such boats shall be equipped in the manner required by and shall be of the description defined in the General Rules *[4(c)]* appended hereto.

(b)   Masters or owners of ships in this class claiming to carry fewer boats under davits than are given in the Table must declare before the collector or other officers of Customs, at the time of clearance, that the boats actually placed under davits are sufficient to accommodate all persons on board, allowing 10 (ten) cubic feet of boat capacity for each adult person, or "statute adult".

(c)   Not less than half the number of boats placed under davits having at least half the cubic capacity required by the Tables, shall be boats of Section A, or Section B. The remaining boats may also be of such description, or may, in the option of the ship owner, conform to Section C, or Section D, provided that not more than two boats shall be of Section D [Rule 1, 4(c)].

(d)   If the boats placed under davits in accordance with the Table do not furnish sufficient accommodation for all persons on board, then additional wood, metal, collapsible or other boats of approved description (whether placed under davits or otherwise) or approved life-rafts shall be carried. One of these boats may be a steam launch, but in that case the space occupied by the engines and boilers is not to be included in the estimated cubic capacity of the boat.

Subject to the provisions contained in paragraph (f) of these Rules, such additional boats or rafts shall be of at least such carrying capacity that they and the boats required to be placed under davits by the Table provide together in the aggregate, in vessels of 5,000 tons gross and upwards, three-fourths, and in vessels of less than 5,000 tons gross, one-half, more than the minimum cubic contents required by Column 3 of that Table [Appendix 4(d)*]. For this purpose 3 cubic feet of air case in the life-raft is to be estimated as 10 cubic feet of internal capacity. Provided always that the rafts will accommodate all the persons for which they are to be certified under the Rules, and also have 3 cubic feet of air case for each person.

All such additional boats or rafts shall be placed as conveniently for being available as the ship's arrangements admit of, having regard to the avoidance of undue encumbrance of the ship's deck, and to the safety of the ship for her voyage.

(f)   Provided nevertheless that no ship of this class shall be required to carry more boats or rafts than will furnish sufficient accommodation for all persons on board.

The Rules' reference to 'under davits' sparked reticence across the industry to issue greater provision for ancillary boats on their vessels – those not stowed within a dedicated set of davits – amid concern the Board may at any time exclude these from the ship's cumulative legal total. Risking also that they may be construed as an 'undue encumbrance' to the deck, the ambiguity of the Act found shipping operators avoiding doubt by deciding against provisioning larger quantities of boats not stowed permanently within a dedicated set of davits: opting to install only sixteen, the minimum required for ships grossing above 10,000 tons. The uncertainty perhaps gave White Star motive to stow two of the four collapsible boats for *Titanic* upon the roof of her officers' quarters 'placed as conveniently' to free them from the deck 8ft 3in below.

4(c): General Rules

The Act also detailed an additional twelve General Rules to give clarity on the classification, acceptability of build, arrangement and apparatus to deploy lifeboats, aboard all classes of vessel.

Rule 1: Boats

All boats shall be constructed and properly equipped as provided by these Rules, and all boats and other life-saving appliances are to be kept ready for use to the satisfaction of the Board of Trade. Internal buoyancy apparatus may be constructed of wood, or of copper or yellow metal of not less than 18oz to the superficial foot, or of other durable material.

Section A [applicable to the fourteen standard lifeboats carried by Titanic]: A boat of this Section shall be a lifeboat, of whale-boat form, properly constructed of wood or metal, having for every 10 cubic feet of her capacity computed as in Rule 2, at least 1 cubic foot of strong and serviceable enclosed airtight compartments, so constructed that water cannot find its way into them. In the case of metal boats an addition will have to be made to the cubic capacity of the airtight compartments, so as to give them buoyancy equal to that of the wooden boat.

Section D [applying to the two emergency cutters]: A boat of this Section shall be a properly constructed boat of wood or metal.

Section E [*four canvas Engelhardt boats*] A boat of this Section shall be a boat of approved construction, form, and material, and may be collapsible.

Rule 2: Cubic capacity

The cubic capacity of a boat shall be deemed to be her cubic capacity, ascertained (as in measuring ships for tonnage capacity) by Stirling's rule, but as the application of that rule entails much labour, the following simple plan, which is approximately accurate, may be adopted for general purposes, and when no question requiring absolute correct adjustment is raised:

Measure the length and breadth outside and the depth inside. Multiply them together and by 0.6; the product is the capacity of the boat in cubic feet. Thus a boat 28ft long, 8ft 6in broad, and 3ft 6in deep will be regarded as having a capacity of 28 x 8.5 x 3.5 x 0.6 = 499.8, or 500 cubic feet. If the oars are pulled in rowlocks, the bottom of the rowlocks is to be considered the gunwale of the boat for ascertaining her depth.

Rule 3: Number of persons for boats

The number of persons a boat of Section A shall be deemed fit to carry shall be the number of cubic feet ascertained as in Rule 2 divided by ten.

The space in the boat shall be sufficient for the seating of the persons carried in it, and for the proper use of the oars.

The number of persons a boat of Section D or Section E shall be deemed fit to carry shall be the number of cubic feet ascertained as in Rule 2 divided by eight.

Rule 4: Appliances for lowering boats

Appliances for getting a boat into the water must fulfil the following conditions: Means are to be provided for speedily, but not necessarily simultaneously or automatically, detaching the boats from the lower blocks of the davit tackles, the boats placed under davits are to be attached to the davit tackles and kept ready for service, the davits are to be strong enough and so spaced that the boats can be swung out with faculty.

Rule 12: Watertight compartments

When ships of any class are divided into efficient watertight compartments to the satisfaction of the Board of Trade, they shall only be required to carry additional boats, rafts, and buoyant apparatus of one-half of the capacity required by these Rules, but the exemption shall not extend to life-jackets or similar approved articles of equal buoyancy suitable to be worn on the person.

The requirements of Rule D would demand, in addition to the lifeboats, a supply of life-rafts and floatation devices equalling the cubic capacity of at least three quarters of the minimum lifeboats required by type Division A – Class 1 vessels exceeding 5,000 gross tons. This would require *Titanic* to furnish an additional 4,125 cubic feet of raft capacity to augment her original allocation of boats due to their failure to provide sufficient accommodation for the total occupancy of people she was certified to carry. However, because the Board were satisfied with the watertight compartmentalisation of *Titanic* this requirement could be mitigated in reward by Rule 12.

On 7 March 1890, to clarify what Rule 12 should construe as 'efficient watertight compartments' the Board had their Bulkheads Committee, chaired by Sir Edward Harland, put forward its definition. The committee answered:

Vessels may be considered able to float in moderate weather with any two adjoining compartments in free communication with the sea, if fitted with efficient transverse watertight bulkheads, so spaced that when two such compartments are laid open to the sea, the uppermost watertight deck to which all the bulkheads extend, and which we will call the bulkhead-deck, is not brought nearer to the water surface than would be indicated by a line drawn round the side at a distance amidships of 3/100ths of the depth at side at that place below the bulkhead-deck, and gradually approaching it towards the ends where it may be 3/200ths of the same depth below it. This line we may call the margin of safety line.

… as an inducement to owners to subdivide their vessels to the extent that we have indicated…we therefore submit that in such case owners might be relieved of the obligation to carry any part of the additional boats, rafts, and other life-saving appliances required by the Rules issued by the Board of Trade under the Merchant Shipping (Life-Saving Appliances) Act, 1888.

Being a vessel exceeding 10,000 gross tons *Titanic* was required to carry a lifeboat capacity amassing at least 5,500 cubic feet. However, since she was not furnished with enough seats to accommodate her entire licensed passenger occupancy Rule D would come into effect. This thereby required her to carry in addition to the base capacity an extra 75 per cent cubic feet of floatation devices, rafts or collapsible lifeboats to increase her minimum lifeboat/raft obligation to 9,625 cubic feet. Although, as *Titanic* was designed to remain afloat with four compartments flooded – as opposed to the committee's minimum of two – and as her bulkheads cleared by double the Board's benchmark of 1.5ft above the waterline, her compartmenting was deemed to be adequately efficient. This being so, White Star could then apply to the Board of Trade to bring Rule 12 into play and halve the additional capacity required by Rule D to 2,062.5 cubic feet. With both Rules D and 12 applied the revised legal threshold for the boats and life-rafts to be carried by *Titanic* would fall to 7,562.5 cubic feet.

In the event, the Board thought it needless to apply either Rule to *Olympic* or *Titanic* since both already exceeded in every respect the two-compartment principle as well as furnished lifeboat capacities surpassing also the extended provisions of Rule D.

4(d): Cubic Capacity

The Merchant Shipping Act contained an appendix to the Rules outlining both the minimum cubic capacity and number of lifeboats required 'under davits' according to a vessel's gross tonnage. Those applying to *Titanic* are highlighted:

Gross tons	Minimum sets of davits	Minimum cubic capacity★	Gross tons	Minimum sets of davits	Minimum cubic capacity★
10,000 +	**16**	**5,500**	3,500–3,750	8	2,600
9,000–10,000	14	5,250	3,250–3,500	8	2,500
8,500–9,000	14	5,100	3,000–3,250	8	2,400
8,000–8,500	14	5,000	2,750–3,000	6	2,100
7,750–8,000	12	4,700	2,500–2,750	6	2,050
7,500–7,750	12	4,600	2,250–2,500	6	2,000
7,250–7,500	12	4,500	2,000–2,250	6	1,900
7,000–7,250	12	4,400	1,760–2,000	6	1,800
6,750–7,000	12	4,300	1,500–1,750	6	1,700
6,500–6,750	12	4,200	1,250–1,500	6	1,500
6,250–6,500	12	4,100	1,000–1,250	4	1,200

6,000–6,250	12	4,000	900–1,000	4	1,000
5,750–6,000	10	3,700	800–900	4	900
5,500–5,750	10	3,600	700–800	4	800
5,250–5,500	10	3,500	600–700	3	700
5,000–5,250	10	3,400	500–600	3	600
4,750–5,000	10	3,300	400–500	2	400
4,500–4,750	8	2,900	300–400	2	350
4,250–4,500	8	2,900	200–300	2	300
4,000–4,250	8	2,800	100–200	2	250
3,750–4,000	8	2,700	0–200	1	125

The table ended with a clarifying footnote stating:

> Where in ships already fitted the required cubic contents of boats placed under davits is provided, although by a similar number of boats than the minimum required by this Table, such ships shall be regarded as complying with the Rules as to the boats to be carried under davits.

Titanic complied already with the minimum requirements for ships exceeding 10,000 gross tons.

The table, originally enacted under the Merchant Shipping (Life-Saving Appliances) Act of 1888, was reprised unaltered in the Rules of 1890; its scale ending '9,000 [gross tons] and upwards'. This was increased to '10,000 [gross] and upwards' for the Act of 1894.

4(e): In Review

Unconvinced that the 1894 Act adequately provisioned lifeboats for ships exceeding 10,000 gross tons, in the autumn of 1910 Horatio Bottomley, Liberal member of parliament for Hackney South, put his concern over the supply intended for *Olympic* in a written question to the president of the Board of Trade, Sydney Buxton:

> To ask the President of the Board of Trade, whether his attention had been called to the fact that the new White Star liner, the *Olympic*, now being built, and a model of which was being exhibited in Piccadilly, was provided with fourteen lifeboats only, being less than a quarter of the number furnished to most other vessels of similar tonnage; and whether he would make a representation to the owners on the matter?

Bottomley was deeply concerned the Act had become dangerously outmoded with the emergence of ships frequently exceeding – by some margin – the upper scope imposed in its Rules. On 22 November 1910 Sir Sydney's deputy, Harold Tennant, parliamentary secretary for the Board of Trade, submitted the reply on his behalf:

> I understand that the *Olympic* will be provided with fourteen lifeboats and two ordinary boats, of an aggregate capacity of 9,752 cubic feet, which is in excess of the requirements of the statutory Rules. I have no information as to any vessel carrying four times this number of boats. The *Lusitania* and *Mauretania* each carry sixteen boats.

Because the sixteen lifeboats planned for *Olympic* aggregated abundantly more cubic footage than required by the Act the answer advised the MP that there was no cause for concern. The reply did not allay Bottomley's apprehension, and indeed suggested proof that the Rules governing the provision of lifeboats was perilously unreasonable for the 45,000-ton *Olympic*.

With that, on 15 February 1911 Bottomley tabled a further question demanding a review to the tonnage scale of the Act:

> Whether he will state the date of the last regulations made by the Board in reference to the number of lifeboats necessary to be attached to passenger vessels; and whether, having regard to the increased tonnage of modern ships, he will consider the desirableness of revising such regulations?

Acquiescing to Bottomley's request, Sir Sydney himself replied:

> These regulations were last revised in 1894. The question of their further revision is engaging the serious attention of the Board of Trade, and I have decided to refer the matter to the Merchant Shipping Advisory Committee for consideration and advice.

The Board then began a lengthy consultation, commissioning a series of reports seeking the opinions of their senior advisors, 'to suggest in what manner the scale should be continued upwards ... so as to provide for vessels of tonnage up to 50,000 tons gross and upwards'.

On 18 February 1911 the Board engaged three principal officers to each issue their thoughts on the matter. The regional principals duly returned their suggestions to encompass ships grossing between 45,000 and 50,000 tons:

Report author and date issued in 1911	Minimum number of fixed lifeboats	Minimum cubic capacity	Including extra 75 per cent capacity	Providing lifeboat seats for
Mr Harris (Glasgow), 24 February	18	9,700	16,975	1,697
Captain Parke (London), 27 February	26	9,500	16,625	1,662
Alfred Young (Liverpool), 3 March	24	10,900	19,075	1,907

On the 28th, also in answer to the Board's request, William David Archer, their principal ship surveyor – incumbent holder of the post since 1898 – submitted his proposal to extend the scale. He recommended that a vessel equal to 50,000 gross tons should carry twenty-six lifeboats amassing 15,500 cubic feet so as to provide enough seating for 1,743 occupants. Should that vessel not then supply enough boats to accommodate the total licensed number of passengers and crew he would apply Rule D as normal, thereby requiring an additional 11,625 cubic feet (twenty extra lifeboats) to provide seating for a further 1,453 people.

Under Archer's plan a ship grossing 50,000 tons could potentially carry forty-six lifeboats, amounting to 27,125 cubic feet, space for 3,196 occupants. The calculation applicable to *Titanic* is highlighted:

Gross tons	Tonnage clearing 10,000 cap	Tonnage clearing 10,000 cap divided by 1,000, times 250	Extra capacity plus 5,500 cubic feet	Including extra 75 per cent capacity
10,000	5,000	1,250	6,750	11,812
15,000	10,000	2,500	8,000	14,000
20,000	15,000	3,750	9,250	16,187
25,000	20,000	5,000	10,500	18,375
30,000	25,000	6,250	11,750	20,562
40,000	30,000	7,500	13,000	22,750
45,000	**35,000**	**8,750**	**14,250**	**24,937**
50,000 +	40,000	10,000	15,500	27,125

Archer's formula was based on adding 250 cubic feet of capacity to a vessel's required lifeboat allocation for every 1,000 gross tons clearing the 10,000-ton cap under the existing Rules. If applied to a ship of similar size to *Titanic* (whose gross tonnage exceeded the upper limit in the Act by 35,000) Archer's proposals would add an additional 8,750 cubic feet to the existing 5,500 base minimum, thereby raising the required capacity for *Titanic* to 14,250 cubic feet. Furthermore, with Rule D applied – since even with this provision was still inadequate for the 3,547 people she was licensed to carry – his incremental proposal would oblige *Titanic* to supply a cumulative lifeboat capacity of 24,937 cubic feet: incidentally proving adequate for all 2,228 occupants aboard her maiden voyage.

Sir Walter Howell, the marine secretary, forwarded the four proposals to the Board's Merchant Shipping Advisory Committee on 4 April 1911 to collate their views on the matter. The panel in turn established a subcommittee on Life-Saving Appliances to formulate the report. Comprising seven members representing various shipping owners, insurers, shipbuilders, naval architects and engineers, the subcommittee met on 19 and 26 May. On 4 July 1911 they presented their proposal for the extension of lifeboat provision to encompass larger ships. Those for *Titanic* are highlighted:

Gross tons	Minimum sets of davits	Minimum number of additional boats	Minimum cubic capacity	Including extra 75 per cent capacity
10,000–12,000	16	0	5,500	9,625
12,000–20,000	16	2	6,200	10,850
20,000–35,000	16	4	6,900	12,075
35,000–45,000	16	6	7,600	13,300
45,000 +	**16**	**8**	**8,300**	**14,525**

The committee's table was then forwarded to Captain Alfred Young, professional advisor at the Board of Trade. Young had been their nautical surveyor since 1891, then senior advisor from 1 September 1911 following the retirement of his predecessor, Sir Alfred Chalmers. During his tenure as principal officer for Liverpool, Young had already, in February 1911, presented his recommendations to extending current provisions to accommodate vessels larger than 10,000 tons (see first table 4(e)). Serving now in this new capacity, he submitted a fresh proposal on 28 March 1912. Those relating to ships equal in size to *Titanic* are highlighted:

Gross tons	Minimum number of boats	Minimum cubic capacity	Including extra 75 per cent capacity
10,000–12,000	16	5,500	9,625
12,000–15,000	18	5,800	10,150
15,000–20,000	20	6,100	10,675
20,000–25,000	22	6,400	11,200
25,000–30,000	24	6,700	11,725
30,000–35,000	24	7,000	12,250
35,000–40,000	24	7,300	12,775
40,000–45,000	24	7,600	13,300
45,000–50,000	**26**	**7,900**	**13,825**
50,000 +	26	8,200	14,350

Young was adamant that the number of lifeboats required 'under davits' in the Act's table should be extended to allow for more boats to facilitate 'a proper and safe transfer of the passengers from one vessel to another in case of adversity'. Averse to provisioning enough boats to account for everybody on board he considered too many sited high above the waterline would undermine the vessel's buoyancy, particularly during inclement weather. Those on *Titanic* were sited 60½ft above her waterline, each wooden boat providing a capacity of 600 cubic feet and weighing an average of 2 tons when empty. It was later calculated that 'about sixty-three' similar-sized lifeboats would have been needed to accommodate all the 3,547 people *Titanic* was licensed to carry. Young believed storing that number of boats would certainly risk the 'undue encumbrance of the ship's deck'. Feeling vessels equal or even exceeding the size of *Titanic* were able to safely stow approximately twenty-six boats among their own sets of davits he surmised that a ship bearing this number, with each providing capacity of 600 cubic feet, would furnish an overall cubic footage of 15,600. Therefore, with Rule D applied, the total capacity for that ship would rise to 27,300 cubic feet – enough seats, if adhering just to the minimum, for 2,730 people.

All the Board's respondents disagreed with Sir Alfred Chalmers' decision of 1904 to maintain the cap at 10,000 tons; their reports concurring that the table in the Act be extended to cater for ships exceeding its original scope. Yet none of the proposals called for a sufficient supply of 'boats for all'. Their findings were based on Rule D still applying to remedy instances where legal minimums fell short of accommodating the total passenger occupancy on board: thereby increasing the legal minimum stipulation in these proposals by 75 per cent. Crucially, under each proposal, Rule 12 could still come into effect and halve any benefit from Rule D should the vessel be deemed to possess 'efficient watertight compartments'.

None of the proposals to extend the table in the Act were implemented as they were superseded by the table in Appendix 4(f) resulting from the government's investigation into the *Titanic* disaster. However, the proposals to extend the scale of the 1894 Act all advised improvement to it, and had any reached the statute book more lives would have invariably been saved from *Titanic*.

How the Act and its proposed revisions would apply to a ship equal in size to *Titanic* and her maximum occupancy of 3,547, is detailed on p.281:

Review	Minimum sets of davits	Minimum cubic capacity	Additional 75 per cent capacity	Combined total capacity+	Total seats provided in lifeboats+
1894 Act	16	5,500	4,125	9,625	962
William Archer	24	14,250*	10,687	24,937	2,493
Advisory Sub-Committee	24	8,300	6,225	14,525	1,452
Captain Young (first)	26	15,600*	11,700	27,300	2,730
Captain Young (second)	26	7,900	5,925	13,825	1,382

* Total if each lifeboat provided 600 cubic feet.
+ Total not including any reduced capacity possibly granted under Rule 12.

Unaware at the time that *Titanic* was lost, the Board acknowledged on 16 April 1912 that it was, finally, 'of the opinion that a very careful and thorough revision of the table should now be made', and that the 10,000 cap would be upwardly revised to 'meet the changed conditions due to recent developments in the size of passenger steamships and in the number of persons which these vessels can accommodate'. This was an admission that saw Lord Mersey's report pull short of branding the Board's maintenance of this legislation culpable for the avoidably high loss of life on *Titanic*.

4(f): Parting of the Ways
Pursuant to Lord Mersey's report, the Board's amended Rules were placed before Parliament on 4 September 1912 and enacted into law on 1 January 1913. From that date the supply of lifeboats carried by passenger liners was instead based on the length of the ship, and no more calculated by gross tonnage or cubic capacity. Rule 12 was repealed.

All emigrant-carrying vessels were henceforth obliged to provide enough lifeboats to accommodate the total number of people it was certified by the Board to carry. The new Rules also required vessels to install a prescribed minimum quantity of davits with at least one boat nested within each set and ready for immediate use. The new table would no longer prescribe a minimum number of boats, but davits, in the hope of encouraging shipping operators to exceed the amount required by law. That relevant to *Titanic* in the new table is highlighted:

Length of vessel (in feet)	Minimum sets of davits
940–1040	26
840–940	**24**
750–840	22
670–750	20
590–670	18
510–590	16
450–510	14
390–450	12
330–390	10
270–330	8
220–270	6
160–220	4
0–160	2

The table still excluded collapsible lifeboats – only wooden boats would qualify for each davit – although the ship was also required to supply enough rafts and lifejackets to cater for all occupants on board. Such provisions guaranteed everyone, regardless of whether the ship was full, access to a floatation device as well as a seat in a boat. The list was also the first occasion that the Board's regulations provisioned for larger currently non-existent vessels likely to appear in the future.

4(g): SOLAS

Out of its findings the British Court of Inquiry examining the loss of *Titanic* established SOLAS, an International Convention on the Safety of Life at Sea, through which it was hoped that regulations on the universal supply of lifeboats would be agreed and harmonised. First convened in London on 12 November 1913, the convention was attended by officials representing thirteen nations: America, Austria-Hungary, Belgium, Denmark, France, Germany, Great Britain, Holland, Italy, Norway, Russia, Spain and Sweden.

The treaty, signed on 20 January 1914, decreed the calculation of cubic capacity be according to the length of the vessel and on the condition that its computation provided enough seats for everybody on board. Forming Article XLIII, the treaty came into effect on 1 July 1915. That relevant to a ship of equal length to *Titanic* is highlighted:

Length of vessel (in feet)	Minimum sets of davits	Minimum cubic capacity
520–550	16	18,720
550–580	16	20,350
580–610	18	21,900
610–640	18	23,700
640–670	20	25,350
670–700	20	27,050
700–730	22	28,560
730–760	22	30,180
760–790	24	32.100
790–820	24	34,350
820–855	26	36,450
855–890	**26**	**38,750**
890–925	28	41,000
925–960	28	43,880
960–995	30	46,350
995–1030	30	48,750

4(h): British Inquiry

The Mersey inquiry identified at the outset twenty-six questions to which the hearings would be dedicated, and the answers were used as a way of recording the loss of *Titanic*. As listed in the report's preamble the questions germane to the provision, manning and occupancy of her lifeboats are detailed here:

2.   Before leaving Queenstown on or about 11th April last did the *Titanic* comply with the requirements of the Merchant Shipping Acts, 1894–1906, and the Rules and regulations made thereunder with regard to the safety and otherwise of 'passenger steamers' and 'emigrant ships'?

3. In the actual design and construction of the *Titanic* what special provisions were made for the safety of the vessel and the lives of those on board in the event of collisions and other causalities?

5. What was the number of the boats of any kind on board the *Titanic*? Were the arrangements for manning and launching the boats on board the *Titanic* in case of emergency proper and sufficient? Had a boat drill been held on board, and, if so, when? What was the carrying capacity of the respective boats?

19. Was the apparatus for lowering the boats on the *Titanic* at the time of the casualty in good working order? Were the boats swung out, filled, lowered, or otherwise put into the water and got away under proper superintendence? Were the boats sent away in seaworthy condition and properly manned, equipped and provisioned? Did the boats, whether those under davits or otherwise, prove to be efficient and serviceable for the purpose of saving life?

26. The Court is invited to report upon the Rules and Regulations made under the Merchant Shipping Acts, 1894–1906, and the administration of those Acts and of such Rules and Regulations, so far as the consideration thereof is material to this casualty, and to make any recommendations or suggestions what it may think fit, having regard to the circumstances of the casualty with a view to promoting the safety of vessels and persons at sea.

4(i): Accountability

Captain Stanley Lord of the *Californian*, often derided as the scapegoat of the disaster, argued in vain that he and his crew had not responded to the distress rockets from *Titanic* because they interpreted them as company signals; non-emergency private flares.

The 1894 Merchant Shipping Act required all shipping operators to register the appearance of rockets used as private signals to avoid these becoming misconstrued as distress flares:

733(1): If a ship-owner desires to use for the purpose of a private code any rockets, lights, or other similar signals, he may register those signals with the Board of Trade, and that Board shall give public notice of the signals so registered in such manner as they think requisite for preventing those signals from being mistaken for signals of distress or signals for Pilots.

The Act could also revoke a certificate of captaincy should a captain be held at fault though any action or inaction resulting in loss of life:

422(1): In every case of collision, it shall be the duty of the master or person in charge of each vessel, if and so far as he can do so without danger to his own vessel, crew and passengers (if any),
(a) to render to the other vessel her master, crew, and passengers (if any) such assistance as may be practicable, and may be necessary to save them from any danger caused by the collision, and to stay by the other vessel until he has ascertained that she has no need of further assistance.

422(2): If the master or person in charge fails without reasonable cause to comply with this Section, he shall be guilty of a misdemeanour, and, if he is a certified officer, an inquiry into his conduct may be held, and his certificate cancelled or suspended.

470(1): The certificate of a master, mate, or engineer may be cancelled or suspended:
(a) by a court holding a formal investigation into a shipping casualty under this part of the Act, or by a naval court constituted under this Act, if the court find that the loss or abandonment of, or serious damage to, any ship, or loss of life has been caused by his wrongful act or default, provided that, if the court holding a formal investigation is a court of summary jurisdiction, that court shall not cancel or suspend a certificate unless one at least of the Assessors concurs in the finding of the court.

The 1894 Merchant Shipping Act would only limit liability for ship owners as long as an official investigation exonerated them of any fault for the loss of lives or goods carried by the afflicted vessel.

503(1): The owners of a ship, British or foreign, shall not where all or any of the following occurrences take place without their actual fault or privity; (that is to say,)
(a) Where any loss of life or personal injury is caused to any person being carried in the ship,
(b) Where any damage or loss is caused to any goods, merchandise, or other things whatsoever on board the ship,
(c) Where any loss of life or personal injury is caused to any person carried in any other vessel by reason of the improper navigation of the ship,
be liable to damages beyond the following amounts, (that is to say,)
(1) in respect of loss of life or personal injury, either alone or together with loss of or damage to vessels, goods, merchandise, or other things, an aggregate amount not exceeding fifteen pounds for each ton of their ship's [gross] tonnage; and
(2) in respect of loss of, or damage to, vessels, goods, merchandise, or other things, whether there be in addition loss of life or personal injury or not, an aggregate amount not exceeding eight pounds for each ton of their ship's [gross] tonnage.

IMPENETRABLE DECADENCE

Bulkhead Configuration of Titanic

Divided by fifteen transverse bulkheads, *Titanic* was considered unsinkable. The inboard profile (top) shows her watertight divisions and key openings and how these divisions neglected to penetrate first-class passenger areas (shaded) in which White Star Line lavished the largest rooms afloat.

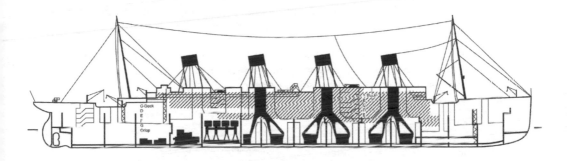

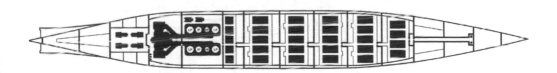

© Allen Gibson

APPENDIX SIX

THE BRIDGE

37 Seconds to Disaster

At the moment the iceberg is sighted, two figures occupy the wheelhouse: Hichens, the helmsman (4) and Moody, the junior officer (3). Concerned he would be unable to sight ice in adequate time, watch commander William Murdoch (1) positioned himself on the starboard navigation wing to achieve a clearer forward view of the ship's path. At this juncture the remainder of the watch was likewise dispersed from the bridge: Boxhall, the navigating officer, sat in the Chart Room (2) recording his earlier position calculations; and the relief helmsman, Alfred Olliver (5), returning to the bridge from checking the compass at its raised platform amidships.

At the rear of the officers' quarters the Marconi suite comprised three rooms: a Silent Room (a) for muffling the set's motorised equipment, transmission room (b) and adjoining a cabin (c) which permitted one operator to rest any given time.

The remaining senior crew off duty and in their berths at the moment of impact were: Captain Smith (6) and officers Wilde (7), Lightoller (8), Pitman (9) and Lowe (10).

© Allen Gibson

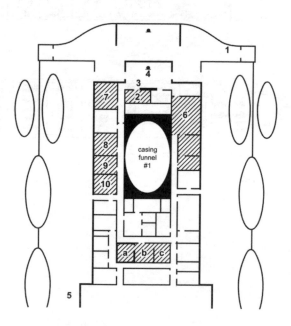

ECONOMY OF PRUDENCE

Lifeboat Configuration of Titanic

Concerned that *Titanic* offered her occupants too few lifeboats, her chief designer, Alexander Carlisle, proposed a deck plan (top) that accommodated thirty-two boats. Believing his ship did not warrant them, his client, Bruce Ismay, provisioned just one boat per davit (bottom; numbered 1–16), the minimum required by law, plus four ancillary collapsible boats (A–D).

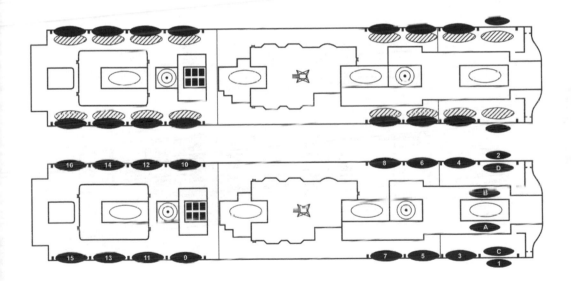

© Allen Gibson

WATERTIGHT SUBDIVISION

Longitudinal vs. Transversal

Titanic (bottom) featured a transverse system of bulkheads that kept her afloat for two hours and forty minutes after striking the iceberg. Fitted with longitudinal bulkheads, the configuration within *Lusitania* (top) was widely deemed to be safer due to their greater isolation of water; whereas she succumbed within eighteen minutes. Aboard each the coalbunkers (shaded) were arranged along these walls; their sodden weight and the compartment's close confinement of water hastened the demise of *Lusitania*.

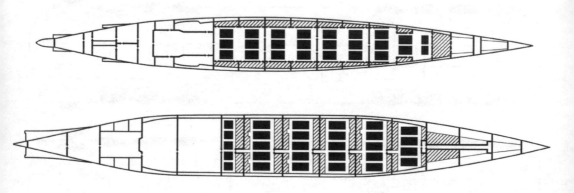

© Allen Gibson

MARGIN OF SAFETY

A Tale of Two Keels

Crosswise mid-section plans comparing the double keel and unrestricted transversely compartmented hull of *Titanic* (right), with the longitudinally protected and double keel of *Lusitania* (left). The formation ensconced within *Lusitania* compromised the buoyancy of her hull due to the longitudinal wall's confinement of water that increased the burden of weight on the damaged side; whereas *Titanic* settled water across her expanse of hull, filling steady and level, with five compartments breached.

© Allen Gibson

APPENDIX TEN

CAUSE AND EFFECT

The Hawke *incident of 1911*

Departing Southampton under the joint command of Captain Smith and the harbour pilot, after skirting its treacherous sandbanks, their navigable limits marked on the surface by buoys, *Olympic* continues into the Solent. At this precise moment Royal Navy cruiser HMS *Hawke* is returning to Portsmouth, the two vessels drawn close by hydrographical 'pull-in' generated by the water displacement of *Olympic*. They collide minutes later.

The incident would showcase White Star's unaccountable faith in Edward Smith who was granted command of *Titanic* the following year despite the dispute over the cause of the *Hawke* collision still wending its way to the highest court in the land.

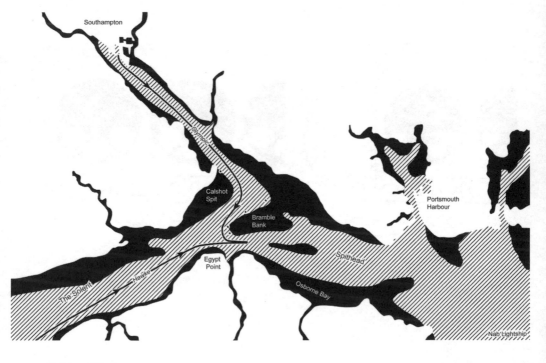

© Allen Gibson

GLOSSARY

aft/atter/abaft	Towards the stern of a ship.
amidships	Middle of a ship.
AST	Apparent Ship Time. Each day clocks at sea are reset to noon upon the sun reaching its highest point in the sky, its zenith, depending on the line of longitude that the ship has reached. One 'hour' of time is equal to 15 degrees of longitude: 24x15 = the 360 degrees of the globe.
ballast	Weight used to stabilise a ship by weighting it low enough in the water to avoid becoming top-heavy. On *Titanic* ballast was water, stored in tanks within her double hull, which could be filled or drained depending on the load of the ship or to adjust stability during fine or inclement weather.
beam	Width of a vessel, usually measured at its widest (extreme) point.
Berthon collapsibles	Canvas-hulled lifeboat held rigid over a longitudinally folding wooden frame; pioneered by Reverend Edward Lyon Berthon (1813–99) Intended to float from the deck should disaster leave no time for crew to assemble or launch, the boat was approved by the Admiralty in 1873 and began production at his manufactory in Romsey, Hampshire, in 1877. The bulkier Engelhardt variety featured planked wooden hulls, and an above-water portion comprising of canvas.
Blue Riband	Originating from horseracing, in 1890 the appellation also became the accolade given to the vessel setting the fastest crossing on the North Atlantic in a race established between rival shipping operators in 1838. Although the competition was itself unofficial and its rules unwritten, two points 3,044 nautical miles apart mark the extent of course: the Ambrose lightship (since 1909) at the southern entrance of New York Harbour and (since 1935) Bishop Rock lighthouse 4 miles west of the Scilly Isles, Cornwall. Previously a variety of European ports (predominately Queenstown) had marked the eastern boundary. The record was split into two; one for the eastbound crossing, the other for westbound.
bilge	Groove where the keel meets the hull and collects water in order to stabilise the ship by reducing its roll.
Board of Trade	British government department established by King William III in 1696 to oversee the administration of commerce and the inspection of American plantations. During the 1850s its remit was broadened to produce and maintain legislation on transportation, merchant

shipping in particular. Renamed the Department for Trade and Industry in 1970, the post of president of the Board of Trade remains the official designation for its Cabinet representative to this day.

bow — Front of a ship.

bridge — Area comprising the wheelhouse and navigation wings on a ship. The Chart Room and accommodation for senior officers are sited adjacent to expedite their constantly required access.

bulkhead — Partition forming a compartment, on ships this being steel walls and sealed to isolate and contain flooding.

buoyancy — Natural force providing a ship with the ability to float; achieved when the volume of water displaced is greater than the weight of the ship itself. A ship is buoyant when the upward force is greater than its opposing gravitational (downward) force.

CQD — The original Morse distress call 'Come Quickly Distress' devised in 1904; it was superseded in 1909 by SOS.

davit — Winching mechanism that hoists a lifeboat from its stowing position on the deck and over to the side of the hull for lowering into water. Operated in pairs/sets, those on *Titanic* each comprised quadrant-geared arms that could incline both inboard and out to easily deploy multiple boats. Sharing the frame of the adjoining set, a switching gear between each davit pair avoided any two adjacent boats being lowered simultaneously.

displacement — Volume of water displaced by the hull of a free-floating and fully loaded vessel. Unlike gross or net tonnage that are measured by cubic volume, displacement tonnage represents actual weight: one displacement ton is equivalent to 35 cubic feet of seawater.

draught — The minimum depth of water a hull requires in which to float clear of the seabed.

expansion joint — A physical joint cut into the superstructure protruding the main hull to give it flexibility to contort with the motion of the sea. Filled with leather, steel and iron the two joints on *Titanic* and *Olympic* were located inward exactly one-third of the Boat Deck's length from the bow and stern. *Britannic* was fitted with three expansion joints.

Fahrenheit — As a comparison, water freezes at zero degrees Centigrade and 32 degrees Fahrenheit, the boiling point of which is 212 degrees. In 1912 all temperature was measured in Fahrenheit. To convert it to Centigrade, deduct 32 then multiply the product by 5 and divide by 9.

fathom — Unit of length, used to measure depth: equal to 6ft or 1.8288 metres.

forecastle — Raised deck at the bow traditionally housing the crew's living quarters.

forward — Looking toward the bow of a ship.

Gigantic — Originating from the word 'gigantes' the mythical giants of ancient Greece.

growler — Floating ice rising between 10ft and 15ft above water but within 25ft in length: most likely the remnants of partially melted icebergs.

gross tonnage — Total of all permanently enclosed space within a ship (including wheelhouse and Chart Room): 1 ton equal to 100 cubic feet (or 2.83 cubic metres) of capacity, which for *Titanic* was exactly 46,328.54 (131,109.85 cubic metres). Often misleading as the phrase does not infer actual weight, the term itself originates from tun – the capacity of an old wine cask, 250 gallons – the standard which determined a ship's carrying capacity for port taxes. *See also* net tonnage.

HAPAG	Hamburg Amerikanische Packetfahrt Actien Gesellschaft (commonly, Hamburg-Amerika Line), a company founded in Hamburg, Germany, on 27 May 1847 and which by 1912 was the world's largest shipping operator.
helm	The wheel that steers a ship.
HMS	His Majesty's Ship: in 1912 the prefix for the name of a vessel in the service of King George V's Royal Navy.
hull	Watertight framed shell of a ship: the term 'laid-down' indicates the date on which construction began on the hull. The decks protruding above the hull are called the superstructure.
horsepower (hp)	System devised by James Watt to measure the power of an engine by calculating the pressure of a steam cylinder: each unit equal to 550 foot-pounds of pressure per second – the pulling power of a single 'draught' horse.
iceberg	Section of floating ice sheered from a glacier of the Polar Regions. Those in the North Atlantic are shed from the glaciers of Greenland's Jakobshavn Fjord and carried south by the Labrador Current. As a rule only ⅛ of an iceberg is visible above water. Those forming the ice field surrounding *Titanic* ranged in height between 50 and 200ft above water and originated from this fjord.
keel	Spine of a ship from which its frame is built. That for *Titanic* was a hollow tube over 5ft thick.
knot	Equal to 1.3mph on land and is the measurement of speed at which a ship can travel 1 nautical mile (6,080ft) in one hour. Such is measured by a Patent Log.
latitude	Unit of distance measured north and south from the Equator in degrees and time: for example, 41° (degrees), 46' (minutes) north (of the Equator). One minute of latitude is equal to 2,027 yards. Pole to Pole latitudes divide the Earth into 180 degrees with the two Poles at 90 degrees, the Equator marking zero degrees – the widest point.
lightship	The modern lightship from 1732 first marked shallow waters at river inlets throughout Britain in locations not possible to build lighthouses. Employed likewise in America from 1820, lightships were first located in open sea from 1828 – marking the approach to New York Harbour until 1985. They carried a powerful light atop their masthead and their hulls painted bright red, adorned with large white lettering (numbers from 1867) to denote their charted position. As many as fifty-six were in use in 1909, those stationed at Sandy Hook, Nantucket Shoals and Ambrose being the most famous.
list	A ship leaning over to one side, transversely.
Lloyd's	1) Lloyd's of London: Insurance market originating from 1688 named after its founder, Edward Lloyd, whose coffeehouse became the focal point for insurers of merchant shipping, sharing and distilling information to evaluate its inconstant state of risk. In 1912 its members underwrote 70 per cent of the world's entire marine insurance.
	2) Lloyd's Register: Likewise deriving its name from Edward Lloyd, the Register of Shipping was first printed in 1764, and was produced to advise building standards across the industry and inform insurers of the seaworthiness of every vessel registered. Among others the Norddeutscher Lloyd Line incorporated Lloyd into their name to

demonstrate that their fleet met the full safety requirements of the Register – thereby akin to a quality mark. IMM was not classified for the Register therefore *Titanic* was neither visited by the organisation's inspectors nor consequently officially complied with its requirements.

load-line
: Height of a hull's waterline when fully laden. Bulkheads extending above this point were considered satisfactorily watertight despite not being sealed at the top.

longitude
: Unit of distance measured east to west in the degrees marking the time in which Earth will complete one rotation. Since 1767 the zero degree Meridian has begun at Greenwich in London, internationally recognised as the point since 1884. The Earth is divided into twenty-four longitudinal lines, each equal to 15 degrees marking one hour of time, 360 degrees in total; for example, 49° (degrees), 52' (minutes) west (of Meridian). Each minute of longitude travelled is equal to 1,520 yards.

longitudinal
: Lengthwise section of a ship, bow to stern.

maiden voyage
: Inaugural fee-earning voyage of a vessel.

Morse code
: System of wireless codes developed by Samuel Morse in 1837. Comprising of dots and dashes it is used to transmit electric pulses as alpha and numeric messages as over radio waves.

nautical mile
: Equal to 6,080ft, 1.15 land miles or 1,000 fathoms. One nautical mile is also equivalent to covering one minute of latitude.

navigation wing
: Small enclosure overhanging the hull to afford crew an unobstructed vantage point along an entire aspect of hull. Located near the bridge it is most often occupied during docking.

net tonnage
: Total cubic tonnage of commercial space available in a ship, such as passenger accommodation, restaurants and cargo areas: 1 ton is equal to 100 cubic feet (2.83 cubic metres), which for *Titanic* totalled exactly 21,831.34 cubic feet (61,482.69 cubic metres). All non-commercial space, such as boiler rooms, ballast tanks, machinery and crew working and living accommodation is deducted from the ship's gross tonnage to determine Net Register Tonnage (NRT). *See also* gross tonnage.

Poop Deck
: Elevated area at the stern of a ship overhanging the rudder: its deck contains the after winching capstans. The term itself originates from the saying a vessel is 'pooped' when a wave has broken over the stern.

port
: Left-hand side of a ship, looking forward: indicated by a red light near the bridge house. Traditionally the side the ship's cargo was loaded and unloaded; 'portside' formally replacing the parlance 'larboard' in 1844 to avoid confusion of its similarity to 'starboard'.

Radar
: Anagram for RAdio Detection And Ranging, invented in 1937 as a detection device that uses electromagnetic waves which rebound off above-water objects.

reciprocating
: Type of steam engine developed in 1812 containing sets of pistons moving up and down in cylinders under the pressure of steam to drive a propeller crankshaft or additional engines. *See also* triple expansion.

RMS
: Royal Mail Steamship; prefix given to a name of a vessel contracted to carry British Royal Mail. The contracts were first awarded in 1840 to vessels able to maintain good speed. The commercial benefit to vessels bearing the prefix, owed to their habitually prompt timekeeping, saw these more sought-after by passengers.

RNR
: Royal Navy Reserve – the voluntary wing of the Royal Navy for

merchant seafarers; founded in 1859. Long service medal Reserve Decoration (RD).

sextant	Instrument used to determine position at sea by measuring the angle of celestial objects in their relation to the horizon. At night stellar observations comprise of measuring the angle of two northern stars (one being the Pole Star) and two southern stars from established constellations. During daytime measurements are taken using both the sun and the horizon. Dating from 1731 the name derives from its frame, one-sixth scale of a full circle containing sighting lines and a small telescope.
SONAR	SOund Navigation And Ranging – developed in the 1940s it employs the use of ultrasonic waves to detect underwater objects by measuring the pitch of rebounding echoes.
SS	Steam Ship: name prefix given to a vessel powered by steam.
starboard	Right-hand side of a ship, looking forward: indicated by a green light near the bridge house. Term originates from early European vessels that employed an oar fixed to the right-hand side of its hull to serve as the rudder: 'steer board'.
stem	Very front of a ship: traditionally the forward-most vertical timber of the hull.
stern	Rear of a ship: the area behind referred to as 'astern'.
Tank Top	The lowest deck on the ship, enclosing water ballast and storage tanks that form the double bottom of a hull.
telegraph	Communication link between the bridge and engine room. Consisting of a lever positioned by an officer on the bridge to activate a dial instructing engineers the speed and direction the engines should be run. Commands either in forward (ahead) or reverse (astern) comprise: full speed, half speed, slow, dead slow, stand by and stop. A bell is triggered each time the telegraph leaver is adjusted thus drawing the crew's attention to the dial as new orders are received.
tender	Small vessel used to ferry passengers and luggage between the dockside and a larger craft at anchorage offshore.
tiller	Horizontal hand-operated bar fitted to a rudder to steer a craft. Used on smaller and older vessels, lifeboats in 1912 were likewise steered in this manner: *Titanic* did not carry any motorised boats.
Titanic	Deriving from the word *titanikos*, meaning colossal, it originates from the Titans, the twelve children of Uranus and Gaea of Greek mythology. One other ship has been named *Titanic*; a more diminutive 280ft-long, 1,608-ton cargo steamer built in Belfast in 1888 by McIlwaine, Lewis & Co. Registered by the Board of Trade as vessel 93171 it was operated by Smith & Service Ltd of Glasgow until 1903. Renamed *Luis Alberto* when sold to a Chilean company, its registration was cancelled in 1928.
trim	Maintaining the vessel an even keel in water.
Trinity House	Institution formed by Royal Charter in 1514 to aid navigation within British coastal waters by providing harbour pilotage, the supply of buoys and the operation of lighthouses.
triple expansion	Type of steam-resourceful engine first developed in 1882 comprising three cylinders of differing sizes, smallest to largest. Because steam is continually reducing pressure through expansion each cylinder is increased in size to maximise the vacuum of the piston head. The

larger the cylinder the lower its internal pressure, those on *Titanic* comprised of one cylinder kept at high-pressure (215psi) with two others at lower pressures (78 and 9psi). The divergent pressures enabled the same steam to feed multiple cylinders simultaneously as well as economise consumption of fuel; typically expending 1.54lb of coal per hour per each shaft horsepower produced.

transverse   Crosswise section of a ship: port to starboard.

turbine   Type of engine first installed on ships in 1897, fed by steam supplied from low-pressure cylinders forced onto a drum of blades that rotate at high speeds to drive a propeller shaft. Turbines run faster and need less energy to run than reciprocating engines. To identify a ship powered solely by turbines its name would bear the prefix TS: Turbine Ship.

U-boat   Unterseeboot: military submarine of the German Imperial Navy (Kaiserliche Marine) developed first in 1906.

Well Deck   Recessed deck in the hull of a ship to allow greater ease for loading and unloading cargoes and supplies.

yard   Measurement equal to 3ft or 0.9144 metres.

BIBLIOGRAPHY

'I consider that he [Thomas H. Ismay] was the most far seeing man of steamers, and I am not sure that the travelling public have ever realised the debt they owe to his foresight. He was the pioneer in introducing most of the comforts, not to say luxuries, which they now take as a matter of course.'

Sir Bertram Fox Hayes, Commodore, White Star Line, 1922/4

Books
Ballard, R.D., *Lost Liners* (Hodder & Stoughton: 1997)
Ballard, R.D., *The Discovery of the Titanic* (Guild Publishing: 1987)
Ballard, R.D., and Sweeney, M., *Return to Titanic* (National Geographic: 2004)
Barczewski, S., *Titanic: A Night Remembered* (Hambledon & London: 2004)
Baxter, B., *Naval Architecture: Examples and Theory* (Charles Griffin & Co.: 1962)
Beesley, L., *The Loss of the SS Titanic* (Houghton Mifflin: 1912)
Beveridge, B., Andrews, S., Hall, S., and Klistorner, D., *Titanic: The Ship Magnificent*, vols. 1 and 2
   (The History Press: 2008)
Booth, J., and Coughlan, S., *Titanic: Signals of Disaster* (White Star Publishing: 1993)
Brown, D., *The Last Log of the Titanic* (International Marine: 2000)
Brown, R., *Voyage of the Iceberg* (The Bodley Head: 1983)
Bryceson, D., *The Titanic Disaster* (Patrick Stephens Ltd: 1997)
Bullock, S.F., *Thomas Andrews: A Hero of the Titanic* (The Blackstaff Press: 1999)
Cameron, S., *Titanic: Belfast's Own* (Wolfhound Press: 1998)
Chirnside, M., *RMS Olympic – Titanic's Sister* (Tempus Publishing: 2002)
Cochkanoff, G., and Chaulk, B., *SS Atlantic* (Goose Lane Editions: 2009)
Dawson, P., *The Liner: Retrospective & Renaissance* (Conway Press: 2005)
Eaton, J.P., and Haas, C.A., *Falling Star* (Patrick Stephens Ltd: 1989)
Eaton, J.P., and Haas, C.A., *Titanic: A Journey Through Time* (Patrick Stephens Ltd: 1999)
Eaton, J.P., and Haas, C.A., *Titanic: Destination Disaster* (Patrick Stephens Ltd: 1996)
Eaton, J.P., and Haas, C.A., *Titanic: Triumph and Tragedy* (Patrick Stephens Ltd: 1994)
Foecke, T., *Metallurgy of the RMS Titanic* (National Institute of Standards and Technology: 1998)
Fox, S., *The Ocean Railway* (Harper Collins: 2003)
Fricker, P., *Ocean Liners* (Thomas Reed Publications Ltd: 1992)
Gardiner, R., *The History of the White Star Line* (Ian Allan Publishing: 2001)
Gardiner, R., and Van Der Vat, D., *The Riddle of the Titanic* (Weidenfeld & Nicolson: 1995)
Green, R., *Building the Titanic* (Carlton Books: 2005)

Griffiths, D., Lambert A., and Walker, F., *Brunel's Ships* (Chatham Publishing: 1999)

Hyslop, D., Forsyth, A., and Jemima, S., *Titanic Voices* (Sutton Publishing Ltd: 1997)

Johnson H., *The Cunard Story* (Whittet Books Ltd: 1987)

Kerbrech R., *Ships of the White Star Line* (Ian Allan: 2009)

Kludas, A., *Record Breakers of the North Atlantic* (Chatham Publishing: 2000)

Lightoller, C., *Titanic and Other Ships* (Nicholson & Watson: 1935)

Lord, W., *A Night to Remember* (Henry Holt & Company: 1955)

Lord, W., *The Night Lives On* (Viking: 1986)

Louden-Brown, P., *The White Star Line* (Titanic Historical Society: 2001)

Lynch, D., and Marschall, K., *Ghosts of the Abyss* (Hodder & Stoughton: 2003)

Lynch, D., and Marschall, K., *Titanic: An Illustrated History* (Hodder & Stoughton: 1992)

Mackenzie-Kennedy, C., *The Atlantic Blue Riband* (William Sessions Ltd: 1993)

Maxtone-Graham, J., *The Only Way to Cross* (Barnes & Noble Inc.: 1972)

McAuley, R., *The Liners: A Voyage of Discovery* (Boxtree: 1997)

McCluskie, T., *Anatomy of the Titanic* (Promotional Reprint Book Company Ltd: 1998)

McCluskie, T., Sharpe, M., and Marriott, L., *Titanic & Her Sisters Olympic & Britannic* (Parkgate Books: 1999)

Mills, S., *HMHS Britannic: The Last Titan* (Shipping Books Press: 1996)

Mills, S., *Hostage to Fortune: The Dramatic Story of the Last Olympian – HMHS Britannic* (Wordsmith Publications: 2002)

Mills, S., *RMS Olympic: The Old Reliable* (Waterfront Publications: 1995)

Preston, D., *Wilful Murder: The Sinking of the Lusitania* (Doubleday: 2002)

Ramsay, D., *Lusitania: Saga and Myth* (Chatham Publishing: 2001)

Reade, L., *The Ship That Stood Still* (Patrick Stephens Ltd: 1994)

Sebak, P.K., *Titanic's Predecessor: The SS Norge Disaster of 1904* (Seaward Publishing: 2004)

Strouse, J., *Morgan: American Financier* (Harper Perennial: 2000)

Ulrich, K., *Monarchs of the Sea* (Tauris Parke: 1998)

Watson, M.H., *Disasters at Sea* (Patrick Stephens Ltd: 1995)

Wilson, D., *The Hole: Another Look at the Sinking of the Estonia Ferry* (Diggory Press: 2006)

Zeni, D., *Forgotten Empress* (Goose Lane Editions: 1998)

Newspapers and Periodicals

Engineering (1 July 1910, pp.14–15)

New York Times

The Shipbuilder

The Times

Haas, C.A., 'Oceanic of 1899: Liner of Luxury', *The Titanic Commutator*, vol. 2, 1979

Lepien, R., 'The White Star Liner Republic', *The Titanic Commutator*, vols. 18 and 19, 1995

Government Papers

Hansard (HMSO: 1910/12)

International Conference on Safety of Life at Sea (HMSO: 1914)

Proceedings on a Formal Investigation into the Loss of the Steamship Titanic (HMSO: 1912)

Report on the Loss of the Steamship Titanic (Cmnd. 6352, HMSO: 1912)

RMS Titanic: Reappraisal of Evidence Relating to SS Californian (HMSO: 1992)

Saving Life at Sea: House of Commons Select Committee Report (HMSO: 1887)

The Shipping Code: being the Merchant Shipping Act, 1894 (National Archives, Kew: ZLIB20/108)

United States Congress; *Hearings of a Subcommittee of the Senate Commerce Committee pursuant to Senate Resolution 283, to Investigate the Causes leading to the Wreck of the White Star liner Titanic* (62nd Congress, 2nd Session, 1912: Doc. 726)

United States Congress; *Report of the Senate Committee of Commerce pursuant to Senate Resolution 283, Directing the Committee to Investigate the Causes of the Sinking of the Titanic* (62nd Congress, 2nd Session, 28 May 1912: Rept. 806)

INDEX